The Lovers' Quarrel

The Lovers' Quarrel

The Two Foundings and American Political Development

ELVIN T. LIM

OXFORD
UNIVERSITY PRESS

Oxford University Press is a department of the University of Oxford.
It furthers the University's objective of excellence in research, scholarship,
and education by publishing worldwide.

Oxford   New York
Auckland   Cape Town   Dar es Salaam   Hong Kong   Karachi
Kuala Lumpur   Madrid   Melbourne   Mexico City   Nairobi
New Delhi   Shanghai   Taipei   Toronto

With offices in
Argentina   Austria   Brazil   Chile   Czech Republic   France   Greece
Guatemala   Hungary   Italy   Japan   Poland   Portugal   Singapore
South Korea   Switzerland   Thailand   Turkey   Ukraine   Vietnam

Oxford is a registered trade mark of Oxford University Press
in the UK and certain other countries.

Published in the United States of America by
Oxford University Press
198 Madison Avenue, New York, NY 10016

© Oxford University Press 2014

CIP data is on file at the LOC
Lim, Elvin T.,
The lovers' quarrel : the two foundlings and american political development / Elvin T. Lim.

9780199812189

9   8   7   6   5   4   3   2   1

Printed in the United States of America on acid-free paper

To my friends

CONTENTS

PREFACE

This is a work of synthesis, out of which a theory of American political development (APD) and American political thought (APT) emerges. It offers a story
of America that I believe is best told by the heuristic of a distinctly American
Lovers' Quarrel. The United States operates on a two-party system not just because of its single-member district, winner-take-all electoral system. Political
scientists tell us that single-member districts incentivize "out" parties to band
together to defeat the "in" and over time, this logic compresses a multiplicity
of voices into a two-party framework. This may be, but the institutional explanation alone does not explain why the Federalists and the Anti-Federalists
settled on the system of representation and governance that they did in the
first place, with one half of the Constitution blithely promulgating powers and
the other half jealously guarding rights.[1] Ideological explanations do a little
better to explain the nature of our politics. Yet our political debates are not
fully captured by the European imports from Hayek or Marx, or even from
Locke or Machiavelli. Even if they were, the question is, why have we selected
thinkers to perpetuate our perennial quarrel about diversity versus unity, *Pluribus* or *Unum*? Philosophers don't pick us; we pick them.

I propose that above all, the nature of APD derives from the historically
contingent fact that America is unique in the world for having democratically
enacted two constitutions in the brief span of seven years. When the Federalists asked Americans in the various states to ratify their proposed Constitution, they were also asking them to invalidate the Articles of Confederation
and the extant conception of union—confederalism, or a league of friendship between fully sovereign states—and to replace it with a more consolidated union whereby the states parted with some of their sovereignty to form
a central government. These questions were answered in the affirmative in
1787–1789, but not for all time. As soon as the new Congress convened, the
Anti-Federalists secured a piece of the First Founding in the new Constitution,

with the ratification of the Bill of Rights in 1791. And so our Constitution has, codified within it, two conceptions of union, one each of our Two Foundings. Federalism and Anti-Federalism would become the foundational philosophies that generations of Americans since have invoked and negotiated to forge their own period-specific understanding of *E Pluribus Unum*.

The Lovers' Quarrel both connects us and separates us. Like a pair of self-consumed lovers, it has always been about us—and there are two of us. We are Federalist; we are Anti-Federalist. If this sounds like Jefferson when he announced in his First Inaugural Address, "we are all Republicans, we are all Federalists," or like Theodore Roosevelt, who used "Hamiltonian means for Jeffersonian ends," it is because both knew, at least at the back of their minds, that they were ensconced in a primordial Lovers' Quarrel. These phrases are more than poetic dyads, because they point to the fundamental bipolarity of the American identity in our conceptions of our union. Are "We" closer to a consolidated nation of "the People" or are "We" more like a compact between "the People of the United States"? The first three or seven words of the Preamble of the Constitution permit one or the other reading.

This ambiguity matters because it has fueled over two centuries of American political debates, including a Civil War. It has even led to perverse and unintended outcomes that neither Federalists nor Anti-Federalists foresaw as each jostled to lock into place their conception of union for all time. For example, it is partly because the Anti-Federalists secured the Bill of Rights that it took so long to build a modern administrative state, and it is because of the administrative state that we now hear renewed calls to respect states' rights. Take another example: at least two of the major problems of American politics today—the allegedly "imperial" presidency and "activist" Supreme Court—stem in part from the Federalists' anticipation of the Anti-Federalist fears of consolidated government and the latter's demands for institutional counterweights to the First Branch.[2] Take a third: whether we are talking about healthcare reform, immigration, same-sex marriage, term limits, or the Voting Rights Act, federalism (or more precisely, the debate over the meaning of federalism) rears its head when we ask whether the federal government has the authority to make national policy, or if the states have the right to go their own way.

History and politicians have conspired well to disguise the Lovers' Quarrel so that we do not read in our books what we feel in our bones. In our collective desire to mythologize the Second Founding and to forget (or reconcile it with) the First, we forget that the Federalists were partisans standing resolutely on one side of the ratification debate, in favor of "a more perfect Union," and by that they meant a more consolidated union than the one the Articles of Confederation had secured. The cost of underestimating the sharp break from our First Founding is that we have also forgotten the "Other Founders," with the combined outcome that we conceive of those who gathered at Philadelphia to write a new Constitution as polite men in powdered wigs who knew only philosophy and no politics. Consider that the canonical, and sometimes only, source for interpreting the meaning of our Second Founding are 85 essays now known as the *Federalist Papers*, most of which Madison, Hamilton, and Jay hurriedly drew up to try to get New York on board with the proposed Constitution.[3] Would our understanding of the news of the day be fair and balanced if we watched only one cable channel?

It has been said, "Americans are fortunate that the antifederalists are the failed, defeated, would-be founders of what would have been a very different kind of nation."[4] True, but these "would-be founders" managed to secure a Bill of Rights, and this was no mean achievement, not least because it was the Bill and the doctrine of states' rights it codified in the Tenth Amendment that made possible the preservation of the "peculiar institution" until the Civil War. At the minimum, the *Federalist Papers* cannot be the major source for recovering the original meaning of the Bill of Rights, one half of the Constitution, because Publius had argued rigorously against it in Federalist 84. Because we have been too successful in depoliticizing the Second Founding, and too dismissive of the legacy of the Anti-Federalists' political thought in American history, I err on the side of highlighting the differences between the Federalists and Anti-Federalists in this book. I err also on the side of synthesizing the various strands of Anti-Federalist thought. If we have assumed a certain coherence to Federalist political thought, fairness requires that we do the same for the Anti-Federalists if they are not to remain in relative obscurity. After all, the Federalists were speaking to a specific group of people, people who refused to ratify the new Constitution. By specifying the ideological differences between the two groups, I hope to demonstrate the paramount significance of us having had not one, but Two Foundings, on the course of American history.

While the Federalists and the Anti-Federalists held many similar ideas— I characterize them as Lovers, after all—the priorities and gradations in their commitments, however fine, were enough to evince an all-or-nothing battle over the proposed Constitution. For example, the Federalists spoke the classical republican language of virtue and the common good, but they did so differently and less confidently than the Anti-Federalists did. The Federalists advocated democracy too, but in less measure and with more skepticism than the Anti-Federalists. I magnify these fine gradations in this book, cognizant that others have called American politics "consensual" and American parties "tweedledum and tweedledee" and accepting that in the grand scheme of things these claims may well be true; but I also want to proffer the not inconsistent claim that Americans have waged very intense and vociferous battles over what others may have perceived to be the littlest things.

Just like the Constitution, in its granting of powers and its codification of rights, is both Federalist and Anti-Federalist, so were some of the framers, on different issues and at different times. A Lovers' Quarrel, after all, pertains to differences between two parties who nevertheless share many values and commitments. Just as some Anti-Federalists, such as Melancton Smith, came ultimately to vote for the Constitution in their state ratifying conventions, others, such as Pierce Butler, and more importantly James Madison, would defect from the Federalist cause. Most Federalists and Anti-Federalists (who formed the Democratic-Republican Party in 1791), however, stayed resolutely on course at least through the Revolution of 1800, which is another reason why there is analytic utility in isolating the archetypes. The Federalists were in favor of a more consolidated union, and the most ardent among them secretly resented its federal components, while the Anti-Federalists wanted a more decentralized union, and the purists among them wanted little more than a military alliance in foreign affairs among independent states.[5] There were possibly more centrists on the compound idea of a federal union than there were purists on the side of total *Unum* or complete *Pluribus*, but the ideal types are helpful in delineating the argumentative scope of America's Two Foundings. I also believe that this was probably how the Lovers' Quarrel was actually lived, since it is always the ideologically zealous who invest their time in and drive the debates of their day. In what follows, there will surely be exceptions to my generalizations, especially in the later iterations of the Lovers' Quarrel when time and a succession of creative resyntheses by talented political entrepreneurs have made the differences between the two sides less stark; however, these generalizations are nevertheless necessary, in my mind, for my goal is to redirect our view from the trees to deliver a view of the forest of what drives American political development. The Lovers' Quarrel is *the* most resilient feature of American politics.

Fortunately, for my purposes, after a 150-year scholarly hiatus, the Anti-Federalists are somewhat back in vogue. Other than an isolated body of scholarship tracing the endurance of Anti-Federalist thought into the Jacksonian era, there had been little if any work tracing their impact on American politics until scholars revived their interest in classical republicanism—of which the Anti-Federalists were strong proponents—as a critique of post-war liberalism and offered the intellectual backdrop to the Reagan Revolution.[6] Two reasons for this long hiatus are the brute facts that the Anti-Federalists lost their battle against ratification and, as I argue in Chapter 4, their third-generation descendants lost again during the Civil War. Certainly, when federal governmental operations began in March 1789, it was no longer politically correct to frontally critique the Federalists' Constitution, which had now become the Constitution of the United States. Rather than launch a politically damaging campaign to disown the Constitution, the Anti-Federalists made the best of an imperfect situation by trying to own it by first amending it in 1791, and then by imposing their "strict" interpretation of the Constitution in the Revolution of 1800. Their cause was aided much, by my telling in Chapter 2, by Madison's (much understudied) conversion in the 1790s and the ensuing entwining and conflation of Anti-Federalist with Federalist political thought that has continued all the way to our own era in the form of the Tea Party movement.

Yet nothing contributed more to the scholarly coming out of Anti-Federalism than the trenchant statism of the New Deal and the Great Society, which caused a conservative movement to coalesce and to draw self-consciously on the nation's first anti-statist template. Collections of the Anti-Federalist papers first emerged in the 1960s. By 1981, political moods had altered enough that Ronald Reagan could unapologetically reverse the conventional wisdom of the preceding decades to declare that "government is not the solution to our problem" and instead that "government is the problem" itself, thereby inaugurating another neo-Anti-Federalist revolution that would reintroduce the repackaged ideas of "New Federalism" and the jurisprudential doctrine of "original intent" into mainstream politics. That same year, Hebert Storing published *The Complete Anti-Federalist*, the largest compilation of Anti-Federalist writings yet, and only the third.[7] Perhaps the nation was far enough along from the divisive debates at the time of the Second Founding that scholars and jurists could now uncover the "Other Founders" and study them in their own right without fear that the universal veneration of Publius would be diminished. Outside of the academy, however, as I will show in the Epilogue on the modern Tea Party movement, the invocation of Anti-Federalism can often still be an undercover, if not a partly unconscious, operation. I have therefore set for myself the task of untangling the distinct ideological strands of Federalism and Anti-Federalism so that we may better understand the central axis of contention of American politics. This book attempts to elaborate on the claim that "if . . . the foundation of the American polity was laid by the Federalists, the Anti-Federalist reservations echo through American history; and it is in the dialogue, not merely in the Federalist victory, that the country's principles are to be discovered."[8] Along the way, I restate and tie together some old arguments, and in doing so, make a few new ones.

As a formal matter, the Anti-Federalists were "simply those who opposed the unamended Constitution as a proposal."[9] They combined a radical Whig, classical republican, "Country" philosophy to defend their idea of the small republic, and added to that an adapted Lockean liberalism that undergirded their opposition to the proposed federal government.[10] Though they would suffer from a martyr's complex once they lost the ratification debate, they may well have constituted a majority of Americans. According to William

Riker, the Federalists succeeded because they deployed their "heresthetics" or agenda-setting tactics to construe a majority in their favor.[11] For example, in Article 7 of the new Constitution, the Federalists flagrantly sidestepped the unanimity rule established in Article 13 for amending the Articles of Confederation, rejected the Articles' contention that the Union was "perpetual," and determined that nine of 13 states could secede from the old Union to make a new one. The Federalists exploited the fact that most states preferred a union of some kind rather than no union at all, and, according to Bruce Ackerman, the threat of secession probably pushed the critical states of New York and Virginia in the direction of ratification.[12] The Anti-Federalists cried foul. As Candidus rightly noted, "Is it not the greatest absurdity to suppose, that the plan offered *cannot* be amended previous to its adoption . . . Would it not be the height of absurdity, to adopt a plan *entire*, in expectation of altering some very essential parts at a future period?"[13] Though his logic did not carry the day, his compatriots did manage to secure a Bill of Rights, which is the lasting legacy of the Anti-Federalists and the basis on which latter-day Anti-Federalists have insisted that the Constitution was a document that limited, rather than granted, as it did in the preceding Articles, the powers of the federal government. In effect, the Anti-Federalists saw the Bill of Rights as the Declaration and the First Founding reincarnated; thus, by 1791, the Constitution had become a bifurcated text and an invitation to perpetual quarrel.

This book is as much a story about the original dissent (as opposed to the "original meaning") of 1787–1789 as it is about the history of American political thought on domestic politics and policy, or modern liberalism and conservatism and their evolution from the principles of our Two Foundings. Readers interested in the modern liberal, Federalist side of the ideological divide may want to read the chapters on the Founding, the Civil War, and the New Deal as evolving faces of what would become modern liberalism based on a new republicanism, repackaged for an extended sphere, and first espoused by the Second Founders. Others more interested in modern conservatism and Anti-Federalism may want to read the chapters on the Jeffersonian Republicans, Jacksonian Democrats, Progressivism, and modern conservatism as appealing to the older republicanism of the First Founders. Once we understand that we have had Two Foundings, then it should no longer be a puzzle why third parties in our history, typically based on single issues, do not stand a chance against the major parties of each era, all of which succeeded because they had grafted themselves onto either side of the Lovers' Quarrel. To the extent that I am focused on fleshing out the "A" in "APD" and therefore integrating APD with APT—the Lovers' Quarrel is both about principles (of the Two Foundings) and their institutional incarnations—my primary focus in this book would be on ideas and only secondarily on tangible institutions or governing authorities, since the latter have been the typical focus of the extant APD scholarship.

This book is also an account of constitutional development, and in particular of its inner logic. The American Constitution sets up a dyadic clock by conjoining, after "reflection and choice," to quote Federalist 1, the principles of the First and Second Founding in the Amendments and Articles, respectively. Perhaps this is why scholars have long since observed rhythms in American history. Arthur Schlesinger, for example, had presented the argument that we alternate between liberal and conservative periods, while Burnham gave us his theory of critical realignments.[14] Huntington offered us an account of creedal passions periods, while Morone argued that the nation vacillates between social communalism and Victorian censoriousness.[15] I too argue that our constitutional rhythm is waltz-like, with the arc of its pendulum swing established on the one side by the First Founding of 1776–1781 (which culminated in the Articles of Confederation) and on the other by the Second Founding of 1787–1789 (which delivered the present Constitution).

As this is a book about *American* political development, it is primarily focused on domestic politics and policy, and the ideas used to defend them. External foes unite Americans easily enough, as they did in 1787; but it is when our conceptions of union collide that our most visceral debates occur. However, this does not mean that the Lovers' Quarrel does not extend to foreign policy, as can be seen in the first face-off between Hamilton and Madison over the Jay Treaty of 1794. From the start, the Anti-Federalists tended to be "idealists," insisting that America should stand with friends, such as France, who shared her values, and know her enemies, such as Britain, who did not. The Federalists, representing mostly the merchant class, were generally "realists" who appreciated Britain's commercial and military power and thought it unwise for a young nation to challenge a global hegemon.[16] If to extend the sphere was also to extend the scope of imagination about conceptions of livelihood and living, Madison was probably correct that the Anti-Federalists were generally more insular and more parochial than were the Federalists.[17] Driven more by economic than philosophical considerations, the Federalists and their descendants have tended therefore to be more cosmopolitan and conciliatory in their outlook in terms of trading partners and immigration, whereas the Anti-Federalists and their descendants, who were concerned about the preservation of their political ideals, tended to possess an "us-versus-them" mentality and were more cautious and insular about the possibility of contagious doctrines infiltrating American shores. Patriotism (or, if we can use the word, "nationalism") has, perhaps paradoxically, tended to be a stronger sentiment on the Anti-Federalist side of American history because it is not so much a deep sense of "us" that binds Anti-Federalists together, but a "them." Foreign and domestic policies are therefore related. Since Andrew Jackson did not believe in a role for the federal government in internal improvements, his nationalism had to stem from the one goal that even Anti-Federalists shared with the Federalists: war and foreign policy. Neo-conservatives, therefore, are not the first to have justified their warfare state by questioning the patriotism of their political adversaries. Though he was no fan of the collective goals of the Union, Jackson would make fun of the "blue light Federalists"—a reference to the friendly signals the Federalists in New London, Connecticut, allegedly sent to the British during the War of 1812, and a charge that, together with the Hartford Convention, discredited and contributed to the demise of the Federalist Party.[18] The descendants of Federalists and Anti-Federalists continue to impugn the patriotism of each other only because their understandings of what America is, what holds us together, and which of the Two Foundings counts as our birthday, are so starkly distinct.

My final prefatory note is to admit that there is a Panglossian hope in this genealogical inquiry, for I believe that setting our heated political battles today against the long stream of the Federalist/Anti-Federalist debate over two centuries may help us see our differences in perspective. Modern liberals need to be less dismissive of conservatives and they will become so if they learn about Anti-Federalism and understand that it is a potent strand of American political thought that long precedes the modern Tea Party and the Confederacy; many conservatives need to rethink their interpretation of "original meaning" and appreciate the fact that far from hating government, Publius and the Federalists created one. As the nation emerges from one pulverizing, negative campaign and looks toward the next, it may be worth considering that things have not gotten irrevocably worse than when the Federalists and the Anti-Federalists were first having at it. Quite the opposite: the arguments we are having today are very similar in substance and tone to the ones of the Second Founding. There are "Two Americas" because and only because we had Two Foundings. So I offer the Lovers' Quarrel not only as a possible frame for understanding the arc of American history from 1776 to the present, but also a gut-checking device for citizens confronting daily claims that we are teetering toward one Armageddon or rushing headlong to another apocalypse. Contrary to Lord Acton, who had observed that "a history that should pursue all the subtle threads from end to end might be eminently valuable, but not as a tribute to peace and conciliation" and that "sharp definitions and unsparing analysis would displace the veil beneath which society dissembles its divisions," this book starts from a different premise that if we must quarrel, we may do so with more mutual respect if we are clearer and more self-conscious about why we do.[19]

ACKNOWLEDGMENTS

I would like to gratefully acknowledge Sonu Bedi, Jim Ceaser, Elisabeth Clemens, Eldon Eisenach, Malcolm Feeley, Alan Gibson, Mark Graber, Jeff Hockett, Sid Milkis, Jim Morone, Bruce Miroff, Michael Mosher, Andrew Rehfield, Patrick Roberts, George Thomas, Elizabeth Sanders, Stephen Skowronek, Rogers Smith, Jeff Tulis, and Michael Zuckert for the conversations and feedback they have shared with me. Thanks are also due to Jason Atsales, Taran Catania, and Jacob Hertz for proofreading and fact-checking the manuscript. I owe thanks also to my colleagues at Wesleyan who have contributed to a supportive and stimulating environment in which to teach and research. Special thanks are due to John Finn, Don Moon, and Nancy Schwartz for reviewing various parts of the manuscript. All remaining errors, of course, are mine.

Many thanks are due to my editor, David McBride, for his patience and his support, and his team at OUP. I am grateful to my former tutors at Christ Church, Oxford—David Hine, Hugh Rice, and Jonathan Wright—where I was introduced to politics and philosophy, and more importantly, thinking. I thank my students for sharing a glimpse of the future they will create and inspiring me to think deeper about where we have come from.

The Lovers' Quarrel: A Tale of Two Foundings

"The year 1776 is celebrated for a revolution in favor of liberty. The year 1787 it is expected will be celebrated with equal joy, for a revolution in favor of government."[1]

The American "Founding" as a monolithic event is a myth, because there have been Two Foundings articulating two distinct and rather irreconcilable conceptions of union, not one. The First Founding started in 1776, when the 13 colonies declared themselves "Free and Independent States," and came together, each with their sovereignties fully intact, to adopt and ratify the Articles of Confederation in 1777 and 1781. *The First Founding of 1776–1781 created a league of nations.* What followed during the Second Founding, in 1787–1789, represented rupture and not continuity, when the 13 states yielded a portion of their sovereignty to create a compound republic, still partly federal but now also national, with a national government sanctioned by "We the People" aggregated across state lines. That this national government was paradoxically called a "federal government" camouflaged the revolution of 1787–1789, for federalism had been completely remade. The Second Founding radically overhauled the older conception of union as merely a compact between 13 sovereign states, by creating a nationalized "We the People" aggregated across state lines and a federal government that would represent them collectively. The United States had become much more than a league of nations. As the Preamble of the new Constitution promised, it was, at a minimum, "a more perfect Union" than was spawned at the First Founding. *The United States had become a nation.*

That we began our world again twice has hounded us ever since; indeed, to decouple the Two Foundings of 1776–1781 and 1787–1789 is to discover the essence of American politics past and present. The Anti-Federalist and Federalist altercation over the necessity of the Second Founding—the former held firmly onto the older conception of union as a compact between states, for principled reasons we will discuss below, while the latter advocated for a national union of individuals distributed across state lines—generated coherent and self-contained philosophies that would become the indigenous core of American political thought that has been reproduced and transmitted across two centuries.[2] I call these philosophies the principles, respectively, of the First and Second Foundings, promulgated first and most comprehensively by the Anti-Federalists and the Federalists during the Second Founding. The Anti-Federalist and Federalist contest over the relative priority of the principles of the Two Foundings would become our own. Our "culture wars," "polarized America," "winner-take-all politics," "disappearing center," "age of fracture," and "divided political heart" are very real and consequential, but they are not of recent origin: they are modern faces of an eighteenth-century Lovers' Quarrel first waged in 1787–1789.[3]

In the presidential election of 2012, an incumbent president successfully defended his Patient Protection and Affordable Care Act on the conviction that we ought to find national solutions for national problems, while his opponent, who had enacted a similar healthcare program in Massachusetts, refused to extrapolate that what worked in one state could be imposed on all 50. It would be easy, because the two sides' arguments now seem so rehearsed, to miss the fact we have had this quarrel before—many times, actually, like a circadian clock of which we are sometimes only subliminally aware. Even though the election seemed very much also like a contest between two personalities, President Barack Obama and Governor Mitt Romney were essentially debating the principles of the Two Foundings. Obama, like the Federalists, saw first the bonds that held the Union together rather than the distinct sovereignty of the states, which predisposed him to privilege the benefits to federal governmental consolidation over its dangers. Romney, like the Anti-Federalists, saw first the sovereignty of the states as cradles of liberty and republican virtue rather than the bonds between them, which predisposed him to highlight the dangers of governmental consolidation rather than the potential benefits of collective action.

At the heart of Romney's claim that what worked in Massachusetts could not work for the whole country was the Anti-Federalist conviction that accurate representation of state interests could not possibly occur at the expanded, national level. This was why the Anti-Federalists refused to ratify the Constitution. That is to say, possibly the greatest meta-historical irony of American politics is that "constitutional conservatives" today who chant to the tune of states' rights are echoing the very arguments of those who vehemently *opposed* the ratification of the Constitution. This is the direct result of our having had a First Founding that won many hearts before it was replaced, less than wholeheartedly, by the Second. As we shall see in Chapter 7, decoupling the Two Foundings helps explain why modern conservatives are simultaneously reactionary and preservationist; because the daughters and sons of the Revolution seek to roll back the principles of the Second Founding by subordinating and interpreting them by what they deem and hope to be the eternal principles of 1776. Whether or not we know it, we are children of Federal Farmer and Publius, still having at it. Mitt Romney and Barack Obama in 2012 were simply taking the side of the Anti-Federalists and the Federalists, respectively, about whether *E Pluribus* or *Unum* was the superior road to "life, liberty, and the pursuit of happiness."[4] I call the theory of American political development presented here a Lovers' Quarrel about the principles of the Two Foundings, because it is one that repeats itself in a way that only two parties who have been together for a long time can have.[5] The repetitious nature of the quarrel would be charming to a third party were it not for the fact that it sometimes looks so heated that a breakup appears imminent. As the United States enters into adulthood and possibly into a midlife crisis, it may be helpful to remind ourselves as we tear into each other that however strongly or fervently held our ideological views, people before us have felt the same, and with the same certitude that if things were not done a particular way, Armageddon was at hand.

To say that we are in some sense locked in the quarrel of 1787–1789 is not at all to imply that we are frozen in the conditions of 1787–1789, or that change does not happen in America. Indeed, in the chapters that follow, I hope to demonstrate that it is precisely and only by way of quarrel that the United States has developed as a polity. The Lovers' Quarrel has operated both as a developmental hurdle as well as a developmental impetus. The Second Founding and the Constitution did not settle the question of democratic legitimacy; rather, it reopened it. To observe this is to offer a rejoinder to the descendants of the Anti-Federalists who have purposefully glossed over the Two Foundings in order to argue that the Constitution had an uncontested and monolithic "original meaning" in 1789. When the Federalists articulated their aspiration to "form a more perfect Union," they were deploying "Union" as a term of art that, unlike the word "nation," which definitively signified a single unit and not a compound, could satisfy both supporters and detractors of the proposed Constitution. As we shall see in the substantive chapters that follow, American political development would not splutter as much in starts and fits between either extreme of *E Pluribus Unum* had it not been for the fact that there had already existed a legitimate but distinct conception of federalism that preceded the one codified in the second Constitution. Through one democratic process, We the People of the States spoke and confederated state sovereignties in the Articles of Confederation, and through another, We the People of the United States in the aggregate spoke very differently, while reinscribing the principles of the First Founding into parts of the Constitution, especially in its second half. Here were two households, both alike in dignity, in a way that no other federal republic in the world can equally lay claim to. These principles from the Two Foundings, codified in our sacred political texts, would establish the developmental boundaries of American politics. For the United States was forged in quarrel; and so too it is remade by quarrel. In what follows, I will argue that American political development (or the prototypically *American* species of political development) occurs *when political actors appeal to and attempt to prioritize one of either set of principles from the Two Foundings*, one originally defended by the Anti-Federalists and the other by the Federalists, *to bring about durable retrenchments or expansions of federal authority*. But before I get there, I must explain what I mean by a Lovers' Quarrel (the first half of my thesis statement focusing on ideas), what it means to develop in a uniquely American way (the second half of my thesis statement focusing on institutions), and how the full statement becomes a theory of American political thought and development.

One Country, Two Texts: Two Foundational Strands in American Political Thought

The Federalists and Anti-Federalists differed so sharply and confidently from each other because each could point to a sacred text of the First and Second Foundings, in the Declaration of Independence and the Constitution, respectively, to ground their claims about the meaning of the American experiment.[6] The Declaration and the Constitution are very different documents even though, together with the Bill of Rights, they are now collectively termed the "Charters of Freedom" and are housed together in the Rotunda of the National Archives in Washington, DC as if they were three consistent gospels of the American nation.[7] In fact, in the tension between the Declaration and the Constitution can be found the life force of the Lovers' Quarrel.

Whereas Publius would boldly proclaim the new Constitution as a radical innovation borne of reason, Jefferson's Declaration bent over backward to proffer a traditionalist justification for the most revolutionary of political acts, born of the passion (or republican virtue) of jealousy. For the Declaration does not begin with its most famous line, "We hold these truths to be self-evident," but with a preamble that belied the fact that if that which followed was really self-evident, then there should hardly have been a need to display "a decent respect to the opinions of mankind" to prepare them for the alleged platitudes to come:

> When in the Course of human events, it becomes necessary for one people to dissolve the political bands which have connected them

with another, and to assume among the Powers of the earth, the separate and equal station to which the Laws of Nature and of Nature's
God entitle them, a decent respect to the opinions of mankind requires that they should declare the causes which impel them to the
separation.

By supplying the archetypically conservative argument—an appeal to God
and the eternal laws—for the most unconservative act possible, Jefferson was
collapsing Hamilton's distinction between "choice" and "force" in Federalist
1 and suggesting that the use of force when operating under the auspices of
God's laws was not revolutionary but entirely unremarkable. Curiously, then,
whereas the Federalists proudly brandished the novelty of their creation, Jefferson understood his creation to be a conservative text.[8] The self-evident
truths he penned, he believed, were not so much deduced from reason, but
intuited from tradition and experience.

But the differences run deeper. While the Declaration and later the Bill of
Rights (the second half of the Constitution the Anti-Federalists pushed through
against Publius' wishes) articulate our *rights against* government, the Constitution enumerates the *powers of* government.[9] The former are negative charters
as the Magna Carta was; the latter is a new kind of charter, one that positively
grants powers to government.[10] The Declaration is at least in part a prepolitical text, drawing its legitimacy from a thin notion of democratic consent, but
mostly from other sources —God, nature, tradition, experience, and so forth.
As Hannah Arendt observed of the paradox of "foundings," "Self-evident . . .
truths are pre-rational—they inform reason but are not its product—and since
their self-evidence puts them beyond disclosure and argument, they are in a
sense no less compelling than 'despotic power.'"[11] This means that the First
Founding was a qualitatively different kind of "founding" than was the Second.
The Constitution, by contrast, is a postpolitical text; it derives its legitimacy
entirely from the democratic sanction of the body politic that ratified it.

The different dating criteria we use to commemorate Independence Day
and the birth of the Constitution indicate that we already understand that
rights, articulated in the Declaration, and powers, enumerated in the Constitution, are antithetical concepts. Rights are in some sense prepolitical, but
legitimate powers are always postpolitical because they must be created by
political contract. And so we do not celebrate the official congressional act of
independence, the Lee Resolution that was adopted on July 2, 1776. If we did,
John Adams would have been correct in his prediction that "The Second Day
of July 1776 will be the most memorable Epocha, in the History of America. . . .
It ought to be solemnized with Pomp and Parade, with Shews, Games, Sports,
Guns, Bells, Bonfires, and Illuminations from one End of this Continent to

the other from this Time forward forever more."[12] Nor is it the case that we celebrate Independence Day on July 9, as George Washington and his army did, after New York, which had abstained from voting on the resolution of July 2, finally delivered its assent. We do not celebrate it on August 2, when most delegates appended their signature to the Declaration, or on August 30, when England received news of the Declaration. Instead, we celebrate Independence Day on July 4, the day the specific wording of the Declaration of Independence was approved. Rights need only be *declared* for their legitimacy to be acknowledged—they do not need to be notarized in a political act of contracting or "founding"—and this is what we celebrate on July 4 each year. For the First Founders, states' rights were prepolitical at least insofar as they preceded the Second Founding; these rights preceded, chronologically and morally, federal powers.[13] Of course, in truth, states' rights were not really prepolitical (or "natural") but were systematically developed and consolidated by the colonists over the century before the Revolution. However, states' rights assumed the prepolitical legitimacy of revolutionary rights because they were announced at the same time as the claim of independence was; and revolutionary rights are, of course, archetypically prepolitical. We possess them whether or not we have previously been bound by political contract.

Power, in contrast, if it is to be legitimate, must be created by consent; it must be postpolitical. This is probably why whereas we chose one of the earliest possible dates to commemorate our independence, we chose among the latest potential dates to commemorate the birthdate of the Constitution. Most Americans do not celebrate the birth of the Constitution on September 17, 1787, when the text of the Constitution was adopted—the criterion used to commemorate the Declaration.[14] We make little of June 21, 1788, when the ninth state, New Hampshire, ratified the Constitution and made it official and binding on all nine states that had ratified it. Instead, 1789 is the year that stands out to designate the Second Founding because on March 4, 1789, governmental operations began; that is, the exercise of legitimate power commenced.[15]

It is not a coincidence, therefore, as I will explore in Chapter 8, that members of the modern Tea Party will more reliably invoke the ideals of "life, liberty, and the pursuit of happiness" than, as President Barack Obama would, the aspiration of "a more perfect Union." Our different dating criteria for the Declaration and the Constitution reveal our collective historical intuition that rights are prepolitical and powers are postpolitical—that our rights come from the First Founding and our powers from the Second Founding—and if so, the Charters of Freedom do not sit as comfortably together as conventionally thought, and most Americans are partial to one over the others.[16] An apprehension of the Two Foundings forces us to rethink the conventional wisdom that the Constitution codified the means and the Declaration asserted the ends of American government. (At the minimum, if the Constitution was really designed to deliver on, rather than partially subvert, the principles of the Declaration, it would have been referenced more in the Federalist Papers. Publius does so only once, in Federalist 40.) Instead, the two texts represent two different and value-laden accounts of the start date of American history: either the covenantal grant of powers at the Second Founding is the first American deed, or the prior articulation of the states' sovereignty in the Declaration of Independence—later codified in a Bill of Rights, the antidote to the perils of consolidated power—is the title deed of American identity. Thus, while the Anti-Federalists refused to compromise their states' sovereignty and insisted that the Articles of Confederation need only be amended but not abolished, the Federalists were convinced of the need to grant greater powers to a new central government and to empower an executive to solve the perceived failures of government that had occurred between 1776 and 1789.[17] Perhaps this is why while the Declaration articulates the less determinate goal of "the pursuit of happiness," the Constitution recommends the more substantive and collective goal of the "general welfare."[18] If 1776 encapsulated the highest ideals of the American (read First Founders') creed, the years from 1781 to 1789 revealed to the Second Founders that idealism was not enough to run a league of states. The Federalists believed that wholesale reconstitution—a Second Founding—was needed to grant new powers to a central government for a polity newly reconceived.

Consistent with the distinction between rights and powers, then, may be observed a insistence in Anti-Federalist political thought that the American political tradition began not in 1789—the year a more consolidated government than ever envisioned by the revolutionaries was created—but in 1776, the year when the original central government, monarchy itself, was overthrown. For the Anti-Federalists, liberty called for destruction, not creation; disestablishment, not consolidation. This is why, according to Charles Kesler, "to the Anti-Federalists . . . the new Constitution looked suspiciously like the British government redivivus, only without the effective checks and balances that it had evolved. A lofty legislature and an ambitious executive did not look to them like the government they had fought for."[19] The Anti-Federalists believed themselves to be the true inheritors of the Spirit of '76, faithful heirs of the First Founding. Like all those who have called themselves daughters and sons of the Revolution ever since, the Anti-Federalists believed that America's revolutionary ideals stand in chronological and moral priority to the Second Founding's (Federalist) principles. Perhaps this was why, in the first presidential debate of 2012, when Mitt Romney referred to both the Declaration of Independence and the Constitution, he took it upon himself to quote only the sacred words of the First Founding, that "we are endowed by our creator with our rights," but not from the Second.[20] As far as where their heart of hearts lie, the First Founders and their descendants are more Declarationist than Constitutionalist.

The distinction between the Constitution and the Declaration is repeated between the Articles of the Constitution and the Bill of Rights, which of course culminates in the Tenth Amendment protecting states' rights. Whereas the Federalists leaned on the ideal of a single diverse community and the collective goals as spelled out in the Preamble of the Constitution, the Anti-Federalists were partial to what John Kincaid has called a "community of communities" reminiscent of the United States after the First Founding, which was why they insisted on a Bill of Rights.[21] So while the Constitution is more concerned with the positive liberty of what the federal government can secure for the collective community and freely grants powers to the federal government to that end, the Bill of Rights (at least until circa 1925) protects the negative liberties of the particular communities against the federal government, much like ancient charters had protected barons against kings.[22] If the Constitution was intended to rectify the vices of the states, the Bill of Rights was intended to protect the states from the excesses of the federal government. And so if 1787–1789 saw a revolution in favor of government, 1791—the year the Bill of Rights was ratified—was a counter-revolution against it. The Bill was a *leitmotif* of the First Founding; it would make the Constitution a bifurcated text.

Federalism Versus Anti-Federalism

The good opinion I have of the frame and composition as well of the Confederation as the several state Constitutions: and that they are, if administered upon republican principles, the greatest blessings we enjoy; and the danger I apprehend of the one proposed is, that it will become the greatest curse.[23]

That we have had Two Foundings means that every major concept in American politics—mostly obviously, federalism, rights, and powers; but also liberalism and republicanism—has had two meanings, one held by the Federalists and another by the Anti-Federalists. The principles of each of the Two Foundings found coherent and explicit expression in Federalism and Anti-Federalism during the ratification debates—the first Lovers' Quarrel—of 1787–1789. Table 1.1 summarizes the fundamental differences on the conceptions of I. union, II. liberty, III. truth, and IV. republicanism between the Federalists and Anti-Federalists to which I will refer in the chapters ahead. For now, I present an initial sketch of these two parallel languages of American politics, each designed to describe the same thing, but almost always in the opposite valence.

Table 1.1 **The Lovers' Quarrel: Federalism Versus Anti-Federalism**

	Conceptions of	Anti-Federalists (First Founding, 1776–1781)	Federalists (Second Founding, 1787–1789)
I.	Union	Preferred to retain "a league of friendship" among small, virtuous republics.	Created "a more perfect Union" of individuals ("We the People") in an extended republic and layered it on top of 13 state sovereignties.
II.	Liberty	Committed to negative liberty, believed that rights are antecedent to powers and were therefore jealous about states' rights, committed to equality only as a start-state condition, rejected the need for a federal government to proffer national solutions, and insisted on the codification of a Bill of Rights to keep federal power in check.	Committed to positive liberty and the need for governmental power to solve collective problems and protect individual rights, understood equality and justice to be end-state conditions guaranteed by government, created a national government and chartered the First Bank of the United States using an elastic interpretation of the Constitution.
III.	Truth	Idealistic and conservative, steadfastly committed to principles derived from custom and experience, believed in an absolute Truth, advocated "seminaries of useful learning" so that civic principles can be cultivated.	Pragmatic and forward-looking, trusted in reason, invented a new "science" and committed only to the relative truth produced when ambition counteracts ambition.
IV.	Republicanism	Distrustful of aristocracy and committed to classical, states-centered republicanism, pure democracy, and majority rights; preferred a mirroring theory of descriptive representation; regarded the Senate and Supreme Court as aristocratic institutions.	Distrustful of "pure" democracy and fearful of majority faction, affirmed a national republicanism, adhered to a trusteeship model of virtuous representation where the passions of the people would be filtered; created the Senate and an unelected judicial branch.

I. UNION

At its root, Anti-Federalism was a conservative ideology committed to the old, peripheralized federalism that preserved the sovereignty of the small republics created by the First Founding, not the new, centralized federalism that Publius was trying to invent for the large republic envisioned in the Second Founding.[24]

II. LIBERTY

The Preamble of the Constitution, which thoroughly contrasts the attitudes of the Federalists with those of the Anti-Federalists, is a statement of optimism that there are things that government can do for us that we cannot do for ourselves, which is to "establish Justice, insure domestic Tranquility, provide for the common defense, promote the general Welfare, and secure the Blessings of Liberty to ourselves and our Posterity." The Anti-Federalists rejected these collective aspirations of We the People and the positive role of government associated with them. These "men of little faith" had only known government, namely monarchy, as a thing to be feared; in contrast, the Federalists believed in the "vigor," "firmness and efficiency of government" and warned of "an over-scrupulous jealousy of danger to the rights of the people" (Federalist 1)—hence the relative commitment to negative and positive liberty (and rights and powers), respectively.[25] Concomitantly, the two sides also understood equality differently: the Anti-Federalists' relative commitment to negative liberty meant that they understood equality as a start-state condition of the various states, not an end-state aspiration to be achieved by way of federal governmental powers.

III. TRUTH

The Federalists were not as confident about human nature as the Anti-Federalists were, at least in the small republic, in part because cultural homogeneity, the checking influence of friends and neighbors, and the limited ambit of sympathies required in the Anti-Federalists' model republic would simply not apply in a large republic. Instead, Publius preferred a trusteeship rather than a mirroring model of representation, which prescribed that representatives ought not simply to mimic their constituents' preferences but should distill the will of the people from the turbulent passions often found in a democracy.[26] As Gordon Wood observed, the Second Founders were pragmatists who adopted "a more modern and more realistic sense of political behavior."[27] One may even say that the Anti-Federalists, like Jefferson, were principled philosophers, while the Federalists, like John Adams, were pragmatic political scientists. The former wanted many virtuous republics, while the latter wanted a stronger union. Since nature provided only a weak and inefficacious union, Publius intended for science to remedy its defects. And so a new "science of politics" (Federalist 9) emerged to justify a new republicanism. Manmade institutions now had to do the work when virtue was sufficient before—institutions that could turn ambition itself into a new kind of virtue.[28] As Gordon Wood observed, the Federalists' extension of the sphere to prevent majority tyranny meant that "the older emphasis on public virtue existing throughout the society lost some of its thrust."[29]

IV. REPUBLICANISM

While all Americans in 1787–1789 were republicans in the sense that they were revolutionaries who had cut off their ties with the British and had just instituted self-government, they disagreed fundamentally on the *type* of republicanism that would work for America: whether it should be of the type that could be exercised in a small republic or the type that would flourish in an extended sphere. The Anti-Federalists possessed more faith in the people of the states than the Federalists, who modified the classical republican idea that while the pursuit of the public good was still the end of government, the multiplication of faction was now necessary to bring it about. The Federalists inverted centuries of inherited wisdom in arguing that republicanism was best preserved by social heterogeneity, not homogeneity—hence *E Pluribus Unum*—though this new republicanism was grafted alongside the older theory that was never entirely displaced.

Republicanism in a small republic was not unlike or at least closer to direct or "pure democracy" (Federalist 10), and so the Anti-Federalists were often (and certainly more often than were the Federalists) also democrats.[30] They were idealistic about human nature in small communities and stout defenders of the virtue of the people when situated within these communities. The Federalists, of course, thought democracy, and its offspring, demagoguery, to be foul words.[31] They had to, not least because pure democracy was impossible in a large republic. Thus, while Madison argued in Federalist 49 against "frequent appeals," Cato worried that "by the manner in which the president is chosen he arrives to this office at the fourth or fifth hand, nor does the highest vote, in the way he is elected, determine the choice."[32] Such Anti-Federalist objections explain why so much of the Constitution addresses the issue of representation, and so much of the *Federalist Papers* was devoted to defending Publius' institutional design for it. In truth, the Anti-Federalists were more interested in preempting the question of representation, which they thought was already settled by the Articles of Confederation, than in finding a new version of it. For in a small republic in which pure or direct democracy could flourish, misrepresentation was nearly as impossible as representation was unnecessary—and this was the model polity for the Anti-Federalists, one that Madison dismissed as nostalgia; "the blind veneration for antiquity" (Federalist 14). The Anti-Federalist theory of representation, then, was that effective and accountable representation could occur only when there is a close or mirror resemblance between the representative and the represented.[33] As Melancton Smith had argued, representatives ought to be "a true picture of the people, possess a knowledge of their circumstances and their wants, sympathize in all their distresses, and be disposed to seek their true interests."[34] And this could occur only in the small republic. Thus, while the Anti-Federalists espoused the classical, states-centered republicanism that highlighted, among other features, cultural homogeneity, negative liberty (from federal authority), community standards of morality, local attachments, and direct democracy, the Federalists' new republicanism adapted for an extended sphere tended to favor cultural heterogeneity, positive liberty, universal (or at least transcontinental) standards of morality, the virtue of empathy across communities, and representative democracy.

Incidentally, identifying Federalism and Anti-Federalism as the native fonts of American political thought also helps us to illuminate the debate about liberalism and republicanism, each of which have taken turns as the dominant tradition in American political thought.[35] Just as there were two republicanisms espoused in the Two Foundings, so there were two liberalisms. Both the Federalists and the Anti-Federalists were liberal, but they differed on whether they relied on the separation of powers or federalism (the horizontal and vertical distributions of power), respectively, to limit the power of government.[36] So the "liberal tradition" in the United States has always contained two liberalisms—one of *limited* government and one of *balancing* government. The first draws more from Locke, who rejected the divine right of kings in his *First Treatise* and proffered a theory of *personal liberty* based on natural law and contract theory in the *Second Treatise*, and the second more from Montesquieu, who theorized on the separation of powers and proffered a theory of *political liberty* based on positive (manmade) law. And so Pangle and Zuckert are right that the (First) Founders were inspired by Locke[37]—but so are Wood and Lutz that the (Second) Founders drew more heavily from Montesquieu.[38] Understanding the "founding" as the Two Foundings helps us to make sense of the liberalism–republicanism debate. Publius' genius was in pivoting from the vertical distribution of power that was the concern of Locke and redirecting his audience's attention to the horizontal distribution or the separation of powers, by borrowing from Montesquieu (whom Publius knew the Anti-Federalists would warm to because of his defense of the small republic) in Federalist 9, 10, and 47.

It is quite possible that Hartz and Pocock were both right, and Americans were more liberal in the years leading up to 1776, and they became in some ways more republican in the years leading up to 1787.[39] In any case, we miss the subtler inflections of *American* political development if we told the story only with theories inherited from Europe without an understanding of how the First and Second Founders adapted and made them our own, creating a pair of parallel languages that we have used against each other ever since. Liberalism and republicanism we inherited from Europe, but Anti-Federalism and Federalism are two strands of American political thought that are unquestionably our own.

Connecting American Political Thought (APT) with American Political Development (APD)

Having discussed the principles of the Two Foundings, we can now link them to the institutions that would embody them and move toward a general theory of APD and APT. There was a time when scholars of American politics did just that, when they searched for a general, unifying field account of the most resilient features of American politics.[40] For causal explanations of political phenomena should also (if not especially) address first causes, or causes of fundamental patterns replete in the landscape. These scholars wove political thought and political development in their overarching accounts of American politics. Louis Hartz, among them, had argued that American politics is trapped in a Lockean trance. Born free, without feudalism, according to him, Americans never learned to develop alternative traditions of thought, such as Marxism or socialism, or a viable third party.[41] Elegant and deceptively simple—and though by no means infallible—Hartz's single-causal account linking the institution of feudalism to political thought and culture explains more about multiple aspects of American politics than most theories that have been posited since. This is in part because he focused not on petty variations, but on the most resilient features of American political thought and development discernible across centuries. Even Sam Huntington, who rejected Hartz's "liberal tradition," nevertheless saw the importance of studying ideas and institutions synchronically. Indeed, it was the gap between ideas and institutions that would turn out to be his explanation for what he termed the "creedal passion periods"—the revolutionary, Jacksonian, Progressive, and countercultural eras—of American politics.[42] Others who followed Hartz, such as V. O. Key and Walter Dean Burnham, paid less attention to political thought and ideas, but they were still interested in the big picture and the resilient features of American politics. Both argued, against Hartz, that significant changes can and do happen in American politics, although they concurred with Hartz that these are periodic punctuations—"critical elections"—in a polity prone to stasis.[43] These days, however, most political scientists, if they are not political theorists, shy away from the study of ideas; they certainly refrain from offering overarching, macroscopic theories of the Hartz, Huntington, Key, or Burnham variety. The theorists who study American politics have mostly settled in their niche in APT or constitutional law, while the behaviorists and institutionalists typically find a period, an institution, or a behavior of interest and try to come up with focused accounts of what, how, and why something relatively specific happened. As a result, we now know a lot about the trees of American politics, but we may have lost sight of the forest. Perhaps there is no forest, and American politics is one random event after another. But it is an aim of this book to make this proposition rather more difficult to sustain.

In an attempt to define a subfield in American politics, Karen Orren and Stephen Skowronek have redirected political scientists back toward the big question of what American politics is about, by defining APD as "a durable shift in governing authority."[44] The phenomenon of "development," perhaps because it is, at least when taken at face value, at odds with the commitment to Burkean conservatism that is implied in written constitutionalism, has been a core idea in the study of American politics. Orren and Skowronek believe that an analytic focus on shifts in authority, and the accompanying changes in institutional forms, helps us to narrow in on the most significant events in American history. We may refer to them and their like-minded colleagues as institutionalists or, more precisely, developmentalists. Others working in APT have tried another approach toward a macroscopic overview, one with an explicit attention to ideas and how they constitute the most resilient features of American politics. We may refer to these scholars as political theorists or foundationalists. Those who study APD and APT do not always see eye to eye (or see each other at all), but together, they take us toward a general theory of American politics.

More recently, George Thomas, a foundationalist, launched a critique of Orren and Skowronek's definition of development, arguing that instead of focusing on institutions, students of American politics ought to focus on ideas, especially the foundational ones encoded in the Constitution. Though equally interested in zooming out from the trees toward the forest of what American politics is fundamentally about, Thomas argued that the principal units of analysis of this forest ought to be ideas, not institutions. The starting point of the political science of a polity ought to be, according to Thomas, the inquiry into the "logic and norms that inhere within the regime."[45] His is a fairly representative critique by the foundationalists of the developmentalists. For the foundationalists, Orren and Skowronek's definition of APD focuses too much on change or development, and institutions, and too little on ideas. To some extent, this is simply a matter of a difference of opinion as to what is more interesting for the respective scholars. While the developmentalists typically set their sights on institutions and thick descriptions of their changes, the foundationalists pay more attention to regime-foundational ideas and normative evaluations of the institutional changes that the developmentalists track.[46] But there is room for overlap, and the results are often quite promising. Thus, for example, Thomas contrasts Orren and Skowronek's approach to Jeffrey Tulis', whose book *The Rhetorical Presidency* focused on systemic health and distinguished development from transformation by suggesting that the former is "change prefigured in the government's original form."[47] Tulis is a developmentalist who is also (if not first and foremost) a foundationalist. Change, then, for Tulis and Thomas, can and should be measured only *after* the baseline of foundational principles has been established. Thus, for another foundationalist, Harvey Mansfield, it is to the Constitution's "soul" that we should be directing our inquiries. To study institutions before their constituting principles is, for the foundationalist, to put the cart before the horse. And so Mansfield believes that "institutional political science needs to be made more aware of its constitutional basis."[48] Tellingly, he observes, "most institutionalists were, and remain, political Progressives [in the modern sense]."[49] For to be committed to foundational ideas is to pay relative homage to the wisdom of the past; to highlight the primacy of institutions is to be drawn to the possibility of change.

But perhaps a synthesis of the insights of those who study APT and APD is possible, and a combined attention to both thought and development offers the most fruitful path toward a reengagement with the big questions, if not the biggest pattern of American politics. Indeed, the foundationalists' critique of the developmentalists may be a latter-day version of a scholarly Lovers' Quarrel that reveals the imprint of the Two Foundings even within the academy. After all, change or no change was exactly the choice the Federalists posed to Americans during the Second Founding. The developmentalists and foundationalists are, in effect, pursuing two strands of inquiry that had their genesis in Philadelphia in 1787: one more open to the possibility of development and therefore the primacy of institutions, and one more partial to continuity and the priority of foundational ideas as a critique of proposed institutions. (Institutions are necessarily manmade; ideas, such as those ostensibly bequeathed by God or by nature, are less clearly so.) Thomas does not fully hit his nail on its head when he suggests that an institutional focus precludes the study of ideas. Actually, in their preface to the inaugural volume of *Studies in American Political Development*, Orren and Skowronek had expressly noted, "*Studies'* historically-institutionalistic perspective is defined broadly to encompass the social and cultural institutions that impinge on government as well as governmental institutions themselves."[50] Developmentalists do study ideas and cultural phenomena; but it is true that they rarely go into normative analysis about the relative fit between a regime's foundational values and its existing institutional arrangements (for to do so is to assume that a regime does indeed possess certain uncontested, fundamental values.) Put another way, the foundationalists' disagreement with the developmentalists is more fundamentally about the different starting assumptions, respectively, of continuity versus change. The foundationalists start with the assumption that political change must be justified and in sync with regime-foundational principles, which is why normative inquiry is near to the heart of their enterprise. For their part, Orren and Skowronek are, in contrast, quite upfront that if "APD does not reject the premise that there is order to be discerned in political affairs, it does demote that premise to the status of a baseline."[51] This of course runs in direct contradiction to foundationalism. As far as generalizations go, Mansfield is probably right that many historical institutionalists and developmentalists are politically progressive—at least in terms of their normative orientation toward change— but he also helps confirm its correlative, that many (though of course not all) foundationalists lean conservative, at least in the sense that seeming deviations from the constitutional order are deemed presumptively invalid until they can be reconciled with "original" principles culled from so-called canonical texts. Developmentalists do revel in the twists and turns of politics; they have tended to observe more flux than foundations. Hence the commitment to "thick-description" and the policy of "greater flexibility in manuscript length" in *Studies*.[52] Foundationalists and theorists of APT, by contrast, are generally more interested in what endures in political life, not in its flux. Hence Thomas' charge that developmentalists seldom stop to ask if the twists are "true, or right."[53]

Because both sides have a point, an account of American politics that explicitly links development with political thought on the one hand, and change and continuity on the other, may enrich our understanding of both APD and APT. Indeed, the distance between Thomas and Orren and Skowronek narrows considerably if we were to contrast both their approaches to rational-choice institutionalism.[54] Although Thomas might disapprove of Orren and Skowronek's focused attention on the superstructure of the "state" over the foundational structure of the Constitution, all three accept that there are fewer avenues for change in the American political order than do Paul Pierson and other rational-choice institutionalists.[55] APD scholars are drawn to odd configurations of authority because it is in these instances that institutional change is halting, tentative, and often convoluted. Thus, if "intercurrence [the simultaneous operation of multiple orders or overlapping authorities] is the purest expression of historically-institutional reasoning," it is because Orren and Skowronek see wholesale change in the American political system as a rather rare thing indeed.[56] APD scholars of the Orren and Skowronek variety tend to resist isolating temporal pivots because they think of "multiple temporal orders," so that every path is *already* the intercurrence of the preexisting and ongoing historical construction of politics. Agency and change are necessarily more limited in such a temporal matrix.[57]

Consider how a perspective deploying "paths" and another centered on intercurrence would differentially characterize the Two Foundings. Paul Pierson designates "paths" (as well as "sequences" and "conjunctures") as demarcated points in a single stream of time so that there is significant room for agency in his theory of politics and time. "Once a country has started down a track," Margaret Levi has similarly argued, "the costs of reversal are very high."[58] She goes on to use the metaphor of climbing a tree with many branches, and suggests that path dependence is registered by the difficulty of jumping across sub-branches once one has traversed up a particular branch. Pierson and Levi would probably characterize the Articles of Confederation as one powerfully path-dependent document, creating positive feedback in the form of "coercive authority" that made it prohibitively difficult, for example, to alter course by way of an amendment.[59]

Pierson and Levi's methodological frame works best in polities least tethered to precedent and constitutionalism, so that political actors are relatively free to initiate new paths. Paths do matter, but a developmentalist reminds us that not every path is a distinct branch of history, and such distinct branches are arguably few and far between. There are also intercurring paths, and they may well form the majority of paths that we see in American history. The years 1776–1781 may have inaugurated a fresh path by creating a constitutional bond—indeed a "perpetual union"—that had never existed between 13 sovereign entities. But 1787–1789 saw a concerted effort by the Federalists to repudiate the earlier path, in the creation of independent executive and judiciary branches when neither had existed before. Positive feedback from the earlier constitution, which had addressed only the legislative power, made the Connecticut Compromise a necessary condition for the ratification of the second Constitution, as were the balancing acts between two conceptions of union contained in Articles 5 and 7 (more below). Pierson's and Levi's conceptual apparatuses can explain this much, but are less helpful for the next step of the Second Founding, when the Anti-Federalists snatched a partial victory from defeat when in the final push toward ratification, they successfully cajoled the Federalists into affirming the fundamental principles of the Articles of Confederation by way of the Bill of Rights as a condition for coming on board. (To be sure, some Anti-Federalists were not satisfied that the Bill in its final form went far enough to address their concerns, but the Bill would likely not have happened had it not been for their agitation.) More so than anywhere else, this part of the Constitution does not represent a reversal or a branching of paths, but the intercurrence of an older commitment with the newer one. The Articles of Confederation can be understood as living in reincarnated form in the second, amended half of the Constitution, where an uneasy affirmation of states' rights now stood alongside a generous grant of power to a new government in the preceding articles. The new federalism, therefore, was only semi-new; it was a *creative* synthesis of the old and the new. Here was the first instance of APD, a new path (in the Declaration and Articles of Confederation), a reversal of paths (in the first half of the Constitution), and the intercurrence of paths (via the Bill of Rights) all in one. This was quintessential *American* political development, a prototype for the remaking of the American compact that—as I will show in Chapters 4 and 6—Civil War Republicans and New Deal Democrats would successfully replicate.

Orren and Skowronek's emphasis on "intercurrence" on the one hand, and Pierson's on "paths" on the other, reveal a marked difference in the way historical institutionalists (mostly developmentalists) and rational-choice institutionalists envision the possibility of change in the American system, with the foundationalists and developmentalists seeing far fewer avenues for agency and wholesale change than do Pierson and other rational-choice institutionalists. Put another way, Orren and Skowronek's relative focus on institutions acting "at the same time" (intercurrence) is closer to the foundationalists' understanding that the Constitution acts *at all times* than Pierson's belief that institutions and actors within them are relatively free to act "in time." In the end, Orren and Skowronek do not find or anticipate as much change as some foundationalists might assign to them. After all, the object of their study is development, not revolution.

Far from being fatal, then, the distance between the foundationalists' critique and Orren and Skowronek's definition of APD narrows if we were to amend the latters' definition of APD to a subset of its original form, to "durable shifts in *constitutional* authority." Orren and Skowronek may disagree, but not as vigorously as one might initially expect. The starting point of concurrence can be found in their insistence on the study of governing structures, because they are "ultimately" where political actors seek to institutionalize their goals into deliverable mandates.[60] The "ultimately" could be pushed one logical step back. If all political actors "ultimately" seek to effect durable shifts in governing authority, then the greatest shift must be in the text or meaning of the Constitution itself, the place where ultimate governing authority or governing "powers" are spelled out. A constitutional amendment (or even a constitutional reinterpretation) would arguably be as durable as any shift could get, and the crowning accomplishment of any political movement. Orren and

Skowronek's definition is not inconsistent with the foundationalists' invitation to focus on the Constitution and its principles because the most durable developments are often those that are etched onto the highest law of the land.

Nonfoundationalists who study the Constitution and patterns in American politics already agree. Bruce Ackerman had offered us one conciliatory way forward (though his work precedes this debate), suggesting that the essential character of our Constitution is not rights foundationalism, but dualism.[61] According to Ackerman, during moments of higher-lawmaking, when the Constitution is amended, rights-foundational claims from a previous "constitutional moment" are rejected or recast in deference to We the People; but during moments of legislative, normal-lawmaking, due reverence is observed of the past's *vox populi*, so the Constitution may be said to be intermittently rights foundationalist and democratic. The "constitutional moments" Ackerman identifies—the Founding, the Civil War and Reconstruction, and the New Deal—are also developmental moments of the first rank that other scholars have long acknowledged.[62] For Key and Burnham, they are "critical elections" and "realignments."[63] For Hofstadter, they are "periodical psychic sprees that purport to be moral crusades."[64] Insofar as Ackerman's account permits us to behold the foundational nature of our Constitution that permits change and yet preserves continuity, he takes the mean position between the developmentalists, who see flux, and the foundationalists, who perceive continuity.

In Search of American Exceptionalism: Defining the "A" in APD and APT

Where I do think both Thomas and Orren and Skowronek fall short is their decision not to interrogate the "A" in APD and APT. This is the lacuna this book hopes to fill. While many events count as durable shifts in governing authority, Orren and Skowronek rely on "durable" and especially "authority" to do the filtering work. Thomas does not use the volatile word "exceptionalism," but given that his concern with ideas is really a battle cry to continue the search for APD qua *meaning* (as opposed to Orren and Skowronek's more limited search for just a definition of the field), perhaps his critique might have been sharper had he posited the foundational features of the Constitution as a supplement to Orren and Skowronek's definition. As such, Skowronek is correct when he observed that Thomas' critique "ups the ante for those . . . who want to preserve and protect inquiry into the 'essential character' of the American regime."[65]

APD is not just about the study of political development *in* America; it is *American* political development. A definition of APD should interrogate the "A" in APD. It should, according to Richard Bensel, "emphasize that all work, however circumscribed in time, place, and subject, must reflect on the *larger tapestry of the American experience in some way* [my emphasis]."[66] In other words, Bensel calls us to identify the resilient features of American politics that comprehensively connect the past with the present.

"PD" is just not the same if it is not "APD." The early luminaries of the field, such as John Burgess, did not shy away from claims about American exceptionalism, and their detractors, such as Charles Beard, did not fail to call them out on their self-congratulation either.[67] From the beginning, APD welcomed foundationalists, like Burgess, who studied the Constitution and the behaviorists (and institutionalists), like Beard, who directed their inquiry at the "interests." Orren and Skowronek do, however, acknowledge the particular nature of APD scholarship and offer tentative though indirect steps in the direction of explicating the "A" in APD. First, the authors argue that APD scholars do not treat history as "a grab bag of examples" but rather that "pattern identification is the sine qua non of the enterprise."[68] Second, Orren and Skowronek note that recurrent or cyclical accounts figure heavily in APD because there is a nagging sense that often, political change in America merely "reshuffle(s) old forms."[69] Third, the authors note that APD is a framework, which embraces "contradictory rules and structures" and "the fugue-like motion of stops, starts, and repetitions."[70] Each of these claims—that there is a constancy, a cyclicity, and a paradoxicality to American politics—are not by themselves definitional, but they are meta-definitional to the extent that they point to the resilient features of American politics. First, organic or unwritten constitutions, such as the British one, which evolved glacially over long stretches of time, are less likely to produce recurring patterns of change discernible across centuries, in part because evolution can take myriad paths in polities unconstrained by written charters. Second, old forms seldom have the luxury of resurfacing or recurring in those countries, such as Venezuela, where wholly new power arrangements established by way of *coups d'état* can quickly and thoroughly displace old hegemonies. Third, paradoxes and contradictions occur less frequently in countries like Switzerland, where a provision for referenda makes it easy for their constitution to be amended.[71]

These features of APD scholarship begin to say something about the "A" in APD—that there is something about the U.S. Constitution in its capacity to constrain and route change in predictable directions, as Hartz, Huntington, Key, and Burnham separately point to in their different theories—but Orren and Skowronek do not follow through. The foundationalists are right to say that to be able to separate a transformation from complete revolution, we need to know we are still on the same "site," to use Orren and Skowronek's term.[72] Orren and Skowronek appear to think that the "site" in question is a matter easily settled by geographical continuity; yet this is exactly where American political identity is most ambivalent, because there are 51 overlapping geo-graphical sovereignties recognized in the Constitution. The unique feature of the American Constitution is not so much that it is dualistic as Ackerman described it, but that it codifies two legitimate ways of characterizing the col-lective American identity: whether the United States is a union of individuals or a compact of states.[73] Over two centuries after the fact, we still cannot agree if the Second Founders meant We the People of the *United* States or We the People of the United *States*.[74]

Defining the "A" in APD and APT

We can only understand that "A" in APD and APT if we appreciated the cre-ative synthesis of the principles and aspirations of the First and Second Found-ings that Publius (with some unsolicited assistance from the Anti-Federalists) would accomplish. To create a United States from a united States, Publius would have to borrow from the legitimacy of First Founding, while at the same time undermining it. He would create new institutions, while also respect-ing some older ones. He would be the first developmentalist, and also the first American political thinker. Publius' principal contribution to APD and APT was the new federalism. The Second Founding layered one conception of dem-ocratic sovereignty onto another that had been codified seven years before, leaving us with two legitimate but antithetical conceptions of union, liberal-ism, truth, and republicanism.

Scholars of federalism, much like rational-choice institutionalists, have tended to characterize federalism as a single-moment bargain or a static division of power between opposing groups. Their accounts rarely address the tempo-ral element—the effect of a prior conception of democratic sovereignty—that made *ongoing* disagreement and contestation about the very nature of federal-ism inevitable. Thus for Martin Diamond, federalism is a *settlement* pointed at "two contradictory ends": the one committed to confederation and the other to complete unity; or, as Martha Derthick called it, a *compromise* "to be both one great nation and many relatively quite small, local communities." When accounting for the origins of the "federal bargain," Riker identifies the desire on the part of the one group advocating territorial expansion, and the desire on the part of another to accept the terms of expansion because of the antici-pation of some external military threat or opportunity.[75] We are left with the impression that as a bargain was struck, so the bargain will stay. These charac-terizations of America's contribution to political theory as a bargain are not so different from "big bang" theories. They highlight the conditions and the ex-periences the delegates brought to the Philadelphia convention, but the focus ultimately is on the deal reached in 1787–1789, not the *continuing* debate about federalism it helped launch.

From a developmental perspective, what is more interesting, and equally consequential, was the pregame before the putative end game. The pregame was the contrasting interpretations of America's initial experience with self-government in the 1780s. Put most starkly, whereas the Anti-Federalists saw only a couple of bumps on the road after Independence, the Federalists saw an unmitigated and conflagrating disaster. Scholars who have studied the "founding" have typically reached back to before 1776, placed the late 1780s in the same celebrated era as 1776, or characterized the 1780s as the disaster, most graphically represented by Shays' Rebellion, from which we were permanently rescued in 1787.[76] Only the second group of scholars at least implicitly addressed the different reactions of the Federalists and Anti-Federalists, when they addressed the successes of the years 1781–1789, where democracy and self-government breathed its first breath here under the Articles of Confederation. This period is of critical importance, for it is only because the Articles of Confederation had enjoyed enough successes that Anti-Federalist attachment to them proved so strong. Between 1776 and 1789 were the critical years of 1781–1789, when Public Enemy Number 1, the British, were gone and Americans, under arguably the first democratically ratified constitution in the world, got used to one conception of federalism—and one that promised "Perpetual Union," no less. Rightly or wrongly, those who refused to sign on to the Second Founding saw this period as the age of original American innocence, when a constellation of 13 sovereign and virtuous republics enjoyed and jealously guarded their hard-won liberties formalized under the Articles of Confederation. On the eve of the American Revolution, well ahead of the ratification of the second Constitution, state sovereignties (later, states' rights) were born when provincial congresses from ten of the original 13 colonies drew up and democratically ratified their state constitutions.[77] Four states, New Hampshire (January 6, 1776), South Carolina (March 26, 1776), Virginia (June 29, 1776), and New Jersey (July 2, 1776), adopted provisional constitutions before the Declaration of Independence and six more, Delaware (September 11, 1776), Pennsylvania (September 28, 1776), Maryland (November 8, 1776), North Carolina (December 14, 1776), Georgia (February 4, 1777), and New York (April 20, 1777), would do so within a year. (Massachusetts waited until 1780 because the first version of its constitution, promulgated by the General Court, was rejected by the citizens, who objected that they had not been consulted on its contents.) By 1777, only Rhode Island and Connecticut were still operating under royal charters (with references to the monarchy struck out) and not by state constitutions ratified by the people of the states.[78] "The unanimous Declaration of the thirteen united States of America" was the first collective expression of fellow feeling among the colonists, though it was one united mostly by a shared commitment to state sovereignty, as registered by the capitalization of "States" but not the "united." This is why, as Tocqueville observed, "it is incontestably true that the tastes and the habits of republican government in the United States were first created in the townships and the provincial assemblies."[79] We the People of the States had spoken many times, in their own state constitutional conventions, before We the People of the United States did.[80]

It is because the Anti-Federalists' conception of confederal or peripheralized federalism had enjoyed over a decade of practice and reinscription in the minds of Americans that the new, centralized federalism would never enjoy the unfettered loyalty of its citizens. The First Founding's conception of democratic sovereignty and collective identity was codified and affirmed by the Articles of Confederation, which was styled a "league of friendship" (in Article 3) between the states. Critically, this constitution codified not only a much looser relationship between the states than the second, but it also boasted a democratic pedigree to rival the one that replaced it.

This, then, is about as close as one can come to staking an empirically verifiable claim about American exceptionalism: the United States is the only federal country in the world to have democratically enacted two and only two constitutions, each specifying a different kind of union.[81] Americans *chose* to be American twice. In other republics, federalism is the means to a (tension-resolving) end rather than an end—the basis of the union's identity—itself. Separatist movements in other federal republics, such as the Mouvement de libération nationale du Québec in Canada, and the Jammu Kashmir Liberation Front in India, tend to be piecemeal conflicts that call only for secession of particular territories, not alternative conceptions of union applicable to all territories. What makes the Lovers' Quarrel more intense here than might arise in other federal republics is that elsewhere language or culture is a basis of local identity while national identity is democratically constructed. In America, state *and* national identities are a matter of democratic construction, entwined in two distinct conceptions of union. Americans quarrel passionately and often unyieldingly about *the same thing*, namely federalism, because there is no other basis for their identity; not blood, not religion. The very thing that binds Americans is also, because of different understandings of it, what divides Americans.

Publius' New Federalism: A Developmental and Ideational Account

Publius in 1787, then, had to perform a delicate dance. His real intention, of course, was to undo the First Founding and the old federalism, but he had to do so respectfully, even surreptitiously.[82] Consider, that in Federalist 15 to 22, he would attack the first constitution's "insufficiency," but he dared not challenge its *legitimacy*. His opponents, the Anti-Federalists, did not return the courtesy, because they had the status quo on their side. Insufficient or not, the Articles and the Confederation Congress that formally operated from 1781–1789 were democratically ordained. Indeed, one could argue that the Articles were a more contemporaneous expression and institutionalization of the Revolution's ideals. It was under the auspices of the Confederation Congress that the American Revolution was conducted and concluded with the Treaty of Paris. Unlike the Constitution, the Articles were unanimously agreed to and ratified without cajoling or procedural tricks.[83] The Articles were drafted by a Committee of the Second Continental Congress in June 1776, and debated for over a year, more than the four months delegates spent at the Philadelphia convention. Once signed by the delegates, the document was sent off to the state legislatures for ratification, and it became official when Maryland became the last state, in 1781, to constitute the unanimity required for ratifying it. Compare the painstaking four years it took to ratify the first constitution and the blitzkrieg strategy occurring over nine months to ratify the second. The Anti-Federalists were up in arms not because they were against the federal idea, but because they believed that Americans in various states had already spoken loudly in favor of one conception of it. It was thus with incredulity that Cincinnatus posed the question, "will any one believe, that it is because we are become wiser, that in twelve years we are to overthrow every system which reason and experience taught us was right?"[84]

The Articles were, in spirit and substance, a very different constitution than the one Publius was recommending. Unlike the Constitution, which devoted over 80 percent of its words to enumerating the powers of the federal branches in its first three articles, the Articles were much more circumspect, spending only about half of that proportion describing the powers of Congress, and only in Article 9. The government created under the Articles had no executive, no judiciary, and no taxing power. Indeed, the united States (the lack of capitalization is advised) government in 1787 lacked a coherent or ongoing identity, but entered into existence only as the delegates of the states were "in Congress assembled."[85] So deeply ingrained was the notion of state sovereignty that some Anti-Federalists even rejected the "republican guarantee clause" (Article 4, Section IV) of the new Constitution. "For though it is improbable," wrote William Symmes, "that any State will choose to alter the form of its government; yet it ought to be the privelege [*sic*] of every State to do as it will in this affair."[86] This is just about the purest affirmation of the old federalism as there could have been: for some die-hard Anti-Federalists, state sovereignty trumped even the hard-won revolutionary ideal of republicanism.

The second Constitution of the United States would, ultimately, be endowed with nearly equal legitimacy; yet it was very different in the conception of federalism and union it proposed. For a new Constitution to replace a preexisting one, the Federalists knew that they had to launch a ratification campaign that could conjure as much democratic sanction in their Constitution as the old one possessed. It would be "the first national campaign in a popularly based, territorially extended, representative government."[87] This was a campaign in the original, multifaceted, coordinative sense, but one that, critically, both sanctioned *and* attenuated the legitimacy of the states in its ratification rule specified in Article 7. On the one hand, Article 7 simply assumed that the states were legitimate units of the Union, of which the concurrence of nine was necessary for ratifying the Constitution. This was an implicit endorsement of the first constitution, an acknowledgement of settled matters after the First Founding. On the other hand, Article 7 explicitly forbade the state legislatures, where state sovereignties were vested, from having a voice in the ratification process. Instead, it was determined that "Conventions of nine states" would be sufficient for ratification. Here was an attempt to generate a higher legitimacy for the new Constitution. By moving away from the state legislatures, the Federalists were reallocating the sovereignty of state houses to the people of the states; by using a ratio of nine out of 13, they were aggregating the people of the states across state lines and creating a national demos. The Federalists conceded that the states were legitimate constitutive elements out of which a majority of nine was made (hence a tip of the hat to the Articles), but also that no one state possessed a veto against decision making (unlike in the Articles). And thus even before ratification was secured, the very rule specified for ratification had already secured "a more perfect Union"—in effect, a different kind of union. For to accept that a majority of citizens spread across state lines can speak for the whole was to accept the linked fate that makes a nation. Article 7, then, was a pivotal item of creative synthesis. With it, the Federalists reconfigured the body politic, creating an aggregated We the People when no such entity existed before, while disguising the creation by affirming the prior legitimacy of the states by using their peoples as part of the democratic aggregating process.

The Federalists also secured the advancing legitimacy of the new federalism by stipulating in Article 4, Section III the authority of the federal government to admit new states and to "make all needful Rules and Regulations respecting the Territory or other Property belonging to the United States."[88] This meant that whereas the territorial boundaries of the 13 original colonies were created by royal decree or charter, the territorial boundary of the United States was not. (This became especially true in 1845, when after Florida joined the Union, there were now more states created by Congress than had been created by the British Crown.[89]) The Federalists had laid the groundwork for a "more perfect Union."

If that had been that, perhaps the Federalists would have had the final word, and we would not have had a recurring Lovers' Quarrel. But the Articles' conception of peripheralized federalism had not only found their way into Article 7, but they were also incorporated, with greater bite, into Article 5. This is significant, for though Publius and Federal Farmer battled with Article 7, which was set up to give Publius the advantage, their descendants would have to contend only with Article 5, which does not provide a clear advantage to either side of the Lovers' Quarrel. The intercurrence of two conceptions of federalism and union, weakly present in Article 7, is particularly evident in Article 5, which also happens to be the place in the Constitution that both constrains and permits change—that is, the place where the polity's developmental potential is laid out. Article 5 stipulates that any amendment to the Constitution must first be proposed by two thirds of Congress or two thirds of the state legislatures to call a national convention, and then ratified by three quarters of the state legislatures or state ratifying conventions, with the method of ratification to be decided by Congress. Two features of the higher-lawmaking method are worthy of note. First, the ratification is always left to the states. In this, the preexisting legitimacy and sovereignty of the states is recognized, an acknowledgment of the order of things codified in 1781.[90] (The only remaining entrenched clause in the Constitution that is still active, that no state shall be deprived of its equal suffrage in the Senate—an analogy to the fact that each state had possessed one vote in the Confederated Congress—vindicates the First Founding's commitment to the sovereignty of each state.[91]) Second and conversely, while the ratification is always left to the states, it is the federal Congress that wields the agenda-setting power in deciding whether the ratifying units would be state legislatures or conventions. Further, once a supermajority is reached, the new amendment is binding even on those states that did not consent to the amendment. This is a sharp departure from the unanimity required in the Articles. As such, the new amendment ratification rule represented a movement toward centralized federalism, and the result was the layering of a new conception of federalism on the old. Ackerman was right that Article 5 is where the heart of the Constitution lies, but contrary to him, its heart is not dualism, but rather the new federalism. It is because Article 5 encapsulates principles from both of our Two Foundings that it effectively ordained that for there to be APD, a Lovers' Quarrel must first occur—a tussle between political actors either to restore the principles of the First Founding (as the Anti-Federalists and their disciples have attempted) or to creatively (re)synthesize the principles of the Two Foundings, by artfully fusing the new with the old (as the Federalists and their descendants have endeavored).[92]

Beyond Articles 5 and 7, the Anti-Federalists secured the greatest enduring legacy of the First Founding in the second half of the Constitution, the Bill of Rights. Publius in Federalist 84 had argued eloquently against a Bill of Rights, suggesting (among other reasons) that a government truly constituted by the people would not need enumerated restraints. But the Anti-Federalists would not back down precisely because they differed on the method of constructing "the People" and insisted, tellingly, on "amendments" (rather than new Articles) or counterweights to the Constitution, which were finally ratified in 1791. All told, We the People spoke twice—in 1776–1781 and 1787–1789—not once. This is why APD can only be durable but never permanent because we have never conclusively settled the question of just who we are. Madison acknowledged as much in Federalist 46 when he said that the "federal and State governments are in fact but different agents and trustees of the people." Similarly, he tried to smooth over divisions between the Federalists and Anti-Federalists by observing in Federalist 39 that the Constitution is "partly federal and partly national." This was intercurrence of the first order, the layering of the artifacts of one era over another that laid the groundwork for future quarrel. "By attempting to confront and retard the thrust of the Revolution with the rhetoric of the Revolution," Gordon Wood astutely observed, "the Federalists fixed the terms for the future discussion of American politics."[93] He might also have added that the rhetoric of the Revolution would in turn become the petard by which the Anti-Federalists and their descendants, as we shall see in Chapter 2 and 3, would hoist the principles of the Second Founding to restore those of the First.

Even though the Federalists won the day, scholars have estimated that the balance of public opinion for and against ratification was probably roughly equal.[94] Of the 55 men who came to Philadelphia in 1787, 16 failed to sign off on the proposed Constitution that was sent for ratification in the states—a fundamental point that Abraham Lincoln makes much of, as I show in Chapter 4. That is to say, even after the agenda-setting of the Virginians, the intense lobbying of Publius, and the procedural tricks of the Federalists such as the insistence on the ratification rule of all or nothing, a full 16 of the "framers" remained uncommitted.[95] For all of Publius' considerable persuasive skills, America's understanding of democratic sovereignty in the 1770s and 1780s enjoyed the positive feedback of the first-mover advantage. And that is why even though the Articles came to be seriously discredited, there were fundamental aspects of the document that were transferred to the Constitution, especially in Articles 5 and 7 and the Bill of Rights, and why two centuries after the fact, there are still nationally prominent figures chanting its *leitmotif*.

If the new federalism, understood as the layering of one conception of union over another and therefore a contested distribution of powers between two levels of government, is the essential and foundational feature of the American Constitution, then changes in the distribution of power between the two levels (i.e., durable shifts in federal authority) are the developmental episodes of the American Constitution. And if what makes America is also what remakes America, a definition of APD also becomes a theory of APD. Readers interested in a more detailed defense of my definition of APD as "durable shifts in federal authority" can consult Appendix I.

Iterations of the Two Foundings

Having argued that the new federalism, or more specifically the consecutive layering of one legitimate conception of union and democratic sovereignty over another in a brief span of time, is the distinctive feature of the second American Constitution, and that development occurs when the Lovers' Quarrel is engaged to bring about durable shifts in federal authority, I turn now to differentiate my theory of APD from another that privileged the Federalists' statist conclusions over the Anti-Federalists' democratic legacy. My point is that *both* sides have contributed to APD. Bruce Ackerman's *We the People* rightly put the American people front and center in elaborating the meaning and development of our Constitution—*but which American people?* Ackerman's constitutional moments are nationalist, "neo-Federalist" moments in which a new state-building or nationalizing milestone was reached, and never the Anti-Federalist ones.[96] His focus was on founding and re-founding, but not on what may be conceived as de-founding or un-founding, when the Federalists' new federalism came up against opposition by those who defended the virtues of the small republic and suffered retreat. Yet for every Federalist moment in American history, there has been an equal and opposite Anti-Federalist moment when the Spirit of '76, and not '89, held sway. Such was the case for the Revolution of 1800, the Jacksonian era, and the Reagan Revolution, when the Anti-Federalists' philosophy of states' rights, democracy, "originalism," fiscal restraint, cultural homogeneity, and so forth held sway.[97] Far from being periods of democratic indolence, these putatively lower-lawmaking moments were typically when "the raving howl of Democracy" was heard.[98] If Ackerman grants more democratic legitimacy to higher-lawmaking moments, it is because he is more partial to the *collective* sovereignty of the American people and large-republic republicanism than to direct or pure democracy, more effectively exercised at the state level, as understood by the Anti-Federalists.

The clearest place where this emerges as a consistency problem is that Ackerman needs to claim *textually* that Article 5 codifies dualism (because without a written constitution that specifies a method of amending the highest law, there cannot be two separate tracks for lawmaking), and yet he also wants to claim *non-textually* that Article 5 invites dualism because he focuses on "il-legalities" or "unconventional adaptations" that transcend the formal require-ments of Article 5. On the one hand, since Article 5 formally demands that a super-majority of citizens be on board before higher-lawmaking can transpire, this allows Ackerman to say that higher-lawmaking is democracy in practice, or moments when the people's sovereignty is exercised. On the other hand, Ackerman also wants to say that majorities can be created by "illegalities" and "unconventional adaptations" of the formal requirements of Article 5, which is really to say that majorities may not be always forthcoming or necessary for higher-lawmaking. So are higher-lawmaking periods moments when We the People speak or not? Here, Ackerman's commitment to neo-Federalist under-standings of democracy is subtler than even he lets on.

If Ackerman thinks that We the People do speak during higher-lawmaking moments, it is because he is keener on national majorities than on pure de-mocracy or concurrent majorities in the states. It is not the quantity of people speaking that is doing the work for Ackerman, but the manner in which they are aggregated. That is to say, his conception of union guides his understand-ing of re-founding episodes. Indeed, the title of Ackerman's books and his selection of "constitutional moments" imply that republicanism, as he un-derstood it, had transpired in lockstep with the "national idea."[99] He is a neo-Federalist, because his idea of national republicanism stands opposed to the Anti-Federalists' states-centered one. The essential dualism of the American Constitution, as it turns out, is not the existence of two tracks of lawmaking, but two democratically sanctioned conceptions of federalism and republicanism.

Ackerman's conflation of two types of republicanism is not uncommon. James Morone's *Democratic Wish* is similarly partial to democracy as a national but not also a local and confederal idea.[100] But he comes closer to acknowledg-ing the two sides of the Lovers' Quarrel than does Ackerman when he observes that "at the heart of American politics is a dread and a yearning" and the story of Americans politics is how Americans mastered their "anti-statist trepida-tions by pursuing their democratic wish."[101] What Morone may have also said is that the dread is mostly Anti-Federalist in origin, and the yearning is mostly Federalist. Anti-statism is not merely a "dread" but a positive political theory. The "myth of *communal* democracy [my emphasis]" scored uneven victories and occasional losses in America because it was opposed by an alternative ideological strand—one that privileged local democracy and the older con-ception of federalism.[102]

Ackerman's and Morone's insights may have been sharpened had they ac-knowledged that the American demos speaks with two voices, and that the "democratic wish" can be either a more national or a more confederal yearning.

Put another way, the democratic ideal assumes that the question of political identity has been settled so that its operationalization by way of a majority is simply a matter of logistics. Ackerman is probably correct that no rights, collective or individual, save for a very few (such as the right of equal suffrage in the Senate) in America are categorical and beyond amendment, but he fails to acknowledge that the powers that determine these rights are themselves subject to contest—hence our recurring tussle about where sovereignty lies. So our Constitution is not rights-foundationalist, as Ackerman correctly notes, but we may still be foundationalistic, as Thomas and others have argued, in the sense that if we somehow became wholly national or wholly federal, America would not have developed, but collapsed. This is a revealing counterfactual—it tells us that the essence of our Constitution lies in its dual conception of union. At the heart of the highest law of our land is a confounding contradiction that the descendants of Publius and Federal Farmer in each political generation have tried to master, but never fully conquered.

Political actors, parties, and movements have attempted to bring about durable shifts in federal authority since 1787–1789, whether this was Henry Clay's "American System," nineteenth-century "dual federalism," "cooperative federalism" during the New Deal, Lyndon Johnson's "creative federalism," or Nixon's and Reagan's "New Federalism" (not to be confused with the Federalists' new federalism, which really suggests that Nixon and Reagan were going after the Anti-Federalists' *old* federalism). Whether it was during the Nullification Crisis, during the Confederacy, or in Ronald Reagan's proud but technically inaccurate proclamation that "We are a federation of sovereign states," Anti-Federalism has been resurrected time and again in American politics.[103] So too has centralized federalism, ultimately the belief that "a more perfect Union" could be deployed to achieve collective, national goals. American "political time" recurs because our twin sets of ideas from our Two Foundings, like information in quantum mechanics, do not disappear; they are merely reworked by new generations, with the information of what they used to be etched onto their contemporary incarnations.[104] Federalist and Anti-Federalist impulses have operated side by side at every moment in American politics. At no moment has one fully engulfed the other, though at any given moment one is usually more dominant than the other.

Chapter Synopses

As Machiavelli wrote of adversity as a prelude to triumph, the Lovers' Quarrel has evinced ideational and institutional demolition as a prelude to renewal and building. In what follows, I survey the two alternating creative/destructive tracks traversed by the Federalists and the Anti-Federalists and their descendants as they commandeered the major breakpoints in our history to bring about durable shifts—retrenchments or expansions—of federal authority. In each iteration, the descendants of the Anti-Federalists and Federalists took a bifurcated stand on union, liberty, truth, and republicanism that ran back to the First and Second Foundings. The parallels between these episodes are briefly sketched in Appendices II and III. I alternate these chapters not because of the particular utility of a chronological account, but because I want to show the tit-for-tat dynamics of the Lovers' Quarrel as it has transpired in two and a quarter centuries: how members of each political generation have successfully repudiated older conceptions of We the People only to be challenged on the terms of their own success by a future cohort. As we shall see, the Anti-Federalists have always tried to rewrite history in the image of the First Founding—and Madison in 1791 and Jefferson in 1800 were the first two to do this—while the Federalists have always sought to creatively reconcile the principles of Two Foundings in the service of the Second. As Norman Jacobson once asked: "What else is national disintegration but a prelude to national rebirth?"[105] Certainly, no one period of history could ever be perfectly compared to another. But this is less true in a nation bound by a written text that fuses the principles of Two Foundings, so that each generation of Americans, if they are to pursue their happiness, must invoke one of two antithetical halves of the Constitution—either its enumerated powers, or the rights that limit them—to do their bidding.

In Chapter 2, I examine the Lovers' Quarrel of the Second Founders in office, who started disagreeing on the meaning of the Constitution as soon as the federal government opened for business, with Washington and Hamilton embarking immediately on an aggressively nationalist economic program. We will explore how Madison's split from Hamilton, and his defection to the Jeffersonian persuasion in what would culminate in the "Revolution of 1800"—in effect, a counter-revolution to the Federalists' overthrow of the Articles of Confederation—would sharpen the lines that had already divided the Federalists from the Anti-Federalists in 1787–1789. Despite Jefferson's conciliatory observation in his First Inaugural address that "we are all Republicans, we are all Federalists," he knew exactly where he stood on the Lovers' Quarrel. Jefferson's attempted retrenchment of the federal government came alongside, and indeed was justified by, a total rejection of the Federalist disdain for democracy that the Anti-Federalists had championed.

In Chapter 3, I explore the continuation of the Jeffersonian surge under Andrew Jackson and the Democratic Party, after the interregnum of nationalism during the War of 1812 and the "Era of Good Feelings" that exemplified a fleeting truce between the disciples of Publius and Federal Farmer. I argue that the Democratic Party would become a potent champion of the rallying cry of this era, states' rights, by abiding by a commitment to fiscal austerity and against internal improvements, and by adopting a theory of enumerated powers for the interpretation of the Constitution. By its decentralized organizational structure and its role in the nineteenth-century "state of courts and parties" which preceded the modern bureaucratic state, the Democratic Party was able to enact a durable retrenchment of federal authority.

In Chapter 4, we examine the greatest Lovers' Quarrel the nation ever engaged; one that took us to the brink of divorce. I will argue, against the grain of established scholarship, that the Confederate States of America represented, even more so than the slave power, the apotheosis of the states' rights doctrine, with the Declaration of Independence, the scripture of the First Founding, figuring heavily in Jefferson Davis and the South's defense of secession. Conversely, Lincoln and the Republicans' most enduring developmental mark was not emancipation or civil rights, but the advancement of a more perfect Union. For though Jim Crow would follow fast on the heels of Reconstruction, secession would never be seriously contemplated again. I will argue that Lincoln's words at Gettysburg have become etched onto the national memory because with those words, and the neo-Federalist philosophy underlying them, he would cross the philosophical bridge into the cherished territory of the Anti-Federalists, the Declaration, and take those principles back in defense of a Union stronger even than the one Publius had dreamt of. Such is the nature and formula for creative resynthesis or political revolution, American style.

In Chapter 5, I examine one of the most enigmatic periods of American history, the Progressive era, which started from the 1890s and spanned the 1910s. I will argue that we cannot make sense of this kaleidoscopic movement unless we incorporate the missing piece to conventional accounts of it: the movement's debt to Anti-Federalism. Both the Democratic and Republican parties could claim the Progressive mantra at the turn of the twentieth century because it was Federalism and Anti-Federalism in more perfect equipoise than possibly any other movement in American history. After all, its followers and spokespersons used, in their own words, "Hamiltonian means for Jeffersonian ends" (just as, incidentally, the Pragmatists amongst them, such as Charles Sanders Peirce and William James, were trying to bridge science and morality). Although the historical consensus appears to be that the era is to be remembered by the fierce "New Nationalism" of Theodore Roosevelt, I argue that it is just as well, if not better, understood by the romantic idealism of Woodrow Wilson's "New Freedom" and the philosophy and spirit of Anti-Federalism. The Lovers' Quarrel transpires even in the most unexpected of places.

In Chapter 6, I examine how the New Deal would dramatically expand the responsibilities of the federal government and forge the greatest arc yet of the neo-Federalist pendulum swing in American history. Though some modern Democrats distance themselves from the Second Founders because the latter tolerated slavery and discounted women—paradoxically enabling modern Republicans to claim the mantle of "constitutional conservatives" walking allegedly in the Federalists' footsteps—they fail to realize that the New Deal was a clear *leitmotif* of the Second Founding. The durable shift in federal authority enacted by the New Deal was perfectly in keeping with Publius' commitment to reason, pragmatism, governmental solutions, and his dynamic dream of "a more perfect Union." Franklin Roosevelt's contribution to the neo-Federalist cause was aided by his success in introducing a distant authority—the federal government—into the family parlors of ordinary Americans, and convincing them that it was not a malevolent phantom to be feared but an institution to be grateful for. Like Lincoln, the New Dealers would transform Jeffersonian ideals and deploy them in the service of Hamiltonian ends.

In Chapter 7, we enter into the contemporary era where Anti-Federalism has waged a long and angry war, under the auspices of the "New Federalism" (not to be confused with Publius' new federalism) and the doctrine of states' rights against the excesses of neo-Federalist modern liberalism. During the Reagan Revolution, the pendulum of federal authority would swing back with the Anti-Federalist cry that "government is not the solution" but the problem itself.

This story continues in the Epilogue, where I explore the battle between modern Democrats and President Barack Obama and the Republican Party and in particular the Tea Party movement. Though the nation is over two centuries old, we can still hear the groans and pangs of our First Founding recycled and repackaged by the Tea Party members. The Patient Protection and Affordable Healthcare Act of 2010, dubbed "Obamacare," which was challenged by 26 states as an unconstitutional grab of authority, of course, represented a serious dent on the wave of Anti-Federalism that swept Washington with the Reagan Revolution. I conclude with some thoughts about the built-in Federalist bias of the Constitution, and the twin legacies of over two centuries of quarreling: the paradox of a formidable national administrative state and a vibrant, cacophonous democracy. The Lovers' Quarrel determines the rhythm of our politics—the Federalists' point and the Anti-Federalists' counterpoint. The playing out of these two impulses over two centuries has created one of the deepest ironies of American politics: a tremendous bureaucracy that would have the Anti-Federalists turning in their graves, and a plebiscitary democracy that would have the Federalists rolling over theirs. The sprawling bureaucratic state we see today is the culmination of the Federalists' advocacy of a more perfect Union, while the plebiscitary style that pervades contemporary politics is the vengeful legacy of Anti-Federalism—a Jeffersonian mitigation of an Hamiltonian imposition.

CHAPTER 2

Federalists, Republicans, & the Revolution of 1800

If by 1787–1789 the contours of the Lovers' Quarrel had been set, by 1824 its dynamics had already propelled both Federalists and Anti-Federalists to their separate days in the sun. Each had their heyday during what historians call the First Party System—the former until around 1798 and the latter until about 1824. But the modern understanding of the early republic would curiously be influenced more by the first two decades of the nineteenth century than the last two of the eighteenth, when government was more energetic than limited, and this is due in no small part to Thomas Jefferson's successful counter-revolution to Federalist principles in 1800. So unlike the Federalists, the Civil War Republicans, and the New Dealers, who were revolutionaries in the modern sense, the Jeffersonian Republicans in 1800 staged a revolution in the ancient sense—a turning of the wheel to restore the vision of limited central government regnant after the First Founding. After the ratification of the Bill of Rights, which was a consolation prize in a decidedly Federalist moment, the Revolution of 1800 would be the first full-throttled Anti-Federalist victory under the new Constitution. Indeed, so penetrating and thorough was this counter-revolution that most of us today know Anti-Federalism only by its most distinguished progeny, Jeffersonian Republicanism.

George Washington and Alexander Hamilton, Federalists

Some defenders of "original meaning" who have no problem referring to Locke or Harrington—who lived in an era closer to the First Founding— are also reluctant to give much credence to events in George Washington's presidency for deciphering the original meaning of the Second Founding. This is selective data mining. To recall what the Federalists stood for, it is not enough to consult the *Federalist Papers*, which were written, after all, to win over, by heresthetic maneuvering, an Anti-Federalist audience. We must look also to their theory put in practice in the first administrations of the new nation if we are to glean their private, unvarnished thoughts for a fuller picture of Federalism.

Though Washington is quite fairly described as a Bolingbrokean president standing above party, even he took a position in the Lovers' Quarrel.[1] Writing to his friend Charles Carter, who had published a private letter between them in a Baltimore newspaper, Washington wrote, "Could I have supposed, that the contests of a private letter, (marked with evident haste,) would have composed a newspaper paragraph, I certainly should have taken some pains to dress the sentiments (to whom known is indifferent to me) [*sic*] in less exceptional language."[2] Washington was quite possibly referring to this sentiment in that private letter: "All the opposition to it [the Constitution] that I have seen to it, is, I must confess, addressed more to the passions than to the reason."[3] He was a pragmatic Federalist—not like the sentimental Anti-Federalists, whose indignation and ire were first aroused by the British, and then later the Federalists, who had cheated them of their birthright as the true and only "founders." Unlike Jefferson, who valued "the spirit of resistance to government" represented by Shays' Rebellion and who "like[d] a little rebellion now and then," Washington joined his fellow Federalists in the conviction that it is reason, not the democratic passion of '76, that went into the creation of a new government in 1787.[4] Indeed, Washington's reaction to Shays' Rebellion could not be more different from Jefferson's:

> What stronger evidence can be given of the want of energy in our governments than these disorders? If there exists not a power to check them, what security has a man of life, liberty, or property? To you [Madison], I am sure I need not add aught on this subject, the consequences of a lax, or inefficient government, are too obvious to be dwelt on. Thirteen Sovereignties pulling against each other, and all tugging at the fœderal head, will soon bring ruin on the whole; whereas a liberal, and energetic Constitution, well guarded & closely watched, to prevent incroachments, might restore us to that degree of respectability & consequence, to which we had a fair claim, & the brightest prospect of attaining.[5]

Washington was an unwavering advocate of an "energetic Constitution" before he became president, and he remained so at the end of his presidency. His Farewell Address promulgated the High Federalist ideology that the United States was and must remain "an indissoluble community of interest as one nation."[6] Alexander Hamilton, of course, ghostwrote the address, and it was on his side, rather than on Madison's or Jefferson's, that Washington stood for most of his presidency.[7] He wrote,

> It is of infinite moment that you should properly estimate the immense value of your national union to your collective and individual happiness; that you should cherish a cordial, habitual, and immovable attachment to it; accustoming yourselves to think and speak of it as of the palladium of your political safety and prosperity . . .[8]

Although he is remembered most for having warned against the "baneful effects of the Spirit of Party" in his Farewell Address, Washington was through and through a Federalist even at this epideictic moment of his presidency, where he reminded his audience that their "individual happiness," bequeathed to them by the First Founding, was secured only by their "national union."[9] Washington's characterization of the "national union" as the "palladium" of the audience's prosperity could not have been more prototypically Federalist. Perhaps this was why, when fellow Republican William Giles wrote to congratulate Jefferson on his First Inaugural Address, he would say, "your Inauguration Speech . . . contains the only American language, I ever heard from the Presidential chair."[10] Presumably, it was an implicit taunt that Washington's and Adams' speeches were less than "American," a charge Andrew Jackson would make of "blue-light Federalists" a generation later.

No sooner than when the new government was called into session would the erstwhile co-authors who had shared the pseudonym Publius enter into a match over where the fulcrum of sovereignty lay between the federal and state governments. To be sure, the discord that would conflagrate in the 1790s was probably already germinating in 1787. Whereas Madison's answer to what was for him the principal problem of the Articles of Confederation, faction, was to "extend the sphere," this answer was still less important than Hamilton's heart's desire, which was "a firm Union."[11] The two saw eye to eye as long as what was the premise to Hamilton's conclusion, an extended republic, remained a common goal. As soon as Hamilton started to move beyond this premise to push a domestic program of aggressive nationalism, their alliance unraveled. And when it did, Washington stood almost always with the leader of the Federalists.[12] When Hamilton proposed in his Report on Public Credit that the federal government should take on the states' revolutionary debt, Madison opposed it because most of the Southern states had already paid off most of their debts. Washington, however, disagreed, and held that since the states were all equally beneficiaries of independence, so the states that endured less fighting ought in return to pay for their neighbors' costs. Like the neo-Federalists after him, Washington never saw the federal government as a specter; his fear was of the states.[13]

Even though he too hailed from the Old Dominion, George Washington is not considered part of the "Virginian Dynasty" of Jefferson, Madison, and Monroe because he was no Republican. On issue after issue, George Washington contributed to the drawing of partisan lines during his administration, even if his intentions might have been to secure the opposite. Washington took the Federalists' side in his support of Britain over France when presenting the Jay Treaty to the Senate, precipitating Jefferson's resignation from his cabinet and fomenting the opposition of the Democratic Republicans, who associated Britain with aristocracy and the antithesis of republican values.[14] He also castigated members of the Democratic Republican Societies (political heirs of the Sons of Liberty during the revolutionary era, and later, supporters of Jefferson) for instigating the Whiskey Rebellion of 1794. He would say to his Secretary of War, "you could as soon scrub the blackamoor white, as to change the principles of a profest Democrat; and that he will leave nothing unattempted to overturn the Government of this Country."[15] Where the Constitution was silent, Washington did not turn to the people for approval but asserted executive prerogative as inherently granted in its ambiguous clauses, such as over his removal power over department heads of the executive branch, or in his Neutrality Proclamation over the war between England and France, thereby adopting an Hamiltonian rather than Jeffersonian understanding of prerogative.[16]

The biggest schism in Washington's first administration, and probably the proximate cause for the birth of partisan politics in the early republic, was the debate over the meaning and scope of the "necessary and proper" clause and whether or not it justified the chartering of a First Bank of the United States in 1791.[17] Hamilton, the new Secretary of the Treasury, took an elastic perspective in interpreting Article 1, Section 8, Clause 18 of the Constitution, while Madison and Secretary of State Jefferson understood the powers of Congress as expressly enumerated, and no more. Washington stood alongside Hamilton, signing the Bank Bill one day after he had read Hamilton's report on it, and against the advice of fellow Virginians Jefferson, Madison, and Attorney General Edmund Randolph.[18] When the sale of script—certificates that entitled their holders to purchase stock in the bank—rose from $25 to $325 in 1791, and while Jefferson and Madison lamented speculation and corruption from their "Country" perspectives, Washington was gratified that the sales revealed that citizens were confident in the new government.[19]

The Anti-Federalist Comeback and the Explicit Versus Implied Powers Debate

One half of Publius, Madison, was always more literal-minded about the Constitution vis-à-vis the vertical distribution of powers.[20] He believed, as expressed in Federalist 43, that "the powers delegated by the proposed Constitution to the Federal Government, are few and defined" while "those which are to remain in the State Governments are numerous and indefinite." This was in keeping with the First Founding's understanding of explicitly enumerated powers, as the second Article of Confederation put it: "Each state retains . . . every power, jurisdiction, and right, which is not by this Confederation expressly delegated to the United States, in Congress assembled."

The other half of Publius, Hamilton, defended an elastic reading of enumerated *and* implied federal powers so that the government would always be up to the task of addressing whatever contingency came its way. Hamilton had previously warned in Federalist 23: "it is both unwise and dangerous to deny the federal government an unconfined authority, as to all those objects which are intrusted to its management." Having noted the utter failure of the Articles of Confederation, Hamilton continued,

> There is an absolute necessity for an entire change in the first principles of the system; that if we are in earnest about giving the Union energy and duration, we must abandon the vain project of legislating upon the States in their collective capacities; we must extend the laws of the federal government to the individual citizens of America.

Hamilton's disquisition on the "energy" of the Constitution is sometimes thought only to have been addressed to the executive, when it applied equally to the federal government as a whole. "There ought to be a CAPACITY to provide for future contingencies as they may happen; and as these are illimitable in their nature, it is impossible safely to limit that capacity," he wrote in Federalist 34. Hamilton believed, therefore, that federalism and decentralization of powers exacerbated the problem of collective action, while Madison feared that excessive centralization would reintroduce the ancient problem of tyranny. So between Federalist 23 and 43, the dispute about whether federal powers were "unconfined" or "few and defined," respectively, was already brewing.

It should be said, though, that the later Madison's faith that the powers of the central government could be explicitly "defined" was hubristic by his own earlier observations. In Federalist 37, Madison acknowledged that "no language is so copious as to supply words and phrases for every complex idea . . . and this unavoidable inaccuracy must be greater or less, according to the complexity and novelty of the objects defined." This was exactly the position of his successor in the White House and prominent Anti-Federalist at the Virginia ratification convention, James Monroe:

> To mark the precise point at which the powers of the general government shall cease, and that from whence those of the states shall commence, to poise them in such manner as to prevent either destroying the other, will require the utmost force of human wisdom and ingenuity. No possible ground of variance or even interference should be left, for there would the conflict commence, that might perhaps prove fatal to both. As the very being or existence of the republican form in America, and of course the happiness and interests of the people depend on this point, the utmost clearness and perspicuity should be used to trace the boundary between them.[21]

In Monroe's warning and Madison's switch are the genesis of the theory of constitutional interpretation falling under the banner of "originalism," or at least the part of the theory that insists that the Constitution's grants of powers are enumerated and explicit, and that there are no implied powers. When Madison joined Jefferson against Hamilton's apparently loose reading of the Interstate Commerce clause in 1791, he was deploying one of the earliest Anti-Federalist adaptations of their political thought in the fledgling republic. Since the Constitution was now a done deal, Madison's only available option, as have been his political descendants', was to dig in his heels and insist (against the Anti-Federalists' warning that it could never be so, it should be said) that the Constitution's text *was* clear, and its boundaries were precisely codified to restrain the mischievous potential of the Federalists' words. In his speech against the Bank Bill, Madison, now a member of Congress, argued that those reading new powers into the Constitution's "necessary and proper" clause to support the bill had "consented to the ratification of the constitution on different principles and expectations" than his own, and professed a more limited estimation of federal powers.[22] In more recent incarnations of this "original intent" theory, contemporary "originalists" have similarly held that the "original *meaning*" of the Constitution has always been clear and defined.[23]

Judging by Madison's protest turning on his earlier "expectations," it is not difficult to imagine why Hamilton and his descendants have always understood "originalism" and its family of theories as after-the-fact attempts to insinuate a precision to the constitutional text that never was thought—either by Federalists or Anti-Federalists—possible. The crucial question to answer, then, is whether the Madison of 1787 was the same Madison in 1791, for if the two can be reconciled, then perhaps the Federalist position was always the Anti-Federalist position; there was no Lovers' Quarrel, and George Washington and his zealously nationalist Secretary of Treasury, Alexander Hamilton, had simply perverted the principles of 1787. But this a difficult case to make. Hamilton's nationalist (some say monarchist) tendencies were not doubted in 1787, or in 1791. In Federalist 9, Hamilton actually defended the federal republic as "an association of two or more states into one state" and then blithely added that "extent, modifications, and objects of federal authority are mere matters of discretion." This was surely an expansive and elastic understanding of federal authority. During the Constitutional Convention, Hamilton had even proposed the abolition of the state governments and an executive with lifetime appointment. He believed that "In every civil society, there must be a supreme power, to which all the members of that society are subject; for, otherwise, there could be no supremacy, or subordination; that is, no government at all."[24]

In contrast, if we compare Madison's writings before and after 1789, there are far more challenges to reconciliation, and if so, our failure to understand Madison's conversion might have clouded or tainted our understanding of the Federalists' political philosophy with elements of Anti-Federalism—exactly what (the later) Madison and Jefferson wanted. The James Madison of 1791 sounded very different than the James Madison of 1787.[25] Indeed, the elevation of James Madison to the "Father of the Constitution" occurred in part because he was arguably the median "founder" who enjoyed the sole distinction of having advocated very publicly on *both* sides of the Lovers' Quarrel before and after 1789.

Madison's views on the national supremacy changed dramatically between 1787 and 1789. To George Washington, Madison wrote in 1787,

> Conceiving that an individual independence of the States is utterly irreconcilable with their aggregate sovereignty; and that a consolidation of the whole into one simple republic would be as inexpedient as it is unattainable, I have sought for some middle ground, which may at once support a due supremacy of the national authority, and not exclude the local authorities wherever they can be subordinately useful.[26]

While the Madison of the 1790s would do an about-face, the Madison of 1787 was unapologetically an advocate of "a due supremacy of the national authority." And to the extent that Madison was not with Hamilton on the "consolidation of the whole," his reasons were nevertheless prudential, not philosophical. Local authorities, for the Madison of 1787, ought to be relevant only where they can be "useful." Indeed, Forrest MacDonald rejected the idea that

Madison has a special claim to being the "Father of the Constitution," when he found that "of seventy-one specific proposals that Madison moved, seconded, or spoke unequivocally in regard to, he was on the losing side forty times."[27] Three major defeats are worth noting. First, Madison stood on the nationalist side in one of the most contentious issues at the Philadelphia convention, the manner of state representation. Madison's plan had called for representation proportional to the size of the free population or the amount of taxes paid by each state, and when the Great Compromise was adopted on July 16, he was strongly against it.[28] The convention had substituted the Virginia Plan's proposal of proportional with equal state representation in the Senate and decided that Senators would be elected by state legislatures rather than by the House. Second, Madison was not a supporter of the principles behind the Tenth Amendment, nor was he in favor of the Bill of Rights, even though he accepted it as a necessary evil for ratification.[29] Consider that in October 1788, Madison was still no fan of a Bill of Rights. He "never felt the omission a defect, nor been anxious to supply it with subsequent amendment, *for any other reason than it is anxiously desired by others* [my emphasis]." He shared James Wilson's "fear that a positive declaration of some of the most essential rights could not be obtained in the requisite latitude" and would end up, paradoxically, diminishing the reserved powers implied in the enumeration of federal powers.[30] But facing a tough congressional race against Anti-Federalist candidate James Monroe, he changed his tune. Six weeks after he had taken the opposite position, in early 1789, Madison would "freely own that . . . [he had] never seen in the Constitution as it now stands those serious dangers which have alarmed many respectable citizens" and it became his "sincere opinion that the Constitution ought to be revised."[31] Whether or not the conversion was heartfelt is beside the point: what matters is that Madison publicly occupied both sides of the Lovers' Quarrel, allowing both sides to claim him as their own and their reading of the Second Founding as the correct one. Third, Madison was also thwarted on one major nationalist provision, a federal "negative," or a veto, over state laws.[32] Madison was not only trying to create a general government capable of common defense and regulating commerce; he was also trying to rectify the vices of the state governments. While others have argued that Madison was more concerned to preempt an ineffective national government than to establish federal supremacy, a federal negative would have created a formidable federal government.[33] One month after the Philadelphia convention, Madison wrote to Jefferson to say that "it is evident I think that *without the royal negative or some equivalent controul* [*sic*], the unity of the system would be destroyed."[34] This was why, looking at the sixth clause of the Virginia Plan, William Riker concluded, "had the Virginia Plan been adopted and successfully imposed, federalism in North America would have ceased to exist."[35]

Madison, the principal drafter of the Virginia Plan, had been the preeminent Federalist figure in the convention, which is probably why Hamilton had approached him to co-author the *Federalist Papers* in the first place. While Madison thought it only fair that the larger states should enjoy greater representation in the House in proportion to their population, he feared that having each state enjoy equal representation in the Senate would encourage centrifugal threats to the integrity of the Union. That is why he concluded his study of the history of confederacies in Federalist 20 with: "a sovereignty over sovereigns, a government over governments, a legislation for communities, as contradistinguished from individuals, as it is a solecism in theory, so in practice it is subversive of the order and ends of civil polity." While Madison was the lead proponent of a system of checks and balances, he believed that the checking should only be happening at the horizontal plane between the federal branches of government, and not, as the Bill of Rights does, at the vertical plane. That is why Madison played a major role in determining that senators would vote as individuals, not as state delegates, and he also rigorously waged but lost the battle to empower the federal government with the authority to nullify state laws. In the late eighteenth century, all examples of confederacy available to Madison's scrutiny had revealed only the tendency of component parts to assert their sovereignty against the whole, and this was just what he sought to temper while drafting the Virginia Plan.

If my account is persuasive that it was Madison who switched his views, and not Hamilton, then "originalism" was not of Federalist origin, but was in fact the Anti-Federalists' reactive strategy of locking down the Pandora's box of national consolidation—as can be seen by the policies of Washington and Hamilton, and as we shall see later, Lincoln's and Franklin Roosevelt's—that the Federalists' Constitution had opened. If the Federalists had appropriated (peripheralized) "federalism" from the Anti-Federalists only to redefine it, the Anti-Federalists retaliated by taking possession of and restricting the "original meaning" of the Federalists' Constitution in order to subvert it. Madison's switch was a godsend for the Anti-Federalists, for he lent credence to the misgivings they had expressed during the ratification debates. More importantly, his switch allowed the Anti-Federalists to camouflage their reinterpretation of the Second Founding under the halo of a converted Second Founder. The Federalist Constitution could now be read with an Anti-Federalist lens. Now, the Constitution could be thought of as a text strictly constructed to limit government, not generously worded to empower it.

Recently, Jack Balkin introduced his theory of "framework originalism," arguing that the Constitution created "an initial framework for governance that sets politics in motion, and that Americans must fill out over time through constitutional interpretation."[36] He was mostly right, though he might have added that "framework originalism" must acknowledge that we began in *original dissent* and the Constitution of 1787 and the Bill of Rights of 1791 was *already* politics in motion. Put another way, "originalism" is not just a method for interpreting the Constitution. It is itself a reinterpretation of the meaning of constitutionalism as an essentially negative rather than a positive project, stemming from the Anti-Federalist side of the Lovers' Quarrel. Together with its rival theory, "living constitutionalism," these understandings of constitutionalism have been an important site of the Lovers' Quarrel. The descendants of the Federalists, such as Daniel Webster, Abraham Lincoln, and Franklin Roosevelt, have tended to interpret the Constitution in relatively elastic terms, because in the end they were confident nationalists eager to wield the enumerated *and* the implied powers of the federal government granted in the first half of the Constitution. They believed, as Publius did, in Federalist 1, that "the vigor of government is essential to the security of liberty." The Anti-Federalists and their descendants from Thomas Jefferson, to Andrew Jackson, to Ronald Reagan have been "originalists" of one form or another because at root they were jealous, states-centered Anti-Federalists who understood federal powers to be strictly enumerated and defined, and were partial to the First Founding and the limiting, rather than empowering, second half of the Constitution, the Bill of Rights.

The Kentucky and Virginia Resolutions

While the halo Washington enjoyed as "Father of the Country" suppressed more talk of his partisanship, his successor in the White House would enjoy no such benefit of the doubt. Within the Adams administration, the president and vice president would be engaged in a Lovers' Quarrel of their own. The Kentucky and Virginia Resolutions of 1798–1799, passed in opposition to the Alien and Sedition Acts of 1798, would become important pronouncements, by Vice President Thomas Jefferson and James Madison, both written in secret, on the doctrine of states' rights that would become the basis of the South Carolina Exposition and Protest of 1828 and its Ordinance of Nullification of 1832.[37]

A decade had passed since Madison lamented that the failure to enact a federal negative had created *imperium in imperio* (Latin for "state within a state"), the same words Hamilton had used to describe the weaknesses of the Articles of Confederation, in Federalist 15. Back then, the author of the Virginia Plan had opposed the New Jersey Plan, which had called for the preservation of the decentralized system set up with the First Founding, and in particular a unicameral legislature with each state possessing a single vote. During the ratification debates, Madison had explicitly rejected the confederalism of the First Founding and countered that "If a compleat [sic] supremacy somewhere is not necessary in every Society, a controuling [sic] power at least is so, by which the general authority may be defended against encroachments of the subordinate authorities."[38] Now, in 1798, he would take exactly the position he had previously feared would threaten the unity of the system. In his report on the Virginia Resolutions, Madison articulated the compact theory of the Union in a way similar to how he once described (dismissively then) the Articles of Confederation:

> The States then, being the parties to the constitutional compact, and in their sovereign capacity, it follows of necessity that there can be no tribunal above their authority to decide, in the last resort, whether the compact made by them be violated; and, consequently, that, as the parties to it, they must themselves decide, in the last resort, such questions as may be of sufficient magnitude to require their interposition.[39]

In Federalist 43, Madison had used very similar language to argue that the Articles of Confederation *could* be superseded without unanimous consent (implying that the new Constitution, contra his views in 1798, possessed a "higher validity" that the states could not casually dismiss):

> A compact between independent sovereigns, founded on ordinary acts of legislative authority, can pretend to no higher validity than a league or treaty between the parties. It is an established doctrine on the subject of treaties, that all the articles are mutually conditions of each other; that a breach of any one article is a breach of the whole treaty; and that a breach, committed by either of the parties, absolves the others, and authorizes them, if they please, to pronounce the compact violated and void . . . the time has been when it was incumbent on us all to veil the ideas which this paragraph exhibits. The scene is now changed, and with it the part which the same motives dictate.

Madison must have known that he was treading on very dangerous ground when he appeared to be suggesting that the union of 1798 (and the rules governing state sovereignty then) was similar to the one in 1781, which is why he threatened only "interposition" or opposition to federal authority, not secession. The Virginia Resolutions explicitly specified the extenuating circumstances under which interpositioning was called for: in "the case of a *deliberate, palpable,* and *dangerous* breach of the Constitution by the exercise of *powers not granted* by it."[40] Even so, the new Madison was still a defender of the horizontal checks and balances and affirmed that "the ultimate right of the parties to the Constitution to judge whether the compact has been dangerously violated, must extend to violations by one delegated authority as well as by another; by the judiciary as well as by the executive or the legislature."[41]

While the Virginia Resolutions deployed the First Amendment to declare the unconstitutionality of Congress's power to regulate seditious speech, the Kentucky Resolutions sought further support from the Tenth Amendment. In this, Jefferson showed his truer Anti-Federalist colors; by reaching deeper into the Anti-Federalist toolkit, Jefferson was emboldened to go further than Madison was prepared. He wrote to Madison in August 1799 to advocate that the Alien and Sedition Acts be rescinded; "were we to be disappointed in this," he continued, Kentucky and Virginia should "sever ourselves from that Union we so much value, rather than give up the rights of self-government which we have revered, & in which alone we see liberty, safety & happiness."[42] Like all Anti-Federalists, Jefferson was strict in his reading of Article 1 but very expansive in his interpretation of the Tenth Amendment. It took a personal visit from Madison in September 1799 to convince Jefferson to drop the controversial sentence from the Kentucky Resolutions.[43] Nevertheless, when the other states failed to join Virginia and Kentucky in their protestations, a second round of Kentucky Resolutions was passed in 1799, which now boldly asserted "That the several states who formed that instrument [the Constitution] being sovereign and independent, have the unquestionable right to judge of the infraction; and, That a nullification of those sovereignties, of all unauthorized acts done under the color of that instrument is the rightful remedy."[44] Like Federal Farmer, Jefferson's greatest fear was that of consolidation. "The natural progress of things is for liberty to yield and government to gain ground," he once wrote.[45] This crisis of two conceptions of We the People did not become a crisis of union only because the Revolution of 1800 interceded.

The Revolution of 1800

The Revolution of 1800 was the pendulum's swing back in the direction of Anti-Federalism. The author of the Declaration of Independence never forgot that his handiwork preceded the Constitution both chronologically and philosophically. Writing to Henry Lee, he recalled "that George Mason was author of the [Virginian] bill of rights, *and of the constitution founded on it*, the evidence of the day established fully in my mind [emphasis in original]."[46] Jefferson understood rights as antecedent to powers, and not, as the Federalists did, the opposite, when the latter created powers first and attempted even to omit a Bill of Rights. As Carey McWilliams observed, "Jefferson represented, for Americans, a guarantee of older ethics; his victory allowed the previously suspicious to trust the modern state."[47] If so, 1800 was also the first proof that there had been a huge ideological leap from 1776 to 1787. "No one in 1776 had predicted or had wanted such a strong government," wrote Gordon Wood. "Such national power was then beyond anyone's wildest dreams."[48] In effect, what Jefferson and his allies waged was a *counter*-revolution. Jefferson compared 1800 to be "as real a revolution in the principles of our government as that of 1776 was in its form" because he believed the Federalists had thwarted the spirit of republicanism all Americans shared in 1776.[49] As a veteran of the First Founding, he understood revolutions more in sociological and cultural terms, and not, as the Second Founders tended to, in intellectual or ideational terms.

In his First Inaugural Address, Jefferson announced that "We are all Republicans, we are all Federalists," after which he proceeded to purge many Federalist office-holders from the federal government. Jefferson would roll back the Hamiltonian program of commercial development directed by the federal government in place of agricultural expansion conducted under the aegis of the states. His aim, as he put in in his First Inaugural Address, was the "encouragement of agriculture, and of commerce as its handmaid." Uttering perhaps the first official formulations of fiscal conservatism, he also said, "a wise and frugal Government, which shall restrain men from injuring one another, shall leave them otherwise free to regulate their own pursuits of industry and improvement, and shall not take from the mouth of labor the bread it has earned."[50] This was an abrupt reversal of Adams' view that "good government is an empire of laws."[51] Jefferson was able to convince congressional majorities to repeal all internal taxes, the internal revenue service (which would only be resurrected in 1913), and with it 40 percent of the Treasury Department personnel in the field.[52] In his first year alone, Jefferson cut the domestic budget by $1 million, or 25 percent. Even despite the $15 million spent on the Louisiana Purchase, the national debt dropped from $86 million in 1803 to $45 million in 1812.[53] By the sixth year of his presidency, Jefferson would be contemplating what he would do with a possible budget surplus, but his Anti-Federalist instincts made him say that for all the virtues of internal improvements and public education, a constitutional amendment was necessary "because the objects now recommended are not among those enumerated in the Constitution, and to which it permits the public moneys to be applied."[54] The upshot of Jefferson's radical retrenchment of the federal government was to deprive citizens of the early Republic of the opportunity (as Hamilton had hoped to engender) to come into contact with the state and ultimately to accept its legitimacy as the preeminent protector of their liberties.

Both major parties in contemporary politics can claim ancestry from the Democratic Republican Party because its founder was a sitting-on-the-fence Federalist with deep reservations during the ratification debates, who within a decade banded with many erstwhile Anti-Federalists to overthrow the Federalists. Jefferson's initial instinct was to oppose the Constitution, but he was kept in the Federalist camp by his friend James Madison.[55] Indeed, Jefferson was possibly spared the unflattering label of "Anti-Federalist" only because he spent the summer of 1787 in Paris, during which he wrote to John Adams to confess "there are things in it, which stagger all my dispositions to subscribe to what such an Assembly has proposed." He further noted that "all the good of this new constitution might have been couched in three or four new articles to be added to the good, old, and venerable fabric . . . which should have been preserved even as a religious relique [*sic*]."[56] The belief that the Articles of Confederation needed only to be amended was, of course, the Anti-Federalist position. Unlike the early Madison, with whom he was also corresponding during the ratification debate, Jefferson was in favor of a Bill of Rights. By December, and probably by Madison's influence, Jefferson came on board, but only grudgingly: "As to the new constitution I find myself nearly a Neutral."[57] With a degree of equipoise not shared by almost any other statesmen of the early republic (with the possible exception of Madison), Jefferson was, by his own admission in his First Inaugural Address, both Federalist and Republican (Anti-Federalist); his political appeal lay in "his ability to provide for the inarticulate a modern foundation for ancient hopes."[58]

These ancient hopes were also ancient fears. "Carried to its logical conclusions," wrote Norman Risjord, Jeffersonian Republicanism "was essentially negative."[59] This would be a consistent feature of the Anti-Federalist bloodline from Federal Farmer to the modern Tea Party movement. Jefferson saw the Constitution not as creating power, but limiting it—which is really to say that he saw its heart in the Bill of Rights, not in the Articles of the Constitution. As he put it, "Confidence is everywhere the parent of despotism—free government is founded in jealousy, and not in confidence; it is jealousy, and not confidence, which prescribes limited Constitutions to bind down those whom we are obliged to trust with power."[60] That was certainly the understanding of royal charters and the first state constitutions that emerged in the First Founding. This explains why, when the Federalist administrations of Washington and Adams began to read more and more powers into the Constitution's clauses, Jefferson came to believe that "the original objects of the Federalists were, 1st, to warp our government more to the form and principles of monarchy, and, 2nd, to weaken the barriers of the State governments as coordinate powers."[61] Like the Anti-Federalists, Jefferson was more concerned about the vertical balance of power than the horizontal. As he explained, "the true barriers of our liberty in this country are the State governments" because "seventeen distinct States, amalgamated into one as to their foreign concerns, but single and independent as to their internal administration . . . can never be so fascinated by the arts of one man as to submit voluntarily to his usurpation."[62] While the Federalists understood the Constitution to be a union of individuals, the Republicans understood the Constitution to be a compact between states; and Jefferson's faith was ultimately in the people of the states.

If the Federalists sought to change the character of Americans, the Anti-Federalists and Jeffersonians sought to preserve or restore their character. This is why the Federalists emphasized institutions and parchments, while the Anti-Federalists opposed the "Federalist Court Party" and put their faith in community and tradition.[63] Admittedly, Jefferson was not a democrat simpliciter enamored by the wisdom of the people, putting him close to the Federalists on this dimension. Although he rejected artificial aristocracy, he did also believe in a natural aristocracy, and that the people's wisdom had to be cultivated. Like many of the Anti-Federalists, however, Jefferson was suspicious of Hamilton's mercantilist leanings, and though he would later build an alliance that included city craftsmen and workers, his heart of hearts celebrated the republican virtues of self-sufficiency and honest toil personified in the yeoman farmer of an agrarian society. To John Jay he once wrote, "Cultivators of the earth are the most valuable citizens. They are the most vigorous, the most independent, the most virtuous, & they are tied to their country & wedded to its liberty & interests by the most lasting bonds."[64] Most Federalists, like Hamilton, looked to manufacturing and commerce as methods not only for cultivating meritocracy and encouraging immigration diversity, but also to hasten the bonds of affection between the states and their citizens. The political economic views of the Anti-Federalists and Jeffersonian agrarians, on the other hand, were not directed toward the goal of an empire of commerce but an "Empire of liberty."[65] And this empire started organically from the ground up; it had no need for the Federalists' artificial (governing) props.

Even Jefferson's self-admittedly unorthodox exercise of prerogative to purchase the Louisiana territories, then, was in service of largely Anti-Federalist ends. "I think our governments will remain virtuous for many centuries," he wrote to James Madison, "as long as they are chiefly agricultural; and this will be as long as there shall be vacant lands in any part of America." The Louisiana Purchase short-circuited the Hamiltonian dream of creating a prosperous, industrial new England aided and protected by a powerful central government, by ensuring that the state governments would not "get piled upon one another in large cities, as in Europe"—for if they did, "they will become corrupt as in Europe."[66] The Purchase might also have facilitated the extension of slavery, by obtaining new lands for the plantation aristocracy.[67] If the Federalists had first extended the sphere to cajole the Anti-Federalists into forming a great commercial nation, Jefferson extended the sphere even further to restore the Anti-Federalists' agrarian vision. The Sage of Monticello was surely one-upping the Federalists who opposed the Louisiana Purchase when he rhetorically asked, "but who can limit the extent to which the federative principle may operate effectively?"[68] In place of a commercial nation, Jefferson hoped to create an even more expansive confederation of small republics, and he would achieve this by asserting his prerogative in the name of the people (of the states).

Republicans and Democracy

Obliged to accept the remnant strength of the Federalists even though the tide against them was turning, Jefferson in the late 1790s had to think of a strategy that could infect Federalism with Anti-Federalism without launching an overt, wholesale repudiation of a Constitution that was mostly written by the Federalists. Publius and his colleagues had created a union of individuals— We the People of the United States—and layered it over the older idea of the people understood only as We the People of the States. The Federalists thus made a strike against the "pure democracy" that existed in the states when they created an extended republic in which the people of the states were no longer directly involved in citizen rule, but were represented instead by a national legislature. Patrick Henry would call the Federalists out on their rhetorical sleight of hand on the ambiguous meaning of "We the People," asking, "What right had they to say, We, the people? My political curiosity, exclusive of my anxious solicitude for the public welfare, leads me to ask, who authorized them to speak the language of *We, the people*, instead of *We, the States*?"[69] Fair point, since the people as an entity that existed across state boundaries did not exist until the architectonic act of the Second Founding was completed.

The Republicans would hoist the Federalists on their own petard. Not to be outwitted by the Federalists, who had already stolen "federalism" (then, confederalism) from the Anti-Federalists and made it their own and, to add insult to injury, were now claiming that they were the true defenders of the people because they had devised a scheme of representation to neutralize the defects of democracy, the Republicans saw that the only weapon equal to the people of the United States was the people of the states. To reinstate the First Founding's understanding of the people, they wisely attacked the most vulnerable part of the Federalist armor, their antidemocratic philosophy and the Second Founders' theory of representation, by chanting a "pure" democratic faith and a mirroring theory of representation that the Federalists thought they had permanently republicanized with an indirect scheme of representation and the new science. In other words, Jefferson and his allies attacked the Federalists' republicanism with Democratic Republicanism—hence the name of their new party. Jefferson believed that "Our republicanism" is found "not in our constitution certainly, but merely in the spirit of our people."[70] His first concern was not in the *Unum* bequeathed to us by the Constitution, but the *Pluribus* of the virtuous citizens of the states—the people who preceded We the People of the United States. As the Federalists created a new conception of federalism and punted on the dual signification the word now possessed, so the Democratic Republicans, in retaliation, exploited the fact that the Federalists had grafted "We the People" ambiguously into the Preamble. They would use these very words to restore the First Founding's understanding of We the People of the States.

The most indirect representatives of the people, of course, were the unelected federal judges. Like the Anti-Federalists, Republicans were especially wary of judges because judges could find meaning in ambiguous constitutional clauses that could enlarge the scope of federal power and thwart the will of the people. The Republicans were particularly miffed at the midnight passage by the Federalist majority in Congress of the Judiciary Act of 1801, which had ended the Supreme Court justices' practice of circuit riding and created 16 new circuit court judgeships in order to assume the state courts' concurrent share of federal jurisdiction prescribed by the Judiciary Act of 1789.[71] On March 16, 1801, Senator William Giles wrote Thomas Jefferson to complain that "the judges have been the most unblushing violators of the constitutional restrictions and their officers have been the humble echoes of all their vicious schemes."[72] The Republicans would repeal the Judiciary Act in 1803.

This battle would play out and unfold in the events leading to the impeachment of Justice Samuel Chase, who was so furious at the Republicans for repealing the Judiciary Act of 1803 that he mouthed off to a grand jury that "the bulk of mankind are governed by their passions not by reason" while warning of "mobocracy, the worst of all possible governments."[73] He was of course parroting the Federalists' trusteeship model of representation and their fear of pure democracy. The Republicans were not impressed and proceeded to impeach Justice Chase for rehearsing the same views that Publius had once expressed.

The Republicans' faith in pure democracy, of course, came straight from the scripture of the First Founding. As Jefferson had sought, in the Declaration, "to place before mankind the common sense of the object, in terms so plain and firm as to command their assent," his surrogates would help him and the Democratic Republicans to harness a popular mandate against the "aristocratical" Federalists.[74] Thus was cultured the germ of populism and anti-intellectualism that Jacksonian Democrats and their descendants would take to new heights. As Bruce Ackerman observed, "1801 marks the birth-agony of the plebiscitarian presidency: for the first time in American history, a president ascended to the office on the basis of a mandate from the People for sweeping transformation."[75] Public opinion, like an electoral mandate from the people that Jackson would later claim, is an extra-constitutional thing; that means it is also an Anti-Federalist instrument. The Democratic Republicans would mobilize this external resource of power for future use by securing passage of the Twelfth Amendment, which paved the way for regularized party competition in the elections to come.[76]

Anti-Federalism and Democratized Prerogative

All this, then, is also to say that Modern Presidency, or the democratization of prerogative, has roots in Anti-Federalism, and Jefferson was but the first practitioner of the backup plan the Anti-Federalists had, albeit grudgingly, negotiated into the Constitution.[77] When Jefferson democratized prerogative in retaliation to the consolidation of the state under the Federalists, he was doing exactly what the Anti-Federalists had hoped the president would do. To see how the Anti-Federalist understanding of democracy would make a comeback under Jefferson's presidency, we need first to see how the Anti-Federalists had first purchased an insurance policy in the Federalists' Constitution against a legislative leviathan by cautiously putting their support behind an independent executive with the veto power.

Taking the Virginia and New Jersey plans as a rough indicator of where the delegates collectively stood at the start of the Philadelphia convention, one observes that those advocating for a stronger national government ended up with one weaker than the one they had proposed, but those advocating for an executive actually ended up with a stronger executive than the one they had proposed.[78] This outcome emerged in part because the Federalists, after compromising on various nationalizing provisions, such as on the manner of representation in the legislature, would push for a stronger executive toward the end of the convention, and some Anti-Federalists were willing to bite. And the latter were willing to bite because they were so concerned about and wary of congressional (read federal) power that they were even willing to look to the executive as a check against federal encroachment. Of "the enormous powers of the President and Senate" a Democratic Federalist observed, he found "TWO EXECUTIVE BRANCHES, each of which has *more or less controul* [sic] *over the proceedings of the legislature*."[79] Even he understood the bitter pill that an effective check on the House could entail. Certainly, some Anti-Federalists did adopt the classical Whig fear of power and took issue with "a president possessing the powers of a monarch,"[80] but the objections were not always about tyranny from on high, but a fear that the president would be partial to one state or region over others—a fear implicated in and inspired by the Lovers' Quarrel. For example, on the president's authority to adjourn Congress, Rawlins Lowndes' concern was that the president could "so arrange things, as to carry a favorite point, by assembling the federal government to the ruin or detriment of those states he meant to crush."[81] Similarly, while Luther Martin objected to the creation of a "king, in every thing but the name" because of the executive's nomination power, his principal concerns were with the mode of election and in particular that the majority rule in the electoral college would predispose the large states to victory.[82] Cornelius' objection to the proposed executive was similarly wrapped up in federalism; namely, he feared "the most violent competitions between individual aspiring men, between particular States, and between the Eastern and Southern States."[83]

These objections leave entirely open the possibility that should the executive reliably and routinely turn out to be a defender of the states and regions from which these Anti-Federalists hailed, or if there were some way to ensure his perpetual impartiality—as the Electoral College arguably did—perhaps they would not have objected as much. As it turned out, and perhaps in support of this supposition, the Anti-Federalists did not spill a lot of ink criticizing the proposed Article 2. Indeed, a major figure among them, Brutus, did not even bother to discuss the executive. The conventional view that the Anti-Federalists were straightforwardly wary of consolidated authority, *including the authority vested in the presidency*, is therefore too simplistic. Like classical republicans, they abhorred tyranny, but they well understood that tyranny came in many forms and from different quarters, not all of which were equally pernicious. Delegates at Philadelphia spent the lion's share of their time hammering out a compromise between the big and small states and in particular the manner of legislative representation. As late as August 31, 17 days before the close of the convention, the delegates were leaning on legislative selection and ineligibility for election for the president, while the proposed Senate still possessed the full treaty-making power. These unsettled matters were delegated to the Committee of Eleven to resolve. The Committee settled on the Electoral College, which would free the executive from legislative selection and made the president eligible for re-election and in charge of the treaty-making power with the advice and consent of the Senate.[84] An important reason why this was possible was that on the eve of creating the most powerful legislature Americans had ever seen, many erstwhile defenders of the view that "power corrupts" were also concomitantly wondering if they needed to fight fire with fire. Thus a Federal Republican held that "the executive should have a check on the legislative for this simple reason—that the executive hath its own limits—but the legislative independent of it, would have none at all."[85] John DeWitt worried that "it is far easier for twenty to gain over one, than one twenty," and "he (the president) will be infinitely less apt to disoblige them (the Senators), than they to refuse him."[86] George Mason, similarly, feared that "unsupported by proper Information and Advice (such as from, as proposed by Federal Farmer, an executive council)," the president "will become a Tool to the Senate."[87] For some Anti-Federalists, acquiescence even turned to advocacy in favor of an independent and strong executive, in part because it was the one body in the Constitution where the classical republican idea of virtue could—without the contortions of a complex scheme of representation devised for the legislative branches—literally inhabit.[88] Since the executive was to be the bulwark against the tyranny of one part of the community over another, James Monroe hoped that the office would be filled with men of "high character" who would "give every quarter indeed every man of the union . . . an equal access to the human heart." He concluded, "The Executive is that upon which, in many respects, we should rest our hopes, for an equal, fœderal, and a wise administration."[89] Like Monroe and Federal Republican, Federal Farmer supported an executive negative (veto), to "prevent hasty laws" passed by two thirds of each of the branches.[90] Brutus concurred: "in a due balanced government, it is perhaps absolutely necessary to give the executive qualified legislative powers."[91] The presidential veto states that even two thirds of *Unum* is not sufficient to override the considerations of *Pluribus*. No wonder, as Skowronek observed, the presidency is ultimately "an instrument of negation" and is most potent when it is directed toward order-shattering enterprises.[92] As an office originally designed to be most powerful when its incumbent said "no," one can see why the Anti-Federalists warmed up to it.

If we scrutinize their writings, we would observe that some Anti-Federalists actually channeled their mirroring theory of representation into their conception of the presidency. Diagnosing the lesser of two evils, since "it is better to suffer the tyranny of one man, than one hundred," A (Maryland) Farmer proposed "a properly constituted and independent executive,—a vindex injuriarum—an avenger of public wrongs" to stand up to the legislature.[93] Stressing the importance of the executive tribune, Monroe urged, "Every possible effort should therefore be use to expell [*sic*] from the hearts of those who fill it, a preference of one part of the community to another." Yet the strongest link from Anti-Federalism to the plebiscitary presidency and modern notions of democracy was Federal Farmer's theory of a "first man" as the focal point for patriotic sentiments. He wrote:

> Independent of practice a single man seems to be peculiarly well circumstanced to superintend the execution of laws with discernment

and decision, with promptitude and uniformity: the people usually point out a first man—he is to be seen in civilized as well as uncivilized nations—in republics as well as in other governments. In every large collection of people there must be a visible point serving as a common centre in the government, towards which to draw their eyes and attachments. The constitution must fix a man, or a congress of men, superior in the opinion of the people, to the most popular men in the different parts of the community, else the people will be apt to divide and follow their respective leaders.[94]

Even before Jefferson, or Jackson, and certainly before the Progressives seized on the idea and routinized its application, the presidency as a place of moral statesmanship, as *"vindex injuriarum*—an avenger of public wrongs," as A (Maryland) Farmer put it, was a vision promulgated by the Anti-Federalists.[95] The Federalists, after all, had placed their chips with the legislature. This is a striking omission from standard accounts of Anti-Federalism that have focused on their generic fear of power, and less on the critical distinction that the Anti-Federalists feared the vertical consolidation of power much more than the horizontal usurpation of power, if that was what it took to impede the federal legislature. Some of them could, albeit cautiously, lodge their faith in the executive because the Electoral College guaranteed at least a modicum of influence of every state in the selection of the chief executive, while the guarantee of Senate election in the case where there was no majority winner was regarded as a gift to the small states. The fear of not being able to control decisions made in other states and districts and therefore the composition of the legislature, in contrast to the direct influence each state could exact in the Electoral College, made the *vindex injuriarum* a palatable counterbalance to the legislature. Further, an institution with a single occupant was also more likely to be filled with someone who would fulfill the Anti-Federalists' descriptive, or mirroring (as opposed to the Federalists' virtuous) theory of representation—a fact that Jefferson and Jackson would exploit in the service of restoring the principles of the First Founding. Legislative elections, by contrast, not only had no chance of securing institution-wide influence, only influence over the senators and representatives for each state; it also required the execution of the Federalists' virtuous theory of representation, since senators and representatives of one state would routinely be called on to vote on matters pertinent to different states across the union. From the beginning, therefore, the horizontal balance of power was explicitly negotiated to service the vertical balance, so that each branch could invoke some authority to speak for the people.[96] The American executive was created on the condition of mutual suspicion and fear between the states, with its method of selection and possession of a legislative veto institutionalizing the idea that the president would be a national officer defending the interests of the states.

Correspondingly and perhaps paradoxically, while the Anti-Federalists expected and insisted that Congress' powers should be enumerated, they did not care to ensure the same for the president because the fear of an overweening legislature overshadowed the fear of a strong executive. That is to say, the Anti-Federalists—as well as Jefferson and Jackson—were particularly "strict" as regards federal powers, but comparatively less so on the separation of powers, because of their apprehension of the off chance that the executive might have to step in from time to time to rein in the legislature. The Federalists, one should note, had little faith in moral statesmanship and were not ready to cross their fingers and wait to see (as in Federalist 51) "if men were angels"; which is why they devised a new science to make a new kind of virtue out of vice. Unlike the Federalists, however, the Anti-Federalists understood the relationship between the executive and democracy—a relationship embraced by Jefferson, Jackson, and Johnson, the three great exceptions to the rule of presidential reticence and restraint in the nineteenth century.[97] All three, it should be noted, were doing exactly what the Anti-Federalists had hoped the office-holder of Article 2 would do, which was to invoke the virtues of pure democracy in defense of states' rights, as the Anti-Federalists had done against the "aristocratical" Federalists. "The nature of our government," wrote Jefferson, "depends mainly on the confidence of the people in their chief magistrate."[98] "Going public" may be a technique afforded by modern technology, but the contestability of exactly who represented the people was already reflected in the first Lovers' Quarrel over the institutional powers of the two elected branches.[99] The Anti-Federalists turned to the people because they did not think the people were legitimately represented by the Federalists' complex scheme.

When Jefferson democratized prerogative, he was merely awakening the sleeping giant the Anti-Federalists had permitted in Article 2 of the Constitution. Whereas Washington and Hamilton had thought that the Constitution's elastic clauses were sufficient to find room for prerogative, Jefferson reached outside of it—to the people—to justify illegal or unconstitutional actions. Jefferson would begin to remake the Constitution in the Anti-Federalist image, by creating a democratic presidency when what was before a constitutional presidency.[100] Consistent with the Anti-Federalists' theory of representation and in contrast to the Federalists' belief that prerogative was inherently justified by the Constitution, Jefferson believed that what was not expressly permitted by the constitutional text had to be sanctioned by the people. And so, an Anti-Federalist suspicion of the Constitution is what explains Jefferson's (and his descendants') seemingly inconsistent commitment to both a powerful presidency and a weak state. Jefferson's recourse to public opinion would set an imprimatur that neo-Anti-Federalist insurgents to come would claim. To roll back a consolidated federal government, a party state, and a liberal welfare state allegedly erected in the name of and in the interest of the people, Andrew Jackson, Woodrow Wilson, and Ronald Reagan would turn to the people for a mandate against the establishment. Washington, Lincoln, and FDR, by contrast, believed that their exercises of prerogative were always within the parameters of the Constitution. Their understanding of prerogative was not populist because their faith was with the Federalist Constitution, which in their mind was sufficient onto itself, and granted them all the power they needed to "form a more perfect Union."

The Jeffersonian Re-Interpretation of the Second Founding

Jefferson's re-reading of the Second Founding would be bolstered when James Madison, the "Father of the Constitution," defected to his side. This defection mattered because on the central and controversial matter of democracy, Madison remained always a Federalist. Despite their "great collaboration," Madison and Jefferson held distinct views of government and human nature.[101] Though Jefferson retained a residuum of Toryism in his belief in a natural aristocracy, he rejected the stakeholder theory of property and more importantly embraced the chaos and disorder that came with his ideology of a "radical democrat." Neither Madison, nor his Federalist co-author, ever did.[102] Even before Jefferson parted company from the Federalists, his commitment to democracy was already more than Madison was comfortable with. His proposed method of constitutional amendment expressed in his *Notes on the State of Virginia* was quoted, disapprovingly, by Madison in Federalist 49, who had judged that "there appear to be insuperable objections against the proposed recurrence to the people."[103] Madison's more Burkean view was that "frequent appeals would, in a great measure, deprive the government of that veneration which time bestows on every thing." Whereas Madison created "auxiliary precautions" on the assumption that men were not angels, Jefferson wrote to William Jarvis in 1820, saying, "I know of no safe depository of the ultimate powers of society but the people themselves, and if we think them not enlightened enough to exercise their control with a wholesome discretion, the remedy is not to take it from them, but to inform their discretion by education."[104] As the Anti-Federalists too had proposed seminaries of learning, the political education of which Jefferson spoke would come in the form of the University of Virginia, where "in the selection of our Law Professor," he insisted to Madison, "we must be rigorously attentive to his political principles."[105]

Jefferson's faith in democracy necessarily made him a weak adherent to the Federalists' doctrine of the separation of powers. If one branch of the national government were unelected, then surely it could not have equal status as the other two. And if another branch of government spoke for all rather than some of the people, than surely it must be *primus inter pares*. And so it was that Jefferson had no real qualms flexing the executive muscle in the name of the people, especially in foreign affairs. There was "one means to unite the local polity and the Enlightenment dream of the great state in an affectionate whole," Jefferson wrote. It was "hostility toward the foreign, unity forged from abstraction into feeling by the greater difference of the alien, fear and suspicion muffled by the menace of war."[106] (To be sure, there were some arch-Anti-Federalists who would disagree down the road.) For the "Old" Republicans, like John Randolph, even Jefferson and Madison were not restrained enough as regards the reach of federal authority, especially in their nationalist foreign policy—most strikingly in the Louisiana Purchase and the War of 1812. After his presidency, however, Jefferson echoed the populist explanation Federal Farmer had voiced two decades ago: "A strict observance of the written laws is doubtless *one* of the high duties of a good citizen, but it is not *the highest*." He continues, because the *"salus populi* [is] supreme over the written law," "it is incumbent on those only who accept of great charges, to risk themselves on great occasions . . . and throw himself at the justice of his country and the rectitude of his motives."[107]

In his First Inaugural Address, Jefferson promised "absolute acquiescence in the decisions of the majority, the vital principle of republics."[108] Like the Anti-Federalists, he was suspicious of the separation of powers because it divided the citizenry. Instead, he preferred that government should operate in local units, and the Democratic Republican Party and its organizational unit, the ward, would be a vehicle for civic education and the cultivating of the fraternity necessary for the conduct of direct democracy. Whereas Jefferson believed that "national unity and fraternal affection should rise out of local devotion," according to Carey McWilliams, Publius turned the argument on its head when he warned of faction arising in local communities.[109] Jefferson was trying to reimpose the virtues of the small town on the large republic. There was a spot in his worldview, though, where Jefferson retained a Federalist imprimatur—his belief in a natural aristocracy. As he wrote to John Adams: "I agree with you that there is a natural aristocracy among men. The grounds of this are virtue and talents. . . . The natural aristocracy I consider as the most precious gift of nature for the instruction, the trusts, and government of society."[110] Even here, though, a distinction surfaces that possibly explains the apparent disjuncture from Jacksonian Democracy and the transition toward it. The natural aristocracy Publius sought were men of reason because the Federalists were pragmatists first; Jefferson, however, tended to privilege the morally superior, not the intellectually superior. Indeed, his privileging of the heart over the head goes some way in explaining the foremost mistake of his presidency, his stubborn refusal to accept the negotiated Monroe-Pinckney Treaty with Great Britain, which led instead to the disastrous Embargo of 1807. "In purely economic terms," Darren Staloff concluded, "Thomas Jefferson had cut off his nation's nose to spite Great Britain's face."[111] Like the Anti-Federalists, Jefferson harkened after visionary ideals, sometimes even over pragmatic programs of action. "Morals," he once wrote to a friend, "were too essential to the happiness of men to be risked on the incertain [sic] combinations of the head."[112] In contrast, because Publius recognized that "Enlightened statesmen will not always be at the helm," he devised "auxiliary precautions" of the institutional kind in Federalist 10. Institutions of course are, among other things, historical reasons set in parchment or stone to preclude the mischief of future passions. To further his argument in favor of extending the sphere, Publius also adopted a more cosmopolitan posture in talent hunting than Jefferson might have approved. In Federalist 36, Alexander Hamilton declared: "There are strong minds in every walk of life that will rise superior to the disadvantages of situation, and will command the tribute due to their merit, not only from the classes to which they particularly belong, but from society in general. The door ought to be equally open to all." Jefferson, on the other hand, was partial to the yeoman farmer. As Darren Staloff surmised, while Madison was immersed in the politics of Enlightenment, "Jefferson had embraced the principled politics of Romanticism."[113]

Conclusion: "Original Meaning" Revised

If, as Sheldon Wolin has argued, the Constitution represented a counter-revolution to restore "political monotheism," Democratic Republicans waged the Lovers' Quarrel to restore the "political polytheism" engendered by the First Founding.[114] 1. *On Union*. Although Publius saw the federal union created by the Second Founding as possessing a "higher validity" than a compact between sovereign states, Jefferson and Madison in the Virginia and Kentucky resolutions challenged the idea that the Constitution was anything other than a compact between states 2. *On Liberty*. The Democratic Republicans articulating the states' right of "interposition" were adopting a negative conception of liberty. They also rejected the constitutionality of the First Bank of the United States and advocated fiscal restraint and a constitutional interpretive theory of explicit, non-implied powers to limit the reach of federal authority. 3. *On Truth*. The Democratic Republicans were idealists who stood on principle with France against England in the 1790s. They were agrarians who romanticized the yeomanry and their values, and Jefferson purchased the Louisiana Territories in part to encourage the expansion of the virtuous republic. 4. *On Republicanism*. The Democratic Republicans were classical republicans who valorized small republics and the majority as "the vital principle of republics." They rejected aristocracy and embraced extra-constitutional but popular innovations like partisanship, public opinion, and democratized presidential prerogative to reinstate the principles of pure democracy from the First Founding.

Herbert Storing was half right when he argued that our nation was "born in consensus but it lives in controversy, and the main lines of that controversy are well-worn paths leading back to the founding debate."[115] The United States was born and then born again in dissent, and this codified dissent is what has been the motivating force behind our politics of reform and reaction in the last two centuries. Jefferson played a critical role in bringing to bear the principles of the First Founding on our understanding of the Second, and in sharpening the competing sides of the Lovers' Quarrel. If "above all," Jefferson taught the American people "what to hate and whom to fight," it was because the author of the Declaration of Independence was a pioneer of reactionism and the Anti-Federalist comeback in American history.[116] Whereas the Anti-Federalists had succeeded only in securing the ratification of the Bill of Rights, the Democratic Republicans in 1800 managed a comeback that constituted a durable shift in federal authority. Perhaps Jefferson's greatest contribution to the Anti-Federalist cause was in extinguishing, for at least a generation and possibly longer, the memory of the aggressive commercialism and nationalism of 1789 to 1801, and resetting public opinion and expectations about the role of federal government in their lives. This legacy is so powerful that when "constitutional conservatives" today talk about "original meaning," they refer to the drastically limited operations of the federal government that commenced not in 1789, but in 1801, as if the decade of Hamiltonian adventurism never even happened.

CHAPTER 3

Anti-Federalism & the Howls
of Jacksonian Democracy

At the dawn of the Jacksonian era, near the end of his life, an old but still partisan Thomas Jefferson rigorously denied the claim that the debate between the Federalists and the Republicans was no more.

> You are told indeed that there are no longer parties among us, that they are all now amalgamated in peace, the lion and the lamb lie down together in peace. Do not believe a word of it, the same parties exist now as ever did. No longer indeed under the name of Republicans and Federalists. The latter name was extinguished in the Battle of New Orleans.
>
> Those who wore it finding monarchism a desperate wish in this country, are rallying to what they deem the next best point, a consolidated government. Although this is not yet avowed (as that of monarchism, you know, never was) it exists decidedly and is the true key to the debates in Congress, wherein you see many, calling themselves Republicans, and preaching the rankest doctrines of the old Federalists.[1]

"Consolidated government," of course, was the specter the Anti-Federalists repeatedly raised.[2] It was echoed by the Democratic Republicans, and then the "Old Republican" faction within it that had separated from the "National Republicans" after the War of 1812. These "Old Republicans" would become the backbone of the Democratic Party, albeit with some adaptations courtesy of Andrew Jackson and Martin Van Buren, while the National Republicans would morph into the Whig Party.[3] And so the stage was set for the Lovers' Quarrel of the Jacksonian era.

Though also a fierce Unionist, Andrew Jackson's greatest legacy stems from his equally adamant defense of states' rights.[4] To facilitate a democracy of men rather than an impersonal republic of institutions, he inaugurated the two-party system and expanded the patronage system that would become the "state of courts and parties"—America's alternative to a bureaucratic state—that administered the country during the long nineteenth century.[5] Jackson was aided in this effort by the "Little Magician," Martin Van Buren. When he left for Washington, Van Buren expressly told his friend, Charlemagne Tower, that his purpose was "to revive the old contest between federals and anti-federals and build up a party for himself on that."[6] He would do just that. Far from pulling together what the Constitution pulled asunder, "The Democracy," as the party was called, would re-inscribe the grassroots democratic paradigm of states-centered federalism that the Anti-Federalists had defended a generation ago. Following the Democratic Republicans, Jacksonian Democrats would inaugurate a second Anti-Federalist moment in American history. It would be the only time in American history when one major Anti-Federalist moment followed another so quickly—with the brief interregnum of the "Era of Good Feelings"—the climactic result of which would be the *reductio ad absurdum* of the states' rights argument, Southern secession, in the era's twilight.

States' Rights and Limited Government in the Jacksonian Era

On the eve of the Jacksonian ascendancy, the Federalist commitment to federal supremacy over state sovereignty had become the prevailing consensus, as seen in the Marshall Court's decisions in *Dartmouth College v. Woodward*, *Sturges v. Crowninshield*, and most famously, *McCulloch v. Maryland*.[7] The presidents before Jackson had embarked on an expansion of federal governmental prerogatives, including protective tariffs, internal improvements, and a robust military establishment. After the War of 1812, almost everyone, even John Calhoun, supported the necessity and constitutionality of the Second Bank of the United States. Whereas in 1791, James Madison had argued that the Constitutional Convention had expressly rejected proposals to grant Congress the power to create corporations, and therefore denied support for the First Bank, by 1816, he had changed his mind. In 1819, John Marshall articulated the nationalist consensus of the Era of Good Feelings in *McCulloch v. Maryland*, which had affirmed that Congress had acted constitutionally in chartering the Second Bank of the United States when it drew on its powers "implied" from the "Necessary and Proper" clause of the Constitution, and that the state of Maryland, in its effort to impede the operations of the bank, did not have the right to impose a tax on the notes of a bank not chartered in the state. *McCulloch* established the supremacy of the federal government over the states when its powers were exercised within its constitutionally sanctioned scope. As Marshall wrote: "If any one proposition could command the universal assent of mankind, we might expect it would be this—that the government of the Union, though limited in its power, is supreme within its sphere of action." Marshall thought that the way to avoid *imperium in imperio* was to have a strict division of labor that was easier to fathom in theory than to practice in reality.

Only a decade later, the nature and meaning of the American Union would come under intense scrutiny, as the Webster–Hayne debate, the intense debates leading up to the Compromise Tariff of 1833, and the Force Bill brought the Lovers' Quarrel about the meaning and future of the Union to the political foreground. Andrew Jackson would declare that federal funding of intrastate building projects such as the Maysville Road as well the idea of a national bank was outside of the federal government's legitimate sphere of action, thereby producing a durable retrenchment in federal authority and ushering in the Golden Age for states' rights.[8]

If the Constitution was an advancement on the Articles of Confederation and Perpetual Union in terms of surpassing the previous goal of perpetuity into one of "perfect[ion]," and assuming that perpetuity is already the superlative on its own spectrum, then the Federalists must have meant that "perfection" was a quality different from and superior to the mere perpetuity of the new Constitution. "Perfection" had to refer to something like the degree of comity between the states of the Union for it to be an improvement on their perpetuity. And it was the Whigs, rather than the Jacksonian Democrats, who stood closer to the Federalists in this regard. In his reply to Senator Robert Hayne, Senator Daniel Webster would intone: "I confess I rejoice in whatever tends to strengthen the bond that unites us, and encourages the hope that our Union may be perpetual," unlike "some persons in the part of the country from which the honorable member comes, who habitually speak of the Union in terms of indifference, or even of disparagement."[9] Andrew Jackson and Democrats of the era were often among the latter kind of persons. Jackson may have been a Unionist—he was after all the chief executive of the national government created by the Federalists—but it is precisely his occupancy of this station that makes his contorted advocacy of states' rights so indicative of the enduring legacy of Anti-Federalism. According to his Second Inaugural Address, there were "two objects which especially deserve the attention of the people and their representatives" in his second term: "the preservation of the rights of the several States and the integrity of the Union."[10] The question, however, is which came first in his mind. Jackson did affirm "the most important among these objects [of the Constitution]—that which is placed first in rank, on which all the others rest—is 'to form a more perfect Union.'"[11]

But his words and actions often indicated that he understood perfection as no more than perpetuity.

Jackson once wrote Governor John Sevier saying, "The moment the Sovereignity [*sic*] of the Individual States is overwhelmed by the Central Government, we may bid adieu to our freedom."[12] He was not, then, a fierce supporter of an organic national community, the way Lincoln was when he reconstituted our political self-understanding and replaced the archaic "Union" with the modern "Nation." Jackson understood the Congress as the "Federal Legislature of 24 sovereign States."[13] For him, the United States was a "Confederacy," whose "strength and true glory . . . is founded on the prosperity and power of the several independent sovereignties."[14] The federal government's strength lay "not in binding the States more closely to the center, but leaving each unobstructed in its proper orbit."[15] When Tocqueville had observed that "the Union is possessed of money and troops, but the states have kept the affections and prejudices of the people," he was merely articulating the legacy of the First Founding that the Second Founding had attempted to erase.[16] But unlike the Federalists, who believed that trust in the federal government could grow and should be nurtured, Jackson, like the Anti-Federalists, started from the assumption that it was best not even to try. In Federalist 17, Hamilton had conjectured that "the people of each State would be apt to feel a stronger bias towards their local governments than towards the government of the Union; *unless the force of that principle should be destroyed by a much better administration of the latter*" [my emphasis]. Hamilton was clearly open to the possibility that federal administration could be more efficient than local administration, even in areas traditionally reserved to local governments. His was a dynamic view of federal responsibilities. Similarly, Whigs such as Henry Clay supported an ever-expanding reading of the Interstate Commerce clause, saying, "All the powers of this government should be interpreted in reference to its first, its best, its greatest object, the Union of these states. And is not that Union best invigorated by an intimate, social, and commercial connexion [*sic*] between all the parts of the confederacy?"[17] Whereas the Federalists and Whigs believed that the federal government would be venerated the more it showed that it could deliver on what the states had failed to deliver on, at the heart of the Jacksonian Democrats' commitment to states' rights was the static and uncompromising Anti-Federalist starting point that the more limited the central government, the more it could be tolerated. In this regard, Jackson, like the Anti-Federalists, was a man of little faith. He believed that "the successful operation of the federal system can only be preserved by confining it to the few and simple, but yet important, objects for which it was designed"—hardly a whole-hearted endorsement of "a more perfect Union."[18]

This is why Jackson invited Congress, in his First Annual Message, to "ascertain what offices can be dispensed with, what expenses retrenched, and what improvements may be made in the organization of its various parts to secure the proper responsibility of public agents and promote efficiency and justice in all its operations."[19] Fiscal conservatism, which never was a goal in and by itself either in the nineteenth century or the twenty-first, was a strategy Jacksonian Democrats used to restrain the size of the federal government. Voicing objection to Webster's argument that public lands ought to be reserved as a permanent source of revenue for the federal government rather than relinquished to the states, Senator Robert Hayne would say, "Sir, an immense national treasury would be a fund for corruption. It would enable Congress and the Executive to exercise a control over States, as well as over great interests in the country, nay, even over corporations and individuals—utterly destructive of the purity, and fatal to the duration of our institutions."[20] Correspondingly, in his First Inaugural Address, Jackson promised to pay down the national debt. In his Second Annual Message, he referred to "the highest of all our obligations, the payment of the public debt," which the government paid off in 1835, though the accomplishment would be negated by the Panic of 1837 and ensuring five years of depression.[21] Thus "every diminution of the public burdens arising from taxation," Jackson wrote, "furnishes to all the members of our happy Confederacy new motives for patriotic affection and support."[22] Jackson's veto of the Maysville Road, of course, was motivated by similar sentiments. He believed the road would not have been interstate in nature and therefore was beyond the scope of Congress's legislative power to authorize. It would also have been a needless drain on the Treasury.

Among Jackson's best-known actions is his veto of Congress's re-chartering of the Second Bank of the United States. In his message explaining his objection, Jackson affirmed the central tenets of Anti-Federalism when he insisted that the bank was "unauthorized by the Constitution, subversive of the rights of the States, and dangerous to the liberties of the people." His denouncement of the bank also included a nativist charge: "It is not our own citizens only who are to receive the bounty of our Government. More than eight millions of the stock of this are held by foreigners."[23] And when Jackson ordered the removal of bank deposits to politically favored state-chartered banks, which arguably led to the Panic of 1837, he revealed where his sympathies lay. By 1841, the only national financial institution in the country was no more. Here was a durable retrenchment in federal authority—the third national bank, the Federal Reserve, would not emerge until 1913. At best, Old Hickory's support of the Union stemmed from utilitarian grounds. At worst, "Jackson sought to persuade his fellow citizens that the ineffectuality of the government was a virtue."[24]

Jackson's and the Democrats' ostensibly negative politics can also be traced to a positive political philosophy and political economy they shared with the "Old Republicans" and Anti-Federalists. Democrats, like the Anti-Federalists, rejected the Federalist vision of a large commercial republic and preferred instead the promotion of a national political economy that would produce virtuous, self-reliant citizens capable of self-government. In this vein, they saw the farmer as the ideal citizen and the fount of the highest virtues, which was why a good amount of their domestic program was dedicated toward the cultivation of a virtuous squirearchy. Jacksonian Democrats revered the patient cultivators of the soil; men who improved the earth on which they labored, acquiring the virtues of independence, frugality, and endurance as they did so. And since an economy consisting of mostly yeoman farmers was an economy in which every man enjoyed the fruits of his labor and no man was exploited, Jacksonian Democrats preferred a political economy that saw no need to import the Marxian distinction between capital and labor, employer and employee, or the socialist ideas of an interventionist state.[25] This also meant, of course, that when greedy speculators challenged this agrarian ideal, Democrats took to arms. Jackson was a defender of the "forgotten man" before Franklin Roosevelt used the term, arguing in his bank veto message that "Every monopoly and all exclusive privileges are granted at the expense of the public, which ought to receive a fair equivalent."[26] Jackson was defending the farmer, however, not the worker, as Roosevelt was. And he defended the farmer precisely so that there would be no need for an aggressive national government to step in to manage an industrial economy. The Democratic Party's valorization of the squirearchy also explains why Jacksonian Democracy proceeded alongside horrific injustices. A virtuous squirearchy needed land, and to that end, Jackson and his successor had no qualms in defying the Supreme Court's judgment that the state of Georgia lacked constitutional authority to pass laws on the Cherokee tribal lands, and even enlisting the federal government to facilitate Indian removal.[27]

For Jacksonian Democrats, the role of government was reasoned backward from what an ideal citizen's occupation and virtues would look like, not what national problems existed for which governing solutions had to be found. This was the position the Whigs took. As Horace Greeley, arguing against free trade, told an audience at Hamilton College in 1844, "'the best government is' *not* 'that which governs least.'"[28] His position was similar to the Federalists', who first saw and diagnosed a problem in society and political economy, and then proposed, literally, a governmental solution to address it. While the Federalists, Whigs, Radical Republicans, and New Dealers saw government as the solution to our problems, the Anti-Federalists, Jacksonians, and Reaganites saw government as the problem itself.

Calhoun, Nullification, and Anti-Federalism

No story of the Anti-Federalist spirit and how its sacred principle of states' rights took form during the Jacksonian era is complete without an account of one of its principal protagonists, the inimitable John Calhoun, Vice President under John Quincy Adams and Andrew Jackson. It was he, son of an Anti-Federalist, Patrick Calhoun, more than any other, who nudged Jackson as close to the edge of the states' rights doctrine as the chief executive of the Union could go.[29] Though Jackson was as strong a defender of states' rights as a federal executive could be, he was not prepared to contemplate disunion. His Vice President, however, may have thought differently. At the 1830 Jefferson Day dinner, Jackson proposed a toast: "Our federal Union, it must be preserved." Calhoun famously replied, "the Union, next to our liberty, the most dear. May we all remember that it can only be preserved by respecting the rights of the states and by distributing equally the benefits and burden of the Union."[30] He might just as well have said, as Patrick Henry, the leader of the Anti-Federalists in Virginia, reportedly did, "Give me liberty, or give me death."

Even though Calhoun came ultimately to stand at the states-centered extreme of the federalism spectrum, between 1822 and 1832, even he swung from arch-nationalism (Federalism) to extreme sectionalism (Anti-Federalism), personifying the Lovers' Quarrel in his own ideological journey in a way not so dissimilar to Madison's, as we saw in Chapter 2. As one of the "war hawks" agitating for war against the British in 1812, even Calhoun saw the need for a national bank, internal improvements, and revenue-generating tariffs to brace the country from another attack from a foreign foe. During this Era of Good Feelings—a time when partisans enjoyed a respite from the Lovers' Quarrel—the prospect of national peril seemed to validate Hamilton's arguments for consolidation, and a wave of nationalism swept aside talk of states' rights. In its place was erected what Henry Clay called the "American System," a mercantilist and nationalist economic plan inspired by Hamilton's economic theories that consisted of a second national bank to establish a national currency and to supply what was called "sovereign credit" (as opposed to credit obtained from the private banking system); a program of internal improvements, which would facilitate interstate commerce; and higher tariffs to encourage American manufacturing.[31] To this end, Calhoun introduced in Congress a bill re-chartering the Second Bank of the United States as well as a "Bonus Bill" proposing federal funds for internal improvements (which Madison vetoed because he wanted a constitutional amendment to codify what he saw to be a new federal prerogative).[32] Calhoun even teamed up with Henry Clay and the Whig Party to pass the Tariff of 1816, and as Secretary of War, from 1817 to 1825, he supported an ambitious program of national defense. In

1824, probably in an attempt to obtain Federalist support for his presidential bid, he would inform the son of Alexander Hamilton that his father's policy "as developed by the measures of Washington's administration, is the only true policy for this country."[33] This was the Calhoun that President John Quincy Adams described as "above all sectional and factional prejudices more than any other statesman of this Union with whom I have ever acted."[34] At this time, the Whigs had artfully comingled the republican idea of virtue with the Constitution's commitment to the "general welfare" to extract sacrifice from the agricultural South, which had less to gain from the Whigs' mercantilist theories of political economy.

No sooner than when the pendulum swung too much in favor of nationalism in the form of tariffs to protect industry did the sons of liberty strike back, as Jefferson had with the Kentucky Resolutions in 1798 after the brief Federalist reign of Washington and Adams. As sectional rivalries intensified, especially after the "corrupt bargain" of 1824, Southerners charged that the Northerners' duplicitous talk of the "general welfare" to justify their calls for higher protective tariffs merely masked their pursuit of wealth and material aggrandizement. Such selfish impulses by aristocratic industrialists were anything but virtuous.[35] Calhoun, favorite son of the future Confederacy, took up his pen and argued in the Exposition that the Tariff of 1828 was unconstitutional because it unfairly privileged manufacturing interests in the North at the expense of agricultural interests in the South.[36] South Carolina followed by passing an ordinance proclaiming the federal tariffs of 1828 and 1832 null and void within its borders, thereby forcing a "replay of the ratification debate" and a re-litigation of Madison's Hamletian disquisition in Federalist 39 that the Constitution is "partly federal, and partly national."[37] This iteration of the Lovers' Quarrel, like all others, was about answering the question begged by Madison's formulation—just how much federal and how much national? Publius did not offer the final words on the nature of American federalism, but in his desire to seek a workable political compromise for the immediate conundrum he faced, Federalist 39 offered only the first of many words exchanged in the Lovers' Quarrel.

However, subtle modulations to the Lovers' Quarrel were already apparent by this time. While Calhoun was arguably the arch Anti-Federalist of his time, he sat in a different place and time than Federal Farmer, who felt no pressure at all to pay homage to Publius' wisdom. "I am not," Calhoun wrote, "prepared to admit a conclusion, that would cast so deep a shade on the future, and that would falsify all the glorious anticipations of our ancestors while it would so greatly lessen their high reputation for wisdom."[38] With the ratification of the Constitution and the Federalists' victory over the Anti-Federalists complete in that one regard, Federal Farmer's descendants have relied on more surreptitious ways to thwart Publius' goal of a more perfect Union. If the Federalists had used similarly crafty means for their creative resyntheses of the Two Foundings in favor of the principles of the Second, Jeffersonian Republicans, Calhoun, and the Democrats of his era would engage in historical revisionism to stealthily restore the principles of the First Founding. As David Ericson astutely observed, "John Calhoun bears the patrimony of the Anti-Federalists. Except, he argues as if they had written the Constitution. His reading of the ratification debate can only be considered odd . . . his historiography makes the Federalists more 'federal' than the real Anti-Federalists."[39] This is spot on—a strategy Calhoun's contemporaries, like Van Buren, and as we shall see later, his political descendants, such as Ronald Reagan and members of the Federalist Society, have adopted with much success.[40] Revisionism worked, of course, only because Anti-Federalist principles were not pulled out of thin air, but directly from the First Founding.

To this end, as the Confederacy would do a generation later, Calhoun invoked the original anthem of democracy, the Declaration of Independence. For Calhoun, "the very idea of an *American People*, as constituting a single community, is a mere chimera. Such a community never for a single moment existed—neither before nor since the Declaration of Independence."[41] But for the fact that it was now too late to cry explicitly over Publius' spilled milk, Calhoun would have concurred with one Anti-Federalist's charge that the Constitution was "not merely a CONFEDERATION of STATES, but a GOVERNMENT of INDIVIDUALS."[42] But in 1831, Calhoun's best bet was to try to rewrite history in the image of the First Founding, and to elide the fact that the Federalists had already won the debate against those who had first launched his argument.

Calhoun's uncompromising insistence on the overriding priority of state over national sovereignty, operationalized in the idea of a "concurrent majority," could not have been further away from Madison's constitutionalism. While Madison had proposed to extend the sphere to conjure a national majority to check the power of state majorities or "factions" within them, Calhoun was trying to achieve the exact opposite—check a potentially tyrannical national majority with a state majority—by arguing that Madison's solution had now become the problem. The idea of a "concurrent majority" as an ostensibly joint condition for granting the constitutionality of federal laws was in fact a single condition whereby each state retained a veto to federal legislation. The historical antecedent of the idea, of course, was the principle from the First Founding that the people of each state possessed a separate and prior sovereignty to the sovereignty of the people of United States, such as expressed in the rule of unanimity required for amendments to the Articles of Confederation.

South Carolina might have lost the nullification battle, but it won the neo-Anti-Federalist war. Although Jackson's response to the Ordinance of Nullification was the Force Bill, which authorized him to take military action, if necessary, to collect tariff duties from the errant state, the tangible result of the crisis was the Compromise Tariff of 1833, which gradually lowered tariffs and increased the list of duty-free goods. Perhaps more importantly, South Carolina's precipitate action meant that the Democratic Party's worship of the states' rights doctrine would continue uninterrupted until the first shots were fired at Fort Sumter. For his contribution to the cause of states' rights and slavery (which he defiantly characterized as a "positive good" as opposed to a "necessary evil"), the Confederacy placed Calhoun's likeness on a one-cent postage stamp.[43]

The Howls of Democracy

The Lovers' Quarrel can be tracked by alternating surges in the consolidation of the national state and democracy respectively. Just as the Union would find a new birth of freedom after the Civil War, the Anti-Federalists' dream of "pure" democracy would reach new heights in the Jacksonian era. Indeed, the major extra-constitutional political invention of the era, the political party, was called "The Democracy." The revolutionaries of 1776, of course, were the first champions of democracy, articulating the principle of consent that was the premise of understanding democracy as self-rule. The election of 1828 extended democracy procedurally by securing universal white male suffrage, though its main impact was to displace the subdued, patrician style of politics that had characterized the decades before.[44] Even more so than the Revolution of 1800, 1828 evinced "the raving howl of Democracy" in unabashed defiance of Madison's observations in Federalist 10 that "democracies have ever been spectacles of turbulence and contention."[45] Madison believed that democracies were short-lived both because they were ruled by passion and also because merely "reducing mankind to a perfect equality in their political rights" without a cultivating a commitment to the commonweal—possibly a veiled reference to the misplaced idealism of the Declaration of Independence—was no guarantee against civil strife. Not surprisingly, as the Federalists had suppressed talk of the Declaration and its Jacobin associations, the Democrats brought it back to life in the 1820s at the same time when pure or direct democracy enjoyed a new birth of freedom.[46] Thus one Jacksonian proudly announced, "there is this remarkable difference between monarchical and aristocratical systems of government on the one hand, and the democratic system on the other, that, while the former are based upon *prescription*, the latter is based on the *right* of the people to govern themselves."[47] Whereas the word was once associated with civil strife and anarchy, Jackson's supporters now dropped the "Republican" part of their party's name and unashamedly called themselves "The Democracy" and adopted the slogan "Let the People Rule" in 1828.[48] "The first principle of our system," Jackson now proudly proclaimed, is "that the majority is to govern."[49] By these new arguments, Democrats successfully inverted the Federalists' understanding of republicanism with their emphasis on indirect rule and schemes of representation (much like the way the Federalists had first inverted the meaning of "federalism" in their own heyday). Instead, the Democrats posited this revised understanding: "where the people are everything, and political forms, establishments, institutions, as opposed to the people, nothing, there, and there only, is liberty; such a state, and such a state only, constitutes republican government."[50]

When nineteenth-century Democrats talked about the people, however, they meant self-government by the people of the states, not the people of the United States—this is an important caveat we will return to in the next chapter. When Democrats talked about democracy, they meant states' rights and majority rule. Today, we understand rights and democracy to be at loggerheads with each other, because we usually think of rights *qua* minority rights.[51] But at the time of the First Founding, rights were held against kings, and thus necessarily a collective and majoritarian concept.[52] As Richard Hofstadter noted of Calhoun's nineteenth-century understanding of minority rights, "Not in the slightest was he concerned with minority rights as they are chiefly of interest to the modern liberal mind."[53] Instead, if rights are understood as majority privileges, the modern antithesis of rights to democracy collapses. Whether these were the rights of Englishmen or those claimed by majorities in the states, rights and democracy understood as self-government were closely related concepts for the Anti-Federalists as they were for the Jacksonian Democrats.

If the Anti-Federalists hoped to strengthen the democratic element in the Constitution with a Bill of Rights, it is no wonder that the Federalists, who shuddered at democracy, also chafed at the Bill. The Anti-Federalists' understanding of rights and democratic self-government as two sides of the same coin is most clearly seen where the criminal grand, criminal petit (trial), and civil jury systems were guaranteed in the Fifth, Sixth, and Seventh Amendments. If, as Tocqueville noted, "the jury is both the most effective way of establishing the people's rule and the most effective way of teaching them how to rule," then at the heart of the Bill of Rights is the principle of democracy as self-government (as opposed to *representative* government).[54] The Anti-Federalists were at pains to extract a Bill from the Federalists because they wanted to preserve the states as bastions of democratic self-government. The importance of jury service was thrice affirmed because such service was both the training ground for citizenship as well as the arena for citizen rule. As Herbert Storing put it, "The question was not fundamentally whether the lack of adequate provision for jury trial would weaken a traditional bulwark of individual rights (although that was also involved) but whether it would fatally weaken the role of the people in the *administration* of government."[55] If the Federalists were concerned with creating institutions that would be, as Federalist 68 put it, "filled by characters pre-eminent for ability and virtue," the Anti-Federalists, in contrast, wanted to make sure that ample opportunities were afforded to the people to administer the laws handed down to them. And so, just as the Anti-Federalists were partial to the lower over the upper house of the legislative branch, so too were they partial to the lower over the upper elements—that is to say, juries versus judges—of the judicial branch.[56] Their faith in pure democracy was unimpeachable.

In their focus on personalities, in their populism, and in their recruitment of career politicians, the elections of 1828 and 1832 became the precursor of modern elections that are the full-fledged culmination of the Anti-Federalists' untrammeled faith in democracy. In the 1828 contest between the plowman versus the professor, the popular rejection of the highly credentialed John Quincy Adams in favor of a frontier duelist with little education and even less political experience may have been the clearest indication yet that the anti-democratic, patrician era of the Federalists was at its twilight.[57] Leaders who helped draft and ratify the Constitution, which everywhere except perhaps in one half of Article 1 emphasized distance between the representative and the represented, were being replaced by career politicians who saw no need to beware the baneful spirit of party, cultivated a closer connection to people, and were more responsive to their sectional demands.[58] Jackson became the first president to open his White House to the public for his inauguration ball, hosting a party so raucous that the crowd had to be lured outside of the White House by strategically relocated tubs of punch.[59] Like Melancton Smith, who believed that "representatives (should) . . . resemble those that they represent," Jackson held a mirroring rather than a trusteeship theory of representation.[60] "I know of no tribunal to which a public man in this country," Jackson would say, "can appeal with greater advantage or more propriety than the judgment of the people."[61] He believed that the way to distinguish Democrats from "Whigs, nullies & blue light Federalists" was to ask whether they "subscribe to the republican rule that the people are the sovereign power, the officers their agents & representatives, and they are bound to obey or resign."[62] With little regard for the Federalists' concerns about demagoguery and the "popular arts," Jackson proposed a constitutional amendment to abolish the electoral college and limit the term of the president to a single four- or six-year term, arguing that "as few impediments as possible should exist to the free operation of the public will" and "the duties of all public officers are, or at least admit of being made, so plain and simple that men of intelligence may readily qualify themselves for their performance; and I cannot but believe that more is lost by the long continuance of men in office than is generally to be gained by their experience."[63] Even Martin Van Buren, always more circumspect about the democratic spirit than was Jackson, would write: "every day convinces me more of the perfect reliance that may, under all circumstances, be placed on the intelligence, patriotism, and fortitude of the people."[64]

In unlocking direct democracy, Jackson and his supporters would deliver a score for the Anti-Federalists. The Federalists believed that power was best checked by separate institutions sharing powers, which is why they constituted a government of laws. The Anti-Federalists, on the other hand, believed that government was best checked from without and not from within, which is why they were ultimately for a government of men. As Lawrence Kohl argued of the Democrats, "that the nation was held together primarily by the artificial bonds of constitutional prescription was inadmissible to them."[65] This is perhaps why Senator Hayne congratulated Jackson that his victory in 1828 was of "the people over corruption," as if also to say that the internal checks of the system had failed to do their work.[66] Similarly, the election ticket for the Jackson delegates from Ohio featured a broom symbolizing a Herculean promise to "sweep the Augean Stable."[67] While Madison had proposed, in Federalist 10, that the defect of "pure democracy," faction, could be solved with republicanism (a system of indirect rule in an extended republic), Jacksonian Democrats countered that the antidote to a corrupted republic was more democracy. Van Buren, for his part, believed that regular party competition would be more effective in checking power than the Constitution's formal separation of powers.[68] This was Anti-Federalism in sharp and sweet revenge, because with the surge in democracy, Jacksonian Democrats could sit in offices created by the Federalist's Constitution at the same time that they averred that no longer was the Constitution the sole source of political legitimacy in the United States. Now, the people were as well. For when Democrats began to claim a mandate from elections, they were also saying that the people's legitimacy-granting sovereignty was no longer locked in the first three words of Preamble of the Constitution.

The Democrats' advocacy of term limits similarly revealed their lack of faith in the allegedly self-regulating mechanisms of the Federalists' new "science." Although the Second Founders were innovators, they were open to dramatic constitutional change as long as it was in frequent; on the other hand, the Anti-Federalists were conservatives who welcomed frequent changes in officers as a brake on constitutional transformation or decay. The latter thought that the Federalists' proposed system of checks and balances was too smart by half and believed that term limits were the only secure bulwark against corruption. Although Madison thought ambition could counteract ambition, Richard Henry Lee was less sanguine and suggested instead that "Abridged duration, temperate revenue, and every unnecessary power with-held, are potent means of preserving integrity in public men and for securing the Community from the dangerous ambition of that too often governs the human mind."[69] George Mason, too, had argued "nothing is so essential to the preservation of a Republican government as a periodic rotation."[70]

When Jackson proposed term limits, however, he was doing more than just parroting his ideological forebears; he was going farther than even they had ventured. If the Anti-Federalists believed that rotation in office prevented corruption, and Jefferson after them had introduced the idea of a purge of the Federalists after the Revolution of 1800, Jackson combined the Anti-Federalists' idea with the Jeffersonian practice to validate yet another new extra-constitutional development—the spoils system of distributing government jobs as an incentive to reward partisan loyalists. In his First Annual Message, Jackson proposed a term limit of four years for all federal appointments, citing "rotation . . . [as] a leading principle in the republican creed."[71] What he did not say was that within a generation, the Anti-Federalist principle of rotation in office would fuse with the routinization of partisan competition to generate the effective truth of the Democratic creed, "to the victor belong the spoils."[72] By this system, the very thing that delivered planned disruptions in officialdom would ensure continuity and loyalty in the party. That is to say, the health and longevity of the political system were now to be guaranteed by something outside of the formal constitutional structure—the party system.

The Birth of the Democratic Party

The greatest tangible departure of the Jackson era from the early republic's constitutionalism, then, was the creation of the Democratic Party. An extra-constitutional if not unconstitutional entity because of its contravention of ex-pressed original intent, The Democracy helped carry the Anti-Federalist ideas of old into the nineteenth century. By supplying the "state of courts and par-ties" in substitution of the earliest shell of a national administrative state that was emerging during the Washington and Adams administrations as well as in the aftermath of the War of 1812, the Democratic Party was an Anti-Federalist godsend that would delay the onset of the modern, bureaucratic state, and the principal beneficiary of the retrenchment of federal authority from the Era of Good Feelings. The "state of courts and parties," ultimately, was a state of states—exactly what the Anti-Federalists were for.

The difference between 1800 and 1828, though, is that while Jefferson had only summoned Anti-Federalist ideas to combat Federalist excesses, Jackson and Van Buren actually formed an Anti-Federalist *organization* to make up for the perceived defect of democracy in the Federalists' Constitution. This innovation was a much more vengeful iteration of the Anti-Federalist spirit than even Jefferson had envisioned. If the early republic's patricians were committed to the idea of political society as an organic whole that could not afford to be divided by faction, Martin Van Buren explicitly broke from the Madisonian framework that was designed to contain conflict *within* the institutions of government.[73] He advanced instead a government of men in which conflict was legitimately played out extra-constitutionally in the form of two-party competition.[74] Writing to a fellow member of the Albany Regency in 1822, Van Buren announced that it was "the proper moment to commence the world of a *general resuscitation of the old-democratic party.*"[75] It is revealing that he chose to use "old-democratic party"—an unabashedly modern name for the "Old Republicans," the name for the conservative wing of the Democratic-Republican Party during the 1810s.[76]

While Van Buren could not make much of the Anti-Federalists' procedural vote against the adoption of the Constitution, he honored them, much as Calhoun had, by resuscitating the substantive theory on which their objection was based. So wrote Van Buren:

> The most auspicious prospects beamed upon the opening administration of the new government, and it is fair to presume that the anticipations thus inspired would have been triumphantly realized if those who had been selected to conduct it, and their successors for the ensuing twelve years, had accepted the Constitution in the sense in which it was known to have been understood by those who framed it, and by the people when they adopted it. *A course thus right in itself . . . would not have failed to conciliate large portions of the Anti-Federal party* [my emphasis].[77]

If Martin Van Buren's most significant contribution to American politics was his justification of the political party to a culture predisposed against "faction," his method to this end was by insinuating an Anti-Federalist reading of the largely Federalist Constitution. As a defender of the First Founding's conception of Union, bound to a text predominantly written by Federalists, Van Buren would attack the new federalism by indirection. According to him, "Alexander Hamilton, the able and undisputed leader of the Federal party, from its [the Constitution's] origin to his death, did comparatively nothing either toward its formation or adoption by the Federal Convention."[78] This observation was not exactly fair or balanced. The author of more than two thirds of the *Federalist Papers* (indeed, the man who convinced Madison and Jay to join him in penning the preeminent publication of American history) would probably have received more credit had he not been "the leader of the Federal party." Conversely, even though Van Buren admitted that Madison "supported, ably and perseveringly, many, if not most of the propositions for the adoption of which the Federal party was particularly solicitous," he nevertheless concluded "there was no time when Mr. Madison can, with truth and fairness, be said to have belonged to the Federal party."[79] This is surely the Lovers' Quarrel waged in sophisticated guise. The reason why Van Buren could not accept Hamilton's contribution to the character of the Constitution is clear: with the continuity of this major personage from Philadelphia to George Washington's cabinet, Van Buren's argument that post-ratification Federalists failed to execute "the Constitution in the sense in which it was known to have been understood" becomes untenable, as we had seen in Chapter 1. Hamilton and his Federalist colleagues could not have been patriots in 1789 and constitutional infidels right after. Van Buren's praise of Madison was, by contrast to his trivialization of Hamilton's role at Philadelphia, superlative. "The character and political career of James Madison was *sui generis* . . . possessed of intellectual powers inferior to none, and taking an unsurpassed interest in the course of public affairs, he seemed invariably to bring to the discussion of public questions a thoroughly unprejudiced mind."[80] This was the same wily Madison who arrived in Philadelphia 12 days ahead of the start of business and requested the same of his fellow delegates from Virginia in order to draft the Virginia Plan and frame the agenda for the convention. As I argued in the previous chapter, Madison was unapologetically a Federalist and nationalist in 1787. His was not an unprejudiced mind.

By sidelining Hamilton, the leader of the Federalists, Van Buren was well on his way to validating the Democratic Party as a necessary antidote to the perversions of the "Federal Party" and inaugurating the "state of courts and parties." When he and Jackson introduced the spoils system, they halted whatever momentum was left from the Hamiltonian effort to create a stable bureaucracy independent from politics.[81] As Van Buren and the Democrats adopted a procedural understanding of their party "that complemented the Constitution's own [alleged] proceduralism," it was also a principled decision to exclude any discussion of the Constitution's substantive commitments that lay dormant until the Civil War.[82] President James Polk's talk of "equal and exact justice" (a quote taken from Jefferson's First Inaugural Address exactly 34 years before) demanded equality of sacrifice, which was a principle so stringent that it made it difficult to legislate collective self-sacrifice in pursuit of the "general welfare," ensuring very little federal governmental action as long as the doctrine remained regnant, especially within the Democratic party.[83] Meanwhile, the shift from the caucus to the nomination system devolved power downward from Congress to local party leaders, while the spoils system entrenched the power of the bosses. In the name of transparency and democracy, Van Buren and Jackson were able to transfer power from King Caucus and send it down to state and local party bosses; and since the president stood at the top of the patronage food chain, he was also able to negotiate a transfer of power from Congress toward the executive.

King Andrew, Defender of the Public Faith

Indeed, it should come as no surprise that the second surge of democracy in American history, after Jefferson's opening act, coincided with another uptick in presidential power. Andrew Jackson summarily dismissed what he deemed to be a false choice in Calhoun's question when the latter inveighed, "it must be determined in the next three years, whether the real governing principle be the power and patronage of the Executive, or the voice of the people."[84] Jackson believed that he could have his cake and eat it. For him, the power of the executive resided in and was derived from the *vox populi*. After the 1832 elections, Andrew Jackson opened his Second Inaugural Address with a narcissism more characteristic of a twentieth- than a nineteenth-century presidential speech, saying, "the will of the American people, expressed through their unsolicited suffrages, calls me before you to pass through the solemnities preparatory to taking upon myself the duties of President of the United States for another term."[85] The election, of course, had been a referendum on his bank veto, and therefore a ratification of his use of prerogative in the Jeffersonian tradition.[86] As the President executes the will of the people, he exists only in a shell until democracy blossoms. As the people begin to rule, so does the president. This is a major Anti-Federalist legacy.

What appeared to be an inter-branch battle between the Whigs, who favored congressional supremacy, and the Democrats, who favored presidential dominance, in this era turned out to be a deeper quarrel about the principles of the Two Foundings. Andrew Jackson took a page from the Anti-Federalists in their suspicion of the separation of powers and the complex Newtonian machine that the Federalists built. He no more believed in checks and balances than in the idea that the popular will could or should be checked. Correspondingly, he styled himself as the defender of states' rights by strictly applying and adhering to the nation's highest law in its vertical or federal dimension, and enforcing this commitment by fluidly interpreting the horizontal separation of powers. Whereas the presidents before Andrew Jackson exercised the veto pen only six times and only on constitutional grounds, Jackson alone would veto 12 bills, simply because he disagreed with Congress on policy grounds. In his veto message explaining his opposition to the re-chartering of the Second Bank of the United States, he noted, "The Congress, the Executive, and the Court must each for itself be guided by its own opinion of the Constitution."[87] Jackson also appointed 24 federal judges and six justices to the Supreme Court, including Chief Justice Roger Taney in 1836. In doing so, Jackson was able to alter the ideological leanings of the judicial branch from one that had been more nationalist under John Marshall to one that would become more sympathetic to states' rights under Taney. The inter-branch jostling was but part of the larger plan to bring about a durable shift—in this case, retrenchment—of federal authority.

It has always been something of a puzzle to modern liberals that modern conservatives—descendants too of the Anti-Federalists—seek limited government in general but do not seek to limit the power of the executive, at least with a zeal equal to their pursuit of the former goal. This is a paradox first observed by the Whigs as they countenanced King Andrew, because they too did not fully appreciate that the Anti-Federalists had prescribed a *vindex injuriarum* empowered with a legislative veto to be the defender of the public faith, as we saw in the previous chapter.[88] When the Jacksonian Democrats distrusted a government of laws and turned to democracy, or a government of men, for a solution, their solution ultimately was a "first man," a person on whom the hopes and dreams of the American people could be pinned.[89] Jackson and Van Buren believed, decades before Woodrow Wilson, that as the president was the leader of the Democratic Party, and as the party represented a constitutional majority, the president enjoyed a privileged interpretive authority over the Constitution. Like Wilson, Jackson did not conceive of the possibility that the people could come to wrong conclusions or that they could constitute a tyranny of a democratic sort. Neither Jackson nor Wilson, of course, saw the tyranny of the majority as any tyranny at all.

If, like the Anti-Federalists, Democrats championed the virtues of democracy, then like the Federalists, the Whigs were deeply suspicious of it. John Whipple, a Whig, expressed the modern liberal's despair at the prospect of irrational voters acting against their own interest. "When I see other hundreds of thousands of houseless free suffrage voters, ready at a call to flock to the standard of these pretended friends of the poor," he once said, "I feel that as a friend to constitutional freedom, I could devote my whole soul to its rescue."[90] From this difference in perspective about democracy emerged the Whigs' and Democrats' different fears about power. Democrats feared organized power, the power of institutions, and government itself. The Whigs on the other hand feared popular power, the power of demagogues, and in particular

King Jackson. Whereas Whigs were quick to point out the inadequacies of the common man, Democrats, like the Anti-Federalists, strongly rejected the idea of a "natural aristocracy." The reason why the Democrats could consistently reject organized power but embrace Andrew Jackson's was because of their belief that the president's power was the people's best bet against the "natural aristocrats" (or "men of distinction") caballing in the nation's capital. Put another way, just as the Whigs and Federalists were comfortable with codified and institutional "powers," Democrats and Anti-Federalists preferred personal power, derived not from the Constitution but from the people. While Jackson shared Jefferson's views about enumerated versus Hamilton's views about implied federal powers, Jackson played fast and loose with the Constitution's horizontal distribution of powers because, like the Anti-Federalists, his overriding concern was the vertical distribution of power.

Conclusion: The Golden Age of States' Rights

If the Federalists and their disciples dominated the eighteenth and twentieth centuries, much of the nineteenth century was triumphantly Anti-Federalist, and this had much to do with the Jacksonian Democrats' successful restoration of the principles of the First Founding. 1. *On Union.* Although Jackson took a strong stance on the perpetuity of the Union, he did not always act in ways consistent with its preservation. He understood the Union to be more of a confederation than a nation, one with very limited powers relinquished by the states to the federal government. 2. *On Liberty.* Like the Jeffersonian Republican Party, The Democracy was concerned principally with negative liberty and states' rights. Indeed, the Democratic Party and the Party State were neo-Anti-Federalist accomplishments because they would perform the functions of and therefore preempt the advent of the national administrative state for nearly a century. To restrain the reach of the federal government, Jacksonian Democrats advocated low tariffs and fiscal austerity and adopted the constitutional interpretive theory that federal powers went only as far as that which the Constitution explicitly enumerated. 3. *On Truth.* Like the Anti-Federalists, Jackson saw no room for negotiation when First Founding principles were at stake. He vetoed the Second Bank, convinced that it was the president's prerogative to judge the constitutionality of public law. Like the Republicans, Jacksonian Democrats prized virtue and believed that it could be found in a squirearchy. As Jefferson had purchased the Louisiana Territories, Jackson and Van Buren would even summon the power of the federal government to facilitate Indian removal and extend Jefferson's Empire of Liberty. 4. *On Republicanism.* Jacksonian Democrats embraced direct democracy wholesale, attempting to give equal if not more authority to the people independent of the Constitution, even practicing the "popular arts" the Federalists had disdained to demonstrate the close relationship between the governing and the governed.

If the aim of the Revolution of 1800 was to put partisanship to rest, the result of the 1828 and 1832 elections was the regularization of party competition and the further institutionalization of the Lovers' Quarrel. Jacksonian Democracy revealed that the Anti-Federalists may have lost the initial battle over ratification of the Constitution, but they had far from lost the ideological war about the proper role of the federal government and its relationship to the people. The Jacksonian era would deliver a durable retrenchment in federal authority from the height it had enjoyed during the Era of Good Feelings. At the end of his presidency, however, Jackson began to worry that the doctrine of states' rights was a Pandora's box. During the preparation of his Farewell Address, Jackson wrote to Roger Taney to express that the preservation of the Union stood at the heart of his concerns. "How to impress the public with an adequate aversion to the sectional jealousies, the sectional parties, and sectional preferences which centring [*sic*] on mischievous and intriguing individuals gave them power to disturb and shake our happy confederacy, is a matter which has occupied my own thoughts greatly."[91] Perhaps Jackson was coming to terms with his complicity in fanning the very sectional jealousies he was countenancing and was taking heed of James Madison's final words to his countrymen written just two years earlier:

> The advice nearest to my heart and deepest in my convictions, is that the Union of the States be cherished and perpetuated. Let the open enemy to it be regarded as a Pandora with her box opened, and the disguised one as the serpent creeping with deadly wiles into Paradise.[92]

CHAPTER 4

The Civil War & Publius Redux

Nowhere is it clearer in the course of American history that there have been two distinct and fervently held conceptions of democratic sovereignty than during the Civil War. One conception, the democratic sovereignty of the people of the whole Union rather than that of its constituent states, would be declared victorious by the war's end. Though the Constitution had promised a more perfect Union, it was really the Civil War that confirmed it in fact. Indeed, it is largely due to the outcome of the Civil War, the nation's second victorious Federalist moment, that Anti-Federalism and its most distinctive battle cry, states' rights, came to disrepute in the North. Yet Anti-Federalism was not vanquished at Appomattox, and to trivialize the states' rights argument would be to fail to understand the deep well of legitimacy that the First Founding conferred to the Confederacy, and, concomitantly, to understate the developmental accomplishment of Lincoln and the Republicans in establishing a more perfect Union.

In this chapter, we will look at how the Confederacy, on the one hand, and the Republicans, on the other, would pit the principles of the First and Second Foundings against each other, and we will examine the creative resynthesis of the Two Foundings that Lincoln would forge at Gettysburg, just as Publius had done in 1787–1788, to bring about a durable expansion of federal authority. The considerable challenges Lincoln and the Republicans faced reveal that the principles of the First Founding are more than just a bad memory, but a deep well of legitimacy that neo-Federalists must contend with. After all, the Second Founding succeeded in part because it did not try to start off from a *tabula rasa,* as the French tried to do in their Revolution, but embraced our *ancien régime* of the states as building blocks of the legitimacy of the new federal government. This was a tricky bargain to finesse; it created the tension that became the Lovers' Quarrel. Lincoln and the Republicans demonstrated that when due homage is paid to the principles of the First Founding, the American people can be persuaded to accept dramatically creative resyntheses of the Two Foundings, which in turn permit the (sometimes surreptitious) advancement of the principles of the Second Founding.

The Civil War and the Lovers' Quarrel

In his introduction to the 1973 edition of *Crisis of the House Divided,* Harry Jaffa defended the view that the Civil War *was* about slavery, and that the Confederacy was in open revolt to the principles of the Declaration of Independence. "Statesmen of the Confederacy in 1861 declared slavery and the theory of racial inequality to be the 'cornerstone' of their regime," he began. "But when the cornerstone was enunciated, it was done with the explicit rejection of the teaching of Jefferson and the doctrine of the Revolution." The Civil War represented "the attenuation of the convictions with respect to a human freedom, rooted in the laws of nature and of nature's God, that had inspired the Revolution."[1] Jaffa puts the cart before the horse in this interpretation; he takes the Republicans' creatively resynthesized meaning of the Declaration's principles negotiated in1863–1868 (roughly from the Emancipation Proclamation to the ratification of the Fourteenth Amendment) and reasons backward that that had always been the meaning of the Declaration since 1776. This interpretation gives rather too much credit to the First Founders, and too little to Lincoln and the Republicans for their creative resynthesis of the principles of the Two Foundings, which made possible the endurance of the republic to this day. After all, the Confederacy's alleged "attenuation" of the Declaration's principles had been permitted for over fourscore years by the Tenth Amendment, the lynchpin of the First Founding that had found its way into the scripture of the Second Founding. At the minimum, indifference to, and at the maximum, outright protection of the slave power was embedded in the First Founding; those who want to argue that the Confederacy was using the states' rights defense as a ruse may perversely end up giving a pass to the uglier side of the First Founding. (Decoupling the Two Foundings, then, permits us to own up to the sordid aspects of the First Founding while allowing us to assign a modicum of credit to the Second Founders, who did make a good-faith effort to roll back the states' right to preserve the institution of slavery.) Oddly enough, in his attempt to identify Lincoln as a foremost figure in American political thought, Jaffa ends up subordinating him to the author of the Declaration of Independence, who by his account had always seen the light. Even if the First Founders had *said* what was right, to give them the benefit of doubt for a rhetorical and symbolic masterpiece designed really only to inspire global sympathy, when they *did* nothing to suggest Jaffa's reading of their enlightened attitudes about natural rights, would be to severely depreciate the ideational and developmental contributions of the neo-Federalists of the Civil War era. For Lincoln did something that Jefferson did *not* do: he extrapolated what were known to be the rights of Englishmen (and only the rights of Englishmen) and applied them, with the help of expanded federal powers, to every individual in the Union, including those who were not previously protected. Jaffa's account underestimates Lincoln and the Republicans' considerable ingenuity in carving out a neo-Federalist justification for emancipation where even Publius had failed.

The legacy of the First Founding meant that there would be a *constitutionally* legitimate language by which slavery was defended, however morally indefensible the institution was. In this sense, slavery was arguably less the "corner-stone" of the Confederacy than was the doctrine of states' rights and the principles of the First Founding.[2] I say this to indict the First Founders on the issue of slavery, not to exonerate the Confederacy. No one can deny that the Confederacy was deeply invested in the institution of slavery, but it is a critical fact for our purposes here that it was able to defend the practice of human bondage in the remorseless language of states' rights—by way of the Declaration of Independence and Bill of Rights, no less. To sell the war to the majority of rank-and-file Southerners who were not slave-owners, higher principles than a sordid tale of racial hierarchy had to be adduced. This is the uglier side of the First Founding that ought not to be swept under the carpet. The Constitution—and especially those parts of it that were necessary tips of the hat to the First Founding—is not and was never moral scripture; it is irreducibly political. To say that secession was justified by a different conception of union than was held by the North is not to exonerate the Confederacy and its defense of slavery; it is to show the resilience of the Lovers' Quarrel even when the answer to another intersecting debate seems so morally obvious.

Scholars have already noted that slavery was not the proximate cause of the war.[3] First, as is well known, the North was not committed to abolition until around 1863, when Lincoln issued the Emancipation Proclamation. Lincoln said it squarely in his debate with Stephen Douglas in 1858 and verbatim again in his First Inaugural Address: "I have no purpose, directly or indirectly, to interfere with the institution of slavery in the States where it exists."[4] Second, if the North was initially concerned only with saving the Union, the Confederacy, as we shall see below, made its case for secession preponderantly in the language of states' rights. The fact is, thanks to the overriding commitment to states' rights, the Second Founding did not and could not outlaw slavery, and the Confederacy could reasonably argue that it was only trying to preserve the constitutional status quo of the antebellum era. Indeed, some actions indicate that the Confederacy was even willing to curb the expansion of slavery. The Constitution of the Confederate States banned the importation of slaves (Article 1, Section 9, Clause 1),[5] and in one of his first acts as president, Jefferson Davis vetoed a bill the Confederate Congress had passed under the Provisional Constitution that would have permitted auctions of illegally imported slaves if no organization were available to return them to Africa.[6] If the Confederacy was ostensibly willing to limit the expansion of slavery within its borders but was insistent on the individual states' right of secession, then it is quite possible that "states' rights was the Southerners' deepest political passion."[7] Even the nomenclatural debate that persists today, over a century after the abolition of slavery but at a time when the Lovers' Quarrel continues to be waged, about whether the war should be called the "Civil War" or the "War between the States" helps to make this point: the war was a war about competing conceptions of federalism, of the very meaning and nature of the United States.[8]

Even if the Thirteenth Amendment might have been the greatest redemptive act of the Civil War era, it was the Fourteenth Amendment that was its greatest developmental legacy. While Karen Orren and Stephen Skowronek were right that "no single act in American history changed so many lives so profoundly as did the Thirteenth Amendment," it is less apparent that "the termination of the master-slave relationship was political development of the *first* magnitude [my emphasis]."[9] Changing lives and introducing new participants to a political community were great and happy accomplishments. The abolition of the master/slave order in American politics did not, however, fundamentally alter the substance and meaning of the American compact. This is especially the case if, as some have argued, the lives of the newly freed women and men were not so "profoundly" changed. Because the Radical Republicans failed to push through land reform, large numbers of freedmen tenants remained under exploitative sharecropping arrangements in the same plantations where they once worked as slaves.[10] As Michael McConnell reminds us, the Reconstruction Amendments were soon to be overtaken by a half-century of Jim Crow laws that enervated the social revolutionary impact of the War.[11] The overtly racist objections raised even in the North to Senator Charles Sumner's Civil Rights bill that passed in 1875 suggest that if the Republicans had been united on the abolition of slavery, they were lukewarm about the civil rights agenda. The Compromise of 1877 turned out to be no compromise at all, as it allowed the Republicans to turn their attention to the economy and their backs on the freedmen.[12]

If so, then perhaps the Reconstruction Amendments, though substantively about civil rights, were jurisprudentially and developmentally about federal powers and states' rights.[13] If one conception of federalism permitted slavery to exist, only a reformed conception of federalism could spell its end. And it took the ratification of the Fourteenth Amendment to deliver this. Whereas Orren and Skowronek find the developmental weight of the Thirteenth Amendment in the first section, that "Neither slavery nor involuntary servitude . . . shall exist within the United States," I argue that it lies in its second section, which authorized that "Congress shall have power to enforce this article by appropriate legislation," and even more so in the Fourteenth Amendment, which stipulated for the first time in the Constitution that "No State shall" make laws of a certain kind when previously the Bill of Rights had applied only to the Congress (that it "shall make no law" abridging various rights). Saying (in the Thirteenth Amendment) that slavery will not exist in the United States remained only a wish until it was matched by the reality of additional congressional, that is to say federal, power (which was granted in the Fourteenth Amendment). This is a pattern that would endure through the New Deal and the Civil Rights era of the 1960s: civil rights are rarely self-activating in American politics; they usually come by way of federal powers. The American compact must typically be remade before new rights can be advanced. Therefore, by my reading, the developmental significance of the Civil War was not so much the white man's reconfigured relationship with the freedmen, but the federal government's relationship with the states. Indeed, this logic is consistent with Orren and Skowronek's account of the Fifteenth Amendment, which made a mockery of legal positivism until the Voting Rights Act in 1965. The passage of the amendment—an attempt to address the embarrassing fact that Northern blacks were still not enfranchised—was proof of the Republican Party's desire to be done with the civil rights agenda. And so the authors rightly concluded, "When the Fifteenth Amendment passed, neither federalism in its essentials nor the incentives of the Republican Party had changed; that was the Amendment's difficulty."[14] Conversely, when the Fourteenth Amendment was passed, stating for the first time that "No State shall" act in certain ways, American federalism was dramatically remade. The Thirteenth Amendment may have passed Orren and Skowronek's significance filter of durability, but it was the Fourteenth that was classic APD as I have defined it. The abolition of slavery certainly mattered as a historical and moral watershed, but the reconfiguration of a constitutional compact—transference of authority from the states to the federal government on the matter of master–slave relationships—ranks higher on the developmental totem pole because every single citizen is implicated when a constitutional compact is remade.

Now, if this observation feels odd and even morally disjointed, then it also reveals the limits of *American* political development and the double-edged nature of the Lovers' Quarrel. After all, the Fourteenth Amendment restricted only state action, not private actors, which meant that states' rights could be curtailed and federal authority enhanced at the same time when racism by private individuals and organizations persisted. APD has generally been more incremental than radical because it is always forged by quarrel and compromise between the principles of the Two Foundings. Indeed, that even the greatest moral issue this country ever had to wrestle with had to be worked out in the contested language of states' rights and federalism reveals the resilience of the Lovers' Quarrel as the master ordering and disordering mechanism of

American politics. And so, for better *and* for worse, as the Supreme Court concluded in the *Civil Rights Cases*, which invalidated the public accommodations provisions of the Civil Rights Act of 1875, the Fourteenth Amendment determined only that "It is State action of a particular character that is prohibited. Individual invasion of individual rights is not the subject matter of the amendment." Delivering the majority opinion of the Court, Justice Joseph Bradley continued, "Positive rights and privileges are undoubtedly secured by the Fourteenth Amendment, but they are secured by way of prohibition against State laws and State proceedings affecting those rights and privileges, and by power given to Congress to legislate for the purpose of carrying such prohibition into effect."[15] The Court did not stymie the moral vision of the Radical Republicans; it merely clarified their developmental goals—the remaking of the relationship between the federal government and the states. The Fourteenth Amendment was therefore developmental, but far from radical. It was classic APD.[16]

It would be too easy to say that the principle of states' rights was a mere artifice freshly invented by the South to protect slavery; to do so might also seem to imply that there was no robust grant of new powers to the federal Congress by war's end. States' rights and federal powers operate in a zero–sum relationship in American politics; one cannot observe more of the latter without recognizing less of the former. So if the Republicans represented the neo-Federalist flank during the Civil War, a parallel line connects the Declaration of Independence and Anti-Federalism to the Confederacy. It was federalism that made it possible for one country to both permit and not permit slavery, and it was federalism that had permitted the socioeconomic differences that others have argued were the cause of the war in the first place.[17] It was federalism that permitted the South to launch its secessionist ambitions, and federalism that structured and made possible the South's reincorporation into the Union. From start to finish, participants on either side of the war wrestled with the constitutional meaning of states' rights in the context of federal power.

The Declaration of Independence and States' Rights

It is no coincidence that just as the Articles of Confederation began by naming every sovereign state party to it, so too did the provisional Constitution of the Confederate States.[18] Both were harkening back to the First Founding's cherished principle of "Free and Independent States" expressed in the Declaration of Independence. When Jefferson Davis declared that the Confederacy "merely asserted a right which the Declaration of Independence of July 4, 1776, defined to be 'inalienable,'" he was reverting to the same document to which George Mason and Elbridge Gerry appealed in their entreaties against the Constitution.[19] Contra Harry Jaffa, the Civil War did not so much fulfill the Declaration's unexecuted principles as it would attenuate its fundamental principle, the supremacy of states' rights.[20] The continuity between the spirit of '76 and the Confederacy can be seen most clearly in the similarity in attitudes between the defenders of slavery in the 1770s and the 1860s. In 1775, the English author and lexicographer, Samuel Johnson, had asked, "How is it that we hear the loudest yelps for liberty among the drivers of negroes?"[21] The answer to that rhetorical question is that the rights and liberties Revolutionary Americans claimed were the rights and privileges of Englishmen. Since these rights were claims against the king, they were necessarily collective rights or privileges that had little to do with the natural, universal, or individual rights of racial minorities subordinated by popular majorities, or modern notions of equality that would enter into modern understandings of the Declaration only after the Civil War.[22] And so, Anti-Federalists such as Philadelphiensis defiantly reversed Johnson's question and countered, "Strange indeed! that the professed enemies of *negro*, and every other species of *slavery*, should themselves join in the adoption of a constitution whose very basis is *despotism* and *slavery*; a constitution that militates so far against freedom, that even their own religious liberty may probably be destroyed by it. Alas! What frail, what inconsistent beings we are!"[23] The slavery that the Anti-Federalists feared was not of human bondage, but of despotism from on high; the rights they proclaimed were not the individual rights of fellow human beings held against each other, but collective privileges that communities held against kings and governments. Similarly, Rawlins Lowndes would remind his peers, "charters ought to be considered sacred things" while at the same time ask, "what cause was there for jealousy of our importing negroes?"[24] In other words, what mattered to the First Founders and the Confederacy were codified rights as immunities operating at the *vertical* distribution of power; the relatively modern idea of rights as a *horizontal* set of claims against fellow citizens—and one may think of the separation of powers as a nascent step in the direction of this modernity—was very far from their mind indeed.

It was with this same understanding of rights that while serving in the South Carolinian legislature, John Calhoun, arch defender of slavery, saw no contradiction in authoring legislation that would make South Carolina, in 1810, after New Jersey in 1792, Georgia in 1798, and Maryland in 1802, among the earliest states that guaranteed universal adult white male suffrage (sans economic qualifications).[25] Calhoun was no champion of individual rights; rather, his neo-Anti-Federalist instincts were that while one rightfully erred on the side of jealousy when encountering governments, one erred on the side of trust when countenancing popular majorities in the states. Calhoun's concern was the vertical dimension of power, for which suffrage was a consistent solution.

A direct descendant of Philadelphiensis, a Confederate soldier applying the same logic to Samuel Johnson's challenge would declare, "we are appealing to chartered rights . . . it is insulting to the English common sense of race [to say that we] are battling for an abstract right common to all humanity."[26] Neither the Anti-Federalists nor Calhoun or this soldier saw a contradiction in yelping for liberty while simultaneously fighting to defend the institution of slavery in each of their separate states, because they understood rights only as collective claims against government, not an individual's trump against another. Their concern was political liberty, not social or economic liberty.

The Anti-Federalists, of course, were the first to have turned the Declaration's list of rights against kings into a defense of states' rights against federal power, which ultimately found expression in the Bill of Rights. Patrick Henry, debating with Madison in Virginia, would paraphrase the Declaration in his defense: "all men are by nature free and independent, and have certain inherent rights, of which when they enter into society, they cannot by any compact deprive or divest their posterity ... our [Virginian] bill of rights contains those admirable maxims."[27] Though it sounds like Henry may have been referring to a set of natural rights, it is noteworthy that he referred to one charter and paraphrased another to ground his claims. He would not "hazard" the loss of Virginians' rights precisely because they were hard earned rather than natural, codified rather than universal.[28] His was the extant and modal understanding of rights in the United States before Lincoln and the Republicans conceived them. Even Jefferson, the author of the Declaration, "historicized rights, locating them in specific civic contexts which—and only within which—the most enlightened and 'civilized' peoples could enjoy them."[29] These men may have cynically deployed the language of universal and natural rights (which inadvertently laid the groundwork for Lincoln and the Republicans' creative resynthesis), but they were not, for the most part, champions of natural, universal, or individual rights; more than anything else, they were guarding the hard-earned rights of Englishmen against despots abroad or at home. Indeed, they even defended these rights at the expense of the natural, universal, and individual rights of slaves. After all, if the revolutionaries were simply asserting their natural rights, there would have been at least 13 separate rebellions— indeed, this is how Daniel Boorstin describes the Revolution.[30] But Americans in 1776 were well past that primordial state, and possessors of the chartered rights of Englishmen. The Declaration does not articulate the rights of a sea of individuals in a state of nature, but "that these United Colonies are, and of Right ought to be Free and Independent States."

Statesmen of the early republic had invoked the Declaration only to affirm the live-and-let-live doctrine of states' rights, not to make modern promises about natural, universal, or individual rights and our obligations to each other.

In a message to the House of Representatives, President James Monroe wrote, "The Declaration of Independence confirmed in form what had before existed in substance. It announced to the world new States, possessing and exercising complete sovereignty, which they were resolved to maintain."[31] The Declaration was for Monroe an articulation of states' rights, not individual rights applicable to all Americans. And so it was for William Henry Harrison, who used the Declaration to defend the rights of the inhabitants of the District of Columbia: "If there is anything in the great principle of unalienable rights so emphatically insisted upon in our Declaration of Independence, they could neither make nor the United States accept a surrender of their [the citizens of the District of Columbia's] liberties and become the 'subject'—as in other words, the slaves—of their former fellow-citizens."[32] In using the word "slave" so cavalierly and typically of his generation, the president clearly understood the Declaration to be a statement of the rights of the descendants of Englishmen, not individual rights applicable to slaves. Affirming the rights of Californians on the eve of the state's incorporation into the Union, Zachary Taylor also understood the Declaration to have been a charter of states' rights: "Any attempt to deny to the people of the State [of California] the right of self-government . . . will infallibly be regarded by them as an invasion of their rights, and, upon the principles laid down in our own Declaration of Independence, they will certainly be sustained by the great mass of the American people."[33] The political result of the Revolution was, according to Franklin Pierce, "the foundation of a Federal Republic of the free white men of the colonies, constituted, as they were, in distinct and reciprocally independent State governments."[34] Presidents Monroe, Harrison, Taylor, and Pierce all understood the Declaration to have espoused the First Founding's fundamental principle of states' rights; they did not believe that the Declaration had championed natural, universal, or individual rights.

Jefferson Davis, president of the Confederate States of America, was operating on firm precedent when he wrapped his Second Inaugural Address in the language of the First Founding and rested it on the doctrine of states' rights:

> When a long course of class legislation, directed not to the general welfare, but to the aggrandizement of the Northern section of the Union, culminated in a warfare on the domestic institutions of the Southern States—when the dogmas of a sectional party, substituted for the provisions of the constitutional compact, threatened to destroy the sovereign rights of the States, six of those States, withdrawing from the Union, confederated together to exercise the right and perform the duty of instituting a Government which would better secure the liberties for the preservation of which that Union was established.[35]

As M. E. Bradford argued, "the fulcrum of his [Davis'] inaugural address is a reading of the choice for independence in 1776 as an insistence upon an historic identity: an assurance that one kind of Englishmen not be treated differently from other sharers in the common blood."[36] To be sure, Davis was conveniently leap-frogging across the years 1787–1789 when a revolution in favor of government was mounted, but that is precisely what makes him a direct descendant of the Anti-Federalists. The latter saw the Constitution as a perversion of the Declaration, not an extension of its principles. "I beg you to call to mind our glorious Declaration of Independence, read it, and compare it with the Federal Constitution; what a degree of apostacy [sic] will you not then discover," wrote A Georgian.[37] A true disciple of Anti-Federalism, Davis' allegiance was to the Revolution and the First Founding, not the Second. He proudly claimed lineage to the Declaration because he, not the Northerner, was the more recognizable heir to the spirit of '76. Like the revolutionaries and Anti-Federalists, he believed that rights preceded powers, not the other way round. Thus the Anti-Federalist, Agrippa, believed that "power is not the grand principle of union among the parts of a very extensive empire; and that when this principle is pushed beyond the degree necessary for rendering justice between man and man, it debases the character of individuals."[38] When Davis reminded his audience that "our colonial ancestors were forced to vindicate that birthright by an appeal to arms," he was appealing to the older conception of union that had preceded the Constitution. When he explained that "we are in arms to renew such sacrifices as our fathers made to the holy cause of constitutional liberty" and when he claimed the "inheritance bequeathed to us by the patriots of the Revolution," he was merely marking the Confederacy's lineage from 1776.[39] It was in the tradition of the First Founding when Davis appealed: "He who knows the hearts of men will judge the sincerity with which we have labored to preserve the government of our fathers, in its spirit and in those rights inherent in it, which were solemnly proclaimed at the birth of the States, and which have been affirmed and reaffirmed in the Bills of Rights of the several States."[40] All told, that the South made its case for secession on legal and constitutional grounds while the North relied increasingly on moral grounds lends some support to the conclusion that "it was a much more straightforward matter for southerners to find historical precedents for their attempt at separate nationhood than it was for northerners to defend their opposition to secession."[41]

Davis and his followers would lose this debate for lack of force but not of logic. Indeed, we observe once again the cost of Madison's equivocation when he had observed in Federalist 39 that the Constitution was "partly federal and partly national." By diminishing the very real differences between a states-centered federalism and a centralized federalism advanced, respectively, by the most ardent Anti-Federalists and Federalists, Madison left room for Davis to characterize the Constitution of 1787 as "a voluntary Union of sovereign States for purposes specified in a solemn compact" rather than as most Federalists characterized it, as a nation sanctioned and created by the *aggregate* republican will of "We the People of the United States."[42]

Davis' more states-centered understanding of federalism also shaped his understanding of what kept the Confederate States together: homogeneity and fraternity rather than, as it was for the Federalists and the North, heterogeneity and strong national institutions. Davis would have concurred with Brutus' judgment that "in a republic, the manners, sentiments, and interests of the people should be similar. If this not be the case, there will be a constant clashing of opinions."[43] Like the Anti-Federalists, Davis highlighted the importance of homogeneity within a republic for effective representation to occur—though of course the republic he oversaw was a lot more extensive than the ones his political ancestors had envisioned. "To increase the power, develop the resources, and promote the happiness of a confederacy," Davis said in his First Inaugural Address, "it is requisite that there should be so much of homogeneity that the welfare of every portion shall be the aim of the whole."[44] In his Second Inaugural Address, he affirmed the same: "To preserve in spirit, as well as in form, a system of government we believed to be peculiarly fitted to our condition," he said, "we determined to make a new association, composed of States homogeneous in interest, in policy, and in feeling."[45] The "community of sentiment" based on fraternity and emotions that Brian Dirck describes as Davis' conception of union is not so different from the homogenous republic of friends and neighbors envisaged in Anti-Federalism or the "harmony and affection" of fellow citizens espoused in Jeffersonian thought.[46] Lincoln's very different conception of Union, which Dirck called a "nation of strangers," was but a corollary of the impersonal republic based on law and reason that the Federalists had created.

Confederate Liberalism and Racism: An Irresistible Link?

If the most passionate advocates of liberty were also the most adamant defenders of slavery, then we need to confront the possibility that liberalism—really, Anti-Federalism—was always a fit with the slave power, and the darker side of the Second Founding comes thanks to the First. If, as Gunnar Myrdal had observed, "an educational offensive against racial intolerance, going deeper than the reiteration of the 'glittering generalities' in the nation's political creed, has never seriously been attempted in America," perhaps it is because the glittering generalities proclaimed in the Declaration were meant to generate self-satisfaction, not doubt.[47] While some scholars have argued that Louis Hartz was wrong about his claim that America's supposed ideological consensus stems from the historical absence of feudalism, I suggest instead that Hartz did not push his conclusion about the liberal consensus far enough in the South, where he characterized the existence of slavery as fraudulent and aberrant, rather than, as I argue, entirely consistent with liberalism as the First Founders understood it.[48] He wrote:

> Long before, in the seventeenth century, America had laid his trap for the Southern thinkers. By being "born equal" by establishing liberalism without destroying feudalism, it [America] had transformed the rationalist doctrine of Locke into the traditionalist reality of Burke, so that anyone who dared use conservatism in order to refute liberalism would discover instead that he had merely refuted himself.[49]

But what if Confederate conservatism understood itself as Lockean liberalism with an American twist—operationalized as states' rights—and the South was not trying to refute liberalism but uphold it? This was certainly the dominant understanding of liberalism, certainly in the South, for fourscore and seven years. It was not that the South "began to break with their Jeffersonian past around 1830" to defend racial feudalism; in fact, it embraced it.[50] Jefferson may have trembled at the hypocrisy of a Declaration that championed the liberty of some men who also perpetrated the enslavement of others, but his moral pause neither affected his prose nor the actions of his generation. The revolutionaries were rather more concerned with their own liberties to have thought for the liberties of others amidst them. Slaves, whether or not they were biologically distinct from the English, certainly did not possess the rights of Englishmen. "As much as I deplore slavery," Patrick Henry began, "I see that prudence prohibits its abolition."[51] To be sure, many Southern delegates to the Philadelphia convention were perfectly happy to argue for the equality of slaves in terms of their economic productivity for the purposes of representation, but such equality did not make them Englishmen.[52] The same concern for English liberty and an indifference to the liberty of the slaves can be found in Jefferson's writing at the end of his life. "The boisterous sea of liberty indeed is never without a wave," Jefferson famously wrote. Yet at the same time he was serenading liberty, Jefferson was also addressing the Missouri Compromise, which he thought was "not a moral question, but one merely of power"—adopting the classical understanding of liberty as a negative concept antonymous to state power (but not to the slave power). Jefferson favored the expansion of slavery to the West because this was what, in his mind, *liberty* demanded. He proceeded in the same letter to address the moral question anyway, offering a revealingly specious argument that would not have given the slaves any comfort, but only to their masters: "All know that permitting the slaves of the South to spread in the West will . . . increase the happiness of those existing, and by spreading them over a larger surface, will dilute the evil everywhere and facilitate the means of getting finally rid of it."[53] Jefferson's liberalism was more, if not entirely, concerned with the liberty of the slave owners, not that of the slaves.

And so, if the liberty that the First Founders championed was the liberty of their forefathers, not those of slaves, so it was that the Confederacy's espousal of liberty, did not, in their minds, apply to those outside of their lineage. As Edmund Burke observed of the American colonists, "they are . . . not only devoted to liberty, but to liberty according to English ideas, and on English principles. Abstract liberty, like other mere abstractions, is not to be found. Liberty inheres in some sensible object; and every nation has formed to itself some favourite point, which by way of eminence becomes the criterion of their happiness."[54] In America, the Declaration became the sensible object and favorite point for the Anti-Federalists and their descendants, who came to understand that the rights articulated there were the rights of Englishmen, not natural, universal, or individual rights applicable also to women, Indians, or slaves. These rights were designed to sound universal to fellow Englishmen and potential allies overseas, but not to Indians or slaves at home. As Stephen Douglas bluntly put it in his debate with Lincoln at Jonesboro, "This Government was made by our fathers on the white basis, by white men, for the benefit of white men and their posterity forever."[55]

If Jefferson had appealed to the "laws of nature and nature's God," it was because American liberalism, as Hartz had argued, did not have to fight to be. In this Hartz was right. The rights of Englishmen were transposed from the Old World to the New, though they *seemed* natural enough, possibly because they operated far away from the reach of the Crown and the institutions of Europe in the virgin territory of the New World. The illusion of freedom proclaimed in the Declaration became an article of national faith in part because those who could have objected to it—Indians and oppressed peasants—were few, while those who would have objected to it—blacks and women—were legally silenced. Though Harry Jaffa makes much of one sentence (the first in the second paragraph) of the Declaration of Independence about "life, liberty and the pursuit of happiness," the overwhelming bulk of the text lists 27 of the King's violations of the rights of Englishmen—the sovereignty of the colonists in each state—not of the natural law. Among these, it was alleged, the King had "forbidden his Governors to pass Laws of immediate and pressing importance," "dissolved Representative Houses repeatedly," "endeavoured to prevent the population of these States," "kept among us, in times of peace, Standing Armies without the Consent of our legislatures," "taking away our Charters, abolishing our most valuable Laws, and altering fundamentally the

Forms of our Governments." Governors, legislatures, and charters—unlike life, liberty, and the pursuit of happiness—are all creatures of English law created and extant in the states, not of nature. As Daniel Boorstin rightly observed, the Declaration was a "bill of indictment against the king, written in the language of British constitutionalism."[56]

Inegalitarian ascriptive traditions have reigned for so long with so little pushback for so much of American history because propertied, mostly Protestant, white males of mostly English descent spoke so authoritatively during the First Founding that their words could not be dismissed by the Second Founders, with the result that American politics remained, for a time, an internal conversation between them that crowded out everyone else. Though Rogers Smith has faulted Hartz and Tocqueville for relegating blacks and Indians to "tangents" in American history, it is not ethnocentric to observe that in terms of the decision makers of history at least until the Civil Rights era, "this is a white man's country."[57] To describe the "was" is not to deny the "ought." Such was the case, for example, in the early republic when, as Sean Wilentz observed, "The Federalists did not hate the Jeffersonians out of antislavery conviction; rather, they sometimes took antislavery positions because they hated the 'Jacobin' Jeffersonians."[58] And as Myrdal astutely concluded, "it is thus the white majority group that naturally determines the Negro's 'place' . . . the Negro, as a minority, and a poor and suppressed minority at that, in the final analysis, has had little other strategy open to him than to play on the conflicting values held in the white majority group."[59] Even the abolition of slavery, then, was an outcome, rather than the cause, of the Lovers' Quarrel.

Though there may well be "multiple traditions" in American culture, it should also be said that liberal and inegalitarian ascriptive traditions have often been the same thing.[60] An excess of liberty has generated an ascriptive heaven (or hell) in the United States, where the absence of *noblesse* has not removed privilege, only *oblige*. The absence of feudalism made America free for most white Americans at the same time that it encouraged racial, ethnic, and gender ascription because the presumption of equality also necessitated a politics of difference. As we saw in the previous chapter, it is precisely because Jacksonian America fixated on the idea that all men (of English, and later, of European decent) are equal that the Democratic Party was able to style itself as an egalitarian party dedicated to equality of opportunity for all white males *while also* defending the institution of slavery. The Declaration, a charter for liberalism, has more than something to do with the country's complacent disregard of master–slave, husband–wife, master–servant, and other hierarchical orders. To be sure, the Declaration also represented a promise, or a check that future generations of historically subordinated groups, such as Martin Luther King Jr. on behalf of African Americans, would take to the bank to cash, as did Elizabeth Cady Stanton, with her Declaration of Sentiments.[61] But this took rhetorical inventiveness, and the callousness by which the Declaration's lofty words were uttered at the same time millions were subjected to chattel slavery cannot fully be scrubbed from our history. Indeed, the legacy of an originally gender- and color-blind proposition that all men are created equal remains with us, so much so that the only way we know to identify or describe subordinated ascriptive classes in America has been to reify distinguishing categories—categories, one should add, that are deviations from the demographical baseline assumed and affirmed in the Declaration. Put another way, the Declaration and the First Founding may have paradoxically committed Americans to the victim-centered language of rights.[62] Consider the title of Myrdal's book, *An American Dilemma: The Negro Problem and Modern Democracy*.[63] The "Negro Problem," of course, was anything but a problem created by the Negro; yet calling it the "White Slaveholding Problem" would hardly have made sense to those in Myrdal's generation who had not benefitted from more recent literature about the pathologies of a victim-centered approach to race relations.[64] Such is the unseen and unspoken cost of the Declaration's lofty ambiguity.[65] Whereas, as Myrdal astutely argues, the "Negro's rationalization [of their racial subordination] . . . has not the same character of a self-deceiving defense construction against one's own moral feelings," the Declaration has been used for a long time, and possibly continues to be used, as a self-deceiving defense mechanism.[66] Perhaps the expression of truth (about the equality of men) in 1776 partly expiated the guilt of committing a sin against it. But saying it was so when it was not yet became a drug that enervated our better angels—certainly in the antebellum era, and possibly even after. This is the unsung legacy of the First Founding.

Lincoln's Reinterpretation of the Declaration and Liberty

It is only when we understand that the First Founding stands as antithesis to the Second that we can fully appreciate Lincoln's pivotal role in reinterpreting the Declaration of Independence for neo-Federalist ends.[67] Some modern conservatives have observed that "on the record of American history since 1858, Lincoln stands convicted as an enemy of the 'founding.' "[68] In a sense, this assessment is correct: Lincoln modified extant understandings of the Declaration, the American scripture of the *First* Founding. But in another sense, the assessment is wrong, because Lincoln's interpretation of the Constitution, the operative text of the *Second* Founding, occurred on a trajectory that Publius himself had initiated. As the Federalists had used the ambiguous language of "We the People" to assert a nationalized "We" to supplant the separate peoples of the States, so too Lincoln invoked his "rightful masters, the American people" to affirm the validity of his conception of union.[69] Recognizing that the Declaration's principles were an external source of political legitimacy that preceded the Constitution, Lincoln and the Republicans' greatest contribution to American political thought was to resynthesize these principles with the Constitution and to turn it into a premise and instrument for federal power. That we see no irony in housing the "Charters of Freedom" together at the National Archives in Washington, DC today—two of which rejected government and one of which affirmed it—is testimony to the creative resynthesis Lincoln and the Republicans must take credit for.

As early as in 1837, Lincoln was affirming a "political religion" that fused the "blood of the Revolution" and the "Constitution and laws" in his speech at the Young Men's Lyceum in Springfield, Illinois.[70] Even then, he was aware of the passage of time from the revolutionary era that necessitated a redefinition of the principles of '76, which he would later call a "new birth of freedom" at Gettysburg. In the Lyceum speech, this redefinition was performed by reconsecration; heresy was concealed by orthodoxy. In supposing "danger to our political institutions," he explains,

> Another reason which *once was*; but which, to the same extent, is *now no more*, has done much in maintaining our institutions thus far. I mean the powerful influence which the interesting scenes of the revolution had upon the *passions* of the people as distinguished from their judgment. By this influence, the jealousy, envy, and avarice, incident to our nature, and so common to a state of peace, prosperity, and conscious strength, were, for the time, in a great measure smothered and rendered inactive; while the deep-rooted principles of *hate*, and the powerful motive of *revenge*, instead of being turned against each other, were directed exclusively against the British nation. And thus, from the force of circumstances, the basest principles of our nature, were either made to lie dormant, or to become the active agents in the advancement of the noblest cause—that of establishing and maintaining civil and religious liberty.[71]

Lincoln understood the Revolution to have been inspired by passions, principally those of hate and revenge. And while these motors for negative liberty did their necessary work against the British, he saw them currently, as the Federalists did in 1787, as a threat to the republic when directed against each other. "Passion has helped us; but can do so no more." He continued presciently, "It will in future be our enemy."[72] (Correspondingly, unlike Jefferson, who understood prerogative as a democratic concept, Lincoln would later adopt a more

Hamiltonian understanding of prerogative, as an inherent emergency power granted by the Constitution.[73]) The speech also reveals Lincoln's understanding of the distinction between revolution and development. If Lincoln believed that "towering genius disdains a beaten path," it was because he echoed the Whiggish fear of demagoguery and the mob and was committed to the consolidation of the Constitution and the rule of law. And so, as Glen Thurow wrote, "whereas the Founders pledged their loyalty to the Declaration of Independence, Lincoln calls for loyalty to the Constitution and laws."[74]

Like the Second Founders and New Deal Democrats, Lincoln would transform Jeffersonian ideals and use them in the service of Hamiltonian ends. In the Gettysburg Address, Lincoln would extract the famous words "all men are created equal" from a Declaration that hitherto had been understood as an expression of states' rights and the rights of Englishmen and turn it into an account of universal rights and a defense of federal authority. Indeed, Lincoln had begun to do this in his speech in Peoria, which had helped launch his political career, when he said, "Let us *readopt* [my emphasis] the Declaration of Independence."[75] For him, rights were not just understood as the *libertas* and privileges of barons or Englishmen against a king, but also an obligation to others in our community who do not yet enjoy such *frei* and privileges. It was this radical move that inaugurated the neo-Federalist activism—"the new birth of freedom"—of the Civil War. Whereas the Anti-Federalists and the Confederates focused on the Declaration's affirmation of government by consent and states' rights, Lincoln focused instead on its assertion that "all men are created equal." The speech was, according to Garry Wills, "one of the most daring acts of open-air sleight-of-hand ever witnessed by the unsuspecting. . . . giving people a new past to live with that would change their future indefinitely."[76] In effect, Lincoln changed the meaning of the First Founding to make it more in line with the principles of the Second Founding. Perhaps this is why another conservative commentator observed, "Lincoln's 'second refounding' is fraught with peril and carries with it the prospect of an endless series of turmoils and revolutions, all dedicated to freshly discovered meanings of equality as a 'proposition.' "[77]

To care about *Unum* is to accept some premise of equality that is shared by the *Pluribus*; and to care about equality is to change our understanding of (negative) liberty. As the Federalists learned that the only way to form a more perfect Union was to change and even invert extant understandings of federalism, Lincoln found that the only way to preserve the Union was to reconfigure previous understandings of liberty. Though "liberty," the word more frequently used in the South, and "freedom," Lincoln's preferred word, are often used interchangeably, their distinct etymologies map roughly onto what Berlin had called "two concepts of liberty."[78] Liberty is more a concept relating to the separated and unrestrained individual with the obligation to use one's independence responsibly, as suggested from the Latin *libertas*.[79] This is perhaps why in his study of Confederate soldiers' letters to loved ones, James McPherson showed that the ideas most frequently invoked even in these private correspondences were liberty and self-government.[80] Freedom, on the other hand, refers more to the benefits and duties of belonging to a community, as suggested by the Norse *fri* or the German *frei*.[81] This is why Lincoln spoke not of the liberty of slaves, but how "in giving freedom to the slave we assure freedom to the free."[82] If liberty is more liberal, freedom is more republican. If liberty does not assume some degree of equality, freedom does, because my freedom has no meaning if my brother or sister is not equally so. While the Declaration and the Bill of Rights affirm liberty, the Constitution is also committed to equality.

Lincoln understood this distinction, which is why he starts off his Gettysburg Address talking about a nation "conceived in *liberty*" fourscore and seven years ago but then ends in a call for a "new birth of *freedom* [my emphases]."[83] This is not a coincidence. Lincoln tells an audience in 1864: "We all declare for liberty; but in using the same *word* we do not all mean the same *thing*."[84] He might have said that the Confederacy was fighting for *libertas* but the Union was fighting for *frei*. When politicians play political theorist, it is likely that they are up to mischief. When they take on the keywords of American democracy, they are playing with the highest developmental stakes. Whereas the Confederacy sought liberty for individual slaveholders and their allies who resented federal intrusion into Southern domestic institutions, the abolitionists first and then, later, Lincoln hoped to extend to disenfranchised members of their community the freedom that the slaveholders already possessed. Lincoln's reinterpretation of the Declaration from a charter of liberty into a battle cry for freedom would set the stage for the more substantive conception of freedom, or the linking of liberty and equality associated with the twentieth century.[85] Consider the fact that in Martin Luther King Jr.'s "I have a Dream" speech, the two times he mentions "liberty" are quotations from the Declaration and from a biblical hymn. "Freedom," however, he invokes 20 times at the steps of the Lincoln Memorial, paying homage to the fact that Lincoln was the first major American statesman to reinterpret the meaning of the Declaration for the cause of freedom. He too understood that the Declaration, once a tool for his enemies, could be reworked to make them his friends.[86]

There are, of course, different interpretations of Lincoln's understanding of the Declaration. Constitutional "originalists," who usually do not give much credence to the Declaration, tend to connect the two texts in a single breath, claiming that, for example, "the American founders aimed to protect natural rights by creating a republican government with limited powers."[87] Declarationists, like Jaffa, prefer to leave some room for Lincoln's innovation and tend to argue that Lincoln "transforms and transcends the original meaning of that proposition (that 'all men are created equal') although he does not destroy it."[88] But this is to walk a tightrope. Either the Declaration's principles are transcendental, and Lincoln can claim no real innovation except for rediscovery, or the Declaration's principles are not transcendental, at least not until Lincoln's reinterpretation made them so. But Jaffa punts, saying, "Lincoln . . . gave a greater consistency and dignity to the position of the signers than was theirs initially," and the end result is to give shorter shrift to the developmental significance of the Civil War than probably the author actually believes.[89] When Jaffa notes that Lincoln "conceives of just government far more in terms of the requirement to achieve justice in the positive sense" rather than just "in terms of the relief from oppression," he comes closer to acknowledging Lincoln's innovation.[90] Jaffa might have been more explicit in observing that there were two antithetical ideological traditions Lincoln was working with. The Declaration, after all, is a statement about collective rights and negative liberty against the Crown. The positive liberty of justice, on the other hand, is a matter deliverable only by a governing authority. The key point is that Lincoln's reading of new rights necessitated an assertion of new powers. In his effort to tie the philosophy of the Declaration and the Constitution together, Jaffa underplays the politics of how they have become so. When President-elect Lincoln responded to Alexander Stephens' invitation to say something to a restless and agitated South, intoning, "A word fitly spoken by you now would be like 'apple of gold in a picture of silver,'" Lincoln ponders in his own notes:

> All this is not the result of accident. It has a philosophical cause . . . That something is the principle of "Liberty to All" . . .
>
> The assertion of that *principle*, at *that time*, was *the* word, *"fitly spoken,"* which has proved an "apple of gold" to us. The *Union*, and the *Constitution*, are the *picture* of *silver*, subsequently framed around it. The picture was made, not to *conceal*, or *destroy* the apple; but to *adorn*, and *preserve* it. The *picture* was made *for* the apple—*not* the apple for the picture.[91]

On the surface, Lincoln appears to be characterizing the Declaration as the "apple of gold" and the Constitution as the subordinate "picture of silver." But it is equally likely that Lincoln was formulating his creative resynthesis of the nation's texts as he discovered that the Declaration's principle "has *proved* an 'apple of gold' to us [my emphasis]." After all, Lincoln's partisan position on the Lovers' Quarrel could not be clearer. In his Cooper Institute address, also around 1860, Lincoln let it be known that in relation to the "original" Constitution, he was a fan neither of the Anti-Federalists nor the Bill of Rights—the constitutional reincarnation of the Declaration of Independence. He asks:

> What is the frame of government under which we live?
>
> The answer must be: "The Constitution of the United States." That Constitution consists of the original, framed in 1787, (and under which the present government first went into operation,) and twelve subsequently framed amendments, the first ten of which were framed in 1789.
>
> Who were our fathers that framed the Constitution? **I suppose the "thirty-nine"** who signed the original instrument may be fairly called our fathers who framed that part of the present Government [my emphasis].[92]

Lincoln was highly unusual among the statesmen of his era, and certainly of our own, to argue that the "fathers" were only the 39 of the 55 who put their signatures to the Constitution. He apparently also had little regard for the Bill of Rights, since it was not part of the "original instrument." (Almost exactly a year later, as we saw, Jefferson Davis, in his First Inaugural Address, would call the revolutionaries of '76, not the Constitution's supporters, the "fathers.") Spoken like a true Federalist, Lincoln understood that the two halves of the Constitution do not sit easily together. A truer "originalist" than today's "originalists," who have more than a soft spot for the Anti-Federalists, Lincoln privileged the views of the majority of 39, rather than the minority, when attempting to decipher the meaning of the Constitution. In doing this, he demonstrated an understanding of the primacy of the Lovers' Quarrel in American history that no president before or after him has matched. In suggesting that those who defend slavery "fix upon the provisions of these amendatory articles, and not in the original instrument," he displayed an understanding of the tension in the powers created in the original Constitution of 1789 and the rights later ratified in the "amendatory articles."[93] It was this sophisticated understanding of the two ideological theses of American history that permitted the creative resynthesis that was to follow. As Storing puts it, "it is a simplification, but not a misleading simplification, to say that the crisis faced by Abraham Lincoln seventy years later required a remixing of the Federalist solution and the Anti-Federalist reservation. And if the major element in the creative resynthesis was still the Federal one, yet it is due the Anti-Federalists to say that it was they, more than the defenders of the Constitution, who anticipated the need."[94]

A Government Of the People, By the People, and For the People

The task of reconciling the Two Foundings has always fallen on the Federalists and their descendants, because they were the innovators of each age trying to persuade citizens, naturally conservative and accustomed to the constitutional status quo, toward a more perfect Union. During the Civil War, Lincoln's political genius lay in his reinterpretation and strategic cooptation of the substantive principles of the Declaration of Independence and his fusion of it to the government structure laid out in the constitutional text, so that the federal government was now poised to use a document the 13 colonies had first drawn up to reject one government, now to empower another. This strategy of hoisting with another Lover's petard is a recurring story of the most successful actors and movements in APD. When he affirmed a "government of the people, by the people, and for the people" in perhaps the most celebrated speech in American history, Lincoln was turning Douglas' theory of popular sovereignty—a Jeffersonian ideal—on its head in service of an Hamiltonian end. With a sophisticated revision and intertwining of Jeffersonian ideals with Hamiltonian ends, his trifecta about popular sovereignty became the most emphatic restatement of national (as opposed to states-centered) republicanism since the Federalists coined and constitutionalized the idea, "We the People." If Lincoln believed in God, natural law, and rights, as a statesman and in his public philosophy, his foremost faith was in "a government of the people, by the people, and for the people." In thrice affirming "government," the Gettysburg Address was a prototypically neo-Federalist speech; more nationally republican than even the Federalists dared to advance.

Though the Federalists did not believe in plebiscitary democracy, unlike many Anti-Federalists, they gave themselves completely over to the idea of self-government as a collective enterprise. They were therefore democratic in conviction, though not in style. This conviction can most clearly be discerned in the fact that they chose to ignore the precedent of several state constitutions and attempted to omit a Bill of Rights, and included only a very sparse schedule of entrenched clauses in the federal Constitution. The Anti-Federalists remained "men of little faith" on this very point.[95] John Smilie's objection to James Wilson's arguments against the need for a Bill of Rights, for example, reveals the sentiment of the Anti-Federalists. "The truth is," he declared at the Pennsylvania ratification convention, "that unless some criterion is established by which it could be easily and constitutionally ascertained how far our governors may proceed, and by which it might appear when they transgress their jurisdiction, this idea of altering and abolishing government is a mere sound without substance." To establish such a criterion, he proposed to his fellow delegates: "Let us recur to the memorable declaration of the 4th of July, 1776."[96] Those who insist that the Constitution's heart lies in its second half and believe the Federalists' "omission . . . to be fatal" remain the disciples of the Anti-Federalists.[97]

The Federalists, on the other hand, generally believed that the people in their collective capacity would get it right, and that there was no need to bind their hands, even if ostensibly for their own good. As John C. Jones argued at the Massachusetts ratification convention, "The federal representatives will represent *the people*; they will be *the people*; and it is not *probable* they will abuse themselves."[98] The same conviction prompted Edmund Pendleton to argue during the Virginian ratification debates that "there is no quarrel between government and liberty" and Edmund Randolph to proclaim that "there can be no liberty without Government."[99] George Washington, for his part, understood that the enemy of liberty was not tyranny but disunion, which is why he had argued in his Farewell Address, "your union ought to be considered as a main prop of your liberty," and the union should be the "primary object of patriotic desire."[100] Similarly, Lincoln's "concept of liberty was an essential part of his description of the union."[101] While the Confederacy understood the people of the states to be the repositories of the virtues and ideology of America, Lincoln and the Republicans would make developmental headway in elevating the *nation* as the embodiment of the people's virtues, and the federal government—expressed most clearly in the Fourteenth Amendment—as their benefactor, not their enemy.

Like the Federalists, Abraham Lincoln battled a political foe, Stephen Douglas, who spoke in the language of popular sovereignty, but couched, perhaps inconsistently, in the rubric of state sovereignty. The Anti-Federalists and their descendants claimed that their hope was in the people of their states. But it is revealing that even in their own state constitutions, they held back, cordoning off areas immune from intrusion in their own bills of rights. Even in their small, homogenous republics, they insisted on boundaries where the people or their elected representatives could not tread, unwilling to freely profess a government "of the people, by the people, for the people." Similarly, for Harry Jaffa, "consent of the governed means the consent of the *enlightened*," and by that he meant only those who understood the laws of nature and of nature's God ought to have a role in creating legitimate government.[102] He too, held back.[103] The Federalists were not against the invocation of God or natural laws or other justificatory principles; they only expected that such principles should hold weight only if they were brought into the public sphere by citizens, should they so choose, placed before the tribunal of, and then sanctioned by We the People. In this way, the "oughts" of our democratic imagination through history have always been achieved by the "is" of our institutions. In American public life, the people in the aggregate decide, not God or any other standard. Like the

Federalists, Lincoln believed that out of the institutional matrix of the American Constitution there emerges the only truth we can know as a people. Lincoln did not turn to rights as an instrument to emancipate the slaves (knowing full well that the Bill of Rights had actually served to prevent that outcome). He turned instead, to paraphrase a line from his Cooper Institute address, to the *might* that comes from right. In this, he revealed that he was the direct descendant of Publius, who was in the business of creating powers, not rights.[104]

National republicanism connects government and the people in a way that no other political philosophy does because it anoints the citizens as the rulers. Indeed, the government and the people are so closely interwoven by Lincoln and the Republicans' account that there is barely a difference between them.[105] Such was the view Lincoln shared with Daniel Webster, who had argued that "the Union is not a temporary partnership of States. It is the association of the people, under a constitution of government, uniting their power, joining together their highest interests, cementing their present enjoyments, and blending into one indivisible mass, all their hopes for the future."[106] And such was the connection between the governing and the governed Lincoln was trying to defend when he resoundingly endorsed "government of the people, by the people, for the people" at Gettysburg. Unlike the Anti-Federalists and their descendants who were populist in style, Lincoln's commitment to democracy and collective self-government was substantive. His characterization of a government of, by, and for the people conjures, like Webster's, a single, timeless, cross-temporal polity that connects the people of the past, the duty of those in the present, toward those who will come in the future. Lincoln's republican trifecta—of, for, and by the people—asserts the foundations, the *modus operandi*, and the purposes of republican government. "Of the people" casts a look back to the Second Founding and posits a government with a democratic pedigree that is *ipso facto* legitimate; "by the people" crystallizes the central working principle of republican government that there is no higher tribunal than the people; "for the people" sets up the ultimate goal of republican government and also the test to demonstrate that the government was indeed of and by the people. Lincoln thus affirms the Federalist and nationally republican idea that it is only as citizens of a republic, rather than as jealous states in possession of our revolutionary rights or in deference to God or tradition, that we may be said to be active participants in our own fates.[107]

Publius Redux: A Revolution in Favor of Union

Richard Henry Lee, the person behind the allonym "Federal Farmer," was probably right when he observed of the Constitution: "It appears to be a plan retaining some federal features; but to be the first important step, and to aim strongly at one consolidated government of the United States."[108] Lee's great-nephew, Confederate General Robert E. Lee, would fight to reverse the course toward consolidation that the former had predicted. Lincoln, on the other hand, would take Publius' plan for a more perfect Union to greater heights. His affirmation of government in the Gettysburg Address stood in stark contrast to the Declaration's rejection of one government and its conspicuous silence on the ideal type of government or political union (except perhaps for the principle of consent). His creative resynthesis at Gettysburg is even more remarkable, then, given that the Declaration said nothing about political forms or structures, yet he would write a new meaning onto it to help him make a neo-Federalist defense of the Constitution's powers, arguably paving the way for twentieth-century statism.[109]

We sometimes forget that perhaps the first reason for federalism's being is the imperative, however weak, to unite. Wherever federalism has occurred in the world, it is because its framers sensed that *because* of the fissiparous tendencies felt among the would-be unit's constitutive parts, more centralization and coordination was preferable to less. Centralization and coordination takes effort because the natural state of all prefederated units is one of independence. The Federalists mounted such an effort in 1787–1789. From the beginning, the Federalists joined the idea of progress to the idea of Union. They believed that a need for common defense and the course of commercial intercourse between the states would lead to an ever-closer bond between them. They hoped that the yearnings of a mystical popular Spirit, We the People, would power the Union's teleology of "a more perfect Union." For the Federalists, the Union—embodied in the Constitution—was more than a means and something of an end to be "venerated," a Grand Design. For the Anti-Federalists, it was no more than the means toward the more lofty ends of life, liberty, and the pursuit of happiness; it was an experiment at best. Whereas the Federalists feared the condition of relative independence between the states and looked forward to a Constitution of mutual dependence, the Anti-Federalists embraced the condition of relative independence between the states and saw no reason to disrupt the status quo.

Like Publius, who had envisioned "a more perfect Union," Lincoln saw the perfectability of the Union as something that was not settled in the past, but an ongoing mission. He thought, for example, of the "central idea" of public opinion, "the equality of men," as always making "a steady progress toward the practical equality of all men," and the union as a dynamic political enterprise.[110] Lincoln, like the Federalists, was no conservative. As he put it, "the dogmas of the quiet past are inadequate to the stormy present. The occasion is piled high with difficulty, and we must think anew, and act anew."[111] Thus he would stretch the limits of presidential prerogative greatly, without much regard for democratic sanction, as was the case for Jefferson, as he believed that the people had already spoken when they ratified the Constitution and granted powers to those elected to sworn to "preserve, protect and defend" it. He accorded due deference to the framers' ideas, but he added, "I do not mean to say we are bound to follow implicitly in whatever our fathers did." As Publius himself had dismissed "veneration for antiquity," Lincoln continued, "To do so would be to discard all the lights of current experience—to reject all progress—all improvement."[112] Lincoln's view is repeated in his First Inaugural Address, where he asserts the important premise for his expansive conclusion, "No organic law can ever be framed with a provision specifically applicable to every question."[113] This parallels (the early) Madison's position when he noted, in Federalist 37, that "no language is so copious as to supply words and phrases for every complex idea." Also like Hamilton, Lincoln found meaning in the Constitution's silences.[114] Lincoln's patriotic faith in the Union, like the Federalists' orientation toward the world, was also of a cosmopolitan kind. Recalling how as a boy he was inspired by America's revolutionary heroes, Lincoln felt that "there must have been something more than common that those men struggled for ... something even more than National Independence; that something that held out a great promise to all the people of the world to all time to come."[115]

Centralized federalism has generally taken the larger and longer victory over peripheralized or states-centered federalism in American history in part because while the Anti-Federalists made persuasive arguments based on the ideals of the First Founding, the Federalists and their descendants often made even better arguments because they took these ideals, instantiated in state capitals, and improved them by extending their applicability across the Union. Consider one of these ideals, sovereignty. Lincoln conceded that the states may have preceded the United States, but he also rightly noted that the legitimacy of the state constitutions ratified at the First Founding paled in comparison to the endorsement by a collective We the People of the United States of the Constitution during the Second Founding. In his message to Congress on July 4, 1861, Lincoln argued,

> The states have their status in the Union, and they have no other legal status. If they break from this, they can only do so against law and by revolution. The Union, and not themselves separately, procured their independence and their liberty.[116]

This was a Federalist talking, though Lincoln was also quite correct. Before their consecration by the Second Founding, the states were creatures of royal authority. Sure, the states would democratically ratify their own constitutions during the First Founding, but they nevertheless inherited their territorial boundaries from royal charters. Only the collective territorial boundary of the United States can truly be said to be a creation of We the People, and not a legacy from the British Crown. In extolling the "government of our fathers . . . which have been affirmed and reaffirmed in the Bills of Rights of the several States," Davis failed to acknowledge that "the government of our fathers" was to a greater or lesser extent still a government of kings, or one whose territorial boundaries were bequeathed by kings.[117] Lincoln may have been a partisan when he made this point—but it was also a compelling point that exposed the relative weakness of the Confederacy's *raison d'être*. He took the Confederacy's idea of sovereignty and turned it on its head.

If the doctrine of states' rights impelled the Confederacy to secession, it also spelt its own breakup as soon as the new government in Richmond began to assert powers over the Confederated States for the execution of war. Davis knew that the government of the Confederate States had to be supreme in order to wage war against the North, which is possibly why, to emphasize its strength, he chose to call the South's equivalent of the federal government that succeeded the "Provisional Government" of 1861 the "Permanent Government" in his Second Inaugural Address. Yet his vice president saw "no differences in principle between the utterances of both men [Lincoln and Davis]; both make necessities of war override constitutional limitations of power."[118] And so, as Drew Gilpin Faust has argued, Confederate nationalism ultimately fell victim to its internal contradictions.[119] Conversely, it was Publius' conception of Union that Lincoln adopted when he pointedly asked, "One party to a contract may violate it [the compact between the states]—break it, so to speak—but does it not require all to lawfully rescind it?"[120]

Yankee Leviathan

As James McPherson noted, the Republican Party "inherited from its Hamiltonian and Whig forebears a commitment to the use of government." It would push through "an astonishing blitz" of laws that "did more to reshape the relation of the government to the economy than any comparable effort except perhaps the first hundred days of the New Deal."[121] In 1861, Congress created the income tax via the Revenue Act; in 1863, the National Currency Act created a single national currency to eradicate the problem of currency fluctuation that occurred as a result of there being different notes issued by state banks circulating at the same time with no predictable lending policy; and in 1864 the National Banking Act introduced bank charters issued by the federal government that would begin to displace the application to and granting of charters by (often corrupt) state legislatures.[122] The federal government also encouraged westward expansion by parceling out farmland and creating the land grant colleges system with the Homestead and Morrill Acts of 1862, and by grants for the construction of transcontinental railroads. To facilitate commerce, the government introduced free mail carrier services to big cities, and operationalized railway mail services and a money order system. The bureaucracy expanded with the creation of the Department of Agriculture (1862), the Bureau of Printing and Engraving (1862), the Office of Comptroller of the Currency (1863), and the Office of Immigration (1864).[123] And as Theda Skocpol has shown, one of the most significant unintended consequences of the Civil War was the inception of the social-welfare state by way of pensions to Civil War veterans, their widows, and dependents as the growing American state became implicated in nineteenth-century patronage politics.[124] The abolition of slavery was a milestone on the road toward the national administrative state because the federal government decisively qualified the states' right argument that a community with an independent democratic pedigree could act in *any* manner to protect its welfare as it understood it.

In the aftermath of war, the victory of the Northern industrial economic system over Southern agrarianism cemented the relationship between and ensured the ascendance of the industrial capitalists and the emerging corporatist state during the Gilded Age.[125] The South's desire to roll back federal power in the realm of civil rights was oddly synchronized with Northern capitalists' desire to coopt it for economic gain. One result was that the period during and following Reconstruction also saw the rapid expansion of the federal judiciary—aided and abetted by successive Republican Congresses—in the service of railroad and corporate interests and against anti-business state laws.[126] This was the great era of plutocratic capitalism, and the state grew as it became a facilitator of economic expansion.[127] The Progressives and the New Dealers helped to build the infrastructure of the state, but this would not have been possible had it not been for the Civil War Republicans who transformed our idea of it, and bequeathed to later generations the "blueprint of modern America."[128]

Yet it is also true that state-building occurs in starts and fits in America because no lover of the two has ever had the last word. The Civil War dealt a serious blow to the doctrine of states' rights, but it was not a fatal one. The period that followed Reconstruction saw a backlash against the centralization and state-building of the preceding years—a fact that should not have surprised the Radical Republicans had they realized that the Fourteenth Amendment may have nationalized the Bill of Rights (at least until the Slaughterhouse cases), but it did not remove the Tenth. Federalism worked for the

North too because it was ultimately more eager to reincorporate Southern whites than blacks into the political process so that America could go on with its business—namely, business. The Compromise of 1877, which installed a Northern president in return for the restoration of home rule, would signal the end of the neo-Federalist episode in the South. Through all the death and destruction, the South lost only one major right, slavery, as a result of the Civil War. The Confederate States (except for Virginia) kept their territorial boundaries and identities after the war, which made it easier for the South to reintegrate back to the Union with an identity that had been constant before, during, and after the war. The South was restored to full membership to the Union and all attendant privileges and was free to reinstate ex-Confederates to positions of power in all sectors of society and even national prominence for at least an entire generation, and to replace slavery with Jim Crow for another three generations. At the same time, the incorporation of the Confederate flag and symbols into state flags rechanneled Southern anger toward the Yankees when once it had been directed at the United States. The perverse result of the Thirteenth Amendment, without enforcement of the second section of the Fourteenth, which would have reduced a state's apportionment for the purposes of representation in proportion to the number of disenfranchised citizens, was that the South gained in political influence what it had lost by the abolition of slavery. Whether or not in retaliation for Reconstruction, the Court in the 1870s and 1880s came to a series of decisions that restored if not enhanced the police powers of the states.[129] And so if the war's causes revealed the danger of states' rights, the war's end demonstrated its resilience. Once again, the Lovers' Quarrel as an instrument of conflict as well as its resolution had done its work, for now.

Because the Union won the Civil War, it has written the history that it fought not for the North, but the Union, and Alexander Stephens' not altogether imprecise appellation of a "war between the states" never caught on. But it is worth remembering that the United States experimented with confederalism not once, between 1781 and 1787, but twice in its history. In the aftermath of the South's military defeat that came about not least because of intrastate jealousies that had marred its war effort, the new, centralized federalism of Publius would gain an even stronger foothold. By the end of the Civil War, we are told, a union of states had become the United States.[130] If during the antebellum period the security of the Union was usually defended on contingent and utilitarian grounds, after the Civil War, it was accepted as a matter of fact. Lincoln himself was fully aware of and partly responsible for the shift. While he had constantly affirmed his commitment to "Union" but not at all to "Nation" in his First Inaugural Address, he would refer to the "Nation" five times in his Gettysburg address, and not at all to "Union."

Conclusion: A New Birth of Freedom

Though James McPherson has dubbed the Civil War the "Second American Revolution," it was really won on principles fundamentally antithetical to those of the First Founding.[131] Lincoln and the Republicans waged a Lovers' Quarrel on the side of the Federalists to secure "a more perfect Union" envisaged by the Second Founders. 1. *On Union*. Lincoln and the Republicans took the rights of Englishmen enshrined in the Declaration and extended them to all individuals, permanently turning the "union," which the Confederacy used to describe a relationship between the states, into an entity, a nation. 2. *On Liberty*. Lincoln saw a tension between the older, negative conception of liberty and equality and therefore proposed "a new birth of freedom." He would thrice affirm the federal government of, for, and by the people, and deployed federal powers liberally, using an elastic understanding of the Constitution's clauses, to save the Union and to protect the liberty of the individuals in it. 3. *On Truth*. Lincoln and the Republicans understood the perfectability of the Union as an ongoing project. They inverted the meaning of the Declaration of Independence from a statement of states' rights into a defense of federal powers, created and relied on new institutions to wage war and to manage the economy, and abolished an institution as old as the republic, slavery. 4. *On Republicanism*. The Republicans dismissed the Confederacy's idea of popular sovereignty and argued that it was the Constitution that granted legitimacy to the states, not the reverse. Lincoln understood his prerogative to be constitutionally granted, not democratically given, and he used it aggressively to pursue his nationalistic understanding of republicanism and to forge new milestones for federal authority.

The Civil War was Federalism versus Anti-Federalism in its angriest incarnation, taking the nation to the brink of divorce. The war was the sharpest iteration of the Lovers' Quarrel because the North and the South took up arms over antithetical conceptions of We the People. The North, like the Federalists, were the more pragmatic and progressive element advocating the preservation of the Union as a whole and later the abolition of slavery; the South, like the Anti-Federalists, were the romantic idealists and principled conservatives standing firm on states' rights. Whatever one may say about the federal government, the fact is that the emancipation of the slaves came by way of federal powers, not states' rights. The solution has its genesis in Publius, not Federal Farmer. If the reason for the Civil War was Anti-Federalist in origin, its resolution and aftermath were firmly, even vengefully, Federalist. The Thirteenth and Fourteenth Amendments stripped thousands of white Southerners of human property that had hitherto been protected by state laws and transferred the authority to grant citizenship and its attendant rights from the states to the federal government.

What did not unmake us, however, succeeded in remaking us, and the ending of the Civil War forged a new equilibrium between the disciples of Publius and Federal Farmer. What emerged was a newfound commitment to the authority of the federal government over the states that Publius had only dreamed of a lifetime ago. He was right that *imperium in imperio* was indeed a "political monster" (Federalist 15). For this conclusion, the Union owes much to the statesmanship of the Republicans and Abraham Lincoln. Like Franklin Roosevelt, who would later speak to what he referred to as "My Friends" in his Fireside Chats, Lincoln would remind the Confederacy, "We are not enemies, but friends." The "mystic chords of memory" he wisely invoked referred to the spirit of '76, a time before the Lovers' Quarrel. "A husband and wife may be divorced and go out of the presence and beyond the reach of each other," Lincoln said in his First Inaugural Address. "But the different parts of our country . . . can not but remain face to face, and intercourse, either amicable or hostile, must continue between them."[132] This is what Lincoln valiantly tried to do from 1863 to 1865. Although a controversial figure in his own time, Lincoln would enjoy "the distinction of bringing the most revolutionary and most reactionary of poets together to pay equal honor to the sole American whom they all agree to honor."[133] The reason why is because he dexterously appropriated the Anti-Federalists' Declaration and creatively resynthesized it with the Federalists' Constitution so that by this artful fusion he became, in time, cleansed of partisanship and levitated out of the Lovers' Quarrel into the realm of national myth. While George Washington was already "great" before he became president, Lincoln would become so only after. Clinton Rossiter was correct that "Lincoln is the supreme myth, the richest symbol in the American experience," because his martyrdom rendered his creative resynthesis of the Declaration and Constitution beyond serious contestation.[134] So durable was this shift in federal authority that few modern Anti-Federalists recognize the radical nature of Lincoln's neo-Federalist creative resynthesis; many even claim him as their own.

CHAPTER 5

Anti-Federalism & the Progressive Creative Destruction[1]

Although a durable shift in favor of federal authority occurred during the Civil War and Reconstruction, the older conception of union envisioned in the First Founding was no more vanquished than was the Bill of Rights, which was retooled by the Fourteenth Amendment. Before North and South was Federalism and Anti-Federalism, and so it has been since; though the successful resolution to the Civil War meant that principles of the Two Foundings, which had been artfully mingled by the unionists, would become increasingly hard to differentiate. This was so especially in the Progressive era, when the United States saw a durable, albeit uneven and convoluted, expansion of federal authority, but became so largely driven by Jeffersonian principles. In this chapter, I will recount a resurgence of Anti-Federalist ideas after the Yankee Leviathan of the post-Civil War years, less in the familiar vessel of the states' rights doctrine and more in the form of classical republicanism, in the least likely of places. My aim in this chapter is, first, to explain why a clear-cut consensus of the era's legacy has not been reached and to show that the enigmatic quality of this era can in part be explained by the Progressives' own internal Lovers' Quarrel between their means and their ends. By doing so, I hope also to demonstrate the enduring and inescapable reach of the Lovers' Quarrel, even when it would seem that the Civil War had settled the debate between the Two Foundings. At the dawn of the twentieth century, the Lovers' Quarrel would begin to take on a more complex and interlocking tenor, as a more mature, participating citizenry began to mix and match the principles of the Two Foundings in the way that statesmen like Publius and Lincoln had done before. Though the Progressives helped to pave the way for the modern bureaucratic state—I will argue that many were really envisioning an "associative state"—and they did so with Anti-Federalist goals in mind, and principal among these was a restoration of a virtuous republic and the advancement of pure or direct democracy. Progressivism's mixed legacy, then, is a reflection of the dyssynchrony, though it is often characterized as a virtue, between its protagonists' self-professed use of "Hamiltonian means for Jeffersonian ends."[2]

"Hamiltonian Means for *Jeffersonian* Ends"

If the Civil War Republicans' conception of centralized federalism was victorious over the Confederacy's, the depth and scope of this victory only expanded in the course of the twentieth century. The conventional view—accurate in my opinion, as I explain in the next chapter—is that the New Deal not only executed the Federalists' and Civil War Republicans' vision of a stronger and more expansive federal government but also went beyond it, altering the balance of power between the federal and state governments and effectively ending the doctrine of "dual sovereignty" that had existed until then.[3] Attached to this conventional view is the interpretation that the Progressives were the forerunners of the New Dealers, partners in crime and descendants of the Federalists in their partiality to the powers of the federal government over those of the states.[4] This liberal-Progressive narrative, partly a result of *ex post facto* reasoning, is somewhat off the mark.[5]

The Progressives were not all statist precursors to the New Dealers. Indeed, those who fall in this camp were the minority in the tribe. Consider the election of 1912, when every candidate purported to be a Progressive. Theodore Roosevelt was the bold nationalist by whom many scholars recall the spirit of Progressivism. "The National Government belongs to the whole American people, and where the whole American people are interested, that interest can be guarded effectively only by the National Government," Roosevelt said in 1910.[6] This was surely a neo-Federalist position, linking the elder Roosevelt to Publius as well as his fifth cousin, Franklin, whose similar beliefs would hold sway 22 years later. But in 1912, Theodore Roosevelt carried only 27 percent of the popular vote. Neither of his fellow candidates, who had also laid claim to the "Progressive" mantle, shared his convictions. William Howard Taft, for his part, repudiated his former boss's strident nationalism, and warned that "social justice involves a forced division of labor, and that means socialism."[7] And in his campaign against Roosevelt, Woodrow Wilson—a Democrat committed to states' rights—would frequently quip, "ours [his 'New Freedom'] is a program of liberty and theirs [the 'New Nationalism'] is a program of regulation."[8] Wilson presaged modern conservatives in his affirmation that "we do not want big-brother government."[9] Between the New Freedom and the New Nationalism, Progressivism itself was waging an internal Lovers' Quarrel; tellingly, it was New Freedom that prevailed. In many ways we shall explore later, Roosevelt's brand of Progressivism was the exception, not the rule.

Scholars have characterized Progressivism as a "sticky smorgasbord of competing enthusiasms" and a "lost promise" in part because there is no clear line from Progressive idealism to New Deal statism.[10] Many prominent Progressives, including Herbert Croly, Louis Brandeis, and Edward M. House, had supported Herbert Hoover for his presidential bid in 1920.[11] Later, such veteran Progressives like Senator Carter Glass of Virginia (who was among Wilson's staunchest allies when he was a member of the House), Senator Josiah W. Bailey of North Carolina, and members of groups like the American Liberty League all saw fit to strongly *oppose* Franklin Roosevelt from the earliest days of the New Deal.[12] Also, while some modern conservatives time the beginning of the end of "strict constructionism" at the Progressives' theory of an organic, Darwinian Constitution, they miss the Progressives' organismic view of society, one evolving "naturally" from the history and traditions of the past, that thinkers such as Woodrow Wilson derived from Edmund Burke and Walter Bagehot.[13] As much as the Progressives were bracing themselves for modernity, they were also idealists looking to restore a past from decades of moral declension. They supplied the critical intellectual bridge from eighteenth-century Anti-Federalism to the twentieth century, just as the "associative state" that they created, one that worked hand in hand with trade associations, professional societies, and other private organizations, was a distinct precursor to the New Deal state.[14]

While the Progressives may have set the stage for the birth and growth of the national administrative state, their accomplishment in this regard was half-hearted, nothing like the full-throttled expansion that the New Dealers would bring. Conversely, while the Progressives left behind only an embryonic administrative state, their democratization of American politics—a clearly Jeffersonian agenda—was significantly less tentative. At a minimum, the Progressives, perhaps more than any other group in American history, were disciples equally of the Two Foundings. A case could even be made that they leaned Anti-Federalist vis-à-vis their goals, and I err on the side of overstating the case in this chapter in part because there is almost no acknowledgment in the extant scholarship of the Progressives' debt to the principles of the First Founding, and that as a proposition seems to me to be highly implausible. Consider that the Progressives were more united in their desire to displace the "state of courts and parties" and restoring America to an uncorrupted Eden than in building its alternative, the national administrative state.[15] In this negative project prompted by restorative goals, they were rather like the Anti-Federalists, and very unlike the Federalists. Publius would not have rested content with the shredding of the Articles of Confederation; he wanted a new Constitution. The same cannot be said of the Progressives, many of whom simply wanted the Party State, and the corruption associated with it, to go away. The administrative (or "associative") state that came to replace it was only one of many solutions, many of which were in tension with each other, that the Progressives proposed and enacted.

While Lincoln had strategically embraced and modified the principles of the First Founding in the service of Federalist ends, his motives were dedicatedly Federalist because his principal goal was a more perfect Union, not a more democratic or virtuous republic. But when the Progressives advocated their "smorgasbord" of reforms to take on corruption, their goals were restorative, even nostalgic. Thus, as the Progressive scholar and Pulitzer Prize winner Vernon Parrington freely admitted in the foreword to the first volume of *Main Currents*: "the point of view from which I have endeavored to evaluate the materials, is liberal rather than conservative, *Jeffersonian rather than Federalist* [my emphasis]."[16] Even Herbert Croly has been dubbed "a liberal reformer with essentially conservative goals."[17] The result of their collective efforts was to nationalize the principles of the small, homogenous republic and to ready the country for modernity. However, unlike the Civil War Republicans and the New Deal Democrats, the Progressives did not wholeheartedly endorse the principles of the Second Founding; indeed, as we shall see, many were contemptuous of the Federalists' handiwork. The Progressives did not formulate a creative resynthesis of the principles of the Two Foundings in the service of the Second; instead they combined Hamiltonian means and Jeffersonian ends in a haphazard manner to leave behind a more convoluted administrative apparatus and attenuated developmental mark than did the Civil War Republicans and New Deal Democrats. (Perhaps the lesson here is that to succeed electorally in American politics, a movement must take a clear-cut stand behind one of the Two Foundings; what is required is either revisionism if the aim is to restore the First Founding or creative resynthesis if the aim is to expand the Second Founding. The Progressives' uncoordinated amalgamation was neither.)

If their goals were largely Jeffersonian, the Progressives' means were not all Hamiltonian either. As Herbert Croly attested, "to nationalize a people has never meant merely to centralize their government."[18] While some among them believed in building an administrative state, the Progressives relied just as heavily on intergovernmental policy instruments, and also possessed a strong sense of what society, and the intermediate organizations between the individual and the state such as corporations, can do to achieve their social gospel ideals.[19] Like Jacksonian Democrats and modern conservatives, the Progressives conceived of the nation as much more than just the national state. As Brian Balogh has argued, "New Liberals viewed unilateral intervention into the economy by the General Government as just one of many forms of associative actions. It was rarely their first choice for such action."[20] The era saw the proliferation of what Eldon Eisenach has called "parastate" institutions—churches, professional organizations, nonpartisan national magazines—to speak for "the collective ends of the national community" rather than to promote the private ends of the bosses. As Eisenach observed, "Both organizationally and culturally, the institutions that consciously articulated and enforced claims of a national public good were established largely outside of formal governing institutions and in direct opposition to the most powerful informal governing institution of them all—the mass-based political party."[21] Indeed, the Progressives' multipronged attack on the Party State—the federal government from the top and "parastate" organizations from the bottom—reveals that they were not standard-variety statists. If the Progressives were willing to put their faith in science, in experts, in the civil service, in churches, or in the people—practically anything or anyone but the party bosses—it was because they were single-minded in their opposition to the Party State, committed to *Pluribus* at least as much to *Unum*.

It may be that "for each of the major institutional reforms of the Jacksonian era, the Progressives sponsored an equal and opposite reform."[22] The two movements may have differed in their means, but they were not so dissimilar in their ends. As we saw in Chapter 2, the Democratic Party had implemented the "spoils system" to purge corruption from government—yet when the Progressives took it on, they did it for the same reason. In fact, the Progressives' attack on the Party State actually bore a striking resemblance to the Anti-Federalists' nostalgic yearnings for an uncorrupted, homogenous, civically engaged citizenry. What many Progressives desired most was not national government *per se*, but freedom from the unaccountable and corrupt Party State, and responsible and virtuous leadership in its stead. So they repackaged some of the fundamental principles of the First Founding to decry and displace the Party State, creating the vacuum that the national administrative state would eventually come to occupy. Unsurprisingly, while the Progressives' positive accomplishment, the associative state that was the first iteration on the route to a national administrative state, was fledgling and tentative, their negative project was spectacularly successful. Like Anti-Federalism, Jeffersonian Republicanism, and Jacksonian Democracy, Progressivism was animated by negative goals.

For their part, the Anti-Federalists were not against all or any state apparatus. They merely rejected the version presented by the Federalists, as the Progressives railed against the one they inherited. As Patrick Henry entreated, "We are come hither to preserve the poor Commonwealth of Virginia, if it can be possibly done: Something must be done to preserve your liberty and mine: The Confederation; this same despised Government, merits, in my opinion, the highest encomium."[23] And so, just as the Anti-Federalists' jealousy of power was a bivalent stance in which suspicion of one type or level of government was counterpoised with advocacy of another, so too the Progressives' commitment to a different kind of state was tied to their antipathy to the Party State. This bivalency mattered not least because during the ratification debates, the Anti-Federalists were focused so much on their negative project to thwart the Federalists that they failed to organize and present a coherent message of what they were *for*. The Progressives traversed a similar path. Herbert Croly exemplified a bivalent attitude against the interests and for the people when he said, "when a group of state or city officials effectively assert the public interest against the private interests, either of the machine or of the local corporations, they are acting just as palpably, if not just as comprehensively, for the national welfare, as if their work benefited the whole American people."[24] We see in Croly's roundabout way of defining the indefinable "public interest" that Progressivism's unifying logic lay, ultimately, in its antinomy to the Party State. It is no coincidence, therefore, that the still unsettled debate about what the Progressives were *for* stands in stark contrast to the consensus on what they were *against*: political and financial corruption. The reason for the consensus on the negative front is that like the Anti-Federalists, Democratic Republicans, and Jacksonian Democrats, the Progressives were principled, social critics before they were social reformers. They were, like each of their forebears, more united by what they were against than what they were for. As Theodore Roosevelt put it, his was the age of "a fierce discontent with evil . . . whether in industry or politics."[25]

Both the Anti-Federalists and the Progressives saw a moral declension in America and looked nostalgically to earlier days for inspiration. At the end of his *magnum opus* on the democratic impetus behind the American Revolution, Progressive historian Carl Becker, quoting the Declaration of Independence, extolled the First Founding:

> It is to those principles—for a generation somewhat obscured, it must be confessed, by the Shining Sword and the Mighty Dollar, by the lengthening shadow of Imperialism . . . it is to these principles, these "glittering generalities," that the minds of men are turning again in this day of desolation . . .[26]

The moralistic tones in Becker's writings are very similar to the Anti-Federalists' jeremiadic warnings. Both shared a deep, conservative commitment to an underlying and unchanging civil religion: the principles of the First Founding. For the Anti-Federalists, the victory of the American Revolution offered not so much a chance to create a new prosperous empire equal to the ones of the Old World, but an opportunity to create a republic of virtuous citizens untainted by corruption, greed, and lust for power.[27] Although the Federalists saw no need to establish a religion to support the political institutions they were creating, just as the Anti-Federalists defended the liberty of conscience, in general, toleration of religious diversity did not, in the latter's case, typically extend to the protection of atheists. Many Anti-Federalists supported the religious establishments that existed in their states and were fearful that if the "barriers of religion" were broken, Americans would become, like the Europeans, "bent on gratification, at the expense of every moral tie."[28] Like the Anti-Federalists, many Progressives sought a renaissance of an earlier America whose values had not been corrupted by the Party State. Many had had religious upbringings that instilled in them evangelical motivations and an aversion to the self-seeking mantra of the Party State.[29] Thus for Hofstadter, Progressivism was "a phase in the history of the Protestant Conscience, a latter-day Protestant revival."[30] It was the changing face of America wrought by industrialization that caused Progressive historian Frederick Turner to "express nostalgia for the old order, for rural small-town America, for agrarian values and lifestyles."[31] Later historians like George E. Mowry argued that the social group most committed to the Progressive program was not farmers but urban elites, though this argument has been challenged.[32] Yet whether or not the modal Progressive was a farmer or an urban elite, s/he "looked back to an older America" and "sought to reaffirm the older individualistic values in all the strata of political, economic, and social life."[33]

The Anti-Federalist and Progressive reverence of an older, beatific America meant that they tended, unlike the Federalists, to diagnose tangible problems with spiritual causes. Both attributed the source of America's problems to the deterioration of the republican spirit and in particular to those "immersed in schemes of wealth."[34] A century before the Progressives came onto the scene, the Impartial Examiner had articulated the quintessential Progressive fear that "If the nation happens to enjoy a series of prosperity, voluptuousness, excessive fondness for riches, and luxury gain admission and establish themselves—these produce venality and corruption of every kind, which open a fatal avenue to bribery."[35] Like many Progressives, Cato believed that "the progress of a commercial society begets luxury, the parent of inequality, the foe to virtue, and the enemy to restraint."[36] As the Anti-Federalists fulminated against the commercial spirit, critics of the Party State decried the greed of the robber barons and the venality of the bosses that had caused Americans to lose sight of the common good.[37] The signature moral issue of Progressivism was, of course, Prohibition, which was passed as the Eighteenth Amendment in a bid to break the influence of the distilling interests on corrupt politicians— "the saloon as a social and political institution"—as well as to restore the moral fabric of society as America braced herself for and then emerged out of the Great War.[38]

Freedom *from* the Party State

The "lost promise" of Progressivism, then, may have something to do with the fact that its participants were clear about and united in what they were against, but less so on what they were for. And there is practically no debate that the enemy *du jour* was the Party State. The Progressive historian Benjamin Parke De Witt recognized three tendencies that united Progressive thought, but he chose to highlight that "The *first* [my emphasis] of these tendencies is found in the insistence of the best men in all political parties that special, minority, and corrupt influence in government—national, state, and city—be removed."[39] These concerns with corruption are Jeffersonian in origin, not Hamiltonian. Similarly, Woodrow Wilson lamented, "The government, which was designed for the people, has got into the hands of bosses and their employers, the special interests. An invisible empire has been set up above the forms of democracy."[40] By "invisible empire," Wilson meant the Party State, an elaborate regime of governance coordinated by the political machines, lubricated by the spoils system, and enforced by the courts. What Wilson called an "invisible empire," the Progressive Party platform called an "invisible government":

> Instead of instruments to promote the general welfare, they [the two major parties] have become the tools of corrupt interests which use them impartially to serve their selfish purposes. Behind the ostensible government sits enthroned an invisible government owing no allegiance and acknowledging no responsibility to the people. To destroy this invisible government, *to dissolve the unholy alliance between corrupt business and corrupt politics is the first task* of the statesmanship of the day [my emphasis].[41]

The Progressives were first and foremost insurgents against the Party State or the unaccountable and irresponsible "invisible government." Their objections to the Party State stemmed from the same republican principle of accountability that the Anti-Federalists had charged was missing in Madison's new "science of politics." In effect, they were adopting aspects of the Anti-Federalists' classical republicanism and applying it to the nation as a whole. Thus Denatus had sounded a Progressive concern when he opined, "the constitution of a wise and free people, ought to be as evident to simple reason, as the letters of our alphabet."[42] But in the Federalist's Constitution, A Columbia Patriot saw a "heterogeneous phantom."[43] Like the Anti-Federalists, the Progressives had neither patience nor faith in Madison's science of politics for two reasons. First, they opposed the Constitution's unwieldy system of checks and balances because it lent itself to exploitation by the Party State at the expense of collective action for the common good.[44] As A (Maryland) Farmer argued, complex governments "seem to bid defiance to all responsibility, as it can never be discovered where the fault lies."[45] And as Centinel argued, "if you complicate the plan by various orders, the people will be perplexed and divided in their sentiments about the sources of abuses or misconduct, some will impute it to the senate, others to the house of representatives, and so on, that the interposition of the people may be rendered imperfect or perhaps wholly abortive."[46] Woodrow Wilson shared these Anti-Federalist concerns for the Constitution's lack of responsibility. He wrote:

> It is, therefore, manifestly a radical defect in our federal system that it parcels out power and confuses responsibility as it does. The main purpose of the Convention of 1787 seems to have been to accomplish this grievous mistake. The "literary theory" of checks and balances is simply a consistent account of what our Constitution makers tried to do; and those checks and balances have proved mischievous just to the extent which they have succeeded in establishing themselves as realities … [The framers] would be the first to admit that the only fruit of dividing power had been to make it irresponsible.[47]

Consider the Sixteenth Amendment, so critical for the agenda of New Deal liberalism and therefore easily mistaken as a reform motivated by Hamiltonian and not Jeffersonian principles. The Progressives were barely thinking about expanding the federal purse or expanding the size of the federal government when they proposed and supported a constitutional amendment that would allow the federal government to levy income taxes on individuals. As Edwin Seligman, a Progressive expert on taxation and campaigner for the Sixteenth Amendment, willingly admitted, "the income tax is assuredly not needed for revenue purposes."[48] According to Elliot Brownlee, "virtually none of the income-tax proponents believed that the income tax would become a major, let alone the dominant, permanent source of revenue within the consumption-based federal tax system . . . and the idea that the tax would enable the federal government to grow significantly was far from the minds of the drafters of the 1913 legislation."[49] Like so many Progressive reforms, their support of the Sixteenth Amendment was motivated by what a federal income tax was going to replace. Titled *"An Act to reduce tariff duties* [my emphasis]," the Progressives supported a federal income tax because they believed that the existing system of tariffs benefitted industrialists (at the expense of consumers and farmers) who were in cahoots with the politicians of the Party State.[50] Progressive reformers believed that tariffs, the "mother of all trusts," were an odious system of government revenue because they were the perfect instruments for members of Congress playing the pork-barrel, distributive politics of the nineteenth century.[51] There were myriad opportunities in the complex tariff schedules for members from both parties to offer subsidies (or penalties) to narrowly defined groups of constituents.[52] That is why the movement for tariff reform was so slow to organize from within the two major parties. The Democratic Party was quicker to cry foul only because its constituents did not benefit as much from the transfer payments and in particular the Civil War pensions the federal government, via the party machine, disbursed from its tariff receipts.[53]

Even though the Progressives embraced an ever-closer relationship between the president and his constituency, thereby adopting the Anti-Federalists' mirroring theory of representation (more on this below), they tellingly adopted a different stance when it came to officials of the Party State. They would advocate for a federal administration of the income tax, and therefore a virtuous system of representation closer to the Federalist view, only because this would diminish the influence of the bosses. As Seligman explained:

> Federal administration is apt to be more successful than state administration. Not only is it easier to secure expert assistance for the larger problems involved in national expenditure, but the contact between official and citizen is not so likely to have that intimate relationship which would exist in the smaller administrative sphere. Above all, the influence of the party boss and of machine methods is obviously less pronounced in proportion as the sway of governmental operations becomes broader.[54]

Similarly afraid that Progressive programs would become captive to the Party State, Herbert Croly also advocated that Progressives concentrate their reforms at the federal level. Again, though, his concerns were more negative than positive: "Almost every member of the American political body has been at one time or another or in one way or another perverted to the service of special interests. The state governments and the municipal administrations have sinned more in this respect than the central government; but the central government itself has been a grave sinner."[55] Croly, like other Progressives such as Louis Brandeis (who had celebrated the states as "laboratories of democracy"), was advocating responsible and competent government, not national supremacy for its own sake.[56]

Consider also the Seventeenth Amendment, which was ratified because of the push factor of corruption, "the greatest evil" motivating the call for direct election of Senators, rather than other positive arguments in favor of it.[57] As one contemporary scholar reported in the *American Political Science Review*, the Seventeenth Amendment "appealed to the people now not so much as a logical extension of democracy, but with far greater force as an expedient method whereby they could exercise more complete control over their state legislatures."[58] The Progressives understood that to dismantle the Party State, they had to attack the root of the problem by divesting party bosses of their king-making power. And the problem of the Senate, according to Henry Jones Ford, was that it had become the "Diet of party lords."[59] As one advocate of the amendment, Senator Albert Beveridge, lamented, "the party boss has become more potent than the legislature, or even the people themselves, in selecting United States Senators in more than one State."[60] The proponents of the Seventeenth Amendment understood that without the gift of office, there could be no *quid pro quo* in spoils. They saw the amendment primarily as an assault on the party bosses who controlled the composition and preferences of state legislatures and only secondarily as an advancement of democracy.[61] So William Riker was correct that the "the proximate cause of variations in the degree of centralization (or peripheralization) in the constitutional structure of a federal system is the variation in degree of party centralization."[62] The Progressives nationalized the party system because they hated the Party State; centralized federalism was only the consequence of achieving their primary goal.

The list goes on. When the Progressives proposed direct primaries, initiatives, referenda, and recall, they were more concerned with curtailing the nominating, agenda-setting, and tenure-administering power of the party bosses than building an administrative state.[63] Indeed, "New Nationalism" Progressives were as willing to send authority upward toward the national bureaucracy as "New Freedom" and agrarian Progressives wanted to decentralize it to the grassroots because of their shared belief that the bosses were the sources of inefficiency and corruption.[64] Even woman suffrage, Progressives believed, could deal a blow to the Party State because expanding the suffrage to citizens as yet unaffiliated to the political parties would increase the common-good-seeking virtue quotient of the citizenry as a whole. This is why so many suffragists relied on the ideology of Republican Motherhood to advance their petition for women's right to vote, and why women's groups paradoxically lost their political salience when suffrage was extended because women lost their claim to the moral high ground and became, like men, tainted participants of the Party State.[65]

Anti-Federalism, Progressivism, and Classical Republicanism

At the turn of the twentieth century, the sharp divide between Progressivism and Conservatism was still not drawn (in part because, as we shall see in Chapter 7, a distinct conservative movement that self-identified itself as such did not emerge until after the New Deal). In this fluid ideological context, the Progressives promulgated both forward and backward looking visions; and many if not most of them harkened back to major features of the Anti-Federalists' interpretation of classical republicanism. Indeed, Progressive historians were among the first scholars to offer a sustained critique of the Federalists and their Constitution, which they saw as the defective underlying infrastructure upon which the superstructure of the Party State was a necessary part.[66] Many Progressives echoed the Anti-Federalist charge that the Constitution was written by and for aristocratic interests, a condition that the patronage-oriented Party State did nothing to ameliorate but only exacerbated. The Progressive Era was, after all, probably the first time in American politics where, upon countenancing the political and economic influence of the Vanderbilts and the Rockefellers, Madison's hitherto ingenious argument of the benefits of extending the sphere in Federalist 10 lost its previous luster. When they saw that even a large republic was no defense against powerful factions or interest groups, the Progressives became skeptics of the new "science of politics" and reverted back to many elements of the Anti-Federalist theory of classical republicanism. As Richard Hofstadter argued, Progressivism was the "the complaint of the unorganized against the consequences of organization."[67] Because Progressives were now convinced that the Federalists' machinery could not do the job of promoting the common good, they too proposed a simple responsive government, liberated from a system of checks and balances that had served only to benefit the interests, to do the people's work. In effect, they attempted to nationalize the small, virtuous, homogenous republic.

The reason why the Anti-Federalists and Progressives opposed complex and invisible government was born of their shared political-epistemological belief that the common good existed as a relatively monolithic, prepolitical reality and their corresponding skepticism that an invisible hand could coalesce a multitude of competing interests toward the pursuit of the common good.[68] Because the Anti-Federalists envisioned a small and homogenous republic, it made sense to speak of a monolithic common good that existed prior to the coalescing influence of (Federalist) institutions. In contrast, the Federalists did not believe that the common good existed as a prepolitical reality, because to do so would have belied any need for the new science. For all their talk of virtue, designed in no small part to play like music to Anti-Federalist ears, the Federalist commitment to building a large, heterogeneous republic necessitated a reconfiguration of republicanism and the classical way of understanding the common good. As Madison recognized in Federalist 10, "[a] landed interest, a manufacturing interest, a mercantile interest, a moneyed interest, with many lesser interests, grow up of necessity in civilized nations, and divide them into different classes, actuated by different sentiments and views. The regulation of these various and interfering interests forms the principal task of modern legislation."

Indeed, the Federalists were in some respect forerunners to modern "interest group pluralists," in their acknowledgment not only of competing interests in society but in the independent value of their Newtonian interaction in delivering democratic outcomes.[69] Madison, in Federalist 14, called the scheme of representation he proposed in the constitution a "great mechanical power" because for most Federalists, the common good had to be *found*. Consider the difference in the Federalist and Anti-Federalist attitudes toward commerce. In Federalist 6 Hamilton argued that "the spirit of commerce has a tendency to soften the manners of men, and to extinguish those inflammable humors which have so often kindled into wars," and in Federalist 12 he advocated "multiplying the means of gratification." By contrast, Thomas Jefferson, who was only temporarily in the Federalist camp, worried about "a system rigged to substitute the countervailing forces of self-interest for the defect of public virtue and supposed dangers of majority rule."[70] Whereas commerce was thought to be a source of antagonism and corruption for both Anti-Federalists and Progressives, the Federalists embraced it as a means of promoting the common good and virtue as they understood it.

For Anti-Federalists and Progressives, the common good had to be rescued from corrupting influences; for the Federalists, it also had to be constructed. Madison believed, as he wrote in Federalist 10, that "the latent cases of faction are thus sown in the nature of man." He did not, at least as much as the Progressives did, believe in moralizing lectures to persuade politicians to set aside their self-interest for the common good, because he saw the way to find the common good via institutions. Intrinsic virtue and moral turpitude, however, were fundamental concepts in both Anti-Federalist and Progressive thought. The Anti-Federalists and many Progressives resisted merely institutional solutions to political problems because they relied on the citizens and the nationally elected president to make the best civic decisions. Both, unsurprisingly, placed a premium on education and the cultivation of civil religion. So, Mercy Warren argued, "if the education of youth, both public and private, is attended to, their industrious and economical habits maintained, their moral character and that assemblage of virtues supported . . . there is not much danger that they will for a long time be subjugated by the arms of foreigners."[71] As the Anti-Federalists feared that an arrogant, power-hungry ruling elite in a distant capital would produce a subservient and degenerated polity, the Progressives believed that only a universally and well-educated citizenry could stand up to the corruption in the country's high places, whether in politics or in the economy.[72] Civic education would restore and instill in citizens a commitment to the public good that had been thwarted by the *modus operandi* of the Party State. A (Maryland) Farmer's recommendation of "seminaries of useful learning, with professorships of political and domestic economy" could just as easily have come from a Progressive reformer. Like the Progressives, he also emphasized the instruction and learning in the social sciences, on "what is useful in this world—the principles of free government . . . the sciences of morality, agriculture, commerce, the management of farms and household affairs," because they believed that self-government could only work if citizens were educated and virtuous.[73]

Indeed, the Anti-Federalists and Progressives alike saw the republic itself "as a school of citizenship as much as a scheme of government."[74] Similarly, the Anti-Federalists wanted a Bill of Rights not only to protect the states, but for its civic educative purposes. "What is the usefulness of a truth in theory, unless it exists constantly in the minds of the people, and has their assent," the Federal Farmer asked in advocating the Bill of Rights.[75] He believed that rights had to be enumerated and codified because he valorized the "effect of education, a series of notions impressed upon the minds of the people by examples, precepts and declarations."[76] The same reasons inspired the Progressives to codify so many of their reforms in amendments to the Constitution so that citizens could transcend their private perspectives and perceive the collective ends of the community.

If the Revolution was a movement against increasing rationalization under the British Crown in favor of "political polytheism," while the Constitution represented a counter-revolution to restore political "monotheism," the Progressives were surely closer to the spirit of '76 but with a twist.[77] Like the Anti-Federalists, the Progressives assumed that there was such a thing as the common good, as expressed in public opinion, which was being thwarted by the Party State. They worried about an "invisible government" because they believed that the faith in an invisible hand had created the very conditions for the pickpocketing hand of the Party State to thrive. They could not see how an "invisible government" held together by partisan loyalties could pull together what the Constitution pulled asunder. They would have agreed with the thrust of Centinel's rhetorical question: "If the administrators of every government are actuated by views of private interest and ambition, how is the welfare and happiness of the community to be the result of such jarring adverse interests?"[78] Most Progressives refused to see America as a conglomeration of interests, but rather as a moral community. If anything, they believed that politicians of the Party State used the spaces created by the constitutional checks and balances to play cat-and-mouse with the common good. That is why they rejected both the need for the Federalists' system of checks and balances and the interest-brokering operating norm of the Party

State. It is also why, incidentally, many Progressives parted company from the New Deal when its proliferating agencies no longer looked like a neutral regulatory state but a stakeout of organized interests and collaborating politicians.[79] Not even the highest science of politics could, in the Anti-Federalist and Progressive mind, turn ambition into virtue. As Chief Justice William Howard Taft put it, "a people must learn to trust their fellows and those of high character," for "without a people so trained, the machinery of self-government, however seemingly perfect, will not suffice."[80]

There was, to be sure, a darker side to the Anti-Federalists' conception of republicanism that derived from a theory of representation that placed a premium on "sameness." Here, the link to Progressivism's idealization of homogeneity is nontrivial.[81] For a system to be representative, the Anti-Federalists believed that there must be a degree of "sameness, as to residents and interests, between the representative and his constituents," and this was possible only in a small republic.[82] As Brutus similarly argued, "In a republic, the manners, sentiments, and interests of the people should be similar. If this not be the case, there will be a constant clashing of opinions."[83] This theory of representation, in turn, assumed and prescribed a homogenous population. The small homogenous republic envisioned by the Anti-Federalists had no place for foreigners because it would then be "composed of such heterogeneous and discordant principles, as would be constantly contending with each other."[84] Agrippa warned that because "Pennsylvania has chosen to receive all that would come there ... [she] has acquired her present extent and population at the expense of religion and good morals."[85]

Even here, the Anti-Federalist legacy on the Progressives was profound. At a time when America was experiencing a new wave of immigration, some Progressives defended their nativist attitudes in ways similar to Anti-Federalists, who had set off a "veritable firestorm" at the Constitution's "no religious test" clause.[86] At North Carolina's ratification convention, David Caldwell had expressed the nativist Anti-Federalist view that "those gentlemen who formed this Constitution should not have given this invitation to Jews and heathens."[87] With a similar commitment to social homogeneity, some Progressives also favored immigration restriction because immigrants were joining the major political parties in droves as they entered the country and sought a social network in which to embed themselves, thereby expanding both the purpose and constituency of the Party State. Thus, the Progressive sociologist Edward Ross complained, "the foreigners constitute an asset of the political machine, neutralizing the anti-machine ballots of an equal number of indignant intelligent American voters."[88] Even women suffragists like Elizabeth Cady Stanton and Carrie Chapman Catt supported literacy tests that not only excluded foreigners but effectively also disenfranchised many African-American women.[89]

Perhaps this is why, incidentally, most of the states that adopted direct democracy reforms—where the Progressive faith in the people was unqualified—were Western states that had homogenously white populations—places that came closest to replicating the small republic.[90] President Woodrow Wilson, of course, was a committed segregationist who reintroduced racial segregation in the civil service when he came into office.[91] Yet that same year, at the semicentennial of the Gettysburg Address, he confidently expressed the Confederate conception of liberty that came from the Spirit of '76, saying, "How complete the union has become and how dear to all of us, how unquestioned, how benign and majestic, as state after state has been added to this, our great family of free men!"[92]

Happily consistent with their attack on the Party State, many Progressives found affinity to and utility in the Anti-Federalist theory of representation and their mutual commitment to "sameness." Because the Progressive aspiration to nationalize democracy was effectively also to homogenize it at least in terms of core ideas and commitments, the assimilability of potential immigrants figured heavily in Progressive debates over immigration. Echoing the Anti-Federalists' concern for "sameness," Edward Ross worried that when a country "admits to citizenship myriads of strangers who have not yet passed the civic kindergarten, questions that were supposed to be settled are reopened." As if he were speaking directly to Anti-Federalist concerns, he called these the problems of "heterogeneity."[93] Thus, Theodore Roosevelt supported only "immigration of the right kind," and the Immigration (Dillingham) Commission he appointed concluded: "it is evident that in the case of the Mexican he is less desirable as a citizen than as a laborer."[94] Many Progressives opposed immigration because they were trying to deprive the Party State of its lifeblood, and because they shared the commitment to homogeneity that was explicit in the Anti-Federalist theory of representation. Even in the area of immigration policy, the Progressives looked rather like their father's son.

Progressivism, Anti-Federalism, and "Pure Democracy"

As Wood had argued, "whatever else may be said about the Antifederalists, their populism cannot be impugned. They were true champions of the most extreme kind of democratic and egalitarian politics expressed in the Revolutionary era."[95] Whereas the Anti-Federalists believed in virtuous citizenship, the Federalists trusted in virtuous representation and were wary of democracy and demagogues. They did not trust in men enough and opted instead for a government of laws.[96] As has often been stated, the Federalists wanted to "extend the sphere" because they feared that the majority in a small republic would tyrannize a minority, and the only way to avoid the problem was to create a republic large enough so that no majority could ever form, and to create a Supreme Court as a bulwark against majority tyranny. In striking at the central operational principle of democracy, factional majorities—since democracies cannot work unless a mechanism of aggregating preferences is decided upon and deemed legitimate—Madison in Federalist 10 was dealing as fatal a blow to "pure democracy" as he could muster.

If the Federalists were relatively more skeptical about human nature and perceived the need to channel ambition via a constitutional framework to turn vice into virtue, the Anti-Federalists were more insistent than the Federalists were on the classical republican belief that there was a font of virtue in citizens that can and ought to be tapped. They believed, as Centinel did, that "A republican or free government, can only exist where the body of the people are virtuous."[97] Because of their starting premise of a small and homogenous republic, the Anti-Federalists were oblivious or indifferent to the possibility of the tyranny by the majority and were far more comfortable with democracy than the Federalists were.[98] This is why some Anti-Federalists opposed the Electoral College, and most worried about the power of the Supreme Court to defend aristocratic interests. On the Electoral College, Republicus asked, "Is it then become necessary, that a free people should first resign their right of suffrage into other hands besides their own, and then, secondly, that they to whom they resign it should be compelled to choose men, whose persons, characters, manners, or principles they know nothing of?"[99] Way ahead of his time, Cato similarly believed that "the representative of the people should be of their immediate choice" and worried that "by the manner in which the president is chosen he arrives to this office at the fourth or fifth hand, nor does the highest vote, in the way he is elected, determine the choice."[100]

A similar faith in democracy led Anti-Federalists to warn (of the Supreme Court) that "those usurpations, which silently undermine the spirit of liberty, under the sanction of law, are more dangerous than direct and open legislative attacks."[101] The Progressives would have agreed with Brutus's worry about the interpretive power of the courts and the provisions for constitutional amendment: "In respect to certain fundamental provisions, which necessarily receive the most rigid interpretation on the part of the courts, it is practically unmodifiable. A very small percentage of the American people can in this respect permanently thwart the will of an enormous majority, and there can be no justification for such a condition on any possible theory of popular Sovereignty."[102]

Sharing the Anti-Federalist concerns about an unwieldy Constitution dedicated to the preservation of aristocratic interests, and further burdened by a Party State incapable of transcending petty interests, the Progressives had no other option but to take their faith in citizens to new heights. They would take a page from the Anti-Federalists in their criticism of the undemocratic elements of the Constitution. Progressives like J. Allen Smith repeated Patrick Henry's objection to Article 5 and expressed the prevailing Progressive view that by insulating the Constitution against amendment, the "framers of the Constitution deliberately intended to dethrone the numerical majority."[103] Smith went as far as to praise the amendment procedure set up by the Articles of Confederation.[104] Even Herbert Croly, who was very sympathetic to the Federalists, criticized Alexander Hamilton, whom he believed "was betrayed by his fears and his lack of faith" for believing that it was "necessary to bestow upon the central government the support of a strong special interest." "Instead of seeking to base the perpetuation of the Union upon the interested motives of a minority of well-to-do citizens," Croly continued, Hamilton "would have been far wiser to have frankly intrusted its welfare to the good-will of the whole people."[105] More importantly, Croly was at pains to clarify that "the nationalization of American democracy does not mean the abandonment of the federal principle, and the substitution for it of a lifeless centralization." Rather, Croly acknowledged that nationalization "has frequently required administrative and legislative decentralization."[106] Even Croly, a Dean of Progressivism, was sold on Jeffersonian principles and tentative on Hamiltonian means.

Perhaps even more than the Anti-Federalists, the Progressives were wary of the most undemocratic branch, the judiciary, because of their belief that they were in cahoots with Congress—the spearheading branch of the Party State—to simply dispose whatever the latter proposed.[107] This is why the Progressives were so strongly opposed, to paraphrase Stephen Skowronek, not only to the state of parties, but also the state of courts. Correspondingly, the Progressive Party Platform of 1912 read: "The Progressive party demands such restriction of the power of the courts as shall leave to the people the ultimate authority to determine fundamental questions of social welfare and public policy."[108]

If the Federalists were at pains to prevent a majority, the Progressives—armed with not a new science of politics but the new sciences of society—were intent on divining and representing it, as we saw in the devolution of institutional power to citizens at both the state and local levels as a result of their direct democracy reforms.[109] For the Progressives, as Eisenach put it, "democracy was a way of life, not a set of public institutions and procedures."[110] The Progressives did not expect their direct democracy reforms at the state and local levels to create a cacophony of heterogeneous voices in part because they believed it was a lesser evil than having the voices of citizens drowned out by machine politics and secret congressional committee hearings, and in part because they assumed that their national leaders, such as Woodrow Wilson, would be able to guide them, if need be, out of their parochialism. Like the

Anti-Federalists, Progressives like Herbert Croly and Theodore Roosevelt tried to tie together public and private imperatives in the project of "nationalizing democracy." They did not reify the public/private distinction at the federal level, just as the Anti-Federalists cared not for it at the state level.[111] As John Dewey put it, "in democracy, at all events, the governors and the governed are not two classes, but two aspects of the same fact."[112] We see in the Anti-Federalist theory of representation a blurring of the public/private distinction as well as the distinction between the ruler and the ruled—in Melancton Smith's proposal that "representatives (should) . . . resemble those that they represent"[113]—just as we find a similar blurring of these distinctions in Woodrow Wilson's "Leadership by Interpretation."[114] Indeed, it was the Progressive introduction of the "rhetorical presidency" as well as the primary nominating process that would complete Jefferson's and Jackson's efforts to reinstate the First Founding's theory of representation, culminating in modern plebiscitary presidents who have indeed, as the Anti-Federalist theory of representation prescribed, come to closely "resemble" those they represent.[115]

Before Theodore Roosevelt and Woodrow Wilson advocated their theories of moral and didactic leadership to bring together a nation of solipsistic individuals and to break the stalemate of partisan wrangling, the Anti-Federalists foresaw the need for "characters who have genius and capacity sufficient to form the manners and correct the morals of the people, and virtue enough to lead their country to freedom."[116] The closeness in the Anti-Federalist and Progressive theories of leadership can be seen in their equal faith in the president as the "*vindex injuriarum*—the avenger of public wrongs."[117] As we saw in Chapter 2, the Anti-Federalist fear of an elected king who would put the country through a frivolous pursuit of empire and glory was balanced by a perceived need to guard against a potential legislative leviathan at home. As James Monroe wrote, "With an executive organized on these principles, *being independent of the legislature* [my emphasis] . . . I should be well content to intrust great powers."[118] Though Theodore Roosevelt's "stewardship theory" of the presidency appeared to look like a variation on Hamilton's understanding of prerogative (in contrast to William Howard Taft's), since he believed that he was free to do what was necessary even if the Constitution offered no "specific authorization" for his actions, what is important is that he was articulating this theory from the Bully Pulpit—a station that was necessarily extra-constitutional.[119] Like the Anti-Federalists who saw room for a strong executive to stand up to aristocratic interests, the Progressives sought a strong executive who would stand up to the political machines and their allies in the Congress, perpetrators of the public wrongs of the nineteenth century. And so, although Carpenter has noted and criticized the pattern, presidency-centered accounts of Progressivism make sense because the presidency was a major actor in the Progressive era.[120] Because Progressives understood full well that a strong legislature (and House speakership) and a weak executive were design features of the Party State, they saw it fit to empower the executive as a weapon against the corrupt politicians. Like the Anti-Federalists, they were quite willing to deliver power to "a first man" so that he could protect the people against the "interests."[121] Woodrow Wilson's intellectual shift from *Congressional Government* to *Constitutional Government in the United States* suggests that he decided that it did not, in the end, matter which branch was spearheading reform. As president, Wilson no longer lamented but even exploited the elusiveness of inter-branch consensus to justify his unique capacity to "interpret" the needs of the public and the corresponding obligations and powers of the federal government.[122]

Conclusion: Hamilton Means for Jeffersonian Ends

As the first to depart from the "Federalist-Whig-Republican point of view" that characterized historical scholarship at the turn of the twentieth century, the Progressives waged an unusual Lovers' Quarrel by retrieving the principles of the Anti-Federalists against the Party State and adapting them in defense of, among other reforms, an "associative state."[123] America's "stateless" condition was (and perhaps could only have been) aborted by the very daughters and sons of those First Founders who had first insisted that power and liberty do not sit well together. It took the descendants of Anti-Federalists, confronting the ineptitude of America's nineteenth-century substitute for a national administrative state, to create the political vacuum it would come to fill. 1. *On Union.* While the Progressives accepted the extended sphere and advocated for a nationalized democracy, they equally encouraged intergovernmental cooperation, local democracy, and "parastate" organizations as constitutive elements of the union. 2. *On Liberty.* The Progressives cared most about destroying the Party State, and they invoked the language of negative liberty against it so that citizens and government could be free from corrupt bosses and interests. Instead of stretching the meaning of constitutional clauses, they codified amendments to secure their policy goals. 3. *On Truth.* The Progressives were idealists who looked nostalgically to an age before corruption tainted the republic. They were distrustful of the checks and balances of the Newtonian understanding of the Constitution and believed firmly in the monolithism of the common good and the uniformity of public opinion. 4. *On Republicanism.* The Progressives had great faith in direct democracy and thought it possible even in a large republic, especially after Wilson promulgated his theory of "Leadership by Interpretation," which blurred the distinction between the ruler and the ruled. They were unfazed by the prospect of majority tyranny and attacked the Supreme Court and Article 5 as undemocratic elements of the Constitution.

Progressivism entered onto the national stage with Theodore Roosevelt and the Republican Party in the 1900s, coursed its way via Woodrow Wilson into the Democratic Party in the 1910s, and then partially returned, as Robert La Follette, Jr. did, to the Republican Party in the 1940s. This by itself should tell us that Progressivism is a protean ideology drawing on a wider swath of intellectual traditions than scholars have acknowledged. We have found it difficult to define the Progressive Movement because so many of its positive goals seemed inconsistent with each other. As Eisenach has observed of the Progressive Era, "Democracy, nationalism, religion, social knowledge, and the march of social justice all get mixed together in ways that equally amaze and offend the modern liberal."[124] Yet if we focused on its negative impulse, Progressivism's reforms take on a very coherent thrust indeed. The Progressives were not so much trying to grant new powers to the federal government as they were trying to wrestle power away from the Party State—a monstrosity so powerful and so entrenched that it admittedly took what would become another behemoth state to take it down. If Lincoln's foremost goal was a more perfect Union, the Progressives' desire was for a more virtuous republic. As Henry May put it, the Progressives "wanted to make a number of sharp changes because they were so confident in the basic rightness of things as they were."[125] Their goals were more restorative than creative.

To take on the state as they knew it in the nineteenth century, many Progressives invoked the arguments of the first generation of anti-statists America ever knew, turning to the Anti-Federalists' understanding of classical republicanism to highlight a theory of virtuous citizenship to contrast it against aristocratic or corrupt institutions. As the Anti-Federalists were wary of a reconfiguration of the world as they knew it, the Progressives were nostalgic for a world before the Party State ruined it. And so if Progressivism was a "lost promise" because it was never a comfortable fit with the goals or accomplishments of modern liberalism, it is in part because many of Progressivism's prominent spokespersons were disciples not so much of Publius, but Federal Farmer. Even if readers continue to see more of the Federalists in the Progressives than they do of the Anti-Federalists after reviewing my account, I hope I have convinced them that the Lovers' Quarrel is still the most plausible *framework* for understanding this most enigmatic of American movements.

Had they used Hamiltonian means to achieve only Hamiltonian ends, the Progressives may have suffered from even more pushback from defenders of the Party State. Like the Anti-Federalists, the Progressives understood that if they wanted to attack a state (or a proposed one), then the people had to be invoked. Direct democracy, for them, was the palliative to Americans' love–hate relationship with the state. So the Progressives continued in the tradition of Anti-Federalists teaching Federalists how to persuade Americans to swallow their bitter Hamiltonian pills. As Lincoln and the Radical Republicans adopted the Party State bequeathed to them by Jeffersonian Republicans and Jacksonian Democrats (who had created the Party State in the name of democracy) with glee and turned it into a formidable governing machine, so New Deal Democrats took the fledging administrative state the Progressives created (also in the name of democracy) and pushed its boundaries to the nth degree. Further, by putting a smile on and attaching a personality to the chief executive, the Progressive presidents, like Jefferson and Jackson, helped mollify the intimidating facelessness of the emerging administrative state, setting the stage for Franklin Roosevelt to use his office to initiate a massive overhaul of the federal–states relationship during the New Deal that many Progressives had not envisioned or intended. Jefferson's, Jackson's, and Wilson's ends—virtuous and accountable representation for the *Pluribus*—would become the means for FDR's Hamiltonian end, *Unum*.

CHAPTER 6

The New Deal & the Nationalized Rhetoric of the Small Republic

The conditions in 1933 were ripe for another "revolution in favor of govern-ment" in American history—a third Federalist moment.[1] Franklin Roosevelt and his coalition were aided by an unprecedented economic depression, which caused eyes increasingly to turn to the federal government for solutions to the country's economic woes—the result of which was a legislative bonanza during the First Hundred Days that remains the *summum bonum* of modern liberal dreams.[2] In a long list of accomplishments William Leuchtenburg credits to the New Deal, the first is that "it gave far greater amplitude to the national state."[3] That is to say, the New Deal launched a durable expansion in federal authority. In the early days, President Franklin Roosevelt received practically everything he asked from Congress, which had been aching for presidential leadership. Senator Lester Dickinson from Iowa complained of the "docility" of the 74th Congress, "a performance never equaled in the history of legislatures since those rump Parliaments which, under the Stuarts, so seriously jeopardized English liberty in the seventeenth century."[4] After a long excursion of *Pluribus*, when private economic motives were allowed to run amok, even Republicans were ready for a dose of *Unum* from the national government. As one opined, "I think we need a 'dictator.' But a dictator is of no use unless he *dictates*."[5]

Capitalism may or may not have been saved in the First Hundred Days of the New Deal, but the American state was eagerly fortified with responsibili-ties that remain among its core functions today. "By using the new materials of social justice we have undertaken to erect on the old foundations a more en-during structure for the better use of future generations," Franklin Roosevelt intoned in his Second Inaugural Address.[6] The old foundations began with the settlement of Publius' quarrel with Federal Farmer, and coursed through Lin-coln's new birth of freedom. In this chapter, I argue that the New Deal's dra-matic expansion of the size and responsibilities of the federal government was motivated by the same philosophy that Publius had once advanced and was made possible by, following Lincoln's innovation, the New Dealers' own neo-Federalist creative resynthesis of rights and powers. By once again adopting and adapting the ideas of the Declaration of Independence, as the Republicans had done during the Second Federalist moment, the New Dealers were able to successfully propose an economic bill of rights and a newly empowered federal government to secure it. And so if Publius had remodeled federalism and Lincoln had reconfigured liberty, Franklin Roosevelt would remake liberalism—all in the service of a more perfect Union. As Harry Hopkins put it, the New Deal "made America over," just as the Federalists and Civil War Republicans had done before.[7] But unlike the Democratic Republicans, the Jacksonian Democrats, and the Progressives, who sometimes used Hamiltonian means for Jeffersonian ends, New Deal Democrats, like the Federalists and Civil War Republicans, would use Jeffersonian means for decidedly Hamiltonian ends.

The Third Age of Government

The New Deal enacted a new contract between citizens and the state that "endowed Americans with new social and economic dimensions of citizenship."[8] The federal government would take on the expanded goals of equality and justice based on an extended understanding of rights. Between the Emergency Banking Act of 1933 and the last of the New Deal measures, the Fair Labor Standards Act of 1938, an entirely new conception of American government emerged. The Wagner Act, which conferred to labor the right to collectively bargain, "put the power of the federal government behind labor as a class."[9] The Fair Labor Standards Act enacted a minimum wage, while the Social Security Act of 1935—the jewel of the New Deal's neo-Federalism—provided a safety net for the unemployed, older adults, and single mothers with children. As one contemporary put it, this expansion of the responsibilities of the state was predicated on a "very far-reaching principle, that of federal assurance of a minimum livelihood for all citizens."[10] Discussing the Social Security Administration, Arthur Schlesinger Jr. noted, "no government bureau ever directly touched the lives of so many million Americans." "With the Social Security Act," he continued, "the constitutional dedication of federal power to the general welfare began a new phase of national history."[11] If before the Progressives had advocated for protection against business wrongdoing, the New Dealers were now actively dedicating the power of the federal government toward "security against the major hazards and vicissitudes of life."[12] This was a dramatic redrawing of the constitutional compact.

In 1937, the Supreme Court ruled that the social security tax was in line with what the Constitution granted to Congress to tax and spend for the general welfare, and the New Deal's redefinition of liberalism was complete.[13] As the Federalists had abolished the old Articles of Confederation and replaced it with a Constitution dedicated to a more perfect Union, the New Dealers radically reconceptualized the scope of federal authority, persuading (or perhaps cajoling) the Supreme Court to come into line even though no formal constitutional amendments were ratified. FDR opposed amending the Constitution and opted instead to "pack" the Court with judges sympathetic to his political philosophy in part because the process was tedious and unwieldy, and in part because, like Hamilton, he did not see the need in explicitly granting new powers to the national government that he believed the Constitution already did. The Federalists, of course, had been the first to try to fill the Supreme Court with their own appointees, as we saw in Chapter 2. Roosevelt, like Hamilton, possessed an elastic understanding of the clauses of the Constitution, and he thought that all the Supreme Court needed was a number of judges who saw things his way. This is a major difference that separates the New Dealers from the Progressives, who thought the Constitution to be archaic and inadequate to the accomplishment of their Jeffersonian ends, and sought amendments to secure them.

The New Deal's durable expansion of federal authority turned significantly on a reinterpretation of the Interstate Commerce Clause. Whereas Article 1, Section 8, Clause 3 of the Constitution states that Congress shall have power "To regulate Commerce with foreign Nations, and among the several States, and with the Indian tribes," the political debate in this country has been scant on the first, Foreign Commerce, and third, Indian Commerce, powers.[14] If the sound of the debates easily misleads us to think that we have only one commerce clause and not three, it is because foreign nations and Indian tribes do not enjoy the same constitutional status of American states to wage battle with the national government. They cannot partake of the Lovers' Quarrel if they cannot claim legitimacy from the First Founding or protection from the Bill of Rights. Even then, for over a century, the Interstate Commerce Clause lay dormant in the Constitution, until Congress invoked it in the Interstate Commerce Act in 1887 to regulate railroads. The power to regulate commerce, however, was not newly created. In *Gonzales v. Raich*, the Supreme Court acknowledged that "the Commerce Clause emerged as the Framers' response to the central problem giving rise to the Constitution itself: the absence of any federal commerce power under the Articles of Confederation."[15] This conclusion, however, was reached only after the Lovers' Quarrel worked itself out in the courts. In 1935, in *Schechter Poultry Corporation v. U.S.*, Justice Cardozo would warn that the obliteration of the "distinction between what is national and what is local in the activities of commerce" would lead "to an end in our federal system."[16] As the story goes, the Supreme Court, after arguing in *Schechter* that the National Industrial Recovery Act interfered with "the domain of state power," and after striking down the government's authority to regulate the mining industry on the grounds that mining was not "commerce" in *Carter v. Carter Coaling Company*,[17] switched itself in time to save nine recalcitrant justices in *National Labor Relations Board v. Jones & Laughlin Steel Corporation*.[18] The Supreme Court was politically pressured to leave it to the people, via their representatives in Congress, to define "commerce," leaving the door open for the steady reinterpretation of constitutional limits on the federal government, and the expansion of the latter's authority to enlist the state governments in the service of an increasing catalog of federal goals and programs. As a result of these new constitutional understandings, the New Deal seriously limited the state governments' control over local and intrastate economic activities. As Bruce Ackerman observed, "before the New Deal, the People had never self-consciously reallocated plenary power over the economy from the states to the national government."[19] Put another way, as George Thomas has argued, "the New Deal reconstruction of liberty was rooted in a 'deconstructive' understanding rather than a positive foundation."[20] It completed the reformation of liberty and liberalism that Lincoln and the Civil War Republicans had commenced.[21]

In his First Inaugural Address, Roosevelt expressed a dynamic and Hamiltonian view of the Constitution, saying, "Our Constitution is so simple and so practical that it is possible always to meet extraordinary needs by changes in emphasis and arrangement without loss of essential form."[22] As we now know, what Roosevelt meant by the "changes in emphasis and arrangement," or what Milkis and Mileur called "a redefinition of the social contract," was in effect a durable and significant shift in federal authority.[23] FDR understood that reconstitution meant reconceiving the demos so as to "prove that democracy could be made to function in the world today as effectively as in the simple world of a hundred years ago."[24] His, of course, was a very different understanding of democracy than that of the Anti-Federalists, who understood self-government as states' rights, not the federal government's obligations to the individuals of the national community. The Federalists, after all, had been the first to conceive of the United States as a Union not only of states, but also as individuals. As Madison had recounted to Jefferson, "It was generally agreed that the objects of the Union could not be secured by any system founded on principle of a Confederation of Sovereign States . . . hence was embraced the alternative of a government which, instead of operating on the States, should operate without their intervention on the individuals composing them."[25] Thus, the germ of the idea of the federal government as a protector of individuals was already there in 1787–1789. Indeed, if the First Founding was primarily about liberty and only secondarily about equality, the Second Founding, written for fear of the excesses of liberty, was also about equality—the equality of branches, the equality of the states, the equality of citizens before the law. A revolution *against* government can guarantee only the removal of oppression from one source, but a revolution *in favor of* government could potentially guarantee a larger set of liberties in part because the government, committed to the equality of contracting citizens, can now help to shelter the weak from the strong. This is why "to look to the arguments of the protagonists of the Revolutionary era for a full and broad sense of what people have conceived to be the ultimate goals and aspirations of American democracy," Spragen suggests, "is to look in the wrong place."[26] The shredding of one ancient contract can generate liberty, but the agreement to a new one must assume a commitment to some notion of equality by all contracting parties as well as the government installed. Consider Federalist 51, where Madison lays out the "auxiliary precautions" necessary in our world, where men are not angels. While Madison admitted the conventional view that the "separate and distinct exercise of the different powers of government . . . [is] essential to the preservation of liberty," his conclusion nevertheless was that "Justice is the end of government." He continued, "It is the end of civil society. It ever has been and ever will be pursued until it be obtained, or *until liberty be lost in the pursuit* [my emphasis]." There may be some rhetorical embellishment here, but it is arguable that for Madison, justice—understood minimally as the principle that a stronger or majority faction should not be able to impose its opinions on a weaker or minority faction—is, as John Rawls, the dean of modern liberalism, has put it, "the first virtue of social institutions."[27] The Second Founders agreed with the First Founders that governments should only rule by consent, but the former added to this another principle, to be enforced by the institutions of the new science: that the strong or the numerous should not have the last word over the weak or the few. The leap from the Articles of Confederation's "league of friendship" to the Constitution's goal to "establish justice" therefore separates the First Founders from the Federalists, because friendship or fraternity relies on intimate connections between known persons and communities, whereas justice is an abstract and relatively more impersonal matter for a larger republic.[28] The establishment of justice is not only different from friendship as the attainable goals of a large republic versus that of a small community; the former is also an inorganic ideal that can be accomplished, as the Preamble of the Constitution professes, only by a national government. Whereas the Anti-Federalists sought liberty by fraternity, the Federalists sought justice by authority and fraternity's authoritarian cousin, paternalism, in the form of a national state. And so, the New Deal's extension of democratic rights to the economic realm was a denouement to the Radical Republicans' dedication to the political equality of all citizens during Reconstruction, which was itself an elaboration of the Federalists' commitment to the equality of individuals and communities across the several states—a collective We the People.

Whereas the First Founding emphasized what a distant government cannot do to us and said little about how we ought to regard each other, the Second Founding directed citizens toward what we can do for each other. Perhaps this was why whereas a neo-Anti-Federalist, President George W. Bush, was loath to call for civilian sacrifice even in war—he had famously asked us to go on living our lives after the terrorist attacks on September 11—neo-Federalist liberals like President John Kennedy invited us to "ask not what your country can do for you—ask what you can do for your country."[29] Kennedy's view was closer to Lincoln's, who not only acknowledged the sacrifice of the soldiers at war but also saw "enough yet before us requiring all loyal men and patriots to perform their share of the labor."[30] His view was also closer to George Washington's, who, as we saw in Chapter 1, stood with Hamilton against Madison in his conviction that the states that did not see war during the Revolution should nevertheless pay their share of the war debts. For the Federalists and neo-Federalists, to stand together was to stand behind the national government that was born on the same day that We the People were born. As Lincoln believed that effort was required to summon the people to heed their better angels in pursuit of the common good, the New Dealers highlighted the principle of equality and the role of the state over traditional conceptions of negative liberty. "The way to get democratic administration is to begin by organizing a central government strong enough to eliminate those conditions which make much of our national life grossly undemocratic," wrote the Brain Trusters Rexford Tugwell and George Banfield.[31] As the Federalists were part of a solidarity movement to shelter the citizens of the United States from the vicissitudes of life on this side of eternity, so too were the New Dealers, who were also "part of another great forward step in that liberation of humanity which began with the Renaissance."[32]

The Third Age of Government was, like the Second Founding and the Civil War, more concerned with real results than abstract principles. Its protagonists were pragmatists, not philosophers. This made sense, for there are arguably more pages written in the history of political thought—at least among those to which the framers of the Constitution had access—warning of the dangers of government and taming its excesses than its virtues. Governments are rarely created from principles alone; they are forged by necessity. And so, in a Fireside Chat in 1938, Roosevelt would offer a utilitarian defense of a stronger government similar to the one Publius had made to the Anti-Federalists a century and a half ago:

> History proves that dictatorships do not grow out of strong and successful governments but out of weak and helpless governments. If by democratic methods people get a government strong enough to

protect them from fear and starvation, their democracy succeeds, but
if they do not, they grow impatient. Therefore, the only sure bulwark
of continuing liberty is a government strong enough to protect the
interests of the people, and a people strong enough and well enough
informed to maintain its sovereign control over its government.[33]

These words could have come straight from Hamilton's mouth. To be sure,
while the New Dealers inwardly recognized that what they were doing had a
deeply moral significance, they often eschewed ethical pretentions and characterized themselves as problem solvers, just as the Federalists were pragmatists
who had created a "Godless Constitution."[34] Musing about how to put a roof
over the heads of "marginal" people, Roosevelt firmly professed, "Private capital cannot do it. It is a field into which Government alone can go, and Government only can do it."[35] Government was, for him, as it was for the Publius, *the*
solution to a nation's problems. (The last thing Roosevelt would have accepted
was the idea that "suffering is part of life," and there is nothing we can do about
it.[36]) Marking the 150th anniversary of the Philadelphia convention in his
Second Inaugural Address, Roosevelt triumphantly declared the purposes of
the Second Founders, who "created a strong government with powers of united
action sufficient then and now to solve problems utterly beyond individual or
local solution." "They established the federal government," he continued, "in
order to promote the general welfare and secure the blessings of liberty to the
American people." Like Lincoln, so convinced was Roosevelt that his was a
government of, for, and by the people that he also would refer to it thrice, as
"We of the Republic."[37] This is possibly why some historians salute "the New
Deal as a genuine expression of the nation's original democratic ideals."[38]

For all the talk of the New Deal's "mongrel intellectual pedigree," one basic
assumption remained constant among its followers: that government was the
solution to national economic problems.[39] The New Dealers therefore dismissed the classical liberal distinction between the public and private sphere,
as did Archibald MacLeish, who had professed that "the public world with us
has *become* the private world, and the private world has become the public."[40] At
the core of the New Deal's statist interregnum was the argument, persuasive at
the time, that on protecting the economic rights of the people, the federal government could and would do better. The New Dealers dedicated themselves
to reducing the differences between the haves and have-nots and promulgated
an "inclusive rather than exclusionist cultural nationalism."[41] Like the Federalists, they were more concerned that the federal government possessed powers
than that the states possessed rights. Both were primarily concerned with
action, not restraint; both were convinced that the consequences of governmental inaction were unthinkable. As Hamilton professed in Federalist 85,

"A NATION, without a NATIONAL GOVERNMENT, is, in my view, an awful spectacle." In this important sense, and as Jeffrey Tulis has rightly noted, the New Deal's commitment to a national government and its promotion of a national economy were "implicit in, and facilitated by, the original design."[42]

Like the Federalists, who believed that civic virtue was not enough, even in a small republic, to restrain the pursuit of self-interest and prevent the rise of faction, the New Dealers understood that corporate ambition could only be counteracted with state regulatory ambition. The latter's innovation was in appropriating the Anti-Federalists' conception of collective or states' rights, expanding it into a corpus of economic and social rights, and then promoting responsive federal action as an extension of these rights. The Radical Republicans and Lincoln, of course, had been the first to link individual rights with national power, having recognized the need to reconcile the foundational constitutional divide between rights and powers. The "commonwealth of hope" that the New Deal wrought was the next extension of the Federalists' argument for "extending the sphere."[43]

The Federalists did not use the same methods as the New Dealers, of course. While the former eschewed faction and party in favor of a national program, Roosevelt used the Democratic Party as a way station toward presidential and bureaucratic government. Nevertheless, the New Dealers shared with the Federalists a faith in manmade institutions that both their political opponents, the Anti-Federalists and the "stand-pat" Republicans, were slower to evince. When FDR said that there is nothing to fear but fear itself, he was not only attacking passion and unreason (as the Federalists too had once done) but also faithlessness in human agency. Roosevelt would call his critics "doubting Thomases," as Cecilia Kenyon called the Anti-Federalists "men of little faith," because the New Dealers and the Federalists were supremely confident that the state was up to the challenge of remedying and managing the political-economic problems of their respective times.[44] As the Federalists audaciously fashioned a new Constitution out of whole cloth despite their charge to amend the Articles of Confederation, the New Dealers "displayed striking ingenuity in meeting problems of governing."[45] Roosevelt was aware of the pedigree of his own confidence:

> Our forefathers ... created a strong government with powers of united action sufficient then and now to solve problems utterly beyond individual or local solution. A century and a half ago they established the Federal Government in order to promote the general welfare and secure the blessings of liberty to the American people. Today we invoke those same powers of government to achieve the same objectives.[46]

The Brain Trust, of course, was the centerpiece of the Roosevelt administration's faith in reason and institutional engineering. Franklin Roosevelt and his aides no more believed in the unregulated hidden hand of the market than Publius, in Federalist 1, believed in a government created by "force and accident." This is why Raymond Moley wanted to rein in a "chaotic competitive system" with "cooperative business-government planning."[47] Rexford Tugwell, for his part, contrasted the hidden hand to "coordination, to rationality, to publicly defined and expertly approached aims."[48] In this, both men were not so different from Publius. Madison's stated goal, after all, was "to erect over the whole, one paramount Empire of reason, benevolence and brotherly affection."[49] According to Richard Matthews, Madison's concern for political stability in the face of the vicissitudes of social and economic change explains his "worship of reason"—the intellectual foundations of the "positive, bureaucratic-administrative state."[50] As I argued in Chapter 2, the early "Madison should be associated almost exclusively with the Constitution of 1787 and not the Revolution of 1776."[51] That the two dates are often conflated as a part of a single "founding" may well be our greatest national myth. As Matthews astutely notes, "Jefferson's democratic rhetoric provides the smoke and mirrors behind which Madison's machine of reason hides."[52] As we shall see below, to bring about a dramatic expansion of the American state, for his part Roosevelt would deploy the Anti-Federalist language of friendship to familiarize fellow citizens with the state of which he was the chief executive. "My friends," he would say, at the start of every Fireside Chat.

The Declaration, Rights, and the New Deal

Roosevelt's understanding of the separation of powers as balancing government but not in guaranteeing limited government is not so distinct from the Federalists' or at least Hamilton's, as we saw in Chapter 1. It is important to view the Federalists' arguments about the separation of powers in the context of selling their plan to Anti-Federalists who were suspicious of this very point. Their actions, therefore, speak at least as loudly as their words. Since there was neither a judicial nor an executive power before the Constitution, the Federalists had a free hand to create these powers and house them in separate branches—yet they chose to create "separate institutions sharing powers" because their principal concern was one of balance.[53] Since the sharing of powers encourages branches to deliberate with each another, there is nothing in the enumerated powers in Articles 1, 2, and 3 that prohibits the possibility that when all branches agree on such matters as the general welfare or interstate commerce—that is to say, when balance is no longer a consideration because consensus prevails—durable and sizeable shifts in federal authority can occur. That the Federalists left open this possibility but declined to comment on or acknowledge it is unlikely to be an oversight. Like Publius and Lincoln, Roosevelt believed that the powers granted by the Constitution to the government are extensive and elastic once consensus could be found between the branches. Roosevelt's "three-horse team" approach acknowledges that there are three branches, but it also conceives of the three branches "pulling in unison"—that is to say, sharing powers—rather than exerting them in discord.[54]

Roosevelt would expand the catalog of rights that Civil War Republicans had already expanded—this time in the economic realm—and convince citizens that the federal government needed to take on new responsibilities for which even more powers were needed. To do this, as Lincoln had done in his Gettysburg Address, Roosevelt understood that he had to take on the Anti-Federalists' Magna Carta, the Declaration of Independence. And when he decided to do so, he was playing with the biggest developmental stakes—because when rights expand, so too must powers—and attempting no less than "a rendezvous with destiny."[55] Like Lincoln, Roosevelt understood that the Declaration of Independence, and in particular its emphasis on the language of rights, was primordial American fodder for symbolic manipulation. Like the Republicans during the Civil War, the New Dealers posited a creative merger of the Declaration and the Constitution to situate an enlarged role for the national government despite the lessons of the First Founding.

Accordingly, in his Second Renomination Speech, Roosevelt extended the Declaration's language that had promulgated the rights of Englishmen to include a list of government-guaranteed rights: "Government in a modern civilization has certain inescapable obligations to its citizens, among which are protection of the family and the home, the establishment of a democracy of opportunity, and aid to those overtaken by disaster."[56] Similarly, in his Commonwealth Club Address, Roosevelt professed that "the role of government in relation to business" was to develop "an economic declaration of rights, an economic constitutional order." In expanding the scope of rights, he was asking his supporters to "recognize the new terms of the old social contract." He bridged Jeffersonian Republicanism and New Deal liberalism when he argued that "even Jefferson realized that the exercise of the property rights might so interfere with the rights of the individual that the government . . . must intervene, not to destroy individualism but to protect it."[57] Roosevelt would restate his expansion of the Declaration's rights in his 1944 State of the Union Address, wherein he advanced a "second Bill of Rights." Like the Federalists, the New Dealers understood that rights do not come only from nature or tradition but are something that government secures by way of the democratic process.[58] When Roosevelt proposed that "the task of statesmanship has always been the re-definition of these rights in terms of a changing and growing social order," he was merely refashioning the powers of the central government in the same way that the Federalists, who were creating one, were necessarily also reconfiguring the First Founding's understanding of collective and states' rights.[59] Had the opposition discerned the pattern of statists such as Hamilton or Lincoln of invoking the Trojan-horse language of rights to achieve untraditional ends, they might have better foreseen what was coming.

Pedagogy and Virtuous Representation in the White House

Whereas Spragens understands American liberalism to mean the "socially 'progressive' and antihierarchical orientation in American politics from Thomas Jefferson and Andrew Jackson through twentieth century Progressivism, the New Deal, the New Frontier, the Great Society, and contemporary social justice-oriented liberalism," his teleological account of liberalism underplays the degree to which the Federalists, the Radical Republicans, and the New Dealers embraced top-down strategies of governance while Jefferson and Jackson belonged to a different tradition.[60] Not unlike the Federalists, the New Deal Brain Trusters revealed their muted faith in mass or direct democracy when they argued that "the survival of democracy depends upon our finding ways of differentiating the mass into publics which are capable of exercising a stable and responsible control of government."[61] Mass democracy, of course, assumes a degree of homogeneity so that the potential gap between individual and majority opinion would not often arise. This is why the Anti-Federalists, defenders of the homogenous republic, could consistently be committed to both the individual and collective, direct democracy. The Federalists, and the New Dealers, however, were more interested in the most pragmatic solutions, to be gleaned from the interplay of proposed possibilities rather than the popular ones. The latter shared the Federalist belief that the long-term public interest can be distinct from short-term aggregate public opinion, which may be tainted by passion and prejudice.[62] "Meaningful political participation," according to Tugwell and Banfield, occurred "through the play of political pressure from a variety of publics upon a government which has power commensurate with its tasks." Like the Federalists, these New Dealers honored the democratic principle not in a straightforward way—by deference to the majority of an undifferentiated mass—but by the interplay of many diverse groups and opinions. They thought, as Madison believed, "the wider the issue, the wider must be the public that decides it."[63]

If under Theodore Roosevelt, the presidency had become the spokesperson of American government, "under [Franklin] Roosevelt, the White House became the focus of all government—the fountainhead of ideas, the initiator of action, the representative of the national interest."[64] While it was the first Roosevelt who had democratized the office, the second nationalized it. This is an important distinction between Teddy's Progressivism and Franklin's liberalism. If Progressivism "marched to the drumbeat of democracy," Spragens correctly maintained, "there was no analogous impulse in the New Deal."[65] Indeed, Franklin Roosevelt incurred the wrath of the loudest populist voices of his time, such as Huey Long and Father (Charles) Coughlin, while in office. When the Democrats abolished the Party's two-thirds rule for the presidential nomination in 1936, they did so not so much for democracy than to unleash a national majority previously constrained by the sectional minority, much as the Federalists had reconstituted a national We the People so that no one state could impede majority rule. The Anti-Federalists have always been the purveyors of democratic procedure and technique, while the Federalists have always championed the more substantive goals of democracy. FDR was populist in his rhetoric, but he did so not to mimic his interlocutors but to educate them of the necessity of a new vision of government hitherto never experienced.[66] While "Jefferson guided America toward a new economic and social system in the rhetoric of the old," Roosevelt nationalized the rhetoric of the small republic to promote his Hamiltonian ends.[67] When he fireside chatted with "my friends," FDR was proposing that the federal government was not a distant bureaucracy to be viewed with distance and suspicion, but a benign and relatable organization representing and working for citizens to remedy the havoc wreaked on lives and families by the Depression. He was trying to change minds, not confirm their prejudices. If Lincoln and the Republicans introduced the basic sentiment of gratitude to the government for freeing the slaves and saving the Union, Roosevelt and the New Dealers built on this newfound receptivity to positive liberty by further cultivating a more advanced sentiment toward the federal government—trust.

The era before the 1960s is regarded as the era of "cooperative federalism" rather than "coercive federalism" in part because Roosevelt gave due deference to the Anti-Federalist strand in American political thought.[68] Perhaps this was because he was authentically steeped in that tradition, having been a traditional Democrat most of his life. Roosevelt was speaking authentically in the Jeffersonian tradition when he said to a reporter in 1911, "the political salvation of the country lies with the country men and boys. Not because they are more honest or more patriotic than their brothers in the cities, but because they have more time to think and study themselves, to know what the country needs."[69] In another address in 1933, he opined that life in the country carried with it the "assurance of a competence, of a sufficient living, of a good life and good neighbors."[70] Roosevelt himself was not an early believer in Keynesian economics. He had campaigned on a balanced budget in 1932, and after the bout of emergency spending in his first term, had tried, unsuccessfully, to balance the budget in 1937. Perhaps it was Roosevelt's own conversion that made him a powerful preacher to those who were not sold quite yet.

As a beneficiary of the Progressives' decimation of the transactional, *quid pro quo* relationship between recipients of patronage and the bosses that had predominated during the party period of American politics, Roosevelt's rhetorical and political genius was in successfully selling the idea that the national state was not a thing to be feared or countenanced in awe, but one to be trusted and loved. Roosevelt artfully deployed the very rhetorical staple of proponents of the small republic who through the course of American history had always resisted overweening federal authority, invoking friends, neighbors, and communities to insinuate, at the national level, the same intimate relationship between the representative and the represented that can be found in a small republic. Much like Publius had sweet-talked the conservatives of his era, FDR would admit during the 1936 campaign that change was sometimes the best way to conserve: "I am that kind of conservative because I am that kind of liberal."[71] Indeed, the reason why Franklin Roosevelt called his governing philosophy "liberalism" and not "progressivism" is because he intended, according to Milkis and Mileur, that "the New Deal should be understood as the expansion, rather than the transcendence, of natural rights."[72] There was much creativity in this seeming continuity, of course. As Publius had introduced a new federalism and Lincoln had forged a new freedom, Roosevelt would complete the transformation of "liberalism" into an ideology stripped of its classical, libertarian shadings. Aided further by the radio, Roosevelt coasted into family parlors across the nation to inaugurate a level of comfort and familiarity with the federal government that citizens had never experienced up until then. As he stated in his Second Inaugural Address after winning a landslide election, "government within communities, government within the separate States, and government of the United States can do the things the times require, without yielding its democracy."[73] By invoking the rhetoric of the small republic, Roosevelt converted a nation for which government was to be feared to one in which many grateful citizens could identify with a government that now ostensibly cared about their lives.

The most famous instrument for his proselytization, of course, was the Fireside Chat. What was most compelling about these was not that they were models of eloquence, but that they were the first time American citizens invited a high official of the federal government into their parlors for a dialog, when before most of their contact with officialdom was with the police power of the state governments. Roosevelt changed that. "He used to talk to me about my government," Eleanor Roosevelt would recall of what people would say of her husband.[74] What H. L. Mencken pejoratively called "crooning" was indeed a calculated, novel strategy to make citizens more comfortable with a federal government that was about to embark on responsibilities never before tried.[75] As Milkis understood it, FDR interpreted his principles as "an *expansion* rather than a *subversion* of the natural rights tradition"—though arguably, the expansion was in many ways the subversion.[76] In other words, "Franklin Roosevelt personified the state as protector," and he worked very hard to make citizens feel that this was a comforting and not a disconcerting thing.[77] Here was a neo-Federalist who had taken lessons from the Anti-Federalist critique of the "federal city," nationalizing, by way of the radio and the White House mailroom, the sense of civic belonging and engagement that the Anti-Federalists were convinced was possible only in the small republic. Calvin Coolidge had gone on the radio too, but we do not remember "Silent Cal's" addresses because he did not use it to bridge the antitheses of the Two Foundings. Roosevelt did just that. To forge a national state not even conceived of by the Federalists, the New Dealers spoke to the concerns of the states-centered republicans among them and still among us.

And so it was that "for the first time," Ted Lowi argued, "the national government established a direct and coercive relationship between itself and individual citizens."[78] When explaining the rise of the Personal President from the observation that "Americans had grown accustomed to big government and no longer saw centralized power only as a threat," Lowi missed the developmental paradox that state-building presidents have learned to invoke the language of rights and democracy in order to prioritize their authority, over that of Congress, to speak for the people to advocate for an expanded state.[79] The Personal President, "an office of tremendous personal power drawn from the people," was but the *vindex injuriarum* Federal Farmer had conceived of a century and a half before to defend the states, though the neo-Federalist Roosevelt now used it to build a national community, not avert it.[80] FDR's most important contribution to the presidency was the Executive Office of the President (EOP) created by the Legislative Reorganization Act in 1939 upon the recommendation of the presidentially commissioned Brownlow Committee. By moving the Bureau of the Budget from the Treasury into the EOP, Roosevelt converted the Presidency "into an instrument of twentieth-century government," ensuring that the president would "fulfill his constitutional mandate of a one-man branch in our three-part government . . . and survive the advent of the positive state."[81] Future presidents, Democratic and Republican, would take their turn to create new units within the EOP under their direct supervision.[82] By creatively adopting the role of the defender of the public faith and introducing new responsibilities to the executive branch and, by extension, the federal government, Franklin

Roosevelt continued the accretion of presidential power that his predecessors, initially the Anti-Federalists, had begun.

Hoover and Anti-Federalism

An important Anti-Federalist standard-bearer of the New Deal era, of course, was Herbert Hoover. Though a Progressive, Hoover shared the Anti-Federalist instinct that it was ultimately men, not institutions, that solved our problems. Unlike Roosevelt and like Ronald Reagan, he believed that the solutions to national problems came from individuals and voluntary associations, not the federal government. In 1922, Hoover had published a book, *American Individualism*, in which he set out the classical antagonism between liberty and power, and distinguished American from European individualism, arguing that the former was committed to equality of opportunity and the latter to equality of outcomes.[83] Here we observe a new phase in the maturation of Anti-Federalism. The original Anti-Federalists were more concerned with collective and states' rights than individual rights. And it was the Federalists, and later the Whigs, who created and affirmed "We the People of the United States" as a community of individuals across state lines, whose fates were linked by the government they created.[84] Until the Civil War, the Anti-Federalists and their descendants defended states' rights because the very legitimacy of the American Union was questioned, based on the idea that if each state was free to compact with others, then it was free also to disengage. As the federal government expanded, and its activities reached past the state governments and into the lives and pockets of more and more individuals, neo-Anti-Federalists began to sound the cry of individual rights alongside the states' rights doctrine now that the latter had lost its antebellum luster. The individualization of the Bill of Rights as a charter that applied also to the states after the Civil War also meant that the older language of states' rights as impediments to federal authority had to evolve to more frequently include the modern language of individual rights in the twentieth century.

What stayed the same, however, was the Anti-Federalists' and their descendants' commitment to limited government. Whether rights were conceived collectively or individually, the Anti-Federalists had always held them against federal powers. Hoover was a president true to the Anti-Federalist cry of small government even when markets appeared to be failing. During the Farm Crisis of 1930–1931, Hoover chose not to support Congressional appropriation of $15 million to fund food loans. He believed that "prosperity cannot be restored by raids upon the Public Treasury."[85] Instead, he put his support behind voluntary organizations such as the Red Cross, appealing to the "heart of the nation" rather than relying on the state.[86] While campaigning against Roosevelt in 1932, Hoover reaffirmed his Anti-Federalist credentials, saying,

> It is a false liberalism that interprets itself into Government operation of business. Every step in that direction poisons the very roots of liberalism. It poisons political equality, free speech, free press, and equality of opportunity. It is the road not to liberty but to less liberty. True liberalism is found not in striving to spread bureaucracy, but in striving to set bounds of it.[87]

Hoover's faith in local and vibrant communities indicate that his foremost desire was for a virtuous republic, not a more perfect Union. The New Dealers' faith, however, was more squarely on the state and its institutions. Unlike the Progressives, New Deal liberals were trying to protect the Forgotten Man, not reform him. They attended to the institutions and structure of society, and not, as the Progressives did, to the soul or nature of man.[88] In this, the New Dealers were rather like the Federalists, who measured progress in structural and material terms rather than by the loftier goal of the "pursuit of happiness," as the First Founding had. Indeed, as the Federalists placed their faith in the perfectibility of institutions more than "the Laws of Nature or Nature's God," the New Dealers saw nothing sacred in Nature. "We must lay hold of the fact that economic laws are not made by nature. They are made by human beings," Roosevelt intoned, and so he believed in bold, persistent experimentation.[89]

Not quite as flexible or as pragmatic as the New Dealers were in dealing with the vicissitudes of the new century, Hoover conceived of a leader as a stubborn, individual figure standing defiantly athwart History, not unlike the Anti-Federalists' *vindex injuriarum*. Like Anti-Federalists, he believed that the proper course of action ought not be surrendered at the altar of collective decision making. "Leadership is a quality of the individual," Hoover wrote. And "no race possesses more than a small percentage of these minds in a single generation."[90] (Though he was not an adherent of descriptive representation, as many Anti-Federalists were, his pre-institutional celebration of human nature was not unlike Jefferson's account of the "natural aristocracy.") Hoover emphasized the importance of equality of opportunity in society so that individual genius can emerge unencumbered by institutions. "Human leadership cannot be replenished like queen bees, by divine right or bureaucracies, but by the free rise of ability, character, and intelligence" and "ideas that lead to progress spring from the womb of an individual mind, not out of the mind of the crowd," he wrote.[91] To this day, conservatives remain partial to Great Men, while modern liberals prefer Great Societies.

The difference between Hoover's faith in collective bodies such as churches and philanthropic societies and the post-New Deal liberal's faith in government is that while Hoover saw the collectivity as an expression of the virtue of individuals (hence the commitment to social institutions), the liberal saw the collectivity as the solution that transcended the provinciality of individuals (hence the commitment to governing institutions). Like the Federalists, who knew men were not angels, at least when operating in a large republic, the New Dealers created or modified institutions to address emerging problems.

Whereas Roosevelt saw the virtue of public institutions, Hoover believed in the virtue of private individuals, in the "divine in each human being," and therefore applauded the "vast multiplication of voluntary organizations for altruistic purposes."[92] He understood "large capital" to be the "mobilization of the savings of the small holder," and so every large conglomerate was reducible to the individuals that constituted it, and every aggregation of individuals was no more than the sum of its members.[93] For Hoover, there was neither magic nor strength in numbers that did not already exist in the individual. But for Roosevelt, as it was for the Federalists, We the People were more than the sum of the individuals who made it up, and the federal government played a fundamental role in perpetuating this myth. If Roosevelt (and John Kennedy) believed that participation in government was what brought out the virtue in citizens, Hoover argued, "democracy is merely the mechanism which individualism invented as a device that would carry on the necessary political work of its social organization."[94] He criticized the "radicals" who "assume that all reform and human advance must come through government."[95] To the extent that Hoover viewed the state in transactional and derivative terms, he was more a democrat and Anti-Federalist than a national republican or Federalist.

The Limits of the New Deal

Evidence of the Lovers' Quarrel abounds even when we countenance the limits of the New Deal. For William Leuchtenburg, the New Deal was a "halfway revolution" because it "left many Americans—sharecroppers, slum dwellers, most Negroes—outside of the new equilibrium."[96] The New Deal, then, may have replaced the "state of courts and parties," but it could not do away with the state of states because the national government still lacked the bureaucratic capacity to implement its programs.[97] And the descendants of Federal Farmer, though outnumbered, were still a vocal minority. Even in the halcyon days of the New Deal in 1933, conservative stalwarts were "opposed to heavy government spending, fearful of the spread of federal bureaucracy, loud in defense of states' rights and individual liberty."[98] They were Jeffersonian Democrats partial to the "agrarian myth" of a nation of independent and virtuous yeomen getting on with their own business without interference from government.[99] Patterson estimated that 10 of the 35 Republican senators of the 73rd Congress were "veteran progressives" and five Senate Democrats consistently opposed the administration in 1933–1934.[100] By Roosevelt's second term, he was up against considerably more opposition.

If the aggressive statism of the New Deal took its cue from Publius, its limits and unraveling stemmed from the legacy of Anti-Federalism, roused once again into reaction and opposition. New Deal concessions to federalism, then, reveal the enduring legacy of the Lovers' Quarrel.[101] It is not surprising that Charles Kesler argues that the New Deal does not "square" with the "founding" principles of American politics, and he looks, predictably, not only to the Constitution but also to the Declaration for guidance as to what these principles are.[102] While most accounts of the New Deal focus on national institutions and the national scene, these accounts are incomplete if not situated in the context of significant resistance and pushback at the subnational level.[103] Scholars have shown that the paradoxical impact of botched or partial Progressive Era reforms at the state level has been to strengthen the influence of local elites, and this in turn has given localism a new lease on life by its postwar linkage to social and racial homogeneity, property or "homeowners" rights, and anti-statism.[104] As it was easier to conceive of fellow white male workers and retired white male workers as industrious co-contributors to the national wealth than to conceive of the same in women or non-white workers, the endurance of traditional liberalism preserved neo-feudal enclaves for the latter groups in the states.[105] On the biggest bloc of voters, FDR insisted on federal responsibility for their general welfare; on the rest, his administration was happy to defer to the states. Unlike the National Recovery Administration (NRA) or the Agricultural Adjustment Administration (AAA), the "categorical" programs created by the Social Security Act, including unemployment insurance (Title III) and grants-in-aid for the indigent old (Title I), blind (Title X), and needy families with children (Title IV), were jointly administered by the federal and state governments. States were left to fund their own unemployment insurance programs in return for federal tax relief. They were also to determine the levels of federal categorical assistance by the mechanism of matching grants—namely, one federal dollar for every two state dollars spent. Multiple orders, and therefore disorder, are the corollary of a federal system. The disappointments of the New Deal, like those following Reconstruction, were inevitable as long as the legacy of the First Founding had to be honored.

The New Dealers, after all, had to throw the states a bone.[106] Speaking of the philosophy behind the Tennessee Valley Authority (TVA), Rexford Tugwell and Edward Banfield observed that "the mistake was in thinking that it would be the policy of President Roosevelt to enhance the federal power . . . at the expense of the states. He seemed to conclude finally that both powers could be enhanced at the same time."[107] In an attempt to finesse a workable, dual federalism, the president created the Federal Emergency Council and the state directors to coordinate the different New Deal agencies as well as their execution across the states.[108] The cost of federalism, however, was that whatever was sent down to the states to implement—education, public assistance programs such as Aid to Dependent Children (ADC) and Old Age Assistance (OAA), and border enforcement—bore the risks of being placed on the public back-burner. Even when there was federal control only, such as in the NRA, the New Deal did not always stray far from the model of the "associative state" championed by Herbert Hoover.[109] New Deal agencies such as the Federal Emergency Relief Administration relied on state agencies to distribute direct grants while creating matching grants of one dollar of federal relief money for every three dollars the states distributed.

Conclusion: A New Deal for the American People

The New Deal brought about one of the greatest and most durable expansions in federal authority the nation had ever seen, as is exemplified by the fact that deep into the Reagan Revolution in 1987, the Supreme Court in *South Dakota v. Dole* was still allowing Congress to attach conditions, in particular 5 percent of the funding to maintain highways contingent on states raising the minimum drinking age to 21, to its grants to the state governments.[110] 1. *On Union.* The New Deal scored a major victory for the Federalist conception of federalism. As the Federalists presented *Novos Ordo Seclorum* to the American people, Roosevelt presented a "New Deal" to the American people by expanding the range of our responsibilities to each other as entailed by a more perfect Union, thereby also adopting new responsibilities for the federal government. As Lincoln universalized the rights of Englishmen, FDR sought a more perfect Union by substantively expanding these rights to include an economic bill of rights for all citizens. 2. *On Liberty.* New Deal Democrats summoned the federal government forcefully to confront the Great Depression. They embarked on fiscal spending to increase employment, created a welfare state to provide a social safety net, and stretched the meaning of "Interstate Commerce" to do much of this. The New Dealers may not have been instrumental in delivering America from the Depression, but they surely changed our perception of the federal government for at least a generation. 3. *On Truth.* Roosevelt was a pragmatist, and the New Deal may have lacked ideological coherence, but these too were quintessentially Federalist attributes.[111] The

New Dealers were not committed to archaic principles but set up a Brain Trust to find solutions for their own Age of Reason. They embraced federalism not to decentralize decision making, but to experiment with new ideas. A newer science of interest-group pluralism would be inaugurated in this era as agencies, interests, and organizations proliferated. 4. *On Republicanism.* The federal government and the president were the coordinators of the national economy. Roosevelt and the New Dealers were confident that left to their devices, the citizenry would only exacerbate the crises of the Depression. Roosevelt used the Fireside Chats not to show that he was of the people, as an Anti-Federalist might have, but to familiarize them with the federal government and the necessity of its actions.

Accounts of the balance of responsibilities between the federal and state governments have typically relied on theories of fiscal federalism, most of which posit that interstate competition and in particular the threat of capital flight make the states better suited for the promotion of economic development, while redistributive social policies are better left to the federal government.[112] Yet fiscal federalism is only a *functional* answer to a *political* question for which there can only be political answers. Just because one level of government does something better than another does not mean that it should be done at all, or so says the modern conservative. The Lovers' Quarrel addresses not questions of efficacy, but the prior question of the legitimacy of the federal government. Similarly, accounts for the success and failures of governmental programs according to state capacity tell us much about the conditions that permit effective public administration, but they seem to assume that if government could "get the job done," there would be no debate that it ought to be the government doing the job at all.[113] State capacity is ultimately an institutional variable; the will of the people is a political matter. The first is a question of efficacy, the second a question of legitimacy. To the extent that even the New Deal, responding to the gravest of crises, could not expand the federal government to such a degree as to vanquish the state governments, it demonstrates that while the Lovers' Quarrel may produce temporary victors, it is unlikely that America will ever transcend it.

FDR and the New Dealers, like Lincoln and the Republicans, were hands-on statists who did not believe in limited government, and contrary to conventional characterization, neither were the Federalists, who invented a government to solve a crisis of their own. After experiencing the debacle created by the Articles of Confederation, the Federalists' primary concern was the institution of *more* government, which is why it is more precise to say that they then saw the secondary need of *limiting* such government, as we saw in Chapter 1. Small-government conservatives, or latter-day Anti-Federalists, put the cart before the horse when they miss this important distinction. Limiting government is not the same as limited government because a brake need not imply a specific or maximum threshold. It is because the Federalists desired a new government with powers never before held that they acknowledged the need to prevent haste and folly by way of federalism and the separation of powers. But they also decided that if the branches and the states have deliberated and concurred to speak with one voice—as the requirements for amending the Constitution demand—Americans can very dramatically empower (or disempower) the federal government when they so choose. This is what happened during the New Deal. As the Second Founders made concessions to the Anti-Federalists by agreeing to a Bill of Rights, FDR and the Democrats presented and sold a New Deal to the American people by making concessions to and even adopting the symbols and language of the Anti-Federalist standard-bearers of their time. Although the New Deal "divided citizenship" along the lines of gender and race, it did narrow the ancient divide between state and national citizenship. The result was a durable expansion in federal authority, a developmental watershed by any measure.

CHAPTER 7

Anti-Federalism & the Reagan Revolution

Durable and sizeable as the New Deal's expansion of federal authority was, it did not vanquish Anti-Federalism. That Lincoln and FDR creatively reconciled the opposing strands of the Lovers' Quarrel does not mean that they created a permanent synthesis, only that they understood the Two Foundings enough to finesse a generational peace, as Publius had done before them. The Constitution, after all, had been the first creative synthesis of the Two Foundings, which also means that as long as the principles of the First Founding codified (mostly) in the second half of the Constitution remain operative—perhaps to the chagrin of some modern liberals—the possibility of durable retrenchments of federal authority will always remain. In this chapter (and continuing into the next), I argue that modern conservatism and its various strands have resurrected the ghosts of the Anti-Federalists, tapping into their political thought to formulate a potent and culturally resonant critique of the consolidated government that emerged as a result of the New Deal and the Great Society. Reagan, following Nixon, would attempt to forge a (not so) "New Federalism" to chip away at the welfare and administrative state by unraveling Roosevelt's creative resynthesis of power and liberty. These modern conservatives inaugurated a fourth Anti-Federalist moment, with contemporary ripple effects I will explore further in the next chapter.

To be sure, no historical parallel is perfect, especially two cases separated by two centuries. To the extent that the Constitution is settled law, we are all Federalists now. Publius' propaganda worked so well that even those who once challenged his premises and arguments would come to accept his conclusion. Perhaps this is why the Anti-Federalists and their descendants were rarely more successful in retrenching the federal government than the Federalists were in creating or expanding it. (More on the built-in Federalist bias of the Constitution in the next chapter.) But, certainly at the ideological level, the battle cries on either side of the Lovers' Quarrel have remain relatively undiluted. Though Thomas Jefferson, who won an election against the Federalist candidate John Adams, declared in his First Inaugural Address, "We are all Republicans, we are all Federalists," he was no more of a Federalist than was Melancton Smith or Elbridge Gerry. John Adams, who refused to attend Jefferson's Inauguration, would have been the first to attest to that.[1] Jefferson went on to affirm his "support of the State governments in all their rights, as the most competent administrations for our domestic concerns and the surest bulwarks against antirepublican tendencies" and his commitment to "economy in the public expense," while also promising "absolute acquiescence in the decisions of the majority, the vital principle of republics."[2] All these claims— deference to the state governments or states' rights, a commitment to direct democracy, and what we now call "fiscal conservatism"—were archetypically Anti-Federalist priorities, as they are modern conservative principles. As we shall see, even though nearly two centuries had passed, the priorities of the fourth Anti-Federalist moment would sound remarkably similar to those promulgated in the first victorious Anti-Federalist moment in 1800. The only significant difference between the Jeffersonian and Reaganite Anti-Federalists is that enough time has passed so that with the old Federalists disbanded and no one to call out the name (re)appropriation, today's Anti-Federalists call themselves Federalists with relatively little pushback. (To be sure, the Federalists had been the first to steal the "federalist" appellation from the First Founders; so the question of who appropriated whose mantra will always be a prototypically American riddle.)

American Conservatism

By one of the manifold ironies of intellectual history, the Anglo-Saxon tradition began as a liberal doctrine: an idea that landed as a slogan for reaction arose as a call for freedom.[3]

In the United States, there have been Republicans and Democrats, Progressives and Liberals. But there had not been, such as in the United Kingdom, France, or Germany, a self-identified conservative movement until the 1950s. Ronald Reagan was arguably the first American statesman who proudly and repeatedly proclaimed himself a conservative. Patrick Henry Lee, Stephen Douglas, and Herbert Hoover did not. As Hartz explains, "the ironic flaw in American liberalism lies in the fact that we have never had a real conservative tradition."[4] But Hartz was only partly right: by "real" he meant "European," and in this he was on point. Burkean conservatism in pure form never really took root in America, for this is a country born of revolution. Consider the fact that in 1932, President Herbert Hoover would enunciate a veritable decalogue of Anti-Federalist principles but come conspicuously short of identifying him-self as a conservative:

> Now, we have heard a great deal in this campaign about reactionaries, conservatives, progressives, liberals, and radicals. I think I belong to every group . . . There is one thing I can say without any question of doubt—that is, that the spirit of liberalism is to create free men; it is not the regimentation of men under government. It is not the exten-sion of bureaucracy. I have said in this city before now that you cannot extend the mastery of government over the daily life of a people with-out somewhere making it master of people's souls and thoughts.[5]

Hoover would declare in a radio address just a week later that "we are a nation of Progressives."[6] As late as in 1955, Dwight Eisenhower was only just starting to introduce "conservatism" into the American lexicon:

> I have tried to find a phrase in which to define what the Republican Party has done at home. I have said we were "progressive moderates." Right at the moment I rather favor the term "dynamic conservatism." I believe we should be conservative. I believe we should conserve on everything that is basic to our system. We should be dynamic in ap-plying it to the problems of the day so that all 163 million Americans will profit from it.[7]

As was the case in previous iterations of the Lovers' Quarrel, Anti-Federalism (modern conservatism) could wax only when Federalism (New Deal liber-alism) was waning. Between 1932 and 1955, one political episode occurred to prod some Republican progressives into claiming the "conservative" mantra—the New Deal and Franklin Roosevelt's remaking of liberalism. Gradually, those who objected to the neo-Federalist, bold experimentation of Roosevelt and his political descendants found refuge in the principles of the First Founding, and would begin to link American "conservatism" to "Anti-Federalism" just as the New Dealers had creatively linked modern "liberalism" to "Federalism." And so Eisenhower's tentative reconfigura-tion of the terms of political ideology was only a little more hesitant than Richard Nixon's (he used the word "conservative" 20 times in his *Public Papers*) or even Ronald Reagan, whose relative deference to modern liberal-ism might be illuminated by the fact that while he took on the Great Soci-ety and Lyndon Johnson, he never explicitly took on the father of modern liberalism, Franklin Roosevelt, and the antecedent to the Great Society, the New Deal.

That "much of conservatism is a reaction to [New Deal] liberalism" means that modern, American conservatism must be a very different thing from its European counterpart.[8] Robert Peel and other British Tory leaders identified themselves as "conservative" because it gave them a title that downplayed their association to the aristocracy and landed gentry. But their American counterparts took to the term for entirely different reasons. From its beginning in the 1950s, the American conservative movement aimed not, as the British Conservative Party has, to preserve the institutions they inherited, but to undo the institutions erected by the New Deal a generation before. To be sure, most modern American conservatives do not ask to roll back the state as much as the Anti-Federalists did, but the parallel is still uncanny. As William F. Buckley, Jr. put it, the mission of the *National Review* and of the conservative movement was to "stand athwart history, yelling Stop."[9] The Anti-Federalists, of course, were the first Americans to yell "Stop" in response to national consolidation. As the Anti-Federalists understood that the expansive powers granted to the federal government by the Constitution had to be reined in by a Bill of Rights, modern conservatives understood that the tide of liberal history had to be stemmed and, better still, undone. This is why, like Anti-Federalism and its Jeffersonian and Jacksonian iterations, modern conservatism is fundamentally a negative ideology: its army is aroused and most potent when arrayed against the forces for change and innovation.[10]

Put another way, American conservatism, even when it came into its own, is *sui generis* because Burkean conservatism does not translate easily for a "First New Nation" forged out of revolution.[11] If Margaret Thatcher could trace her political ancestry through Churchill and Disraeli back to Burke with relative ease, it took Russell Kirk and Robert Nisbet to construe an awkward lineage from Barry Goldwater via William Howard Taft and John Adams back to Burke.[12] Yet these Europhilic accounts of conservative intellectual history are amiss because they fail to grapple with the critical fact that the first political act of America's first political generation—Federalists and Anti-Federalists alike—was one of severance, itself a culmination of a century and a half of immigrants from England and Europe kicking the sands of the Old World from the back of their sandals as they sailed to the New World. Before the label was ever adopted, when, then, did a conservative ideology of any form first arise in the United States? It was precipitated when the Second Founders tried to undo what the First Founders established, and the Anti-Federalists cried foul. At precisely the moment when conservatism was turned upside down from what it was in Europe, American conservatism was born: when the Anti-Federalists, in 1787–1789, battled to preserve the post-revolutionary status quo against the Federalists' machinations toward a partial reconsolidation of the American Union. America's first conservatives, the Anti-Federalists, were ardent Lockean liberals who jealously guarded their severed relationship from the Crown and saw no need to create a new consolidated authority. Recognizing that there were Two Foundings, then, allows us to explain the seemingly paradoxical assessment that the Anti-Federalists were both revolutionary *and* conservative. It also explains modern conservatism. Understood in the light of the Two Foundings, conservatism, contra Hartz, has always existed on this side of the Atlantic—though it was conservatism, Anti-Federalist style. What the Anti-Federalists were trying to preserve were the liberal principles of the First Founding; and this is why the "liberal tradition" has also largely also been the Anti-Federalist, and the *American* conservative tradition.

There is, to be sure, still an element of Burke in American conservatives, who, like their Anti-Federalist ancestors, have always been wary of reason, as opposed to tradition or experience, as the guide to action. Though Patrick Allitt has argued that the Federalists thought that Jefferson "seemed too willing to experiment politically and take a rationalistic approach to politics rather than trust experience and the wisdom of former ages," it was really the Federalists who were the rationalists, and the inventers of the new "science of politics" they used to overthrow the order of 1781.[13] The Anti-Federalists espoused and practiced a greater humility of intellect than the Federalists, who thought they could conquer even human nature. As Carey McWilliams argued, the Anti-Federalists defended "conservative democracy which feared innovations and which, like the mass of the people themselves, sought guidance from custom and the wisdom of the past."[14] The Second Founders who accomplished in 1787–1789 what had never been attempted before were apostles of reason, not experience. In Federalist 31, Publius went as far as to claim that his conclusions, derived by deduction, possessed "the same degree of certainty with those of the mathematics." Between Publius and Federal Farmer, of course, it was the latter who advocated the conservation of the status quo. As we saw in Chapter 1, the Federalists knew full well that they were attempting something extraordinary with their new Constitution. In the first place, they had exceeded the charge of the Continental Congress to only amend the Articles of Confederation, and not create an entirely new constitution. Second, the Articles had required unanimity for amendment and not the assent of only nine states, and certainly not by ratifying conventions in only nine states.[15] Trying to make a virtue out of perceived vice, Alexander Hamilton boasted of the audacity of the Federalists. In the first paragraph of Federalist 1, we find the opening shot of his Lovers' Quarrel:

It has been frequently remarked that it seems to have been reserved to the people of this country, by their conduct and example, to decide the important question, whether societies of men are really capable or not of establishing good government from reflection and choice, or whether they are forever destined to depend for their political constitutions on accident and force.

Though many conservatives have claimed Hamilton as one of their own, he and Madison were in this important regard fundamentally unconservative. While Hamilton's highlighting of the Enlightenment virtues of "reflection and choice" was not set alongside a direct charge against the Anti-Federalists, Madison in Federalist 14 put the matter more pointedly as a matter of progress versus traditionalism by suggesting that those defending the Articles and the ancient theory of the small republic "suffered a blind veneration for antiquity, for custom, or for names." If Hamilton was unwilling to aggressively surrender his conservative mantle, Madison was:

> But why is the experiment of an extended republic to be rejected, merely because it may comprise what is new? Is it not the glory of the people of America, that, whilst they have paid a decent regard to the opinions of former times and other nations, they have not suffered a blind veneration for antiquity, for custom, or for names, to overrule the suggestions of their own good sense, the knowledge of their own situation, and the lessons of their own experience? To this manly spirit, posterity will be indebted for the possession, and the world for the example, of the numerous innovations displayed on the American theatre, in favor of private rights and public happiness.

If the Federalists were revolutionary in 1776 and again in 1787–1789, the Anti-Federalists (and their descendants) were revolutionary *only* in war but not in the peace that followed. Like the Anti-Federalists, modern conservatives believe that American history began in 1776, and the experience in self-government in the decade following presented a more reliable guide for self-government than the reason and social engineering of the Federalists or the New Deal Brain Trusters.

Infusing the Federalist Papers With Anti-Federalist Thought

Like Jefferson, who had rather disingenuously posed as both a Federalist and a Republican, and like Martin Van Buren, who used the post-1789 Madison to help him rewrite the meaning of the Second Founding, the intellectual entrepreneurs of the modern conservative movement have sought to restore the principles of the First Founding by supplying an Anti-Federalist reading of Federalist political thought. Indeed, this is arguably the signal accomplishment of modern conservatism, which has been far more successful at the level of ideas than at tangible retrenchments of federal authority.

One example may help to clarify this point. Consider the conservative public intellectual Charles Kesler's introduction to his best-selling edition of *The Federalist Papers*, in which he calculatedly split the *Papers* into two volumes—the first volume (numbers 1–36) addressing the "Union" and the second (numbers 37–85) addressing "the proposed Constitution"—and privileges the second.[16] By this seemingly innocuous organizational move, Kesler would marginalize the Federalists' overriding desire for a stronger Union, which is most strongly expressed in the first half of the *Federalist Papers*, and simultaneously upgrade what had been enticing and peacemaking overtures to the Anti-Federalists, which occur mostly in the second half, into the Federalists' allegedly first-order commitments. Kesler, like Jefferson and Van Buren, understood that the Federalists' creative resynthesis of the principles of the Two Foundings could be used back against them, for borrowed legitimacy opens up a two-way street.

By Kesler's reading, "the Union may be necessary for our 'political prosperity,' but what was 'most honorable for human nature' was disclosed by Publius in the case for the Constitution and its principles, not in the case for the Union."[17] Kesler was suggesting that the Constitution's principles are morally prior to its end, "a more perfect Union," disregarding the distinct possibility that the vision of "a more perfect Union" was *the* first principle and purpose of the Second Founding. This is why he characterized Publius' reasoning to be merely "axiomatic" in Numbers 1–36; but weightier matters, apparently, are the focus of the second half of the *Papers*: "it is only in *The Federalist's* second volume that Publius begins consistently to look at matters from a higher point of view," he wrote.[18] This is, of course, debatable. Given that most of the first volume was written by the aggressively nationalistic Hamilton highlighting the dangers of having a weak national government and that only two of the first 36 *Federalist Papers* were single-authored by Madison, another reading might be that Kesler was selectively highlighting the views of the framer with a more moderate commitment to a consolidated government.[19] He was also taking the phalanx of Publius' charm offensive in the second half of the *Papers*, which obviously was crafted to sound more balanced for it to be persuasive, and representing it as the Federalists' deep philosophy. Simply put, Kesler's organizational bifurcation allowed the Federalists to appear less nationalist, or at least more tentative in their agenda to centralize the Union. "*The Federalist's* second part" exhibits "the freedom to deliberate on the various means or institutions actually proposed in the Constitution," Kesler wrote. He continued: "in contrast to the proud confidence in human knowledge displayed in the first part, the second volume begins by questioning, in No. 37, how and what we can know," suggesting that the Federalists (writing, on Hamilton's initiative, to convince New Yorkers on the eve of their ratification convention) had not already made up their minds. Kesler, a philosopher, like the First Founders, believed that the ends matter more than the means, even if the means happened to be the Constitution itself.[20] By trivializing the end of a "more perfect Union" and inviting the reader to focus instead on the Constitution's principles, as if the two were separable, Kesler was rewriting Federalism itself.

The less partisan Publius sounds, then, the more Anti-Federalist he can be made to sound. Perhaps this was why Kesler preferred to further the myth that the Federalists were bewigged patricians devoid of partisan leanings, ignoring the possibility that some if not much of what we can glean of Federalist political thought as penned by Publius was but the eighteenth-century version of political correctness. According to him, "the convention must have enjoyed, in a very singular degree, an exemption from the pestilential influence of party animosities; the disease most incident to deliberative bodies." By Kesler's telling, Publius "chooses to speak in moderate tones to moderate men," as if he knew no politics, only philosophy.[21] Yet alongside Kesler's interpretation of the Constitution's principles is an inconvenient historical footnote: the case for a more perfect Union was *the* proximate motivation for Publius' undertaking, and his downplaying of "party animosities" was but a rhetorical overture to mollify the Anti-Federalists. Further, *The Federalist Papers* did not merely try to make "the case for the Union," as Kesler had suggested—since a Union already existed with the Articles of Confederation and Perpetual Union (the use of the full title is advised)—but *a more perfect* Union.[22] This is why the "principles" Publius adduces cannot be understood independent of "the case for the Union."

The calculated depoliticization of the Second Founding was a necessary precursor to the mingling of Federalist and Anti-Federalist political thought. By sweeping under the carpet the animating point of contention between the Federalist and the Anti-Federalists—the need for a more perfect Union as deliverable by the new Constitution—Kesler left himself free to rewrite the "principles" of the Constitution in Anti-Federalist terms. Like Richard Weaver, who had argued that "a constitution is and should be a primarily negative document"—in which case the Bill of Rights ought to have preceded Articles 1, 2, and 3, as they do in a number of state constitutions written at the time of the First Founding—Kesler understood the Constitution more in the way that the Anti-Federalists rather than the Federalists understood it, as a document primarily about rights, and only secondarily about powers.[23] Consider, most illustratively, that Kesler found a right to revolution in the Constitution. He wrote: "the people have the precious right, under the Constitution, of exercising their sovereign opinion over the whole government through

regular elections, and they may amend the Constitution according to the procedures outlined in Article V or newmodel it according to their revolutionary
right under the natural law (*Federalist* No. 43, p. 275)."[24] The third of these
options and the alleged basis of the opinion cited in parentheses is striking
and deserve attention—for its pedigree is decidedly Anti-Federalist in nature.
The whole point of Article 5 was to render unnecessary any future revolutions
beyond the Second Founding. Indeed, even the post-ratification Madison was
less Anti-Federalist than Kesler makes the pre-ratification Madison out to be.
An examination of Federalist 43 shows that Madison's invocation of "the transcendental law of nature and of nature's God," a phrase taken from the Declaration of Independence, was expressly intended only to justify his limited
proposition that the Articles of Confederation could be superseded by a new
Constitution ratified by nine states:

> Two questions of a very delicate nature present themselves on this oc-
> casion: 1. On what principle the Confederation, which stands in the
> solemn form of a compact among the States, can be superseded with-
> out the unanimous consent of the parties to it? . . .
>
> The first question is answered at once by recurring to the absolute
> necessity of the case; to the great principle of self-preservation; to
> the transcendent law of nature and of nature's God, which declares
> that the safety and happiness of society are the objects at which all
> political institutions aim, and to which all such institutions must be
> sacrificed. *Perhaps*, also, an answer may be found without searching
> beyond the principles of the compact itself. It has been heretofore
> noted among the defects of the Confederation, that in many of the
> States it had received no higher sanction than a mere legislative rati-
> fication. The principle of reciprocality seems to require that its obli-
> gation on the other States should be reduced to the same standard.
> A compact between independent sovereigns, founded on ordinary
> acts of legislative authority, can pretend to no higher validity than a
> league or treaty between the parties. It is an established doctrine on
> the subject of treaties, that all the articles are mutually conditions of
> each other; that a breach of any one article is a breach of the whole
> treaty; and that a breach, committed by either of the parties, absolves
> the others, and authorizes them, if they please, to pronounce the com-
> pact violated and void.

Madison was clearly distinguishing the text and legitimacy of the First Founding from those of the Second. The right to revolution may have been retained
by the people of the states against the Articles of Confederation, but Madison

did not think that such a right was retained by the people of the United States against the new Constitution. (This was in part why he did not support South Carolina's Ordinance of Nullification of 1832.) In proposing that "an answer might be found without searching beyond the principles of the compact itself," Madison was arguing in 43 that because the Articles were ratified by the state legislatures and not by the people, it could "pretend to no higher validity than a league." This would not be the case for the new Constitution, which would enjoy a "higher validity" because it would be ratified not by state legislatures, but by popular conventions in the separate states.[25] Duly ratified by We the People, with specific provisions for amendment enumerated in Article 5, it would be self-contradictory to speak of the Constitution granting to We the People the right to revolution against ourselves, unless of course, We the People of the states retained their revolutionary rights *in spite* of the Second Founding. If Kesler thought that the principles of the First Founding were still relevant after the Second, it is probably because he did not believe that the Second superseded the First.

The Madison of 1787–1789, however, was unambiguous in his remarks at the Philadelphia convention, when he asserted: "the doctrine laid down by the law of Nations in the case of treaties is that a breach of any one article by any of the parties, frees the other parties from their engagements. In the case of a Union of people under one Constitution, the nature of the pact has always been understood to exclude such an interpretation."[26] Madison did not believe that individual parties "under one Constitution" possessed the unilateral right to dissolve the Union of which they are a part, even if one of the parties had acted in bad faith. He considered "the difference between a system founded on the Legislatures only, and one founded on the people, to be the true difference between a league or treaty and a Constitution."[27] Since the Articles constituted a league of sovereign nations, Madison was happy to concede that a right to revolution existed as long as one party had acted in way that voided the compact. But to speak of a right to revolution against a Constitution ratified by the people is to assert an absurd right to revolution against ourselves, unless—as was the position of the Anti-Federalists—the "self" of the Second Founding was not the same "self" of the First Founding. Thus for the Federalists, the Anti-Federalists' insistence on a Bill of Rights perversely implied (among other things) that the states were not actually sovereign at the time when they signed up for the national compact, which had set out the conditions for ratification and the terms of constitutional amendment, for only by conceding such would it then be consistent for the states to advocate the retention of a wild card to second-guess their earlier commitment to ratification. No Federalist would have felt comfortable suggesting that the Constitution operated alongside a right to revolution.

The Anti-Federalists, of course, did not buy Madison's distinction between a league and a Constitution, because they refused to accept that the states had outgrown the principles of '76. Elbridge Gerry observed, "if nine out of thirteen can dissolve this compact, six out of nine will be just as able to dissolve the new one thereafter."[28] It is no coincidence, then, that when seven decades later the Confederate States articulated a right to revolution, they appropriated Madison's understanding of the Articles *qua* a league, which in Federalist 43 he had characterized as a "compact between independent sovereigns," and willfully misapplied it to the Constitution, despite Madison's insistence that the rules that bind a league are different from the rules that govern a Constitution. By inserting a comma to the preamble of their constitution, "We, the People of the Confederate States" denied that there ever was an aggregated people, or a nation, that preceded the people of the states, and so the Federalist Constitution was no more a league of sovereign entities than was the arrangement under the Articles of Confederation. Not surprisingly, in his First Inaugural Address, President Jefferson Davis argued that the South's secession "illustrates the American idea that government rests upon the consent of the governed, and that it is the right of the people to alter or abolish a government whenever it becomes destructive of the ends for which it was established."[29] So that there was no question as to the document to which he was referring, he continued to say that the Confederacy "merely asserted a right which the Declaration of Independence of 1776 defined to be 'inalienable.'"[30] Kesler may have been editing *The Federalist Papers*, but in finding a right to revolution in it, he was doing so with distinctly Anti-Federalist sympathies, because his understanding of popular sovereignty is closer to the Confederacy's understanding of "We, the People" and not the Federalists' understanding of "We the People."[31] His position, however, is shared by a wide swath of the conservative base today. Indeed, multiply Kesler's revisionism by those mounted by other conservative public intellectuals across the land through the 60s, 70s, and 80s, and one may understand why many modern liberals have come to concede that conservatives are the true defenders of the Constitution and the disciples of Publius.

Modern Conservatism and the First Founding

The modern conservative animus toward the federal government comes straight from the Spirit of '76, and not 1787–1789. In part because the old language of states' rights had been somewhat tarnished by the Union's victory during the Civil War, and in part because the federal government in the twentieth century began to interact directly with most citizens, Federal Farmer's modern descendants began to modulate their cry of negative liberty to include the language of individual and natural rights. As their forebears did, modern conservatives happily found support for this evolved understanding of the tension between power and liberty, previously centered on collective, majoritarian rights, in the Declaration of Independence. This expanded understanding of rights to now include individual rights gave new wind to Anti-Federalist sails. Thus Ronald Reagan was among the first in the modern conservative movement to make the career-making lamentation: "our natural, inalienable rights are now considered to be a dispensation of government."[32] In this, he was arguing for a reversal of the Federalists' causality—that the Constitution's powers, properly understood, exist for no other reason but to protect our natural rights. Rights came *before* powers: this was neo-Anti-Federalist revisionism, because in the Constitution, powers are articulated before rights. If the Second Founders were really overridingly concerned with natural rights or any rights at all, they would have insisted on an individual bill of rights in the Preamble of the Constitution, and not dragged their feet about appending a statement of states' rights after the last Article of the Constitution.

Nevertheless, Kesler's and Reagan's reinterpretation of the Second Founding in the image of the First has become the conventional wisdom, and this is a considerable accomplishment. Even Jack Balkin has accepted the reigning wisdom that "there is no text that is more a part of our Constitution . . . than the Declaration," and "the Constitution exists to fulfill the promises made by the Declaration" affirms Reagan's account.[33] Similarly, Lee Strang has proposed, even as he was consciously making a modest claim, that "given our society's commitment to originalism, the Declaration's role in constitutional interpretation is limited to one of the sources of the constitutional text's original meaning."[34] Of course, by my telling, the Declaration set alongside the Constitution demonstrates original dissent, not meaning, and conflating the two texts conceals the Lovers' Quarrel, the politics in American politics. If for the Federalists, to act as if nothing happened between 1781 and 1789 to temper our revolutionary ideals and our talk of rights was to miss a critical stage of American history, Anti-Federalists downplayed the disruptions that transpired in these years. Similarly, while modern conservatives harken back to 1776, they gloss over the governing disaster of the Confederation Congress that met between 1781 and 1789. Hence Kesler argued:

> *The Federalist* elucidates the kind of politics and constitutionalism that are needed in order to rescue the cause of the American Revolution and to vindicate the Declaration of Independence, which after all proclaimed not only "that all men are created equal" and "are endowed by their Creator" with certain inalienable rights, but that in defense of those sacred rights, good men ought to pledge their "sacred honor."[35]

Because there is no better template for anti-statism than the original one conceived by the signers of the Declaration of Independence, modern conservatives and their allies have deployed it for their particular anti-federal-governmental ends and downplayed the fact that while the Declaration very quickly caused Americans to revert to an anarchic condition of mutual distrust, the Constitution rescued us from it. Indeed, Ronald Reagan did not conceive of the American Revolution and its aftermath under the Articles of Confederation as an imperfect prelude to a compact written by We the People, but as the consummating act itself. He would say: "The American Revolution continues as we continue to push back the barriers to freedom. We, like the patriots of yesterday, are struggling to increase the measure of liberty enjoyed by our fellow citizens. We're struggling, like them, for self-government—self-government for the family, self-government for the individual and the small business and the corporation."[36] On a day intended to celebrate the bicentennial of the Constitution, not the Declaration, Reagan could not resist reaching back to the ideals articulated in the document articulated a decade earlier:

> It wasn't the absence of problems that won the day in 1787. It wasn't the absence of division and difficulty; it was the presence of something higher—the vision of democratic government founded upon those self-evident truths that still resounded in Independence Hall. It was that ideal, proclaimed so proudly in this hall a decade earlier, that enabled them to rise above politics and self-interest, to transcend their differences and together create this document, this Constitution that would profoundly and forever alter not just these United States but the world.[37]

As Ronald Reagan was not a fan of consolidated federal power, but a champion of the rights that preceded the creation of such power, his affinity was toward the Declaration. Similarly, because the Anti-Federalists championed rights over powers, they believed that a dose of rebellion was a healthy thing for democracy. Such was the case for the most famous Federalist convert to Anti-Federalism, Thomas Jefferson, who was after all the protégé of Richard Henry Lee, Federal Farmer himself. Warning his compatriots to stand up against the proposed Constitution, A (New Hampshire) Farmer wrote, "A merchant or mechanick [sic] may dispose of his goods, or pack them up in trunks, and remove to another clime in the course of a few months; but you cannot shoulder your lands, or dispose of them when you please, it therefore behoves [sic] you to rouse up, and turn your most serious attention to this Constitution."[38] Anti-Federalists and their descendants believe that the Constitution did not settle the distribution of power in America for all time. Rather, the Revolution lives on, or so they hope. In a speech, Reagan told his audience that "Two centuries ago, America was born in a rebellion against unfair taxation," as they now stood on "the eve of the second American revolution."[39] Reagan even issued a proclamation commemorating January 25, 1987, the 200th anniversary of Shays' Rebellion, which he termed "the defense of Springfield," a day Federalists recalled with infamy.[40] Like the founder of the Republican Party, Reagan's storytelling moved seamlessly between the First and Second Foundings. But unlike Lincoln, his affections lay with the First.

Reagan and modern conservatives' celebration of jealousy is pure Anti-Federalism. As Patrick Henry claimed, "suspicion is a virtue, as long as its object is the preservation of the public good."[41] Whereas the Federalists generally equated good government with efficient government, the Anti-Federalists saw suspicion of government as a necessary virtue in a healthy republic. As Candidus wrote, "It must be a melancholly [sic] crisis when the people are tired of guarding their liberties; and are resigned to whatever government is *dealt to them.*"[42] This jealousy is well captured in their insistence on the Second Amendment—a favorite also of modern conservatives, and evidence that the latter are in some ways still living in the 1770s, not the late 1780s and beyond, when the virtue of jealousy was rendered obsolete, according to the Federalists, after a government of the people was constituted. The Anti-Federalist commitment to states' rights was, of course, inextricably linked to their commitment to the right to bear arms.[43] In the Virginia ratifying convention, Patrick Henry proclaimed, "O sir, we should have fine times, indeed, if, to punish tyrants, it were only sufficient to assemble the people! Your arms, wherewith you could defend yourselves, are gone . . . Did you ever read of any revolution in a nation . . . inflicted by those who had no power at all?"[44] Henry believed that freedom from oppression was predicated on the right to bear arms. Federal Farmer opined, similarly, that "to preserve liberty it is essential that the whole body of the people always possess arms and be taught alike, especially when young, how to use them."[45] Federalists like John Adams tended to differ on this point. "To suppose arms in the hands of citizens, to be used at individual discretion, except in private self-defense . . . is to demolish every constitution, and lay the laws prostrate, so that liberty can be enjoyed by no man; it is a dissolution of the government. The fundamental law of the militia is, that it be created, directed and commanded by the laws, and ever for the support of the laws."[46]

As the First Founders saw an antithesis between power and liberty, so too did Barry Goldwater: "Absolute power does corrupt, and those who seek it must be suspect and must be opposed. Their mistaken course stems from false notions of equality, ladies and gentlemen. Equality, rightly understood, as our founding fathers understood it, leads to liberty and to the emancipation of creative differences. Wrongly understood, as it has been so tragically in our time, it leads first to conformity and then to despotism."[47] The conception of equality Goldwater was speaking of was the equality of citizens engaged in collective self-government. For him, equality was the start-state condition shared by all citizens, not the end-state goal of the federal government. Thus when Goldwater accepted the Republican nomination in 1964 and proudly declared, "extremism in the defense of liberty is no vice," it was clear that his heart was with Patrick Henry, who had intoned, "Give me liberty, or give me death."[48]

That jealousy is a civic virtue also translated to a healthy appetite for conspiracy in both Anti-Federalism and modern conservatism. If power corrupts, then one can never err too much on the side of suspicion. The very first conspiracy theory was, of course, launched by the Anti-Federalists against the Federalists, who were moving very quickly to convince the states to ratify their proposed Constitution without amendment. One Anti-Federalist called himself "None of the Well-Born Conspirators."[49] Federal Farmer was similarly suspicious. "Men who wish the people of this country to determine for themselves, and deliberately to fit the government to their situation, must feel some degree of indignation at those attempts to hurry the adoption of a system, and to shut the door against examination. The very attempts create suspicions, that those who make them have secret views, or see some defects in the system, which, in the hurry of affairs, they expect will escape the eye of a free people."[50] The Anti-Federalists believed that the new federal government and the raising of a national army would portend the end of state governments.

The Anti-Federalists' and modern conservatives' suspicion of consolidated power (which liberals characterize as the "politics of fear") comes not from ignorance, but wariness of the mischief Federalists and neo-Federalists could do with a Constitution that was after all written by Federalists, with as much ambiguity for future expansion in meanings and federal power as the latter could get away with. As we shall see below, the different forms of "originalism" that neo-Anti-Federalists have espoused have been efforts less to honor the intent of the first Federalists than to guard the Constitution from neo-Federalist adventures with federal power.

States' Rights, Direct Democracy, and Fiscal Conservatism

No person has united the modern conservative moment more effectively than did Ronald Reagan, and this has at least something to do with the fact that he validated fellow conservatives with the oldest home-born principles of America, Anti-Federalism. Reagan was not the only figure of his revolution, but he was its central, unifying figure. Part of his magic, and those who have come to mimic him, came from the fact that Reagan allowed his followers to forget about their obligations to the sea of individuals in the Union that liberals had for so many decades imposed on them. Instead, he gave his followers leave to cherish their private rights, and to shrug off liberal guilt. (By doing this, Reagan also helped his followers to nurse their patriotism to the Union, a method not dissimilar to Jackson's recommendation that the less the federal government did, the more it could be beloved. This is possibly why modern conservatives are fiercely patriotic, but, excepting the neo-conservatives, not necessarily nationalistic.) Whereas the country had been trying since the New Deal to fulfill our communitarian obligations to each other, Reagan offered his followers a liberating, Anti-Federalist breath of fresh air when he announced that America had no problems that had to be solved other than the government trying to solve her made-up problems. Instead of always trying and striving, it was easy to be American again, like Mom and apple pie. Conservatives (and incidentally, libertarians too) shared the Anti-Federalist intuition that politics and representation should be easy, and not reliant on representational flights of fancy or sympathy. So on income inequality, employment discrimination, global warming, and rising healthcare costs, the collective conservative response has been "it's not that bad, let it alone"—rather like the Anti-Federalists' position on the Articles of Confederation. And like the Anti-Federalists of yore, conservatives turned to states' rights, direct democracy, and fiscal conservatism to secure their vision of America as bequeathed to us by the First Founding.

STATES' RIGHTS

Even though Hoover, as we saw in the previous chapter, had grafted individual rights onto the states' rights template, modern Anti-Federalists have not forgotten about the original anthem of the First Founding. Reagan repeatedly referred to the United States as a "federation of sovereign States"—37 times, by my count—in his *Public Papers*.[51] As he put it: "Our Founding Fathers devised a system of government unique in all the world—a federation of sovereign States, with as much law and decision-making authority as possible kept at the local level."[52] The President did not make a distinction between the two federalisms of the Two Foundings, so in effect he was trying to recapture the term "Federalist" from the Federalists, who had themselves stolen it from the Anti-Federalists, defenders of the older conception of federalism under the Articles of Confederation. Perhaps Reagan was using "a federation of sovereign States" as a term of art, but he was nevertheless affirming what the first substantive provision of the Articles of Confederation guaranteed—that "each state retains its sovereignty"—exactly the problem that drove the Federalists to Philadelphia. The Federalists would have opted for the more limited route of amending the Articles of Confederation if they did not think that nothing short of reconstitution would create the governing apparatus for "a more perfect Union." Perhaps Reagan was able to recall the sovereignty of the states so brazenly only because the Federalist Constitution was beyond contestation two centuries after the Second Founding. Yet his words resonated only because the modern Sons of Liberty picked up on the anthem of 1776.

The Anti-Federalists' commitment to state sovereignty of course implied a disdain for the capital. "For it is to be remembered that there is to be a *federal* city, and the inhabitants of it will be the great and the mighty of the earth," Brutus had warned.[53] This has become a familiar refrain for modern conservatives. Thus Ronald Reagan quipped, "Washington is not the fount of all wisdom and authority in the Nation."[54] In a speech for the Goldwater campaign that would launch his own career, Ronald Reagan affirmed his allegiance to the First Founders, saying: "This is the issue of this election: Whether we believe in our capacity for self-government or whether we abandon the American revolution and confess that a little intellectual elite in a far-distant capitol can plan our lives for us better than we can plan them ourselves."[55] In contrast to modern conservatives' disdain for Washington, consider Bill O'Reilly's nostalgic account of the capital of the Confederacy:

> Richmond was a proud city and perhaps more distinctly American than even Washington, D.C. It could even be said that the United States of America was born in Richmond, for it was there, in 1775, in Richmond's St. John's Episcopal Church, that Patrick Henry looked out on a congregation that included George Washington and Thomas Jefferson and delivered the famous "Give me liberty or give me death" speech, which fomented American rebellion, the Revolutionary War, and independence itself.[56]

Coursing through O'Reilly's account of the First Founding is the battle cry of Anti-Federalism—liberty. The virtues he celebrated were pride, love of country, religiosity, sacrifice, passion, defiance, and the courage of men. These are the virtues of the First Founding. He did not valorize choice, deliberation, reason, collective decision making, reconciliation, or federal authority. The First Founders, after all, promulgated different theories of republicanism and representation than Publius did. In predicting the peoples' distrust of their representatives in a remote "Federal City," Brutus defended the mirroring theory of representation that modern conservatives have adopted:

> Being so far removed from the people, their station will be elevated and important, and they will be considered as ambitious and designing.

They will not be viewed by the people as part of themselves, but as a body distinct from them, and having separate interests to pursue; the consequence will be, that a perpetual jealousy will exist in the minds of the people against them; their conduct will be narrowly watched; their measures scrutinized; and their laws opposed, evaded, or reluctantly obeyed.[57]

Thus in his 1964 nomination acceptance speech, Barry Goldwater would similarly reiterate the theory of closeness between the representative and the represented articulated long ago by the Anti-Federalists:

Thus do we seek inventiveness, diversity, and creativity within a stable order, for we Republicans define government's role where needed at many, many levels, preferably through the one closest to the people involved. Our towns and our cities, then our counties, then our states, then our regional contacts—and only then, the national government. That, let me remind you, is the ladder of liberty, built by decentralized power. On it also we must have balance between the branches of government at every level.[58]

On election eve in 1980, Reagan similarly asked reporters: "Would you laugh if I told you that I think, maybe, the people see themselves and that I'm one of them? I've never been able to detach myself or think that I, somehow, am apart from them."[59]

DIRECT DEMOCRACY

The populism of modern conservatism, then, has its roots in the Anti-Federalists' theory of representation. The flip side of the Anti-Federalists' suspicion of power was their commitment to pure or direct democracy, laced with a strong dose of anti-establishmentarianism and anti-intellectualism. According to his son-in-law, Patrick Henry "detested the projects of theorists and bookworms. His prejudices against statesmen of this character were very strong."[60] The bookworms, of course, had taken their learning to Philadelphia when they tried to design the new Constitution. The populist and anti-intellectualistic strand of Anti-Federalism would evolve and culminate in the plebiscitary politics in which "going public" and the "permanent campaign" became routine features of American politics from the 1970s onward.[61] Certainly, just as there were patrician and plebiscitarian Anti-Federalists such as, respectively, Elbridge Gerry and Richard Henry Lee, there are Tory and populist conservatives today. These American Tories are, at least on this front,

possibly as much Federalist as they are Anti-Federalist. Unlike the social conservatives, American Tories such as William F. Buckley, Jr. have typically been
more guarded in their attitudes toward direct democracy, preferring to find
virtue in the dispassionate patrician elite. For example, referring to Federalist
49, in which Madison argued that "frequent appeals would in great measure
deprive the government of that veneration, which time bestows on everything," Garry Wills predicted that "if this passage were shown to anyone only
vaguely acquainted with eighteenth-century literature, it is a safe bet it would
be attributed to Edmund Burke."[62] Like Wills, Harvey Mansfield emphasized
the importance of "political distance" so that legislators could act like trustees
and not be subject to the whims of constituency demands, making him more
of a Federalist on this front.[63] But these neo-Federalist conservatives (if they
were that) were always a minority. In order for what was only an intellectual
movement to become a political one, modern conservatism rid itself of most of
its Tory and Federalist predilections and eased into its contemporary populist
mode around the time when Richard Nixon invoked a "silent majority" and
when Jerry Falwell discerned that "pro-moral people have been the sleeping
giant."[64]

That many conservatives today are in favor of term limits suggests as much.
Most probably agree with Federal Farmer that a representative ought to mirror
the views and opinions of his constituents, and frequent contact between them
was the only way to ensure responsive representation at the nation's capital. In
advocating a system of rotation for the Senate, Federal Farmer reasoned, "In a
government consisting of but a few members, elected for long periods, and far
removed from the observation of the people . . . they become in some measure
a fixed body, and often inattentive to the public good, callous, selfish, and the
fountain of corruption."[65] In arguing for term limits for the presidency, he reasoned: "A man who must, at all events, thus leave his office, will have but few
or no temptations to fill its dependant [*sic*] offices with his tools, or any particular set of men; whereas the man constantly looking forward to his future
elections, and, perhaps, to the aggrandizement of his family, will have every
inducement before him to fill all places with his own props and dependants
[*sic*]."[66] Like Jefferson and Jackson, modern conservatives have been strident
supporters of term limits. In supporting term-limit reform, George Will had
argued, "the worst feature of professionalism in politics is that it obliterates
the proper distance between the representatives and the represented."[67] Newt
Gingrich's "Contract with America" and Senator Tom Coburn's two-term
pledge were attempts to bring Will's vision to fruition.

Modern conservatives' faith in democracy can also be seen in their suspicion of "judicial activism," and it is especially clear here that they have taken
a leaf out of the Anti-Federalist playbook. The Anti-Federalists were afraid of

a monarchical presidency and an aristocratic Senate, but above all, they predicted that the Supreme Court was "more in danger of sowing the seeds of arbitrary government in this department than in any other."[68] They did not see the Court, as Hamilton did in Federalist 78, as "the least dangerous branch," but the one with the most transformative potential. From the very beginning, Brutus foresaw the danger of ambiguity in the text of the Constitution, and as an attempted solution in response to which the ideas of enumerated powers and judicial restraint were born:

> the judicial power of the United States under the first clause of the second section of article eight, would be authorized to explain the constitution, not only according to its letter, but according to its spirit and intention; and having this power, they would strongly incline to give it such a construction as to extend the powers of the general government, as much as possible, to the diminution, and finally to the destruction, of that of the respective states.[69]

The Anti-Federalists worried, in particular, about the ambiguous extension of the judicial power enumerated in the Constitution "to all Cases, in Law and Equity." They saw "Equity," which was the principle in the English common-law tradition that judges possessed the leeway to mitigate the harsh application of the law, as "an arbitrary power of discretion in the judges, to decide as their conscience, their opinions, their caprice, or their politics might dictate."[70] The most famous and probably the most significant historical example of this was the second *Brown v. Board of Education*, which fused the principle of equity with that of "equal protection" to produce the new formula of "equality *by* the law" instead of "equality *under* the law"—a major sore point for modern conservatives.[71] "It is true, the laws are made by the legislature; but the judges and juries, in their interpretations, and in directing the execution of them, have a very extensive influence for preserving or destroying liberty, and for changing the nature of the government," wrote Federal Farmer. He was among the first who warned of what in our modernity has been called "judicial activism"—namely, that "we must leave a vast deal to the discretion and interpretation—to the wisdom, integrity, and politics of the judges."[72]

Today's "originalists" similarly echo Brutus' fear that Supreme Court justices would feel "empowered, to explain the constitution according to the reasoning spirit of it, without being confined to the words or letter."[73] While Brutus was wrong that judges would turn to the Preamble of the Constitution to find the words to justify their decisions, his description that it "seems to include all the objects of government"[74] and his fear that the proposed Constitution was "conceived in general and indefinite terms" would correctly predict the Supreme Court's use of the "Supremacy," "due process," "general welfare," and "necessary and proper" clauses.[75]

What Brutus did not predict, however, is that the power of the courts has since been used for both Federalist and Anti-Federalist ends. The modern conservative movement has learnt, probably from FDR's foiled court-packing and successful court-replacing example, that "this power in the judicial, will enable them to mould the government, into almost any shape they please."[76] Many, like Jacksonian Democrats did, have also proposed amendments to rewrite the Constitution, just as the Anti-Federalists did with the Bill of Rights. Thus we observe the pattern in American history where the Federalists have typically justified new federal powers by way of creative resyntheses of the Two Foundings, while the Anti-Federalists have played catch-up, with a Bill of Rights, a theory of enumerated powers, or personnel or ideational court-packing of their own—all in the service of restoring the principles of the First Founding.[77] By last century's end, Jack Balkin and Sanford Levinson observed "a veritable revolution in constitutional doctrine" had occurred in the Rehnquist Court, due in no small part to the appointment of Justices Antonin Scalia and Clarence Thomas in 1986 and 1991, to fill the vacancies left by Warren Burger and Thurgood Marshall respectively.[78] Gerald Gunther and Kathleen Sullivan observed an "Anti-Federalist revival" in Supreme Court decisions, while Finkelman found that all the references to the Anti-Federalists made by Supreme Court justices were made by conservative justices in dissent.[79] Anti-Federalism had fully morphed into "constitutional conservatism."

FISCAL CONSERVATISM

As Jefferson and Jackson understood, the surefire way of rolling back the federal government was simply to deplete its coffers. Thus Robert Collins has observed that "the Reagan administration's persistent efforts to dismantle social programs by restricting eligibility, slashing benefits, and privatizing activities met with only uneven success, but where direct assault failed, fiscal policy succeeded by indirection."[80] Not a few shrewd political observers, like Senator Daniel Patrick Moynihan, recognized Reagan's indirect methods.[81] For his part, and well before he had accumulated a stream of annual deficits, Reagan indicated that he too knew the method in the fiscal madness. In a speech in 1982, he said, "Increasing taxes only encourages government to continue its irresponsible spending habits. We can lecture it about extravagance till we're blue in the face, or we can discipline it by cutting its allowance . . . Feeding more dollars to government is like feeding a stray pup. It just follows you home and sits on your doorstep asking for more."[82] Indeed, between 1982 and 1995, the federal government was forced to shut down 12 times—a fact that inspired more than a few enthusiastic tax-cutters in the second Bush and Obama administrations. Reagan's defiance of the federal government and of the administrative branch of which he was the head was breathtaking. He even seemed to condone tax loopholes. "Thirty and forty years ago you didn't hear people brag at social get-togethers about how they got their tax bill down by exploiting this loophole and engineering that credit. But now you do. And it's not considered bad behavior. After all, goes this thinking, what's immoral about cheating a system that is itself a cheat? That isn't a sin, it's a duty."[83] Reagan continued: "But what is the broader purpose of our tax proposal? Well, I'm glad to be standing in front of the House of Burgesses as I address that question. The members who spoke in this capital said no to taxes because they loved freedom. They argued, 'Why should the fruits of our labors go to the Crown across the sea?' Well, in the same sense, we ask today: Why should the fruits of our labors go to that Capitol across the river?"[84] Reagan acted as if between the First and Second Founding, We the People had not expressly and legitimately granted legislative power to that Capitol across the river, and made it our own.

Social Conservatism and Civic Virtue

As conservatives and Anti-Federalists both are jealous of power, both place their hope in more relatable, ostensibly reliable, and tangible crucibles of virtue, such the church, community, family, and even markets, rather than—as their political rivals, the Federalists and modern liberals, were more willing to do—in the state. This is why conservatives do not seek a more perfect Union, but a more virtuous republic.

Incidentally, the reason why social conservatives and libertarians are willing, occasionally, to become strange bedfellows with one another is because they were born to the same ideological parents—Anti-Federalists who advocated limited government and feared corruption in high places (as libertarians do) and loved virtue (as social conservatives do), invoking the age-old dichotomy that while the powerful are corrupt, the people are virtuous. It is true that libertarians are a relatively modern breed, but this is not to say that they are not offspring of the Anti-Federalists. Indeed, like the Anti-Federalists, they emerged as a reaction to an ever-expanding central government. Self-styled libertarians are a relatively modern breed because the libertarian language of individual liberty could gain traction only in the twentieth century, and begin to displace the older states' rights mantra, because it was only at this time when individuals began to take notice of and interact with the federal government as a result of, among other developments, the Sixteenth Amendment and the emergence of the national security state. Libertarians and states rights advocates, however, share an important common link to Anti-Federalism because of their negative conceptions of liberty, their commitment to rights, and unwavering principle.

So Reagan was only nearly right when he said, "the very heart and soul of conservatism is libertarianism."[85] If libertarianism is conservatism's heart, then Anti-Federalist is its molten core, because the Republican Party's rejection of government comes with a political philosophy that reaches to America's deep past, connecting modern Republicans' valorization of the small-business owner to Jackson's yeoman farmer and Jefferson's physiocratic views. Though some modern Democrats are accustomed to thinking of business and agriculture as opposite interests, what should not be missed is that modern conservatives, together with some libertarians, came together to give the old, Jeffersonian, agrarian philosophy a facelift, and are now defenders as much of the rural farmer as the small-business owner. The link between the virtuous farmer and the virtuous business owner comes from their common ancestry in Anti-Federalism. Both nineteenth-century Democrats and twentieth-century Republicans wanted citizens to engage in the type of economic activity that would help them to cultivate the republican virtues of thrift, industry, and independence necessary for a self-sustaining and flourishing republic. They believed that only a virtuous citizenry could sustain republicanism. The small business is archetypically a "Mom and Pop" business in which the owners of the business are also the employees who reap the full fruits of their labor. Like the yeoman farmer, who was lord and peasant on his own land, the small-business owner is proprietor and worker at the same time. If nineteenth-century Democrats hoped to cultivate a virtuous squirearchy, twentieth-century Republicans hoped to cultivate a virtuous entrepreneurship. It is not so much, therefore, that libertarians or modern Republicans are blind to social inequality (and the case for redistributive policies it spawns), but that their reasoning for the limited role of government arises from the shared desire to create conditions conducive to cultivating virtues such as thrift and industry, and not to solve and possibly perpetuate existing social and economic problems by way of state "handouts."

While the Anti-Federalists cared about virtue and goodness that sprang authentically and organically from its source—the people in small, uncorrupted republics (states)—the Federalists were skeptical that they could tap into it directly. If virtue in citizens and representatives was enough, the state governments and the Articles of Confederation would not have failed so miserably, or so some Federalists thought. The state constitutions had failed, according to the Federalists, because of their naive reliance on the people's virtue, which even when forthcoming did not prevent faction. In Federalist 10, Madison noted, "complaints are everywhere heard from our most considerate and virtuous citizens . . . that our governments are too unstable, that the public good is disregarded in the conflicts of rival parties." "Neither moral nor religious motives can be relied on as an adequate control," Madison continued, because even virtuous people could well deploy moral or religious arguments on behalf of their factious ends. As Madison argued, "A zeal for different opinions concerning religion, concerning government, and many other points . . . have, in turn, divided mankind into parties, inflamed them with mutual animosity, and rendered them much more disposed to vex and oppress each other than to co-operate for their common good." This is possibly why, while most of the state constitutions (as well as the Declaration of Independence) incorporated religious and moral exhortations and some even contained provisions for the promotion of religion and morality, by the time Federalists and Anti-Federalists had parted company, we find that the Constitution the Federalists proposed made no reference to God.[86]

Although Madison saw fit to trust the people in their choice of their representatives in the House, when considering a solution to how to settle violations of the separation of powers between the branches, Madison in Federalist 49 explicitly rejected Jefferson's proposal to bring the matter before the people. The whole point of the separation of powers, Madison argued in Federalist 49 and 50, was to allow government to be conducted without interference and independently from the people. If the Federalists trusted in virtue, it was not the virtue inherently possessed by men or emanating from communities but a virtue reconfigured when funneled through the interplay of institutions. Federal institutions, one might add. If the Federalists, including the early Madison, divided power between the federal and state governments, between branches, and then divided it internally again in the first and most powerful branch—it is difficult to argue that this preponderance of caution sat alongside an expectation or commitment to virtue as hitherto understood. And if they did not completely eschew talk of virtue, it was at least in part because they realized that it was the language that Anti-Federalists could understand and therefore be persuaded.

Before the Religious Right came into being, then, there was Anti-Federalism. "Without the prevalence of Christian piety, and morals, the best republican Constitution can never save us from slavery or ruin," wrote the Anti-Federalist Charles Turner.[87] Both the Federalists and the Anti-Federalists believed in the freedom of religion, though the Anti-Federalists were also against the freedom not to have a religion, for religion was a fundamental source of virtue. Like the Anti-Federalists, modern conservatives trust not the state, but some other more reliable font of goodness. Liberals, like Federalists, tend to be more secular because they believe that the state can solve our temporal problems. To be sure, until the 1970s, most Christian or social conservatives stayed outside of politics, but they did so only because they took a page from George Mason's adamant refusal to serve in either the Continental Congress or the U.S. Senate and took heed of Mason's advice to his sons in his will to "prefer the happiness of private Station to the troubles and vexations of public business."[88]

But Ronald Reagan and his followers would bring religion back into the public sphere. In his first Inaugural Address, Reagan said, "I am told that tens of thousands of prayer meetings are being held on this day, and for that I am deeply grateful. We are a nation under God, and I believe God intended for us to be free. It would be fitting and good, I think, if on each Inauguration Day in future years it should be declared a day of prayer."[89] Reagan learned that he could reconcile states' rights advocates with traditionalists and Christians by romanticizing the small town and its values—a common thread that connects various strands of conservatism, most of which stem from Anti-Federalism. He tapped into these values when he said, "During the 1960s, there were those who scoffed at small-town values—at family, the talk of family and God and neighborhood. And they said those things in which we believe are old-fashioned and corny. Well . . . people are discovering that those basic values we hold so dear are stronger than the fads that make a big splash one day and evaporate the next."[90] To be sure, conservatives before him had laid the groundwork for this fusionism. As Kirk attested, "The conservative will do everything in his power to prevent the further diminution of our rural population; he will keep as many men and women as possible close to the natural and customary world in which tradition flourishes."[91] Or, as the conservative commentator (who did not even think Madison and Jefferson were Anti-Federalist enough), M. E. Bradford argued, "There is theory in the private history of free Americans living *privately* in communities, within the ambit of family and friends: living under the eye of God . . ."[92] Foreshadowing an anti-intellectualism that George W. Bush and Sarah Palin would one day adopt, Bradford continued, "Our scholars, most of them rationalists, and neo-Federalists, had a vested interest in producing [Patrick] Henry's present reputation: that he was a simple-minded country politician turned demagogue, a Populist trimmer whose talents happened to serve his more far-sighted contemporaries when the Revolutionary crisis came. That Madison was the fellow to read, and Jefferson before him—or certain selected Boston radicals, as reprinted under the auspices of the Harvard University Press."[93]

Conclusion: Government Is Not the Solution to the Problem

When modern commentators make such claims as there having been a "decline in reverence for the American founding," they rarely consider the all-important and prior question, "which one?"[94] Reagan and the Republicans waged the Lovers' Quarrel on the side of the Anti-Federalists to restore the principles of the First Founding. While conservatism was hardly a label any politician embraced before the 1950s, today, Americans are almost twice as likely to identify themselves as conservative than liberal.[95] This is a dramatic change in political attitudes that owes much to the coalescing influence of the Reagan Revolution and its movement leaders' rediscovery of Anti-Federalism.

The Reagan Revolution's durable retrenchment in federal authority was more muted than was the New Deal's expansion; nevertheless, Reagan's anti-statist mantra would become entrenched enough that a Democrat, Bill Clinton, found political incentives in "ending welfare as we know it" over a decade later.[96] At the level of ideas, however, Reagan and his compatriots in the conservative movement were spectacularly successful in simultaneously presenting themselves as the true defenders of the Constitution while reinterpreting it. 1. *On Union.* The Reagan Revolution would introduce a new "New Federalism" to counter the Second Founders' new federalism. Like Jefferson, Jackson, and Jefferson Davies, Reagan characterized the Union as a "federation of sovereign States," and he did so 37 times in his *Public Papers.* 2. *On Liberty.* Reagan and the Republicans understood the federal government not as the solution to problems, but the problem itself, and grafted the language of (negative) individual rights onto the traditional defense of states' rights. They attempted to roll back the welfare state, advocated low taxes and fiscal austerity, and oversaw the growth of "originalist" understandings of the Constitution. 3. *On Truth.* Reagan and the Republicans were conservative and principled. They trusted not in the wisdom of man, but of custom, the virtuous entrepreneurship, and/ or God. 4. *On Republicanism.* Plebiscitary democracy flowered in this era, as conservative politicians practiced the mirroring theory of representation that by this time had soundly overtaken the Federalists' more aristocratic theory of representation. In the name of the people, Reagan and the Republicans would attack liberal paternalism and judicial activism, obstacles to the pure democracy the Anti-Federalists had championed two centuries ago.

In 1789, the Anti-Federalists lost the argument that they were the true federalists and the Federalists, nationalists. So Jackson Turner Main astutely observed that the defeat of the Anti-Federalists could be observed in "the attachment to them of a word which denotes the reverse of their true belief."[97] Today, their descendants have similarly denied the "Anti-Federalist" label, in an effort to honor and restore the good name of their forebears by indirection and ideological revisionism. Instead, by no coincidental turn of fate, the Anti-Federalists of the Reagan era boldly called for a "New Federalism" and became members of the Federalist Society. Modern conservatism is Anti-Federalism nationalized, paradoxical as it may sound. Today's Anti-Federalists are different from the original ones insofar as they argue from offices and podiums in the

"Federal City" itself, and very often in the capacity (or the impending capacity) of federal officers. Modern conservatism has deftly updated Anti-Federalism for its modern followers, who by and large now accept the core responsibilities of the federal government (and even a few more). But in their ideas about the Constitution and their foundational commitment to the Declaration of Independence, in their opposition to governmental tyranny, in their support of states' rights and direct democracy, in their dedication to fiscal conservatism, and in their commitment to virtue in the polity, we may observe that modern conservatives are descendants less of Publius than of Federal Farmer.

CHAPTER 8

Epilogue: The Tea Party, Obama, & Beyond

The men who create power make an indispensable contribution to the Nation's greatness, but the men who question power make a contribution just as indispensable, especially when that questioning is disinterested, for they determine whether we use power or power uses us.[1]

We cannot properly understand American politics if we continue to refer to a single "founding" when the fact that there were two tells us so much more. In 1776, the American colonies, with all authority over them consolidated in a single nexus in London, displaced the Crown and replaced it with the most decentralized of American unions, the Confederation of the United States—this was the outcome of the First Founding. If elsewhere, such as in France, monarchy was restored after a failed experiment with republicanism, in America a subtler restoration occurred during the Second Founding. Countenancing the chaos that ensued and suffering from revolutionaries' remorse, the Federalists mounted an effort, to quote Ralph Emerson, "to build an equal state" to replace the one they had separated from a decade before. When the Anti-Federalists insisted on a Bill of Rights to protect the will of popular majorities in the states as a condition for ratification, they successfully mounted a counter-revolution that placed constitutional limits on national "consolidation"—this was a defounding in pursuit of the principles codified in the First Founding. Thus ended the third act of the Two Foundings, producing a Constitution that is both a peace treaty between Federalism and Anti-Federalism and an invitation to quarrel—war by healthier means.[2] Much of American history has been a tale of these two sets of ideas funneled through the political, economic, and social issues of the day.

If the reader remains unconvinced of my account of American history because I may have placed one group or another in the wrong camp in the preceding chapters, I should say that I would already have accomplished most of what I have set out to do. Maybe Jacksonian Democrats were predominantly Federalists, not Anti-Federalists, and maybe the Progressives were too; but the objection would already concede that all must draw primarily from the two dominant strands of American political thought codified in the texts of the Two Foundings. Of course there was political thought before the Two Foundings, such as was brought to American shores by the Puritans. But these ideas were neither explicitly codified, democratically sanctioned, nor as repeatedly invoked through history in the way the principles of the Two Foundings were. And of course there were variations within Jacksonian Democracy and within Progressivism. But I submit that no set of ideas have recurred with more consistency and frequency in American politics than the principles of the Two Foundings. Correspondingly, and as this chapter hopefully demonstrates, over two centuries later, the Lovers' Quarrel continues apace in modern America. It rages with sound and fury because it is an existential debate going to the core of who Americans are. Knowingly or not, most citizens take a stand on one half of the nation's original motto, *E Pluribus Unum*. Clinton Rossiter believed that Americans have "always put a higher call on *unum* than on *e pluribus*."[3] Paul Nagel has argued the same.[4] So did Barack Obama, when in his victory on election night in 2012, he said, "What makes America exceptional are the bonds that hold together the most diverse nation on Earth, the belief that our destiny is shared."[5] On the other side, Richard Weaver stood for *Pluribus* when he proposed, "a constitution is and should be a primarily negative document."[6] Hans Kohn concurred in his belief that Americans have always resisted the idea of unity.[7] And so small matters in America get conflagrated into deep differences over fundamental principles, because Americans disagree about the most basic question of political life—how We the People are constituted. Modern liberals sometimes forget that there is a legitimate, alternative conception of democratic union out there, because they start off from the Second Founding's premise of finding national solutions to national problems. Conservatives, on the other hand, tend to revise the "original meaning" of the Second Founders in part because they cannot wholeheartedly admit their ancestry in Anti-Federalism—the ideology of the "Other Founders." There is no group for which this is truer than members of the modern Tea Party movement. In this final chapter, I shall try to make sense of the vociferous politics of recent history as our own Lovers' Quarrel, and offer some concluding remarks about where the nation stands after over two centuries of quarreling.

The Modern Tea Party Movement and Anti-Federalism

Consider the opening words of a book written by the co-founders of the largest Tea Party group in the nation, Mark Meckler and Jenny Martin:

> WE THE PEOPLE. With those three words, our nation began ... We, the people of the United States of America, felt threatened. We felt angry. We felt helpless as we watched our beloved nation—the greatest nation in world history—slip away.[8]

Here was an attempt to substitute the Second Founding with the First, by taking the first three words of the Constitution back from the Federalists, and enveloping them in the indignant tone of the Declaration of Independence. Because we usually do not think of ourselves as having had Two Foundings, it would be easy to miss the rhetorical strategy being deployed here. "We the People" are the first three words of the Second Founding, but they were crafted more than a decade after "our nation [first] began." In 1787, there was no immediate foreign threat as there was in 1776, and the American people were perhaps disillusioned, but they were not angry. The Second Founders were anything but helpless; quite the opposite, they were possibly the most empowered and privileged in their generation (and possibly most generations in the history of the world) to have had the luxury of gathering by "reflection and choice" to write a new Constitution. The only people who "felt angry" were the Anti-Federalists.

If the Federalists and their disciples have specialized in creative syntheses and resyntheses, and layering new meanings on old ones, the Anti-Federalists and their descendants have always responded with historical revisionism. Since the First Founding came first, their followers never felt obligated to engage in any reconciliation with the innovators of their age. As Jefferson took it as a badge of honor that he would "never turn an inch out of my way to reconcile them [the Federalists' leaders]," today's Anti-Federalists are similarly unflinching in their commitment to (what they believe to be and indeed fittingly call) "first principles."[9] If Grover Norquist is uncompromising and inflexible, he is no more so than another earlier neo-Anti-Federalist, John C. Calhoun, who was so rigid he was called the "cast iron man."[10] Meckler and Martin were only doing what Madison, Jefferson, and Calhoun did, when they first insinuated Anti-Federalist meanings out of Federalist words, in the debate about the First Bank in 1791, the Revolution of 1800, and the Nullification crisis, respectively. Theirs was the same strategy Herman Cain deployed, if less wittingly, when the latter alleged, in a speech announcing his bid for the Republican presidential nomination in May 2011, "For the benefit for those that are not going to read it because they don't want us to go by the Constitution, there's a little section in there that talks about life, liberty and the pursuit of happiness."[11] That section is actually in the Declaration of Independence. Here was another disciple of the First Founding who could not think of the Second Founding as legitimate on its own terms, but who believed that it needed to piggyback on the legitimacy of the First. Consider, also, the web page articulating the "Core Principles" of the John Birch Society, where the Declaration of Independence is twice cited and the Constitution not at all.[12] Consider, finally, Governor Mike Huckabee's anti-federalization of Federalism at the Republican National Convention in 2012:

> So fearful were they [the Second Founders] that government would grow beyond their intention that even after crafting our magnificent Constitution, they said, "We can do even better." They added amendments that we call the Bill of Rights that limit what the government can do and guarantee what "We the people" have the unimpeded right to do—whether to speak, assemble, worship, pray, publish, or even refuse intrusions into our homes.[13]

Only an Anti-Federalist, original or modern, would see the Bill of Rights, which Publius had argued vigorously against, as an improvement on the Constitution. The frequency and predictability of the foregoing *faux pas* tell a deeper story, especially now that we have seen the pattern of revisionism that (the post-ratification) Madison, Jefferson, Calhoun, Van Buren, and others in the Anti-Federalist tradition had pioneered. The modern Tea Party and the conservatives who share the movement's views are Anti-Federalists in their newest guise; their conflation of principles from the Declaration with words from the Constitution is merely the most recent attempt to do a makeover on the 1787 revolution in favor of government, which, as Gordon Wood rightly noted, had done no less than "shattered the classical Whig view of 1776"—the view espoused by the Anti-Federalists.[14]

Even as the Second Founding is over and settled—since most Americans now concede by their actions that we do not have a constitutional right to revolution—we have nevertheless inherited a primal instinct to rebel from our First Founding. Revolution is in our blood, because we are the daughters and sons of revolutionaries. What the Anti-Federalists were recalling among those rights the Declaration of Independence held "self-evident" was "that whenever any Form of Government becomes destructive of these ends, it is the Right of the People to alter or to abolish it, and to institute new Government." No movement in American politics has successfully exercised this revolutionary right since the Second Founding, but there are sections in the country that have never stopped believing in it. Today's Tea Partiers, therefore, did not come from nowhere, and their ancestors predate the Confederacy. They possess a fiery temperament and an absolutist attitude they share with Patrick Henry, who had once asked for liberty or if not, death. If Rush Limbaugh was "ecstatic" about Representative Joe Wilson's (R-SC) indecorous outburst in the middle of President Obama's speech to a joint session of Congress on September 9, 2009 (when he yelled "you lie!"), it is because both were part of a movement of unyielding principle and radical democracy.[15] When Governor Rick Perry charged that Chairman of the Federal Reserve, Ben Bernanke, would be committing treason if he authorized more "quantitative easing" (increasing money supply by purchasing financial assets), he was merely threatening to do what Andrew Jackson did to Nicholas Biddle and the Second Bank of the United States.[16] What some (modern liberals) today see as incivility is for others (Tea Partiers) an ancient virtue—jealousy. This can be seen most clearly in the Anti-Federalists' and their descendants' unwavering commitment to the Second Amendment as an important bulwark to the symbolic and moral priority of the First Founding. As Newt Gingrich professed at the national convention of the National Rifle Association in 2012, "the right to bear arms comes from our creator, not from our government. It is one of the inalienable rights alluded to in our Declaration of Independence."[17] Vigilance and jealousy of power are the virtues of the First Founding, not the Second. Defenders of gun rights believe that citizens should enjoy the presumption of virtue, not governments.

Like Jacksonian Democrats and the Confederacy, at the heart of the Modern Tea Party Patriots' cry is a return to constitutionalism and "originalism." As Elizabeth Foley argues, "they [Tea Party members] have a unique and intense desire to learn about, honor, and preserve the Constitution."[18] But if we take the Tea Partiers at their word, we would misunderstand the side they are taking in the Lovers' Quarrel. The theory that the Constitution enumerated only explicit, non-implied powers, as we saw in Chapter 2, was the method Jefferson had first used to limit the mischief made possible by the document the Federalists had drafted to supersede his Declaration. Like the Anti-Federalists, the Tea Partiers' hearts are with the First Founding, not the Second. As one of the Senators the movement successfully sent to Washington in 2010 revealingly wrote, "If the Constitution and common sense still have any bearing, the Tea Party isn't the least bit radical—the federal government is."[19] Yet the Constitution of 1787 was just what created the federal government; the two share an inseparably linked fate. What Senator Rand Paul (R-KY) was presenting was American history, Anti-Federalist style.

So when Jill Lepore observed that the Tea Party "wasn't just kooky history; it was *anti*history," she was exactly right. It was not coincidental that Sean

Hannity, whom she quoted, referred to a Liberty Tree graphic he showed to viewers on FoxNews as "built upon the roots of life, liberty, pursuit of happiness, and freedom."[20] Predictably, Hannity's affections were attached to the scripture that preceded the Constitution of the United States. Like the Anti-Federalists and the Tea Partiers, he believed that America was founded in 1776, not 1789. Yet, contrary to Hannity, in American history, *not* "all roads lead to the Revolution."[21] Only Anti-Federalist ones do. By revising history the other way round, Hannity was trying to reenact the status quo that the Anti-Federalists were trying to preserve. Or, as the name of one Tea Party group in Maine, the Maine ReFounders, tellingly suggests, Tea Partiers are really trying to refound or, more precisely, defound the nation along Anti-Federalist lines.[22] Their sense of grievance and their visceral desire to "take back" America stems from, I argue, the atavistic memory of a victory that the Federalists had first snatched from their forebears. This affinity toward the First Founding and the Declaration might well explain why, in late 2010, Tea Party activists were particularly offended that Barack Obama had misquoted the Declaration of Independence, omitting reference to "the Creator." This led one commentator from the *Weekly Standard* to ask,

> Does the president believe in the Declaration? . . . His presidential victory speech last Election Night incorrectly dated this nation's existence from the writing of the Constitution, not from the signing of the Declaration. His Independence Day remarks in 2009 managed to avoid mentioning, or quoting from, the Declaration at all.[23]

A modern Federalist would have cared less. These charges come from a Declarationist and son of the First Founding. They parallel the firestorm Justice Samuel Chase provoked (leading directly to the 8th Article of his impeachment) when he told a grand jury in 1803, "there could be no rights of man in a state of nature previous to the institution of society; and . . . liberty, properly speaking, could not exist in a state of nature."[24] Barack Obama is a Constitutionalist and a Federalist first, and the modern descendants of the First Founding resent the fact that he, as Samuel Chase had similarly done to offend the Jeffersonian Republicans, had glossed over the history of the First Founding and so callously replaced it with the principles of the Second. Certainly, Obama occasionally spoke (and sometimes botched up, as we shall see below) the language of Anti-Federalism, as most liberal politicians have learned to do, but he did so only when he needed to bring to his side the half of the country who did not identify with his governing philosophy. What Tea Party members failed to appreciate is that a failure to properly quote or understand the Declaration of Independence—which possesses absolutely no legal status—is strictly an irrelevant matter for interpreting the Constitution of the United States (except that the former is in many respects the antithesis of the latter).

As the Anti-Federalist and Jeffersonian philosophies were fundamentally negative, so too is the modern Tea Party philosophy. The Anti-Federalists adopted the "Country" as opposed to the "Court" philosophy of the opposition to Walpolean England because it suited well their own negative orientation toward power. So committed were they to their negative politics that both Jeffersonian Republicans and Jacksonian Democrats continued to think of themselves as outsiders even after their victories in 1800 and 1828. In this, they revealed an intuition that the Federalist Constitution was never and could never really be their own. In their own way, the Tea Partiers have conceded just as much. It is perhaps why when chastising the Republican Party, Rand Paul would say, "We desperately need a *real* 'party of no.'"[25] Senator Paul and his supporters maintained that the Tea Partiers were the truest defender of the Constitutional faith, and at the heart of this faith was the principle of limited government, codified in the movement's favorite provision, the Tenth Amendment, which was an affirmation of the eighteenth-century Radical Whig idea that power decentralized is power legitimate, while power centralized is power tyrannical. "The entire purpose of the Constitution," Paul wrote, "was to limit the power the federal government had over the states . . . so strong is the regard for the Tenth Amendment, that various offshoots of the Tea Party have formed completely devoted to it."[26] Never mind that nearly the entire purpose of the Constitution was to create a federal government because the Confederation Congress had no authority over the states. Clearly, the Tea Party's loyalties are not to the federal government, but to the states, which enjoyed their golden age from 1776 to 1788.

The Tea Party is not, therefore, a fringe party, but a more enthusiastic champion of many of the values that the Republican Party has espoused for decades. Indeed, the wisest in the party will understand that while the Tea Party will come and go, Anti-Federalism—the grandparent of all the conservatisms that have found a home in the Republican Party—will not. Thus the Party's 1964 Platform opened with this ancient anthem against power: "even in this Constitutional Republic, for two centuries the beacon of liberty the world over, individual freedom retreats under the mounting assault of expanding centralized power."[27] Similarly, in September 2010, the Republican Party released a "Pledge to America" (reminiscent of Newt Gingrich's "Contract with America" in 1994) promising to "honor the Constitution as constructed by its framers and honor the original intent of those precepts that have been consistently ignored—particularly the Tenth Amendment, which grants that all powers not delegated to the United States by the Constitution, nor prohibited by it to the states, are reserved to the states respectively, or to the people."[28] Major spokespersons in the party share this position. On April 15, 2009, Governor

Rick Perry (R-TX) told reporters: "When we came into the Union in 1845, one of the issues was that we would be able to leave if we decided to do that. My hope is that America, and Washington in particular, pay attention. We've got a great Union. There's absolutely no reason to dissolve it. But if Washington continues to thumb their nose at the American people, who knows what may come of that?"[29] Perry appeared to think that our Union is no more than a league of friendship, with each state retaining its full measure of sovereignty, as the states did before 1789. In a similar tip of the hat to the First Founding, in his victory speech after winning the New Hampshire Republican primary in 2012, Governor Mitt Romney (R-MA) told supporters that while Barack Obama "takes his inspiration from the capitals of Europe," he looked to the "cities and towns across America."[30] Or consider the re-interpretation of the meaning of the Constitution in the language of the Declaration displayed in the Republican Party Platform of 2012:

> We possess an owner's manual: the Constitution of the United States, the greatest political document ever written. That sacred document shows us the path forward. Trust the people. Limit government. Respect federalism. Guarantee opportunity, not outcomes. Adhere to the rule of law. Reaffirm that our rights come from God, are protected by government, and that the only just government is one that truly governs with the consent of the governed.[31]

After two centuries, there remains one side of America that continues to believe in the primacy of the federal government, and another side that insists on the precedence of federalism and limited government. The Tea Party is passionate and even choleric about its agenda, and these too are Anti-Federalist traits. For if the Second Founding was an extended moment of reflection, 1776 was a time of passion. While it is true that principles ancient and modern equally weighed on the Second Founders' minds when they deliberated and delivered at Philadelphia, the Federalists were more sanguine about the "Machiavellian moment" of their modernity, and pragmatic about its given facts, while the Anti-Federalists were more nostalgic, attentive to the connection between the regime and the character of its citizens philosophized since antiquity, and more wedded to absolute truths than achievable goals. Hence whereas the Federalists saw a pragmatic need for the new Constitution, the Anti-Federalists were idealists who opposed it as a matter of principle. This is perhaps why Madison, in Federalist 10, in proposing the multiplication of factions to mitigate the influence of the most powerful one, effectively denied that there was an objective hierarchy of values that government ought to protect. He might have been what a conservative today would call a moral relativist.

While the Federalists were dedicated to maintaining community peace, the Anti-Federalists, like today's conservatives who denigrate liberal political correctness, were not.[32] The First Founders, after all, had launched a war to overthrow a king; the Second Founders mounted an intellectual revolution to rewrite the meaning of the American Union.

At the center of the Tea Party's charge that America has been hijacked is a deep animus toward President Barack Obama and a deep, neo-Anti-Federalist intuition that he is not "one of us." This is why, even though the Bush administration had also contributed to the federal budget deficits and had started the "bailout" of the banks during the financial crisis of 2008, the Tea Party movement emerged only after Obama's first inauguration. The movement's distrust of Obama can be found in the claims by the "birthers" that Obama is not a natural-born citizen of the United States or in the charge that he is a Muslim, both of which have traceable roots in the Anti-Federalist theory of representation that held that effective and accountable representation could occur only when there is a close resemblance between the representative and the represented.[33] Though the president's race might have something to do with these sentiments, it does not tell the whole story because the Tea Party's objection to Obama's policies is both personal *and* substantive. These fears of Obama as an outsider were put on display when Obama announced plans to broadcast a speech to schoolchildren on the first day of school in September 2009, and he was accused of propagandizing a "socialist" ideology.[34] Many parents feared that the President was trying to indoctrinate young children with corrupt ideas. "Socialism" is but the modern name for "consolidated" government, a condition that Anti-Federalists feared would render citizens as unthinking subjects of a tyrannical government. Like the Anti-Federalists, these parents believed that schools were critical to the cultivation of virtuous citizenship, and needed therefore to be insulated from ideological contagion with particular care. This episode paralleled the anti-communist sentiments Republicans espoused in the 1950s. When he was the president of Columbia University, Dwight Eisenhower was hesitant about the idea of federal aid to schools because he feared that "unless we are careful, even the great and necessary educational purposes in our country will become yet another vehicle by which the believers in paternalism, if not outright socialism, will gain additional power from the central government."[35] If Eisenhower was not clear exactly what functions our public schools performed, John H. Cowles, testifying before the same committee to whom Eisenhower was addressing, was: schools were "the bulwark of our free institutions" whose responsibility was to "impress upon the minds of the pupils the ideals and traditions of our country."[36] The Lovers' Quarrel, then, has played out even in education policy. While Democrats have generally advanced education reform as the solution to social and economic inequality, Republicans have tended to value education less instrumentally and more intrinsically for its role in cultivating civic virtue. As the Republican Party Platform of 2012 put it, "The principles written in the Constitution are secured by the character of the American people."[37] While Democrats have concentrated their reform efforts on affirmative action and access, Republicans have focused on school prayers and fighting liberal indoctrination of schoolchildren to ensure a virtuous citizenry capable of self-government.

The populism and anti-intellectualism of the Tea Partiers are also offshoots of the Anti-Federalists' theory of representation. The latter fiercely rejected the Federalists' proposals of virtuous representation, whereby the preferences of the people were to be distilled to leave out the passions and defects of democracy, because of their fear of domination by the "better sort." Their descriptive theory of representation therefore led the Anti-Federalists to push for a more plebiscitary form of government. The Tea Party, by proposing to "take back" Washington for the people, has insinuated that there is a higher source of legitimacy than the Constitution itself—namely, the people. This is a view the movement shares with Jefferson, Jackson, Wilson, and Reagan. When presidential candidate Rick Santorum, speaking at a forum hosted by Americans for Prosperity, a group affiliated with the Tea Party movement, accused President Obama of being a "snob" for suggesting that every American should go to college, he was merely practicing Melancton Smith's theory that "representatives (should) . . . resemble those that they represent."[38] (Conversely, the problem with John Kerry's image in 2004 was not that he was wealthy, but that he was not a wealthy rancher in a cowboy hat, as George W. Bush and Ronald Reagan were.) Populism and anti-intellectualism, then, are not uniquely Republican or Tea Party qualities; they stem from the Anti-Federalist theory of representation.

Whereas most scholars characterize Tea Party members as possessing inconsistent beliefs—such as a pick-and-choose attitude about when government is desired—I suggest that their beliefs are mostly consistent, and their only error is the failure to appreciate (or admit) that the lion's share of their beliefs run back to the "Other Founders."[39] The movement is also more than a top-down movement, even if it has sponsors in high and powerful places.[40] To be sure, this descendant of an authentic homegrown ideological tradition—unlike, say, European imports such as communism or even Lockean liberalism—is one so deeply ingrained that its adherents seldom pause to reflect on the pedigree of their ideas. This too is testament to the enduring legacy of the First Founding and the cultural transmission of its values through the centuries despite the Second Founding. When members of the Tea Party rail against federal spending, it is because they do not think the spending comes back to them. They are harkening back to their primordial identities as members of small republics or states, trying to rewrite history only because the Federalists had first rewritten federalism. They see "death panels" as constituted by malevolent bureaucrats because they think the "Federal City" breeds cabal and vice with malign intentions to "spread the wealth." As Theda Skocpol and Vanessa Williamson report,

> Despite their fondness for the Founding Fathers, Tea Party members we met did not make any reference to the intellectual battles and political compromises out of which the Constitution and its subsequent amendments were forged . . . nor did they realize the extent to which some of the positions Tea Partiers now espouse bear a close resemblance to those of the Anti-Federalists . . . The Tea Partiers we met did not show any awareness that they are echoing arguments made by the Nullifiers and Secessionists before and during the U.S. Civil War . . .[41]

The Tea Partiers appear to be proffering their claims in bad faith because they have not admitted, or perhaps will not admit, their ancestry in Anti-Federalism, for to do so would be to concede the difference from and priority of the values of the Second Founding compared to their own. Yet the best way to make sense of the movement and its commitments is to acknowledge that its members hail come from a long line of American reactionism that began in 1787, when their ancestors stood athwart History and the Federalists, yelling "Stop." In the Lovers' Quarrel, old grudges die hard.

Barack Obama, Federalist

The Era of Obama has seen the defenders of the First and Second Foundings scrimmaging tooth and nail. The debates over stimulus packages for the economy, the budget deficit, and public debt, serious and enormous as they are, are variations on the Lovers' Quarrel. The signature achievement of President Barack Obama's first term—the Patient Protection and Affordable Care Act—represents a surge in federal authority that places Obama squarely in the Federalist camp and our era as a neo-Federalist era. Indeed, at no point in the nation's history has the Supreme Court determined it consistent with the Constitution that Congress's taxing and spending powers permit it to tax as many as over 40 million Americans, should they fail to purchase a product, in this case health insurance.[42]

A brief look at Obama's writings and speeches suggests that he has always been a disciple of Publius. In a book specifically written to introduce himself to voters on the eve of his presidential campaign, Obama was careful not to step on Republican toes, but he did little to hide his neo-Federalist identity. Politicians can fudge or change their positions on specific issues, but whether or not they are Federalist or Anti-Federalist runs to the core of their identity and is not something they, or most Americans, can easily disguise. So in the section of *The Audacity of Hope* where Obama discussed the Declaration of Independence and rights, he observed, like a true Federalist, "a declaration is not a government; a creed is not enough."[43] His faith was in the Constitution, which had created governmental powers, not the Declaration, which had articulated our rights. Like the Federalists and unlike the Anti-Federalists, he considered the basic problem of political life as starting from a position of heterogeneous interests. Since the Anti-Federalists believed in a small republic, it was but an implied afterthought that political communities should be socially homogenous, so there would be no need for a government to be the arbiter of interests. The Federalists, on the other hand, in extending the sphere, not only had to accept heterogeneity as a given, but also had to find a new argument in defense of the new and much-enlarged political community they were envisioning. In this tradition, Obama wrote: "if my notion of faith is no better or worse than yours, and my notions of truth and goodness and beauty are as true and as good and beautiful as yours—then how can we ever hope to form a society that coheres?"[44] Obama was no idealist insistent on The Truth, but a pragmatist committed only to the truth that could hold a society together.[45] Discussing the scourge of slavery, Obama opined, "it has not always been the pragmatist, the voice of reason, or the force of compromise, that has created the conditions for liberty."[46] He understood that when Publius et al. extended the sphere, they also enlarged the ambit of our sympathies from those in our communities and states, to those in every state of the Union. This is why we would find out later that "empathy" was the virtue Obama prized in his vetting of judges for the Supreme Court. Empathy is a modern liberal virtue, as it was a Federalist virtue.[47] Conversely, conservatives do not buy that empathy is a virtue; instead, these modern Anti-Federalists believe that the fellow-feeling one feels authentically for one's brother or neighbor in the family or a small town is a natural sentiment far superior to the paternalistic artifice that is empathy. ("Compassionate conservatism," an attempt by the second President Bush to extend the scope of conservatives' sympathies and therefore the size of their electoral coalition, proved to be a relatively short-lived affair.) If the Anti-Federalists were correct that it was difficult if not impossible to cultivate fellow-feeling among, and responsive representation for, diverse peoples across an extended sphere, the Federalists can be lauded for trying—because *Pluribus*, not *Unum*, is the natural human path of least resistance.

Like the Federalists, who invited fellow Americans to imagine a *Unum* when there was only *Pluribus* about them, Obama understood that the Constitution "is not a static but rather a living document, and must be read in the context of an ever-changing world."[48] He was committed to the Constitution's "elaborate machinery" because it was "designed to force us into a conversation."[49] He understood that the Constitution's design implied "a rejection of absolute truth," for that was the best way that the many could become one. If Obama thought the "Founders" were "suspicious of abstraction," he must not have considered the author of the Declaration of Independence as a Second Founder (and Chapter 2 made the case that Obama was right in his assessment).[50] When, on the last page of his book, Obama canonized the service of those who "laid down their lives in the service of perfecting an imperfect union," the reader is left with the distinct impression that he could think of no higher calling.[51] In his victory speech in 2012, he affirmed this conviction, saying, "tonight, more than 200 years after a former colony won the right to determine its own destiny, the task of perfecting our union moves forward."[52] Similarly, in his Second Inaugural Address, Obama cited the sacred text of the First Founding, saying, "We hold these truths to be self-evident, that all men are created equal," and continued, "today we continue a never ending journey to bridge the meaning of those words with the realities of our time. For history tells us that while these truths may be self-evident, they've never been self-executing."[53] To accomplish that, we needed a Second Founding. Obama may have started his speech with the Declaration of Independence, but he cited the fundamental idea of the Constitution, "We the People," five times.

At his core, Obama believes in the commitment of the federal government to the protection of every individual in the Union. In 2011, he gave an indicative speech at the dedication of the Martin Luther King Jr. Memorial in Washington, where he proffered a neo-Federalist rehearsal of the aspirations of the American people, and an invitation for the nation to focus, as King had, on the liberal and aspirational "ought" rather than the conservative "is." Quoting King, Obama affirmed Union as a nation of individuals "caught in an inescapable network of mutuality, tied in a single garment of destiny." "In this democracy," Obama continued, "government is no distant object but is rather an expression of our common commitments to one another."[54] And so, he pragmatically and optimistically observed in his First Inaugural Address, "the question we ask today is not whether our government is too big or too small, but whether it works."[55]

None of this is to say that Obama did not learn to speak the rhetoric of states-centered republicanism to appeal to independent and conservative voters, only that his fundamental worldview is archetypically Federalist. Indeed, if Obama is occasionally eloquent, it is because he, like Lincoln, FDR, and Martin Luther King Jr., understood the seductiveness of the language of the small republic, and that American political eloquence is a function of the speaker's ability to interweave and reconcile the antithetical principles of the nation's Two Foundings.[56] For example, in May 2012, Barack Obama completed his personal evolution on the issue of gay rights and declared his support for same-sex marriage, but at the same time held that states should be allowed to decide on the matter for themselves. He thought it was a "healthy process" that "states [are] working through this issue—in fits and starts, all across the country. Different communities are arriving at different conclusions, at different times." He predicted that "this is an issue that is gonna [*sic*] be worked out at the local level, because historically, this has not been a federal issue, what's recognized as a marriage."[57] Here was a Federalist making music to Anti-Federalist ears.

The best example of Obama's creative resynthesis of the Federalist and Anti-Federalist traditions occurred in his celebrated keynote address at the Democratic National Convention in 2004. There, he quoted the self-evident truths of the Declaration (this time with reference to the "Creator" intact) and laid on thick the Anti-Federalist rhetoric of the small republic: "a faith in simple dreams . . . an insistence on small miracles; that we can tuck in our children at night and know that they are fed and clothed and safe from harm." But like Lincoln had done at Gettysburg, he proceeded to pivot from Anti-Federalist ideals to Federalist ends:

> Now, don't get me wrong, the people I meet in small towns and big cities and diners and office parks, they don't expect government to solve all of their problems. They know they have to work hard to get ahead . . . but they sense, deep in their bones, that with just a slight change in priorities, we can make sure that every child in America has a decent shot at life and that the doors of opportunity remain open to all.[58]

Obama wrapped himself in Americana, the cloak woven from neo-Anti-Federalist dreams, and used it to lead his audience to the less familiar territory, just as the Federalists had done before. And so he would say, "alongside our famous individualism, there's another ingredient in the American saga, a belief that we are all connected as one people." This other ingredient, of Federalist origin, is "what allows us to pursue our individual dreams, yet still come together as a single American family: 'E pluribus unum,' out of many, one." And so, in perhaps the most remembered part of this speech, he said,

> The pundits like to slice and dice our country into red states and blue states: red states for Republicans, blue states for Democrats. But I've got news for them, too. We worship an awesome God in the blue

states, and we don't like federal agents poking around our libraries in the red states. We coach little league in the blue states and, yes, we've got some gay friends in the red states . . . We are one people, all of us pledging allegiance to the stars and stripes, all of us defending the United States of America.

By tapping into the two indigenous strands of American political thought, Obama captivated the electorate in 2008, paving the way for his attempt at American political development when he came into office. His 2008 election theme, "hope," after all, had made its first cameo appearance in this speech. Hope, of course, was what the Anti-Federalists felt about the citizenry. The Federalists, on the other hand, with their darker view of human nature, at least when operating in an extended republic, put their faith in the new science. Obama took the Anti-Federalists' hope in the people and stretched it to include a newfound faith in the powers of the federal government. This creative resynthesis persuaded voters that 2008 would be the dawn of a new Federalist moment, a new age of government.

President Obama's speeches since have often come short of the one that paved his meteoric rise to the White House, in part because his subsequent invocations of Anti-Federalism seemed more perfunctory and even dismissive, rather than incorporative or genuine. Healthcare reform was of course the landmark legislation of Obama's first term, and debate about it lined up squarely along Federalist/Anti-Federalist lines. In his speech to Congress on healthcare in 2009, he attempted to do what he had done in 2004, but with a small but significant difference. "The danger of too much government is matched by the perils of too little," he said. Like the neo-Federalist presidents before him, Obama took on the arguments of the other side and gave them fair hearing. "One of the unique and wonderful things about America has always been our self-reliance, our rugged individualism, our fierce defense of freedom and our healthy skepticism of government," he said, paying homage to the Anti-Federalists. But unlike his 2004 convention speech, he posited a contrast rather than a creative *link* from Anti-Federalism to Federalism, saying that there was also another American ideological tradition he called "large-heartedness—that concern and regard for the plight of others . . . too, is part of the American character," and that "sometimes government has to step in to help deliver on that promise."[59] "Large-heartedness," like the virtue of empathy, is a Federalist ideal—not something that appeals to Anti-Federalists, and a contrast without a bridge does not creatively resynthesize but exacerbates the Lovers' Quarrel.

On another occasion, in 2009, Obama even mocked the Anti-Federalists in our midst when at a fundraiser in San Francisco, he explained, "they cling to guns or religion or antipathy to people who aren't like them or anti-immigrant sentiment or anti-trade sentiment as a way to explain their frustrations."[60] Though he was not entirely wrong in that modern Anti-Federalists share the same jealousy of power and the mirroring theory of representation of their forefathers, Obama made the cardinal mistake of disrespecting the principles and adherents of the First Founding, while missing an opportunity to make the case for why the alternative conception of government he held was not malevolent but benign. Obama showed his partisan hand again at another campaign event three years later when he said, "there is a certain crowd in Washington who, for the last few decades, have said, let's respond to this economic challenge with the same old tune . . . one that speaks to our rugged individualism and our healthy skepticism of too much government. That's in America's DNA. And that theory fits well on a bumper sticker. But here's the problem: It doesn't work."[61] The President might have gained more converts had he started from Anti-Federalist premises and conscientiously built an intellectual and emotional bridge toward Federalist conclusions, as Lincoln and Franklin Roosevelt had successfully done before. At his best, Barack Obama can sound more like Madison than Hamilton, and in these moments he has been relatively successful in convincing Anti-Federalists that it is possible to have faith in a government that they do not yet love.

The Constitution's Federalist Bias I: Limits to the Tea Party's and Neo-Anti-Federalist Fortunes

The Lovers' Quarrel has proceeded for over two centuries, with each iteration looking remarkably similar to the one before. Here, near the end of our inquiry, it is time for this author to explicitly take a side, or rather, to report a side that History has already taken. The Federalists did win the ratification debate. They won the day in their argument in favor of more and not less government against their contemporaries, and they secured the weight of words and the priority of placement in the Constitution not only to prove it, but also to bequeath to succeeding generations who would build on their qualified victory. This is perhaps why the expansions of federal authority brought about by Publius, Lincoln, and Franklin Roosevelt's coalitions were of greater amplitude and durability than the retrenchments of federal authority attempted by Jefferson, Jackson, and Reagan. Put another way, as a document written by Federalists and only modified by Anti-Federalists, it was no wonder that the Constitution contained more opportunities for neo-Federalist than neo-Anti-Federalist adventures in the future. This is the built-in bias of the Lovers' Quarrel, a path dependent on the victory of the Second Founders.

In the last paragraph of the last Federalist Paper, number 85, Hamilton laid bare his conclusion after weeks of argumentation. "A NATION, without a NATIONAL GOVERNMENT, is, in my view, an awful spectacle." In the end, a nation and a national government were the ultimate ends of the Federalists, and the more insistent among them probably believed that it was the latter that made possible the former. The Tea Party and modern conservatives' view that the Second Founders stood for limited government, then, is a distortion of the latter's position. And this is perhaps why the Party's relatively unadulterated Anti-Federalism (compared to, say, the neo- or religious conservatives, who see a role for a muscular state at least in foreign or social policy) cannot go very far if their members and spokespersons do not reconcile their beliefs with at least some of the principles of the Second Founding. The First Founding created only 13 "Free and Independent States." There was no United States as a single nation until the Second Founding, which simultaneously created the federal government. So unless the Constitution is undone, there will forever be a linked fate between the American nation and its national government. This is the deep meaning of the Constitution Lincoln acknowledged when, in his Gettysburg Address, he used the word "government" emphatically and interchangeably with the word "nation," as Publius had done a lifetime before.

Constitutions are supposed to be higher laws that apply equally to everybody, ensuring, as Jefferson put it, "equal and exact justice" to all who fall under their protection. Yet in establishing the rules of the political game for any given polity, constitutions also presume a particular conception of the good and the ends of government for which certain powers are granted. To the extent that the framers disagreed vehemently on what these ends are—given that 16 delegates out of the 55 who gathered at Philadelphia either left early or refused to endorse the new Constitution, as Lincoln notes—then it should not be apostasy to say that the Constitution is about two parts Federalist and one part Anti-Federalist. Yet it should also be said that by the very standards of the "originalists"—who place credence on what was deliberated on and approved in Philadelphia—the Articles of the Constitution, ratified in 1788, must take legal and normative precedence over the Bill of Rights, which Publius had argued against, and was only ratified later, in 1791. If context matters, it matters especially at the beginning, and the original intention of Publius was *not* to include a Bill of Rights, and the original meaning of the Constitution in 1788 literally excluded it.[62]

It is not the Declaration but the Constitution that is the supreme law of the land, and this is why followers of the First Founding face a natural ceiling as to what they can accomplish. "No taxation without representation" is an ancient British constitutional principle to which the Bostonian colonists were legitimately appealing in 1773. These colonists objected to the Tea Act passed by the British Parliament in 1773, on grounds that the act violated their right to be taxed only by laws passed by their elected representatives. But this situation does not apply to modern Tea Partiers. Not only does every single member of the modern Tea Party movement have a representative and two senators representing her or him at the federal level, residents of the nation's capital do not even fully enjoy such representation. While the Boston Tea Party was a protest against the British government from America, the modern Tea Party is a protest against American government in her capital city. The appropriate historical parallel is not 1773, but 1800 or 1828.

The Tea Party claims that it wants to make Washington irrelevant to the lives of Americans. Yet on September 12, 2009, tens of thousands of Americans gathered at the national mall, a culmination of a 7,000-mile bus tour that had started two weeks before in Sacramento, California, to protest the tax and spending policies of the Obama administration.[63] The movement called this a "March on Washington" to mimic Martin Luther King Jr.'s historic march in 1963. King believed that the federal government was the solution to our problems, and not the problem itself. So a solution he sought, and a solution, by way of the Civil Rights Act, was found. But consider the grand meta-historical irony of the Tea Party's march in 2009. For better or for worse, the descendants of the Anti-Federalists, even if they are champions of state capitols, must now bring their march to Washington, the nation's capital. Those who still see the District of Columbia as the swamp it used to be must nevertheless seek power in the "Federal City" if only to relinquish it. Thus an enduring legacy of Publius is that even as modern conservatives have fought back to introduce a "New Federalism," they must now organize nationally in order to do so. There was a time when federalism meant that there were as many ways as there were states to implement a particular policy, so that federalism meant diversity and inequality.[64] But this has changed, as surely as the Federalists' plan for a more perfect Union has come to fruition. Unlike Calhoun, today's conservatives and Tea Partiers can no longer speak from the perspective of a particular state, but the perspective of the states, and often from that of a nation. Like the Anti-Federalists who took up positions as representatives and senators of a new government they had previously deemed illegitimate in order to prevent even more Federalist antics, the reactionaries to the New Deal have had to accept the premises of a battle thrust on them by organizing nationally to defeat neo-Federalism. As Tulis noted, "The 'New Federalism' is a *national* policy adopted by the national government and changeable in the future by the national government."[65] Almost every major policy, even a conservative one to roll back government, must first start in Washington as a federal initiative. Thus, to take another example, when Rick Santorum insisted that Mitt Romney was the worst Republican the party could put up against

Barack Obama in 2012 because of "Romneycare" in Massachusetts, he was extinguishing the state/federal distinction that the Anti-Federalists defended years ago—implying that what is unacceptable at the national level ought not to be practiced at the state level, even if Bay Staters had democratically decided otherwise.[66] The Anti-Federalists would have seen no contradiction or hypocrisy in Romney supporting one policy at the state level, but not its counterpart at the federal level. This is exactly what the old federalism stood for. But today's successful or nationally prominent Anti-Federalists must sing to a different tune. Washington matters now, and neo-Anti-Federalists understand more than ever that they must convince not just their states, but the nation if they are to find their way into Washington to then restore their vision of the First Founding. Santorum, then, was paradoxically defending the principles of the First Founding by nationalizing them, implicitly conceding by his updated reasoning that the cards are now stacked against the pure, unfettered Spirit of '76. While Andrew Jackson looked out into the Potomac and still saw swamps around him, modern Anti-Federalists confront the nation's capital as a metropolis rivaling any European city with its opulent piazzas, federal buildings, statues, and monuments attesting to the might and expanse of the federal government of the twenty-first century. This is why some conservatives are even using Hamiltonian means for Jeffersonian ends; for example, in advocating for a one-size-fit-all, top-down constitutional amendment about the meaning of marriage as between a man and a woman.

There are therefore two related reasons that limit the odds of Tea Party success deep into the future. First, the Tea Party's anti-establishment philosophy lends it to being represented by hundreds of groups, with no clear leadership. Speaking as a fan and major spokesperson, Rand Paul offered a clue as to why the movement has likely peaked: "the Tea Party sprang in each state de novo. It wasn't created by a network. It wasn't created by a billionaire. It came from the people. It has no single leader; is often adamantly against leadership and threatens the power structure of both political parties."[67] A movement that does not believe wholeheartedly in national organization is less likely to succeed under a Constitution that was written to provide national solutions. Second, especially at the presidential level, voters are more likely to choose someone who offers a positive national vision, not a negative or parochial one. As Hamilton noted in Federalist 27, as "the extension of the spheres of election will present a greater option, or latitude of choice, to the people," it is likely that more and better candidates will emerge from among those who share the *Unum* persuasion to compete for national elections, compared to those of the *Pluribus* opinion, who are more likely to devote their service to the states. A viable candidate for national office offering national solutions is simply less likely to arise from an ideology dead set against top-down solutions from Washington. Perhaps this was why all the Tea Party candidates for the Republican presidential nomination were found wanting in 2012.

This does not mean that the Tea Party is impotent, only that it is a movement more likely to succeed in opposition politics, rather than in government itself, and in congressional and local rather than presidential and national races. The Tea Party—true to its commitment to the Declaration's principles of negative liberty—is most powerful when it is in attack mode, during off-year elections and in local races, in keeping with its mantra that all politics is, and ought only to be, local. And attack it did in 2010, with much success in "throwing the bums out." But the Tea Party is a lot less comfortable with itself when in governance mode, when a movement of anti-incumbents becomes the incumbents. When this happens, a celebrated movement of No becomes derided as a Party of No.

While the Civil War established the ceiling of the Anti-Federalist impulse beyond which it cannot go, the Federalists and their descendants have been pushing their boundaries for over two centuries because encoded in the Federalists' Constitution was the open-ended promise to build "a more perfect Union"—by which they really meant, but did not want to say, a more *consolidated* Union—and this is the trajectory we continue to be on. Polities constituted by a written Constitution are more deeply republican in one sense than monistic polities, such as the UK, where popular sovereignty is vested in parliament, can ever be. In the United States, the Constitution embodies and encourages the ever-growing intergenerational consensus of We the People, constantly adding to the legitimacy of living majorities that alone empower governments elsewhere. And so while it is often said that limited suffrage qualified the Second Founding's republican legitimacy, the Second Founders also laid a path by which future generations could articulate their own generational consensus while also sharing and adding to their predecessors'. Even Tea Partiers are less incensed about Medicare and Social Security than they are about "Obamacare" because the former programs have allowed them to come into contact with the federal government and ascertain for themselves that it is not such a malevolent phantom. If the provisions of the Patient Protection and Affordable Healthcare Act are enacted, it may well follow in Medicare's and Social Security's trajectory. As the Federalists had hoped, time has often proved to have a tranquilizing effect on Anti-Federalist fears.[68]

When the Supreme Court affirmed, in part, the Patient Protection and Affordable Care Act in June 2012 to have been in accordance with Congress's power to "lay and collect taxes," it merely recognized, as perhaps Chief Justice Roberts did, that the Constitution, written by the Federalists to replace the weak Articles of Confederation, enumerated very considerable powers to Congress indeed—powers that now included the authority of Congress to tax individuals who failed to purchase a private (insurance) product. Although some conservatives rejoiced that Roberts had joined the other conservative justices in declining to expand the meaning of "interstate commerce" to cover the individual mandate, this was cold comfort because the Supreme Court upheld the highly unpopular provision with the most undisputed of Congress's powers—the power to tax and spend—which "gives the Federal Government considerable influence even in areas where it cannot directly regulate."[69]

Nevertheless, the Supreme Court rarely has the final word on matters decided by two factions of We the People. The history of federally and uniformly implemented programs such as old age insurance versus decentralized programs such as Aid to Dependent Children, implemented at the state level, suggests that the individual mandate may not be as successful as a public option would have been. Without some uniformity of implementation by a federal authority and with plenty of opportunities for state actors to displace the intentions of national policymakers, beneficiaries may not grow to think of healthcare as a privilege of national citizenship.[70] The same can be said of the Affordable Healthcare Act's provision on the expansion of Medicaid to individuals making 33 percent above the poverty line, which the Supreme Court had determined the federal government had no authority to mandate of the states. Arguments about the relative efficiency of the national or state governments to deliver welfare services are part of the Lovers' Quarrel, but the real issue has always been about trust. Federalists and modern liberals trust the federal government and decry the discriminatory and feudalistic patterns of implementation at the state level, while Anti-Federalists and modern conservatives trust the state governments more, because they are literally closer to home. It is no surprise that about 40 percent of the residents of Washington, DC are self-identified liberals—10 points higher than the most liberal state in the Union, Massachusetts.[71] Liberals congregate in the "Federal City" because they believe that government is the solution, and they disagree heartily with Reagan in his conviction that "Washington is not the fount of all wisdom and authority in the Nation."[72] Instead, they believe, as Hamilton did in Federalist 17, in the "splendor of the national government."

If the Anti-Federalists' difficulty has always been the challenge of nationalizing their *Pluribus* ideals or least packaging it into a coherent governing agenda, the Federalists have always wrestled with the corresponding burden of personalizing and selling their aspirations for *Unum*. Although Suzanne Mettler may have been right that "policymakers who seek to incorporate citizens into the polity in ways that might promote the sense of social solidarity so fundamental to civic life should heed the lessons of the New Deal," she does not and perhaps cannot offer an answer to the prior question of how policymakers can convince the followers of the First Founding that national solidarity is a goal worth seeking in the first place.[73] Only the American people, working through our Lovers' Quarrel, can decide if healthcare reform ultimately creates a more perfect or a more fractured union, and whether or not we are entering a durably Federalist moment in our history.

The Constitution's Federalist Bias II: The Presidential Pattern

Beyond the limits to how far the modern Tea Party can succeed in restoring the First Founding, presidential history has also demonstrated the Constitution's Federalist bias. I look to the executive branch for clues to the built-in biases of the Lovers' Quarrel because it is there that the major legacies of the Two Founders—democracy from the Anti-Federalists and the state from the Federalists—are equally evident. And when we look to when American political development has occurred, we find that in each instance, the day is won only when federalism is redefined, not when a branch utters the final word or when a war is won. A quick look at the "great" or "near-great" presidents of American history corroborates this account. The names that are often at the top of any list are Washington, Jefferson, Jackson, Lincoln, Franklin Roosevelt, and Reagan.[74] All took on the Lovers' Quarrel—a necessary though not sufficient condition for "greatness" (for the top three in rank) or "near-greatness." All oversaw durable shifts in federal authority, either upward toward the federal government or downward toward the states. It is only because each took a stand on America's developmental fault-line that they were afforded a shot at "greatness." More importantly, a pattern within this pattern lays bare America's developmental logic. Every one of the "great" presidents—Washington, Lincoln, and FDR—oversaw the expansion of federal authority over the states with a more nationalist vision of the Union, while those who fought on the side of the states have always been relegated to no more than "near-greatness." John Whipple offered the same reasons discussed above about the Tea Party for why some presidents hit a "near-great" ceiling. Of Jackson's presidency, he had observed,

> He had money, and popularity, and power to an unlimited extent. What use did he ever make of either, except for party purposes? He pulled down and demolished much of what his predecessors had built up, but what did he build up himself? What public improvements of any kind did he propose or adopt? What did he do for national roads, for internal facilities? What for trade, for education? Has not his whole administration been the work of demolition?[75]

Even the great "Reconstructor" presidents, then, were not all created equal.[76] At the crux of every presidential worldview is an answer to a fundamental American question: does the president embrace or reject the role of the federal government as *the* solution to governing problems? The reason why Jefferson, Jackson, and Reagan hit a ceiling was because they were the Anti-Federalists' political descendants, personifying the tension of a Constitution that had codified two conceptions of democratic sovereignty. All three were national executives granted powers from the Federal Constitution; yet they possessed ideologies that committed them to speaking up for the states. The tension between the source of their power from an aggregated We the People and the decentralized direction of their hearts toward the people of the states allowed neo-Anti-Federalist presidents to periodically recalibrate the nationalistic bias of the Federalists' Constitution and hence to achieve "near-greatness," but it also placed a ceiling on how "great" they could be. Thus, as it had been for Jackson, Herbert Croly would similarly observe, "Jefferson, who had been a lion in opposition, was transformed by the assumption of power into a lamb."[77] The President of the United States is after all the Chief Executive of the *Federal* government; if she or he seeks the particular power only to renounce the general powers therefrom, an opportunity to synergize the power of the executive and the powers of the national government is missed. I do not mean to say that this a good thing to which all presidents should aspire, only that it is a developmental fit between vertical and horizontal centralization that coheres with the Federalists' aspirations for a more perfect Union. When the President affirms the energy in her or his office and deploys it to enact the program of the federal government, the spoils of national state-building redound to her or his office; personal and formal powers act in unison to make "greatness" more likely, though of course it is not guaranteed. What Jefferson, Jackson, and Reagan tried to do, in effect, was to aspire to greatness by the auspices of a *prior* democratic sovereignty. To the extent that that prior conception had roots in the First Founding, they were able to successfully invoke an impulse that preceded the Constitution, giving themselves a surge of democratic legitimacy. But to the extent that the Federalists' Constitution enjoyed the weight of words, it meant that those presidents who oversaw the horizontal and vertical consolidation of powers—incidentally, those presidents who oversaw Ackerman's "constitutional moments"—were more likely to rise to "greatness."[78]

Correspondingly, the "near-great" presidents who have fought for states' rights have tended to be remembered for their personalities or democratic political techniques, and less for the institutions they left behind—they would probably not have had it otherwise. So we think of the eponymous *Jackson*ian era, or the *Reagan* Revolution. The great Party Builder and the Great Communicator both reached outside of the Federalist constitutional toolkit to renegotiate the relationship between the federal government and the states. Conversely, as Spragens rightly argued, modern liberalism has been "less centered on procedural norms of democratic legitimacy" and more centered on "substantive goals of expressive liberty and social and economic equality" because these goals can only be achieved by state-building.[79] For the Anti-Federalist presidents, however, democracy and state-building are antithetical ideals that do not, or at least should not, go together. So they are remembered not for the institutions they build or leave behind, but for their ability to imitate or mirror the people they represent, which is also to say that they are more often than not celebrated for their personalities and their political techniques.[80] In contrast, "Great" as Lincoln and Roosevelt were, we refer to the "Civil War and Reconstruction" and the "New Deal" eras. The names resonate, yet they are not used to identify the eras in which these men lived. We remember instead the national programs more than the presidents not only because institutions outlast men, but also because these presidents brought more individuals under the protection of, and therefore felt a newfound affinity to, the federal government than had existed in the status quo before. To do so, on the one hand, Lincoln and Roosevelt presented themselves as trustees, rather than delegates, of the people, which, by increasing the distance between the representative and the represented, also allowed them to bring more individuals under the protection of the state—a move anticipated in the Federalists' new science. It is no coincidence, on the other hand, that our most populist presidents—those who adopted a mirroring theory of representation—were those who stood on the Anti-Federalist side of the Lovers' Quarrel. Thomas Jefferson and Andrew Jackson both played the part of the *vindex injuriarum*, and in doing so they established the unimpeachable democratic pedigree of the presidency as the defender of the public faith, and made possible a Rhetorical Presidency that future presidents would enact for either Federalist or Anti-Federalist ends. They did not, however, build the state, and that is why our affections run to them, but not to their programmatic legacies.

That some eras are better remembered for their state-building outcomes while others are remembered for their political techniques reveals the enduring relevance of the Lovers' Quarrel in the exercise of the powers of the executive. Reputation and legitimacy figure so heavily in accounts of the presidency and American politics in general because the mandate presidents seek for their actions comes from a source that has always been differentially constituted; for We the People are divided as to who we are. The perpetual search for legitimacy in American politics occurs because what Skowronek calls the "persistent order" of the Constitution, constitutional time itself, was *already* an intercurrence, as I argued in Chapter 1.[81] Although each is a critique on the other, what connects Corwin's account of "powers" to Neustadt's account of "professional reputation" and Skowronek's account of "warrants" for action in "political time" is the centrality of legitimacy in constitutional, secular, and political times.[82] "Political time" is cyclical because the Constitution's legitimacy comes from two opposing traditions, and legitimacy fluctuates for the American presidency because her or his authority to speak for We the People is contingent on resolving the prior and even more confounding ambiguity of just who the people are. And this may be why prerogative has exhibited such wide latitude in presidential history. Whereas the Lockean understanding of prerogative allows leaders to poach discretionary authority only from those spaces in which legislative acts have not yet addressed, American presidents are able to tap into an even deeper ambiguity—the very contested meaning of We the People. As we saw in Chapter 5, Woodrow Wilson's version of the Modern Presidency theory, "Leadership by Interpretation," had addressed and exploited just this conundrum when he proposed that the president alone had a national constituency and that was why he spoke with more legitimacy than do members of Congress, whose understandings of the needs of We the People were more parochial.[83] The ambiguity from which Wilson derived an extra boost of legitimacy came not from Locke or Machiavelli, but from the quarrel between Publius and Federal Farmer.

The Maturation of the Lovers' Quarrel: A Formidable State & a Plebiscitary Democracy

After over two centuries of tit for tat and give and take, the Lovers' Quarrel has matured, and it has yielded mixed-blooded progeny too. Most Americans today have internalized the principles of both Publius and Federal Farmer, typically picking one sphere of politics, either economic or social, to emphasize *Pluribus* and another to reify *Unum*. Modern liberals may believe in collective governmental solutions and conservatives may reject the need for them on economic issues, but when it comes to some social issues, conservatives have learned to agitate for collective governmental solutions if not pronouncements, while liberals tend to prefer that individuals be left alone to do as they please in the privacy of their own homes or body (though it is consistent with the Lovers' Quarrel that most of the rights liberals care about are often held against state governments, not the federal government). It is as if each side understood the draw of both sides of *E Pluribus Unum*; over time, citizens and parties, as well as statesmen, have undertaken their own creative resyntheses of the principles of the Two Foundings.

When Thomas Jefferson observed that "the natural progress of things is for liberty to yield and government to gain ground," he did not conceive of the possibility that government could also grant (positive) liberty, though he was right that the Federalists' momentum could not easily be halted.[84] The Federalist victory in 1789 has, with ups and downs, generally been consolidated in time. These days, thoroughgoing states' rights conservatives calling for secession are a rare breed, and they seldom espouse their creed of negative liberty and small government from the particular perspective of a single state. Instead, they champion such values uniformly on behalf of all 50 states. Libertarians who call for limited government nevertheless recognize the value and role of the federal government. Or consider that during the New Deal, bureaucrats were culled from the private sector where technocrats had been trained during the Industrial Revolution; but today, former members of the public sector transition out of government into lucrative jobs in the private sector. Like it or not, experience in government now counts as something that the business world values. The American state is no longer weak or intangible, but a formidable player in the market.

If Anti-Federalists have gradually learned, since the Revolution of 1800, that they can coopt the federal government to pursue their Jeffersonian ends, the Federalists, for their part, picked up that democracy could be used to sell their Hamiltonian ends. And as the presidency was initially a platform for the propagation of Anti-Federalist ideas, so it has also been a place where Anti-Federalism has left its greatest legacy—democracy. To reject the Federalists' state-building ambitions, the Anti-Federalists invoked democracy and a mirroring or descriptive theory of representation to register their distrust of Federalist schemes. As a result, as the state has grown, so too has democracy in reaction to it. The more Jefferson, Jackson, and Reagan managed to place a face on the state, the less their followers felt estranged from it. These Anti-Federalists helped make more palatable the growth of a bureaucratic state by making its representatives and especially its chief executive appear more accessible and less malign.

Most Federalists have caught on. The legitimacy of the First Founding, sanctified in the Declaration and codified in the Bill of Rights, demanded that if neo-Federalists like Lincoln and FDR wanted to move forward, they first had to reach backward to the First Founding for sources of political justification. By an Anti-Federalist twist of fate, it is now reserved mostly to presidents, harnessing the creative and destructive energies of the *vindex injuriarum*, to implement Americans' alternating love–hate relationship with the state. And so the modern executive is possibly the starkest incarnation of the twin legacies of the Lovers' Quarrel. In America, the state fueled democracy and democracy made the state. Together, they make the grandest irony of American politics. If the American state, of which the president is chief, was the culminating legacy of the Federalists, democracy was the Anti-Federalists' revenge. The institutional winner, of course, has been the presidency. If the energy in the executive comes from its potential to invoke the people's sovereignty in one of two ways, the unitary executive has arisen both because of the growth of the national state and the expansion of democracy.[85] To the extent that Congress represents the part and the president the whole, the flow of powers from former to the latter occurring in lockstep with an expanding bureaucratic state and the march of democracy points to America's maturation and convergence from many localized democracies to a national, consolidated democracy.[86]

We may therefore be reaching a plateau in terms of state-building and plebiscitary politics. The maturation of the Lovers' Quarrel has meant that we are no longer adolescents loving quickly and spurning hastily, but like an older couple quibbling over the wrinkles in a relationship in which some fundamental commitments—our democratic faith, Anti-Federalist in origin, and our reliance on the state, Federalist in origin—are increasingly beyond debate. On the one hand, because democracy is here to stay, so is the "permanent campaign," and every neo-Federalist aspiration stands or falls by it.[87] On the other hand, since we no longer revisit the fundamentals of our commitment to the state, the order shattering and creating energies of presidents has been somewhat muzzled.[88] Anti-Federalism has matured, and it is for the most part a nationalized ideology today.[89] All-out attacks on the legitimacy of federal institutions are rarer today than they were in the nineteenth century. Whereas Andrew Jackson challenged the legitimacy of the Second Bank of the United States, even the fiscal hawk and Republican vice-presidential candidate, Paul Ryan, defended Medicare against cuts made in the Affordable Healthcare Act on the 2012 campaign trail.[90] As more and more of the institutions and programs of the federal government are locked in place, buffered by the growth of their own clients and constituents, and legitimated by the passage of time, the cordoned-off area of the state resistant to Anti-Federalist attacks has grown. Stuck with a state we no longer wish to completely dismantle, and a boisterous democracy we have come to embrace, we have become, after two centuries of quarrelling, a government of laws *and* men. Federalists and Anti-Federalists can both claim the last laugh.

Conclusion

Maybe there is a better way to connect the numerous dots of American history than the one I have proposed in this book. But I stand by the Lovers' Quarrel because, as Aristotle reminds us, "there is quite as much trouble in the reformation of an old constitution as in the establishment of a new one, just as to unlearn is as hard as to learn."[91] We do not live each moment in a vacuum, and however much we may have mythologized our Second Founding, we have not forgotten the First. I have stressed the differences between the Declaration and the Constitution, rights and powers, or the invisible line between Article 7 and the Bill of Rights in this book because there is where American politics occurs. The Federalists might have thought that they had routed the first constitution of the United States, but the Lovers' Quarrel of the last two centuries and a quarter stands as formidable evidence that they did not. And they could not, because unlike many other nations, America's independence did not coincide with our Second Founding. While other new nations have adopted aspects of our system in theirs, they have not been able to replicate perhaps the most important and yet the most inimitable contingency of the American "founding"—that there were two.

Vociferous as our debates have been, then, our Quarrel may have produced some beneficial consequences. A possible reason why the American system has lasted is that Anti-Federalism justifies destruction and Federalism demands creation, and creative destruction is necessary for a polity committed to both constitutional perpetuity and evolving reality. Whereas some nations took a few constitutions to get it right, it has likely been integral to the longevity of the second Constitution, paradoxically, that it followed on the heels of and as a response to the first. In the Constitution's first half, the Federalists affirmed the necessity and value of power; its second, the Anti-Federalists warned against its excesses. When Tocqueville distinguished American patriotism in the 1820s as more of a "rational sentiment," in contrast to the "instinctive passions" of European nationalism, he may have been alluding to the fact that Americans were always debating about their original principles.[92] The Constitution has survived because each conception of democratic sovereignty infused within it is legitimate enough to hold its own against the other account. Machiavelli believed that if a republic was to last forever, it must renew itself periodically by reflecting on its "original principles."[93] By a stroke of luck along with some perspicacity, Americans have been forced to engage with our original principles because they were never settled at America's "Machiavellian moment," when the Second Founders gathered to secure their republic's temporal finitude.[94] Whereas destructive and creative impulses have caused extraconstitutional convulsions elsewhere, the Lovers' Quarrel has channeled these energies against each other. As a bloated federal bureaucracy or a legislative leviathan, with their roots in Federalism, pose a threat to the republic, so too does pure democracy and demagoguery, with their roots in Anti-Federalism. The Lovers' Quarrel has kept both tendencies in relative check by making possible the "continued coexistence of reformism and reaction" in American politics.[95] It has done so by grounding us in perhaps the most important and probably the oldest question of political life—what is the relationship between power and rights?

The greatest civilizations are those that were better able to solve their collective action problems than did their rivals. In an era of upheaval and revolutions, the Second Founders reconciled those who wanted a big republic and those who wanted a smaller one, thereby fermenting the Lovers' Quarrel in the Constitution and creating the very conditions of peaceful revolution that Thomas Jefferson had once whimsically hoped for. The Second Founders peered further and deeper into the future, and chose to consolidate the sovereignty of the several states so that they could stand a chance, as a large republic, against their foreign foes, building an empire that would one day rival that of England or France. "Join, or Die," as Benjamin Franklin put it in his famous political cartoon.[96] The Anti-Federalists, for their part, looked to the past and saw that every state powerful enough to stand up to its foes had also become powerful enough to become its own enemy. The larger and more populous a republic, the tougher would be its coordinating challenge, the more urgent its need for a central government, and the more insoluble its democratic legitimation puzzle.[97] The Federalists' solution—a creative synthesis of the opposing principles of the Two Foundings by the invention of a new federalism—made possible the United States' growing economic and military dominance in the nineteenth and twentieth centuries. Other communities have tried different solutions. The European Union has attempted but appears to be suffering from the travails of confederation that America attempted at her First Founding. It may be in need of, if it is possible or desired, a Second Founding. China's collective action problem is twice as large as Europe's, but it appears to have found a relatively stable solution by way of an authoritarian Communist Party. Whether or not *Pax Americana* persists in the twenty-first century turns on whether or not some other great power is able to fashion a superior collective action solution that would be better able to simultaneously manage the different aspirations and unleash the potential of its population than the Lovers' Quarrel was able to do for Americans in the last two centuries. Suffice to say for now, that insofar as America's global hegemonic status outpaces what Rome or England were ever able to achieve, the Lovers' Quarrel may be among the greatest political innovations the world has ever seen. That this is so may have something to do with the fact that America is as externally strong in exerting power over other nations as it is internally weak in exerting power over its inhabitants. We have the Federalists to thank for the former, and the Anti-Federalists to thank for the latter.

Americans are not going to stop bickering, but this conclusion is not entirely tragic. Set against the arc of our history, the Lovers' Quarrel reveals the bittersweet story of how we have tried to live with each other. Bipartisanship and compromise are not really American traits, whatever the politicians may say. (Indeed, they are qualities more Federalist than Anti-Federalist.) Instead, our solutions are either restoration or creative resyntheses, depending on whether the disciples of the Anti-Federalists or the Federalists of each generation win their day. Creative resyntheses—the closest Americans can come to compromise—have been rarer than restorative episodes in our history because the principles of the Two Foundings are not easily harmonized, but they will occur again when the Federalists of a new generation create new meanings that marry the previously irreconcilable principles of the First and Second Foundings, and satisfy the Anti-Federalists of the era that they do not have to sacrifice their principles on the altar of the Second Founding. Three times *Unum* and *Pluribus* have been creatively reconciled in our history—when Publius remade federalism, Civil War Republicans remade liberty, and New Deal Democrats remade liberalism—all in the service of creating a more perfect Union. Creative resynthesis is no easy task, because the Anti-Federalists, standing on principle and on older understandings, will always be around to call the Neo-Federalists out on their inventiveness. Either way, the dominant party of each generation will likely continue to be the one that more artfully and successfully defends the principles of one of the Two Foundings, and American political developments will likely continue to be registered in durable shifts in federal authority.

In his preface to *The Semi-Sovereign People*, E. E. Schattschneider sagely observed that "we shall never understand politics unless we know what the struggle is about."[98] He was referring to a different struggle, to be sure; but I hope this book invites fellow political scientists to return to what citizens already routinely do, which is to ask the big question, "what is the struggle about?" I have argued that American history and especially the "founding" has been so fiercely contested because we have had Two Foundings, each delivering a legitimate but distinct conception of union. The cleavages in American politics have often been described in binaries or in combination of binaries: South/ North, Red/Blue, Rural/Urban, and so forth. These are modern binaries emanating from the original one. American political development happens when and only when what makes America is periodically remade, following a Lovers' Quarrel. A theory of American political development and political thought that highlights the contested principles of our Two Foundings as the central axis of American politics will spur citizens and scholars to be more self-conscious of which side of the Lovers' Quarrel we stand on when we make certain value judgments about the purposes of government, the scope of rights claims, "lost promises," "unfinished revolutions," and so forth. To do so, we need to understand that when we began our world again in 1787, we were not fighting monarchy, but an earlier version of ourselves.

Appendix I

A DEFENSE OF APD DEFINED AS DURABLE SHIFTS IN FEDERAL AUTHORITY

The account of APD presented in this book takes off from the conceptual tools introduced by Karen Orren and Stephen Skowronek, who had defined APD as "durable shifts in governing authority."[1] I have argued that the most thoroughgoing "shift" in governing authority, short of total revolution, would be the remaking of the terms of the original compact itself, and in particular, the settled understanding of federal authority. This was what the Second Founding achieved, when the compact between the states was formally abolished and the relationship between them was reconfigured by layering a new conception of democratic sovereignty—of the collective We the People of the United States—over the old one. The Second Founding would become the template for all developments to come because the constitutional text that was drafted to codify for posterity the relationship between the federal government and the states placed enough in there for advocates of either federal "powers" or states' "rights" to invoke their half of the document for a future battle. It further locked both conceptions of union in Article 5, which made amendments to the Constitution prohibitively difficult so that a Lovers' Quarrel at the ideational level had to ensue along and only along original lines before development, at the ideational and institutional level, could occur. Political actors must *search* for APD because nothing in the words of the Constitution guarantees victory to either conception of federalism promulgated in the Two Foundings. Put differently, since APD must occur on "site," the two uniquely American sites that are *primus inter pares* against all other sites are the federal government and the state governments, the twin pillars of the American polity enshrined in Article 5.[2] This definition may be more restrictive of what counts as APD than some would like, but it does so in the service of identifying the greatest developmental stakes so as to discriminate trivial change from development, and development from *American* political development. While it may be open to debate whether or not durable shifts to or from other authorities are developmental, it is impossible to argue that durable shifts in authority from the federal to the state governments or vice versa are not developmental. Durable shifts in federal authority are the greatest attainable goal of American political mobilization, because they remake America's social compact.

The APD field's preoccupation with institutions and, in particular, the American state already points to this conclusion. By "governing authority," Orren and Skowronek "mean the exercise of control over persons or things that is designated and enforceable by the state."[3] Their instinct to focus on the state is correct, though it needs elaboration. The "state" is exactly what is contested and elusive in America because federalism confounds its meaning, and unpacking it reveals a definition within the definition. This is possibly why APD scholars have long interrogated Marx and Weber, asking if they were wrong or if America is simply *sui generis*.[4] And unsurprisingly, generations of scholars have grappled with and rendered different accounts of the oddity of the American state.[5] "Weakness" was probably not the most precise description, but, William Novak notwithstanding, the contrast with Europe's states was no myth.[6] Yet the explanation as to why was always closer to home than our comparative forays had yielded. Once we recognize that with divided sovereignty comes a divided state, we would know, as Stephen Skowronek and Brian Balogh did, to look beyond conventional bureaucratic structures and the nation's capital for manifestations of the American state kept "out of sight."[7] To say that democracy came before bureaucracy here is also to say that for most of the nineteenth century, the Anti-Federalists and their descendants defending states' rights and a different conception of confederated sovereignty spoke more loudly than the descendants of the Federalists. America did without a bureaucratic state in the nineteenth century not because citizens were too free to have bothered to build one, but because the Second Founding came on the heels of the First, and the new federalism acknowledged and institutionalized so many veto points in the political system that it encouraged battles over policy to become battles of jurisdiction—the accumulation of which would be a bare-bones, anemic state compared to those in Europe.

To be sure, something happened during and after the Progressive Era, when the "state of courts and parties" came under intense attack, and this is possibly the reason why the era draws so much scholarly attention from the APD community. There are relatively few books in the APD canon that focus on the period before the Civil War, because the federalism of the 1800s was a relatively eventless equilibrium until the onset of "Yankee Leviathan," "Building a New American State," and the "Forging of Bureaucratic Autonomy."[8] APD was at the vanguard of "bringing the state back in" because scholars in the field have always understood the state to be the preeminent site at which developmental innovations come together.[9] If so, the essential cause that underlies existing accounts of an "exceptional" state on both historical ends of the Progressive interregnum, before which the American state was "out of sight" and after which the American state emerged as a convoluted maze, was the alternating rhythm of the Lovers' Quarrel.

Three benefits emerge from my definition of APD as "durable shifts (expansions or retrenchments) of federal authority." First, understanding the new federalism as the master ordering and disordering mechanism in American politics accounts for the paradoxes that feature so often in American politics. In particular, this definition is consistent with why APD so frequently amalgamates the new with the same-old, why one step forward often also coincides with two steps backward, and why America's moral saga is so bittersweet. The familiar story of how national goals were executed by parochial administrators, for example, explains the racialization of ADC (Aid to Families with Dependent Children), but it also highlights the ubiquity of the federalism explanation.[10] In particular, this account of APD clarifies the different methodological approach of Orren and Skowronek and another APD scholar, Paul Pierson. If Orren and Skowronek highlight the confluence of different historical legacies impinging on the present, Paul Pierson's approach of "placing" an event in time—even though he introduces the useful concepts of "sequences," "junctures," and even "multiple paths"—conceives of time as a single stream.[11] Pierson's goal of encouraging methodological scrupulousness and generalizable propositions that can "travel . . . beyond a specific time and space" is a worthy one, and one shared by APD scholars.[12] However, the "placement" perspective takes a neater and more unidirectional view of time than other developmentalists normally do, and supplies a more limited framework for analyzing reversals and cycles in political time—key features in American politics. In unraveling the developmental sequences of the Two Foundings, the theory of APD and APT presented here embraces Orren and Skowronek's challenge to put "politics at the center of developmental analysis."[13] The deep contradictions of our constitutional tradition are not just evident in the institutions of one era and the needs of the next, as the Progressives were the first to argue, but they were there at the beginning, and have been with us since.[14] This account of APD, then, encourages us to zoom in on the rough and tumble, the twists and turns that attend to the doing and course of American politics. The Federalists' new federalism, the oxymoronic layering of national over confederated-state sovereignties, is much more than an institutional boundary condition; it is both the thing political actors fight to define and the method by which the fight is fought. It is the "master problematic" of APD, permitting change amid fundamental continuity in American politics because the lynchpin of the compact is itself the site of as well as the means for political contestation.[15] When Madison declared the Constitution to be "partly federal, partly national" in Federalist 37, he was trying to make a contradiction go away at the same time when he and his compatriots were creating a tangled knot. The Constitution did not create a compound republic in which the partly federal and partly national elements were stably and constantly integrated. Ours is a colloidal republic in which the powers of its component parts were never conclusively fixed because from the beginning, as Madison put it in Federalist 37, "no language is so copious as to supply words and phrases for every complex idea." The new federalism was quintessentially such an object.[16]

Second, this account of APD clarifies the field's distinction from History, and helps us center on the most resilient features of American politics. Like History, APD revels in the twists and turns of causal sequencing, but unlike History, my account of APD focuses on the first cause of American politics. Contingency is real, and it matters, of course, but APD, by my account, consists in the study of the most frequently recurring, or the most resilient causes. Whereas durable shifts in governing authority could conceivably occur by chance, durable shifts in federal authority cannot occur by chance any more than the Constitution—in either its written or interpreted form—can change by chance. If there is one thing in American politics that has never altered as a result of chance, it is conscious higher-lawmaking by We the People to determine the nature of the nation's political identity. From the beginning, Americans were conscious about their constitutional endeavors, whether they were directed in the drafting of royal charters or state constitutions. This jealousy followed the skeptics of the new Constitution into Philadelphia, where Hamilton would later claim that it was by "reflection and choice" that seeming reconciliation was found. The new federalism, the first product of the new science, encapsulated the primacy of reflection by making the contest of sovereignties the burden (or the privilege) Americans have had to face ever since. Madison was correct in Federalist 51 when he asked, "But what is government itself, but the greatest of all reflections on human nature?" The citizens of the small republics (states) and the large republic of which they became a part have been debating this prompt for over two centuries. Put most simply, my account of APD guides us from the infinite variety of historical facts and helps us to identify the most significant among: those that implicate the foundational question of American politics—the question of national identity.

Third and finally, articulating the nation's developmental fault line also gives us a concrete standard to make interpretive sense of American politics, an underlying impulse in much of APD scholarship.[17] Examining the political development of any country, not just America, "is tantamount to interrogating the national premise," as Orren and Skowronek noted.[18] If so, to define development as durable shifts in federal authority is also to identify what is exceptional about our particular species of political change. Whereas for some other polities, development is the midway accomplishment between revolution and stasis, *American* political development occurs on our own unique axis between consolidated federal authority and the principles of the Second Founding versus confederated state sovereignties and the principles of the First Founding. By joining political thought, or the principles of the Two Foundings, with political development, the theory of APD and APT presented here aims to explicitly connect and theorize the relationship between cultural/normative and institutional/empirical enquiries.[19] It also articulates the normative standards by which development is judged, helping us think through what political victory means in the America context. Though we are not locked in Locke, Hartz was correct that Americans are locked in a developmental frame, and one created by our start-state conditions. But Hartz was wrong to say that we are a nation of consensus, because while the *framework* of the Lovers' Quarrel is shared, the sides are most definitely not. My definition invites us to stop thinking of culture as merely a "boundary condition," but rather as the contested or bifurcated source of political justification in the United States.[20] When we appreciate the indigenous driver of APD—a Lovers' Quarrel that is both anachronistic and antagonistic—we need no longer see "development" as an oxymoron. As long as the two sovereignties are on the same page, American political development can produce, and indeed probably has produced, changes far beyond what even revolution can produce. Foundationalists and developmentalists can each have their day. This is why there are no permanent truths; only generational truths. There are no permanent winners or losers in APD, only the circadian rhythm of the Lovers' Quarrel.

What "Durable Shifts in Federal Authority" Excludes

It may be useful to identify some implications of the definition of APD presented here. By my account, APD occurs when the federal government is empowered to do that which it could not do before, or when the federal government loses the authority to do that which it could do before. *American* political development cannot occur unless the zero–sum game between federal and state authorities is played to produce a new equilibrium, though of course political development of a generic variety will continue to transpire whether or not the Lovers' Quarrel occurs. One implication that follows is that in domains where federal authority has been relatively unilateral because the problem of collective action prevented a viable states-led alternative, such as in foreign relations (where federal authority is oriented externally) and to some extent in postal delivery and old-age insurance (where federal authority is oriented internally), there has been less vociferous of a Lovers' Quarrel, and therefore more scope for neo-Federalist intervention.[21] Another implication is that two important kinds of "shifts"—power shifts between state and society, and inter-branch shifts at the federal level—are not, strictly, APD. Both exceptions point to the all-consuming nature, for better or for worse, of the Lovers' Quarrel.

Let me explain why. Any definition, including Orren and Skowrone's, which focuses on shifts in *authority*, would entail that APD is not, directly, about power shifts between state and society. To say that APD is defined with durable shifts in federal authority is to say that APD is not directly concerned with the governed, such as measured by the rights and liberties of those burdened by authority, but it is concerned with authority, as Orren and Skowronek rightly note.[22] This is an implication of the fact that while private citizens or groups of citizens organize to influence the nature of the authority under which they live, they do not, by themselves, possess formal authority. Rights in and by themselves are rarely mandates for actions; they are certainly not self-enforcing. Indeed, individuals could have no part in the Lovers' Quarrel until the Fourteenth Amendment because the Constitution, up until then, was concerned only with federal powers and states' rights. The story of the expansion of civil rights is a major story in American history, to be sure, but it is a story at most about political development, but not *American* political development until the account addresses the plot of how federal authority shifted to bring about such expansion.

Although I do not intend for this definition in any way to trivialize the efforts mounted by generations of civil rights activists, I do hope it helps to explain the perception, held by most modern liberals and neo-Federalists, that America has always dragged her feet and remains one step behind Europe in terms of race relations, the welfare state, women's rights, and so forth.[23] As authority is "plenary," in America it is shared between the federal and state governments in a zero–sum relationship that permeates the United States territorially and legally.[24] Corporations, interest groups, individuals, and even Indian tribes are creatures of one or the other sovereignty or both, and their causes can advance only if they petition one or both sovereignties, and if their political agenda is successfully grafted onto the national compact newly reconfigured to make space for it. This may also explain why not every constitutional amendment would count as an instance of APD; only the ones that altered the nature of the federal compact or the powers of the federal government vis-à-vis the states were. These may include the Bill of Rights and the Fourteenth, Fifteenth, Sixteenth, Seventeenth, and Twenty-Third Amendments.

One further implication of this definition, then, is that interest-group politics and social movements that do not graft their claims unto reconstitutional agendas are likely to hover in the shadow of the two preeminent identities that crowd out all other debates and claims. For example, consider the Civil War and race relations, sometimes posited on the one hand to satisfy certain criteria to be a watershed moment in American politics, and yet often also thought of as an unfinished movement or even one overturned by backlash.[25] As I argued in Chapter 4, the Civil War and Reconstruction era was developmental not because of the Thirteenth Amendment, morally significant as it was, but because of the Fourteenth Amendment, which triggered a seismic reconfiguration of what the federal government can do by turning the Bill of Rights from a guarantee of states' rights to an instrument of federal authority. This is what happened when the North won the war, and the Radical Republicans passed the Reconstruction amendments, remade liberalism, and turned the United States into a singular noun when it was plural before.[26]

Indeed, my definition illuminates why of the "organization of private interests" in America, John R. Commons observed, "no other country in the world presents so interesting a spectacle."[27] This spectacle emerged in part because the American state often could not do what was asked of it; when the boundaries of the public are subject to rigorous contest, the private must step in to perform the public work. This is why a sizeable portion of the literature on American politics, at least since Tocqueville, has examined the role of parties, voluntary associations, and interest groups as the critical intermediary between the state and society. The people need parties because the Constitution invites political struggle and organization to determine who the people are and what they want.[28] Interest groups and other "parastate" institutions harness ideology and interest to form coalitions so that they can influence policy at the local and national levels.[29] And the study of parties and "parastate" institutions and the nature of American federalism intersect because the problem of collective action is particularly heightened (and the study of political science especially interesting) in a large republic constituted by two conceptions of We the People. If the United States were a purely confederated system, all politics would be local; and if it were a purely unitary system, all politics would be national. Because American politics must be both, it is often also neither, and so actors and groups from other sectors of society must be called in when the Lovers' Quarrel is trapped in impasse. So much of our politics is driven by kaleidoscopic and disparate configurations of citizens organizing themselves to bring about durable shifts in federal authority because there are two (and often contradictory) points of access in a federal system and it is unclear which levels of government represent "The People." Understood in this context, parties in the nineteenth century and the partial displacement of these parties with the explosion of other political organizations during the Progressive Era represented variant answers to the same confounding structure.[30] State and local parties in the nineteenth century and interest groups in the twentieth century were period-specific ways of organizing coalitions of voters in line with reigning conceptions of union that had privileged distributive issues and confederative democracy in the nineteenth century, and regulatory or redistributive issues and national democracy in the twentieth century. The interrelated stories of the decline of parties, the rise of interest-group pluralism, and the administrative state describe and explain the reconceptualization of federalism and the expansion of federal authority that would begin at the turn of the twentieth century.

Other than shifts from state to society, durable shifts in inter-branch authority also do not directly count as APD, by my account. Scholars have typically lumped federalism with a string of institutional features, such as the separation of powers, checks and balances, and judicial review, which jointly describe the American political system, as if these innovations were of equal magnitude and part of the same explanation for how Washington works (or fails to work). Typically, the textbook language of the "division of authority between the federal and state governments" emphasizes the parallel to the separation (and hence division) of powers.[31] But the horizontal and vertical distributions of power in the Constitution are very different. Advocates of states' rights can call on the First Founding to ground their doctrine; no one branch of the federal government can. This is why differences over conceptions of federalism led once to Civil War on the one hand, while differences over the meaning and scope of the separation of powers has not. Indeed, the separation of powers operates in the orbit of the Lovers' Quarrel. The reason, I propose, is that when the framers gathered in Philadelphia, they were not dealing with a *tabula rasa* with regard to federalism, though to a much greater extent they were when it came to the separation of powers. The Federalists understood the Anti-Federalists' fear of consolidation, which was why they wisely and calculatedly proposed horizontal dispersion in return for vertical concentration. It was the latter proposal, of course, that proved to be the major source of quarrel; and this had much to do with the fact that while there was a prior conception of federalism, there had not been a separation of powers until the Second Founding. As Richard Neustadt has noted, the separation of powers is better understood as the blending of powers ("separate institutions sharing powers").[32] As I argued toward the end of Chapter 2, the Second Founders had a free hand to mix and match because the prior situation was wholly unseparated. The Articles had neither an executive nor a judiciary (with the trivial exception that Congress had the authority, by Article 9, to appoint courts "for the trial of piracies and felonies"), so the debate over the horizontal division of powers was a relatively abstract debate with malleable sides because no one had had a prior experience of what they were proposing at the federal level. On the one side, since there was no executive (just a president of the Congress) in the Articles, any reform, as long as it included an executive, would have been an infinite (from nothing to something) improvement for the Federalists who were looking for more "energetic" government. On the other, because there was no separation of powers to begin with in the Articles—since there was only a single, unicameral legislative branch—any new system that introduced at least a modicum of separation would have been an improvement for the Anti-Federalists, who acknowledged the weaknesses of the confederation but feared legislative Leviathan. As a result, at the start of the convention, there was general agreement that an executive branch and the separation of powers were necessary, and this was a consensus registered in both the Virginia and New Jersey plans.[33] There was some disagreement, but not a Lovers' Quarrel, about the separation of powers.

Federalism, however, was an entirely more divisive matter. The Virginia Plan proposed centralized federalism and a bicameral legislature, while the New Jersey Plan proposed peripheralized federalism and a unicameral legislature with each state equally represented with a single vote, as the states had been under the Articles.[34] The conventional metaphor for federalism understood as the "splitting" of the atom of sovereignty misleadingly implies that the atom was not already split in 1787, and that the Federalists were the ones who had discovered federalism in any of its variant forms.[35] While powers, previously vested entirely in the legislature in the Articles of Confederation, were divided in 1787, sovereignty had *already* been split by 1787. The Federalists can take no credit for the latter. If anything, the Second Founders were trying to pull together what the First Founders had left apart by inventing a new federalism in contradistinction to the old confederalism. As a result, the conservative, Anti-Federalist response to this innovation set up a very different bargaining game than the one over the separation of powers. Any new constitution, as long as it created and layered a new sovereignty on the old, meant a net loss of state autonomy for the Anti-Federalists.[36] It should not be surprising, then, that while the Federalists got as much if not more than they asked for in the unity and strength of the executive, they ended up with much less than they wanted in the strength of the Union. In fact, the debate over the executive and the separation of powers in 1787 and 1788 ultimately fell in the shadow of the Lovers' Quarrel, with modulations in the former debate necessitated by the outcome of the latter (such as most clearly seen in the composition of the Electoral College).

Appendix II

THE FEDERALIST LEGACY

	Federalist	Civil War Republican (Second Federalist Moment)	New Deal Democratic (Third Federalist Moment)
I. Union	Created "a more perfect Union" of individuals ("We the People") in an extended republic and layered it on top of 13 state sovereignties.	Universalized the rights of Englishmen to apply to all individuals in the union, turned the "union," which the Confederacy used to describe a *relationship* between the states, into an *entity*—a stronger nation.	Expanded the meaning of the American social contract and offered a "New Deal" for the American people to include a "second [economic] Bill of Rights" for all citizens.
II. Liberty	Committed to positive liberty and the need for governmental power to solve collective problems and protect individual rights, understood equality and justice to be end-state conditions guaranteed by government, created a national government and chartered the First Bank of the United States using an elastic interpretation of the Constitution.	Proposed a "new birth of freedom" in place of a previously negative conception of liberty, celebrated a government of, for, and by the people, used federal powers liberally to save the Union and to liberate individuals bonded in slavery.	Summoned the federal government to face the national crisis that was the Great Depression, embarked on fiscal spending to increase employment, created a welfare state to provide a social safety net, stretched the meaning of "interstate commerce."

continued

(continued)

	Federalist	Civil War Republican (Second Federalist Moment)	New Deal Democratic (Third Federalist Moment)
III. Truth	Pragmatic and forward-looking, trusted in reason, invented a new "science" and committed only to the relative truth produced when ambition counteracts ambition.	Understood the perfectability of the Union as an ongoing project, created and relied on new institutions to wage war and to manage the economy, stood on the fence initially about slavery and then abolished it.	Set up a Brain Trust, embraced federalism not to decentralize decision making but to experiment on new ideas, inaugurated interest-group liberalism.
IV. Republicanism	Distrustful of "pure" democracy and fearful of majority faction, affirmed a national republicanism, adhered to a trusteeship model of virtuous representation where the passions of the people would be filtered, created the Senate and an unelected judicial branch.	Dismissed the idea of "popular sovereignty," argued that it was the Constitution that granted legitimacy to the states and not the reverse, adopted an Hamiltonian understanding of prerogative to set new milestones for federal authority.	Understood the Constitution's clauses to be elastic, used the Fireside Chats to educate the people about governmental policies and to familiarize them with the federal government, attempted to pack the Court.

Appendix III

THE ANTI-FEDERALIST LEGACY

	Anti-Federalist	Jeffersonian Republican (First Anti-Federalist Moment)	Jacksonian Democratic (Second Anti-Federalist Moment)	Progressive (Third Anti-Federalist Moment)	Reagan Republican (Fourth Anti-Federalist Moment)
I. Union	Preferred to retain "a league of friendship" among small, virtuous republics.	Insisted that the Constitution was a compact between states.	Understood the Union to be a Confederacy with very limited powers given to the federal government.	Accepted a Union of individuals and advocated nationalized democracy (like the Federalists), but also encouraged local democracy and "parastate" organizations.	Advocated a "New Federalism," called Union a "federation of sovereign states."
II. Liberty	Committed to negative liberty, believed that rights are antecedent to powers and were therefore jealous about states' rights, committed to equality only as a start-state condition, rejected the need for a federal government to proffer national solutions, and insisted on the codification of a Bill of Rights to keep federal power in check.	Asserted the states' right of "interpositioning" in the Kentucky and Virginia Resolutions, rejected the constitutionality of the proposed First Bank of the United States, advocated fiscal restraint, and understood federal powers only to be those enumerated and not implied by the Constitution.	Fierce defender of states' rights, advocated low tariffs and frugal government, preempted the advent of the bureaucratic state by creating the "state of courts and parties," and understood federal powers only to be those enumerated and not implied by the Constitution.	Believed in freedom from the corrupt bosses and the party state as they built an "associative" and fledgling bureaucratic state and other nongovernmental institutions, codified constitutional amendments instead of stretching textual meanings interpretively.	Believed that government is the problem and not the solution, grafted the language of individual rights onto the traditional language of states' rights, attempted to roll back the welfare state, advocated low taxes and fiscal austerity, committed to "originalism."

	Anti-Federalist	Jeffersonian Republican (First Anti-Federalist Moment)	Jacksonian Democratic (Second Anti-Federalist Moment)	Progressive (Third Anti-Federalist Moment)	Reagan Republican (Fourth Anti-Federalist Moment)
III. Truth	Idealistic and conservative, steadfastly committed to principles derived from custom and experience, believed in an absolute Truth, advocated "seminaries of useful learning" so that civic principles can be cultivated.	Stood on principle with France against England in the 1790s, mounted the Counter-Revolution of 1800, celebrated the values of the yeomanry, and purchased the Louisiana Territories in part to encourage the expansion of the virtuous republic.	Unconvinced that internal improvements were necessary, vetoed the Second Bank, asserted the president's duty to judge the constitutionality of public law, and facilitated Indian removal to cultivate a virtuous squirearchy.	Nostalgic about an era before corruption tainted the republic, distrustful of the checks and balances and the Newtonian Constitution, believed in the monolithism of the common good and the uniformity of public opinion.	Conservative and principled, cultivated the Religious Right to promote values rather than reason, trusted in the wisdom of the virtuous entrepreneurship.
IV. Republicanism	Distrustful of aristocracy and committed to classical, states-centered republicanism, pure democracy, and majority rights; preferred a mirroring theory of descriptive representation; regarded the Senate and Supreme Court as aristocratic institutions.	Understood majority as "the vital principle of republics," embraced extra-constitutional entities like parties and public opinion, democratized presidential prerogative.	Created the Democratic Party, understood rights as majority rights; practiced the "popular arts" so that the Election of 1828 would be the precursor to modern, personal campaigns.	Possessed an unfettered faith in direct democracy and public opinion, inaugurated the Rhetorical Presidency, advocated the theory of "leadership by interpretation" that blurred the distinction between the ruler and the ruled, attacked the Supreme Court and Article 5 of the Constitution.	Oversaw the flowering of plebiscitary democracy, adopted the mirroring theory of representation, rejected liberal paternalism, objected to judicial activism.

NOTES

Preface

1. Although some might prefer "Antifederalist," I follow Herbert Storing and Forrest MacDonald in using the hyphenated "Anti-Federalist" to designate the group and philosophy. I do this to highlight the distinction between them and the Federalists, that the one defines the other, and that it is the very meaning of federalism that animates the quarrel between the two. See Herbert J. Storing and Murray Dry (eds.), *The Complete Anti-Federalist*, 7 vols. (Chicago, IL: University of Chicago Press, 1981), 1: 79; Forrest MacDonald, "The Anti-Federalists, 1781–1789," *Wisconsin Magazine of History*, Spring 1963, 206–214, 206. When New Hampshire became the ninth state to ratify the Constitution in June 1788, most Anti-Federalists acquiesced in the legitimacy of the Constitution; when they did, they became former Anti-Federalists. But most did not become Federalists. The two famous exceptions, of course, are John Hancock and Edmund Randolph, who were converted to the Federalist cause, possibly, by the potential rewards of the vice presidency and attorney generalship respectively. The majority of former Anti-Federalists, as I show in Chapter 2, became critics of the Washington and Adams administration, and would soon transition into the Jeffersonian Republican persuasion and party.
2. David J. Siemers, *The Antifederalists: Men of Great Faith and Forbearance* (Lanham, MD: Rowman & Littlefield, 2003), 6.
3. The *Federalist Papers* may not even fully capture the Federalist position, since the arch Federalist posture can sometimes be found only in more private and obscure writings. A welcome expansion to the genre is Colleen A. Sheehan and Gary L. McDowell (eds.), *Friends of the Constitution: Writings of the "Other" Federalists, 1787–1788* (Indianapolis, IN: Liberty Fund, 1998).
4. Paul Finkelman, "Turning Losers into Winners: What Can We Learn, If Anything, From the Antifederalists?" *Texas Law Review* 79 (2001): 849–894, 854.
5. For a proponent of the view that the purists among the Federalists were the majority, see Martin Diamond, "The Federalist's View of Federalism," in George C. Benson (ed.), *Essays in Federalism* (Claremont, CA: Institute for Studies in Federalism, 1962), 21–64.
6. On Anti-Federalism through the Jacksonian era, see Richard E. Ellis, "The Persistence of Antifederalism after 1789," in Richard Beeman, Stephen Botein, and Edward C. Carter (eds.), *Beyond Confederation: Origins of the Constitution and American National Identity* (Chapel Hill, NC: University of North Carolina Press, 1987), 295–314; Saul A. Cornell, "The Changing Historical Fortunes of the Anti-Federalists," *Northwestern University Law Review* 70 (1989): 39–74; John A. Aldrich and Ruth W. Grant, "The Anti-Federalists, the First Congress, and the First Parties," *Journal of Politics* 55 (1993): 295–326. On republicanism, see Gordon S. Wood, *The Creation of the American Republic: 1776–1787*

(Chapel Hill, NC: University of North Carolina Press, 1969); J. G. A. Pocock, *The Machiavellian Moment: Florentine Political Thought and the Atlantic Republican Tradition* (Princeton, NJ: Princeton University Press, 1975); Paul A. Rahe, *Republics Ancient and Modern: Classical Republicanism and the American Revolution* (Chapel Hill, NC: University of North Carolina Press, 1992).

7. Morton Borden (ed.), *The Antifederalist Papers* (East Lansing, MI: Michigan State University Press, 1965); Cecelia Kenyon (ed.), *The Antifederalists* (Indianapolis, IN: Bobbs-Merrill, 1966); Storing and Murray Dry (eds.), *The Complete Anti-Federalist.*

8. Storing and Dry (eds.), *The Complete Anti-Federalist*, 1: 72.

9. Siemers, *The Antifederalists*, 1.

10. For an account of this synthesis of American revolutionary thought that pervaded what I call the First Founding, see Michael P. Zuckert, *Natural Rights and the New Republicanism* (Princeton, NJ: Princeton University Press, 1994).

11. William H. Riker, *The Strategy of Rhetoric: Campaigning for the American Constitution* (New Haven, CT: Yale University Press, 1996).

12. Bruce Ackerman, *We the People: Transformations* (Cambridge, MA: Belknap Press, 1998), 34.

13. Candidus, 12/6/1787, in Storing and Dry (eds.), *The Complete Anti-Federalist*, 4: 126 (4.9.8).

14. Arthur M. Schlesinger, Jr., "The Tides of National Politics," *Paths to the Present* (New York: Macmillan, 1949), 77–92; Walter D. Burnham, *Critical Elections and the Mainsprings of American Politics* (New York: W. W. Norton, 1970).

15. Samuel P. Huntington, *American Politics: The Promise of Disharmony* (Cambridge, MA: Harvard University Press, 1981); James Morone, *Hellfire Nation: The Politics of Sin in American History* (New Haven, CT: Yale University Press, 2003).

16. Paul A. Varg, *Foreign Policies of the Founding Fathers* (East Lansing, MI: Michigan State University Press, 1963), 73–79.

17. For Madison's attack on the Anti-Federalists as mediocre leaders contriving to preserve their privileges in their small political ponds, see Drew McCoy, *The Republic in Peril* (Chapel Hill, NC: University of North Carolina Press, 1976), 121–132.

18. David S. Heidler and Jeanne T. Heidler (eds.), *Encyclopedia of the War of 1812* (Annapolis, MD: Naval Institute Press, 1997), 181.

19. John E. Acton, *The History of Freedom and Other Essays* (London: Macmillan and Co., 1907), 62.

Chapter 1

1. Pennsylvania Gazette, 9/5/1787, cited in Isaac Kramnick (ed.), *The Federalist Papers* (New York: Viking Penguin, 1987), 16.

2. For accounts of Anti-Federalist political thought, see Herbert J. Storing and Murray Dry (eds.), *The Complete Anti-Federalist*, 7 vols. (Chicago, IL: University of Chicago Press, 1981), 1: *passim*; David J. Siemers, *The Antifederalists: Men of Great Faith and Forbearance* (Lanham, MD: Rowman & Littlefield, 2003); Saul Cornell, *The Other Founders: Anti-Federalism and the Dissenting Tradition in America, 1788–1828* (Chapel Hill, NC: University of North Carolina Press, 1999); Jackson Turner Main, *The Anti-Federalists: Critics of the Constitution* (New York: W. W. Norton, [1961] 1976).

3. James D. Hunter, *Culture Wars: The Struggle To Control The Family, Art, Education, Law, And Politics In America* (New York: Basic Books, 1992); Nolan McCarty, Keith T. Poole, and Howard Rosenthal, *Polarized America: The Dance of Ideology and Unequal Riches* (Cambridge, MA: MIT Press, 2008); Jacob S. Hacker and Paul Pierson, *Winner-Take-All Politics: How Washington Made the Rich Richer—and Turned Its Back on the Middle Class* (New York: Simon & Schuster, 2010); Alan I. Abramowitz, *The Disappearing Center: Engaged Citizens, Polarization, and American Democracy* (New Haven, CT: Yale

University Press, 2011); Daniel T. Rodgers, *Age of Fracture* (Cambridge, MA: Belknap Press, 2011); E. J. Dionne, Jr., *Our Divided Political Heart: The Battle for the American Idea in an Age of Discontent* (New York: Bloomsbury, 2012).

4. *E Pluribus Unum*, or "out of many, one," was the *de facto* motto of the United States found on the Seal of the United States that was first publicly used in 1782. The motto was changed in 1956 when, at the height of the Cold War against communism (and therefore atheism), Congress passed a law (36 U.S.C. 302, see http://www.gpo.gov/fdsys/pkg/CRPT-112hrpt47/html/CRPT-112hrpt47.htm, accessed 10/12/2012) adopting "In God We Trust" as the nation's official motto. By my telling, the older motto bears the true imprint and puzzle of American identity.

5. In their introductory textbook to American Government, Marc Landy and Sidney Milkis had also characterized the debate over the Constitution as a "lovers' quarrel." However, they present the debate as between rights and democracy, and not between Two Foundings, or two conceptions of union and federalism. See Marc Landy and Sidney M. Milkis, *American Government: Balancing Democracy and Rights*, 2nd Edition (New York: Cambridge University Press, 2008), 79.

6. The Articles of Confederation had fallen into relative disrepute by 1787, so the Anti-Federalists and their followers turned first to the Declaration, and later also to the Bill of Rights, as the foundational texts of their faith.

7. Jefferson generally thought that the Bill of Rights was the Declaration by another name. "With respect to the declaration of rights," he wrote, "I suppose the majority of the United states are of my opinion: for I apprehend all the antifederalists, and a very respectable proportion of the federalists think that such a declaration should now be annexed." That he referred to the Bill as a "Declaration," I suggest, reveals the rough equivalence in his mind, since both the Declaration and the Bill of Rights were negative instruments, immunities against consolidated power. See Thomas Jefferson to F. Hopkinson (3/13/1789), in Thomas J. Randolph (ed.), *Memoirs, Correspondences, and Private Correspondences of Thomas Jefferson* (London: Henry Colburn and Richard Bentley, 1829), 2: 442.

8. To cut down on the number of footnotes, I do not fully cite the *Federalist Papers* I quote in this book. The full text of these *Papers* can be found, among numerous other places, at http://thomas.loc.gov/home/histdox/fedpapers.html (accessed 7/1/2012).

9. For more on the distinction between rights and powers, see Sonu S. Bedi, "Judging without Rights: Public Reason and the Counter Majoritarian Difficulty," *Studies in Law, Politics, and Society* 58 (2012): 1–28.

10. In its attention to collective community goals, the Constitution is also rather more like Magna Carta's lesser known but equally important companion text, the Charter of the Forest issued in 1217, which protected the people's access to the commons. See Peter Linebaugh, *The Magna Carta Manifesto: Liberty and Commons for All* (Berkeley, CA: University of California Press, 2008).

11. Hannah Arendt, *On Revolution* (New York: Penguin, 1963), 33; see also B. Honig, "Declarations of Independence: Arendt and Derrida on the Problem of Founding a Republic," *American Political Science Review*: 85 (1991): 97–113, 98. Arendt's insightful analysis about the coercive nature of self-evident truths might have been further sharpened had she acknowledged the distinction between the Two Foundings. For Arendt, "foundings" are ineluctably political, illegal, contingent. But Publius partially and quite uniquely escapes this charge because of the Two Foundings. What Arendt called "Sieyès's vicious cycle"—the idea that those who create a new constitutional order must, paradoxically, have first stood outside of it and appealed to a different authority which, by the law of transitivity, would assume higher moral precedence than the creation it helped sanction—was averted in the Second Founding because the Second Founders were able to borrow from the legitimacy of their half-brothers in the regime, the First Founders. Because the First Founding had already reached for ancient sources

of legitimacy external to the regime to establish the sovereignty of the states, the Second Founders did not have to appeal to God, natural law, or some other higher authority. Instead, they were able to ride on, while partially displacing, the sovereignty of the states in their delivery of the new United States. The cost of escaping the vicious circle of constitutional and extra-constitutional sources of legitimacy, of course, has been a Lovers' Quarrel about the principles of the Two Foundings. But at least this is a debate internal to the American regime and arguably less prone to convulsive outcomes. With the Second Founding, politics became the American answer to revolution.

12. John Adams to Abigail Adams, 7/3/1776, in John Adams, Abigail Adams, and Charles F. Adams, *Familiar Letters of John Adams and his Wife Abigail Adams, During the Revolution* (New York: Hurd and Houghton, 1876), 193–194.

13. This is also to say that the First Founding was a qualitatively different kind of "founding" than the Second, because it drew its legitimacy from *beyond* the people and the act of contracting—hence the value of distinguishing between the Two Foundings. Those, for example, who argue that the "founding" was based on God's law or natural rights belong to this tradition. The Second Founding, in contrast, draws its legitimacy *entirely* from the architectonic act of "founding" by We the People. The Second Founding is more substantially performative than the First because it does more than declare a state of affairs; it also *constituted* a new nation.

14. Congress in 2004 established September 17 as Constitution Day and Citizenship Day (36 U.S.C. 106), but the holiday has not caught on; it pales, certainly, in comparison to the symbolic pull of July 4. This too, is revealing, for it tells us that most Americans' hearts are with the First Founding, even if their minds are (or should be) with the Second. The Lovers' Quarrel transpires within individuals too. See http://www.law.cornell.edu/uscode/text/36/106 (accessed 10/4/2012).

15. Therefore, the American constitutional ontology privileges federal powers first, states' rights second, and individual rights at a distant third, relevant only to the extent that the third would be coopted by and conjoined with the first after the Civil War. Since the states' bills or declarations of rights are a statement of individual (and not states') rights, it is instructive to observe how late some of them were enacted. Although five states (Maryland, North Carolina, New Jersey, Virginia, and Pennsylvania) were quick to enact such bills either as separate texts or as part of their state constitutions in or around 1776, quite a few took their time. Massachusetts (1780), Connecticut (1818), and Rhode Island (1842) were late because they were equally late in enacting their first constitutions, so they tell us a little less. However, it says something about the relative unimportance of individual rights in America's constitutional ontology that New Hampshire ratified its own Bill of Rights in 1783, New York in 1787, Delaware in 1792, Georgia in 1861, and South Carolina only in 1970.

16. Of course, the principles of the First Founding were not, technically, prepolitical, though they felt more natural and unforced than those of the Second Founding in part because the colonies had already been organized as communities (later states) for over a century by the time they cast off the British yoke.

17. Charles Thach, *The Creation of the Presidency, 1775–1789* (Baltimore, MD: Johns Hopkins University Press, 1922); Roger H. Brown, *Redeeming the Republic: Federalists, Taxation, and the Origins of the Constitution* (Baltimore, MD: Johns Hopkins University Press, 1993).

18. So a functionalist account of the ideological difference between the Federalists and the Anti-Federalists is that while the former were interested in the pursuit of non-rivalrous, non-excludable public goods such as common defense that return a positive externality to all states in the union, the Anti-Federalists focused on guarding particular goods such as the right to bear arms with little or no externality impact. On how the nature of goods lined up best with the level of governmental provision, see Ronald McKinnon and Thomas Nechyba, "Competition in Federal Systems: The Federal Role of Political and Financial Constraints," in John Ferejohn and Barry R. Weingast (eds.), *The New*

Federalism: Can the States be Trusted? (Stanford, CA: Hoover Institution Press, 1997), 3–65, 5–9. On functionalist versus political theories of federalism, see Paul Peterson, *The Price of Federalism* (Washington, DC: Brookings Institution Press, 1995).

19. Charles R. Kesler and Clinton Rossiter (eds.), *The Federalist Papers* (New York: Penguin Putnam, 2003), xxviii.

20. CNN Political Unit, Transcript of Wednesday's presidential debate, 10/4/2012, available at http://www.cnn.com/2012/10/03/politics/debate-transcript/index.html (accessed 10/4/2012).

21. John Kincaid, "Federalism and Community in the American Context," *Publius* 20 (1990), 69–87, 71. Kincaid's account of federalism stands closer to the Anti-Federalist, confederal archetype than the Federalist one. After all, the idea of *communitas communitatum*, though a medieval idea, has, since the early modern era, been almost exclusively used to characterize a single state. On this, see John N. Figgis, *Studies of Political Thought from Gerson to Grotius, 1414–1625* (Cambridge, UK: Cambridge University Press, 1907), 51.

22. On positive liberty, see J. David Greenstone, "Political Culture and American Political Development: Liberty, Union, and the Liberal Bipolarity," *Studies in American Political Development* 1 (1986): 1–49. The Supreme Court had held, in *Barron v. Baltimore*, 32 U.S. 243 (1833), that the Bill of Rights applied only to the federal government. This would change, as I argue in Chapter 4, with the ratification of the Fourteenth Amendment after the Civil War. A more trenchant expansion in the applicability of the Bill of Rights to state governments would occur in *Gitlow v. New York*, 268 U.S. 652 (1925), when the Court upheld a New York law that made it a crime to advocate for the overthrow of government by force. Critically, however, the Court invoked the "due process" clause of the Fourteenth Amendment—a legacy of Reconstruction—to affirm that the First Amendment applied to both the federal *and* state governments. The Court would go on to incorporate more rights under the banner of "due process" in *De Jonge v. Oregon*, 299 U.S. 353 (1937), *Wolf v. Colorado*, 338 U.S. 25 (1949), and *Gideon v. Wainwright*, 372 U.S. 335 (1963).

23. Sidney II, 2/21/1788, in Storing and Dry (eds.), *The Complete Anti-Federalist*, 6: 97 (6.8.10).

24. William Riker has argued that what changed from the first to the second Constitution was "peripheralized federalism" to "centralized federalism." See Riker, *Federalism*, 5.

25. Cecilia Kenyon, "Men of Little Faith: Antifederalists on the Nature of Representative Government," *William and Mary Quarterly* 12 (1955): 3–43.

26. This distinction also translates, roughly, to the "person to person" versus "issue-oriented" representative styles observed in Richard Fenno, "U.S. House Members in their Constituencies: An Exploration," *American Political Science Review* 71 (1977): 883–917.

27. Gordon S. Wood, *The Creation of the American Republic: 1776–1787* (Chapel Hill, NC: University of North Carolina Press, 1969), 606.

28. J. G. A. Pocock, *The Machiavellian Moment: Florentine Political Thought and the Atlantic Republican Tradition* (Princeton, NJ: Princeton University Press, 1975), 522.

29. Wood, *The Creation of the American Republic*, 610.

30. Madison understood the opposite of an extended republic to be "simple democracy or a pure republic." See James Madison to Thomas Jefferson, 10/24/1787, James Madison, *Letters and Other Writings of James Madison*, 4 vols. (New York: R. Worthington, 1884), 1: 350.

31. James Ceaser, *Presidential Selection: Theory and Development* (Princeton, NJ: Princeton University Press, 1979).

32. Cato IV, 11/8/1787, in Storing and Dry (eds.), *The Complete Anti-Federalist*, 2: 115 (2.6.30).

33. Gerald De Maio and Douglas Muzzio, "The Will of the Community: Theories of Representation at Founding and in Recent Political Practice," *Commonwealth* 5 (1991): 32–56.

34. Speech of Melancton Smith, New York Ratification Convention, 6/21/1788, in Storing and Dry (eds.), *The Complete Anti-Federalist*, 6: 157 (6.12.15). Contrary to Yarborough, who had argued that the intellectual descendants of the Anti-Federalists are the proponents of interest-group representation, I propose that the Anti-Federalists did not take the next logical step of advocating proportional representation *because* they were committed to majoritarian rule. Madison, after all, had charged in Federalist 10 that "theoretic politicians, who have patronized this species of government, have erroneously supposed that by reducing mankind to a perfect equality in their political rights, they would, at the same time, be perfectly equalized and assimilated in their possessions, their opinions, and their passions." See Jean Yarborough, "Representation and Republicanism," *Publius* 9 (1979): 77–98, 88.

35. Hartz, *The Liberal Tradition in America*; Wood, *The Creation of the American Republic*; Joyce Appleby, "What is Still American in the Political Philosophy of Thomas Jefferson?" *William and Mary Quarterly* 39 (1982): 287–309; Rahe, *Republics Ancient and Modern*; Daniel T. Rodgers, "Republicanism: The Career of a Concept," *Journal of American History* 74 (1992): 11–38.

36. See Greenstone, "Political Culture and American Political Development," 6. Greenstone argues that republicanism is consistent with liberalism because of shared commitments such as the fear of government, and the importance of the independent citizen. On how the liberalism–republicanism scholarly debate has contributed little to our understanding of the American Union, see Rogan Kersh, *Dream of a More Perfect Union* (Ithaca, NY: Cornell University Press, 2001), 3–4.

37. Thomas Pangle, *The Spirit of Modern Republicanism: The Moral Vision of the American Founders and the Philosophy of Locke* (Chicago, IL: University of Chicago Press, 1990); Michael P. Zuckert, *Natural Rights Republic: Studies in the Foundation of the American Political Tradition* (Notre Dame, IN: University of Notre Dame Press, 1997).

38. Wood, *The Creation of the American Republic*; Donald S. Lutz, "The Relative Influence of European Thinkers of Late Eighteenth-Century American Political Thought," *American Political Science Review* 78 (1984): 189–197. Lutz had found in his study of American revolutionary literature from 1760 to 1805 that Montesquieu was cited more often than any other thinker, followed by Blackstone and Locke. Locke, however, did dominate in the 1760s. Although the Anti-Federalists frequently invoked Montesquieu in support of their objections in particular to the Senate and also to make their case for a small republic, they did so because Madison drew even more heavily on the "great oracle" (Federalist 47) in support of the importance of institutional design (the separation of powers) as a safeguard against human passions.

39. If the Federalists and Anti-Federalists were espousing two theories of liberalism and republicanism with opposite features, Hartz and Wood may both be correct. The Anti-Federalists were liberal in their attitude against the federal government and committed to republican self-rule within their state boundaries, while the Federalists were nationally republican across state boundaries and liberal in their attitude toward factions that could dominate in state legislatures. Relatedly, Rogers Smith's argument that American history is a synthesis not only of a liberal-democratic tradition, but also "illiberal" ones, may arise from the fact that our conceptions of who we are have always been a mixture of Federalist theories of representation, which relied on the heterogeneity of a large republic to prevent the tyranny of the majority, as well as Anti-Federalist theories of representation that highlighted the homogeneity of small republics as a bulwark against misrepresentation. See Rogers Smith, *Civic Ideals: Conflicting Visions of Citizenship in US History* (New Haven, CT: Yale University Press, 1997).

40. On the concept of resilience, see "Resilience as the Explanandum of Social Theory" in Ian Shapiro and Sonu Bedi (eds.), *Political Contingency: Studying the Unexpected, the Accidental, and the Unforeseen* (New York: New York University Press, 2007), 79–96.

41. Louis Hartz, *The Liberal Tradition in America* (New York: Harcourt Brace, 1955).

42. Samuel P. Huntington, *American Politics: The Promise of Disharmony* (Cambridge, MA: Harvard University Press, 1981).

43. V. O. Key, "A Theory of Critical Elections," *Journal of Politics* 17 (1955): 3–18; Walter D. Burnham, *Critical Elections and the Mainsprings of American Politics* (New York: W. W. Norton, 1970).

44. Karen Orren and Stephen Skowronek, *The Search for American Political Development* (New York: Cambridge University Press, 2004), 123.

45. George Thomas, "What is Political Development? A Constitutional Analysis," *Review of Politics* 74 (2011): 275–294, 288.

46. For a discussion of certain types of ideas that are typically offered in political discourse as first principles beyond justification, see James W. Ceaser, "Foundational Concepts and American Political Development," in James W. Ceaser, Jack N. Rakove, Nancy L. Rosenblum, and Rogers M. Smith, *Nature and History in American Political Development: A Debate* (Cambridge, MA: Harvard University Press, 2006), 5.

47. Jeffrey K. Tulis, *The Rhetorical Presidency* (Princeton, NJ: Princeton University Press, 1987), 7.

48. Harvey C. Mansfield, Jr., *America's Constitutional Soul* (Baltimore, MD: Johns Hopkins University Press, 1991), 8.

49. Mansfield, *America's Constitutional Soul*, 5.

50. Karen Orren and Stephen Skowronek, "Editor's Preface," *Studies in American Political Development* 1 (1986): vii–viii, vii.

51. Orren and Skowronek, *The Search for American Political Development*, 14.

52. Orren and Skowronek, "Editor's Preface," viii.

53. Thomas, "What is Political Development?" 281.

54. On the differences between historical and rational-choice institutionalism, see Peter A. Hall and Rosemary C. R. Taylor, "Political Science and the Three Institutionalisms," *Political Studies* 44 (1996): 936–957. There are, of course, those in the APD camp who do not accept Orren and Skowronek's definition and its focus on institutions, and simply understand the field more generally to be about "Politics and History," or the historical study of politics. There are certainly valid methodological and even strategic reasons for a more inclusive and expansive definition of the field. However, I do not enter into direct conversation with these scholars because my concern is with the A in APD (and APT)—what is unique about American political development as opposed to political development writ large.

55. Paul Pierson, *Politics in Time: History, Institutions, and Social Analysis* (Princeton, NJ: Princeton University Press, 2004).

56. Orren and Skowronek, *The Search for American Political Development*, 113.

57. Pierson's term for "intercurrence," "conjunctures," is illuminative of the difference in perspective. Whereas "intercurrence" for Orren and Skowronek refers to an *ongoing* impingement of older over newer governing arrangements, "conjunctures" connotes a *momentary* "intersection." Even though Pierson rejects "snapshot" account of politics, his account nevertheless privileges a series of snapshots over the observation of simultaneously operating temporal orders. Pierson's interpretation of Orren and Skowronek's perspective belies a different type of institutionalist thinking (of institutions acting only "in time") than the one shared by them (of institutions acting also "over time" and especially "at the same time"). See Pierson, *Politics in Time*, 56; Orren and Skowronek, *The Search for American Political Development*, 81.

58. Margaret Levi, "A Model, a Method, and a Map: Rational Choice in Comparative and Historical Analysis," in Mark I. Lichbach and Alan S. Zukerman (eds.), *Comparative Politics: Rationality, Culture, and Structure* (New York: Cambridge University Press, 1997), 19–41, 28.

59. Pierson, *Politics in Time*, 31.

60. For a discussion of why APD focuses only on change that "ultimately registers its developmental significance in altered forms of government," see Orren and Skowronek, *The Search for American Political Development*, 24.

61. Bruce Ackerman, *We the People: Foundations* (Cambridge, MA: Belknap Press, 1991).

62. Bruce Ackerman, *We the People: Transformations* (Cambridge, MA: Belknap Press, 1998), 409.

63. Key, "A Theory of Critical Elections"; Burnham, *Critical Elections and the Mainsprings of American Politics*.

64. Richard Hofstadter, *The Age of Reform: From Bryan to FDR* (New York: Alfred Knopf, [1955] 1959), 17.

65. Karen Orren and Stephen Skowronek, "Have We Abandoned a 'Constitutional Perspective' on American Political Development?" *Review of Politics* 74 (2011): 295–299, 299.

66. Richard Bensel, "The Tension between American Political Development as a Research Community and as a Disciplinary Subfield," *Studies in American Political Development* 17 (2003): 103–106, 104. Oddly, though, of his own proposed definition, Bensel went on to suggest, "the modifier *American* could be replaced by any other national adjective or dispensed with altogether" (105).

67. John Burgess, *Political Science and Comparative Constitutional Law* (Boston, MA: Ginn, 1902); Charles Beard, *An Economic Interpretation of the Constitution* (London: Macmillan, 1913).

68. Orren and Skowronek, *The Search for American Political Development*, 6, 7.

69. Orren and Skowronek, *The Search for American Political Development*, 7.

70. Orren and Skowronek, *The Search for American Political Development*, 144.

71. The second Swiss constitution of 1874 had undergone over 140 revisions before it was updated and replaced by the new constitution of 1999.

72. See also John Finn, "Transformation or Transmogrification? Ackerman, Hobbes (as in Calvin and Hobbes), and the Puzzle of Changing Constitutional Identity," *Constitutional Political Economy* 10 (1999): 355–365. Orren and Skowronek appear to assume that geographical continuity is sufficient to establish that we are still at the same site.

73. Ackerman is right that the story of America's constitutional development has a lot to do with the episodic story of We the People, intermittently engaged in higher-lawmaking and lower-lawmaking (hence "dualism"). However, dualism as he understands it is a *structural* feature of any written constitution, because any polity that has codified a higher law and a method of its amendment would automatically have two lawmaking tracks. Ackerman is correct in his negative theses that our conflicts are political and not social, and that we are neither rights foundationalists nor monists, but he does not spell out *what* our struggle is about. Dualism does not explain why "unconventional adaptations" are the telltale features of our "constitutional moments." The Two Foundings, I propose, does. Unconventional adaptations occur exactly at the time when the principles of the Two Foundings are being forcibly reconciled, or creatively resynthesized. At such moments, APD is afoot.

74. During the Virginia ratification debates, Patrick Henry asked, "who authorized them to speak in the language of We, the People, and not We, the States . . . the people gave them no power to use their name." See Jonathan Elliot (ed.), *The Debates in the Several State Conventions on the Adoption of the Federal Constitution as Recommended by the General Convention at Philadelphia in 1787*, 4 vols. (Philadelphia, PA: J. B. Lippincott, 1836), 3: 54.

75. Martin Diamond, "The Ends of Federalism," in William A. Schambra (ed.), *As Far as Republican Principles Will Admit: Essays by Martin Diamond* (Washington, DC: American Enterprise Institute, 1992), 145; Martha Derthick, *Keeping the Compound Republic: Essays on American Federalism* (Washington, DC: Brookings Institution Press, 2001), 10; William Riker, *Federalism: Origin, Operation, Significance* (Boston, MA: Little, Brown, 1964), 12–13.

76. For the first group, see Bernard Bailyn, *The Ideological Origins of the American Revolution* (Cambridge, MA: Belknap Press, 1992); Paul A. Rahe, *Republics Ancient and Modern: Classical Republicanism and the American Revolution* (Chapel Hill, NC: University of North Carolina Press, 1992). For the second group, see Merrill Jensen, *The Articles of Confederation: An Interpretation of the Social and Constitutional History of the American Revolution 1774–1781* (Madison, WI: University of Wisconsin Press, 1940); Gary J. Schmitt and Robert H. Webking, "Revolutionaries, Antifederalists, and Federalists: Comments on Gordon Wood's Understanding of the American Founding," *First Principles* 9 (1979): 195–229. For the third group, see Alexis de Tocqueville, *Democracy in America*, 2 vols. (New York: Alfred A. Knopf, [1835–1840] 1945), 1: 112–114; John Fiske, *The Critical Period of American History 1783–1789* (Boston, MA: Houghton Mifflin, 1888); Max Farrand, "The Federal Constitution and the Defects of The Confederation," *American Political Science Review* 2 (1908): 532–544; Thach, *The Creation of the Presidency, 1775–1789*. The argument advanced by this last group, that the First Founding was a disaster to be superseded by the Second, was of course the one advanced by Publius in Federalist 15–22.

77. This was, to be sure, an outgrowth of the tradition of constitutionalism that the colonists inherited from Britain. Since the Glorious Revolution of 1688, British subjects in the United States had developed a distinct sense of their rights as Englishmen, who had overthrown the already limited British monarchy and replaced it with a constitutional monarchy, unlike the French, who had yet to overthrow absolutism. See Hannah Arendt, *On Revolution* (New York: Viking, 1963), 154.

78. Willi Paul Adams, *The First American Constitutions: Republican Ideology and the Making of the State Constitutions in the Revolutionary Era* (Lanham, MD: Rowman & Littlefield, 2001), 3. The two exceptions actually prove the rule. Connecticut's and Rhode Island's charters may be construed as their first state constitutions because they were secured by local leaders, and represented the most liberal charters secured from the Crown among the colonies, guaranteeing fundamental freedoms and self-government. Both colonies, for example, were the only ones that did not have royal governors and judges installed. Connecticut's Fundamental Orders of 1638–1639 was the first document written by a representative body in North America setting up a framework for government—it was the first American constitution. The Charter of 1662 was written by Connecticut's governor and leaders, modeled after the Fundamental Orders, and presented to Charles II. Indeed, in 1776, Connecticut's Governor Trumbull was the only governor who supported the Revolution. Having already humbled the Crown over a century ago, Connecticut's General Assembly saw no need for a new constitution and simply had it enacted "that the ancient form of civil government contained in the Charter from Charles the II, King of England, and adopted by the people of this state, shall be and remain the civil constitution of this state, under the sole authority of the people hereof, independent of any king or prince whatever." (See http://www.churchstatelaw.com/historicalmaterials/8_1_2_1. asp, accessed 7/12/2011.) Rhode Island, similarly, enjoyed among the greatest degree of independence from the Crown. Its Charter of 1663 was the first among the colonies to guarantee that "all and every person and persons may, from time to time, and at all times hereafter, freely and fully have and enjoy his and their own judgments and consciences, in matters of religious concernments." (See http://avalon.law.yale.edu/17th_century/ ri04.asp, accessed 7/12/2011.) Rhode Island was also the first to declare independence (on May 4, 1776) from the British Crown, jealous as it was of its liberties, so it is not surprising that it would be the last to ratify the Constitution (on May 29, 1790) among the 13 colonies/states.

79. Tocqueville, *Democracy in America*, 1: 164.

80. For an account of these constitutional conventions, see John J. Dinan, *The American State Constitutional Tradition* (Lawrence, KS: University Press of Kansas, 2006), 8–9.

81. The United States is also one of only three countries (with Jordan and Sri Lanka) that enacted the two and only two constitutions of their history, democratically or otherwise, in seven or fewer years. This meant that the different conceptions of union codified in the Articles of Confederation and the Constitution were starkly on display to the same political generation, undisguised by the passage of time. The federal countries of the world are, with the number of constitutions enacted in parenthesis, Argentina (3), Australia (1), Austria (3), Belgium (1), Brazil (7), Canada (1), the Federated States of Micronesia (1), Germany (5), India (1), Malaysia (1), Mexico (6), Nepal (4), Pakistan (3), Russia (6), Saint Kitts and Nevis (1), Switzerland (7), United Arab Emirates (1), United States (2), Venezuela (25). The list of countries to have enacted only two constitutions are Bahrain (1973, 2002), Bavaria (1808, 1818), Cote D'Ivoire (1960, 2000), Finland (1919, 1999), Gambia (1970, 1996), Iran (1906, 1979), Iraq (1958, 2005), Ireland (1922, 1937), Japan (1886, 1946), Jordan (1946, 1952), Kyrgyz Republic (1993, 2006), Liberia (1847, 1986), Libya (1951, 1969), Maldives (1968, 1998), Myanmar (1962, 1974), Philippines (1976, 1986), Senegal (1963, 2001), Seychelles (1979, 1993), Sri Lanka (1972, 1978), Swaziland (1968, 2005), Sweden (1809, 1974), Tuvalu (1978, 1986), Transvaal (1856, 1906), Trinidad and Tobago (1962, 1976), and the United States (1781, 1787). There are only six democracies in this set (Finland, Ireland, Japan, Sweden, Tuvalu, and the United States), as measured by a total Freedom House aggregate (political rights and civil liberties) score of 70. The time elapsed between the U.S.'s two constitutions is seven years, while the average time elapsed between the two constitutions of the other five democratic countries was 85.6 years. Data from Zachary Elkins, Tom Ginsburg, and James Melton, *Chronology of Constitutional Events, Version 1.1. Comparative Constitutions Project.* Last modified: May 12, 2010. Available at: http://www.comparativeconstitutionsproject. org/index.htm (accessed 7/25/2011).

82. Indeed, Publius' considerable achievement was exemplified in "the attachment to them [the 'Anti-Federalists'] of a word which denotes the reverse of their true belief." See Main, *The Antifederalists*, xl.

83. On these, see Ackerman, *We the People: Transformations*, 34–39.

84. Cincinnatus IV, 11/22/1787, in Storing and Dry (eds.), *The Complete Anti-Federalist*, 6: 20 (6.1.21).

85. As Article 2 of the Articles of Confederation stated, "Each state retains its sovereignty, freedom, and independence, and every Power, Jurisdiction, and right, which is not by this confederation expressly delegated to the United States, in Congress assembled."

86. William Symmes to Capt. Peter Osgood, Jr., 11/15/1787, in Storing and Dry (eds.), *The Complete Anti-Federalist*, 4: 61 (4.5.2).

87. William H. Riker, *The Strategy of Rhetoric: Campaigning for the American Constitution* (New Haven, CT: Yale University Press, 1996), 24.

88. This was an affirmation of the principles of the Northwest Ordinance of July 1787, which stripped all existing states' claims to the territory, provided government under the jurisdiction of Congress for the area north of the Great Lakes, west of the Ohio River, and east of the Mississippi River, secured a guarantee of the rights of the inhabitants, and paved the way for the westward expansion of the United States by the inclusion of new states rather than the expansion of the existing states. See Peter S. Onuf, *Statehood and Union: A History of the Northwest Ordinance* (Indianapolis, IN: Indiana University Press, 1987).

89. This, to be sure, was the Northern position as perhaps indelicately espoused by Lincoln when he argued before Congress on July 4, 1861, "By conquest or purchase the Union gave each of them whatever of independence and liberty it has. The Union is older than any of the states, and, in fact, it created them as states." See John G. Nicolay and John Hay (eds.), *Abraham Lincoln Complete Works*, 2 vols. (New York: The Century Company, 1894), 2: 64. By 1863, Lincoln had learned the error of his rhetorical ways, and harkened back to "four score and seven years ago" (1776), an era dear to the heart of the Confederacy.

Discerning presidents have followed suit to reach into the deep past of 1776, to a time before the Second Founding, to creatively reconcile the two sides of the Lovers' Quarrel.

90. For a contrary (neo-Federalist) view that posits that the states *fully* gave up their sovereignty in 1787–1788, see Akhil R. Amar, *America's Constitution: A Biography* (New York: Random House, 2006).

91. The other entrenched clause, regarding any amendments prohibiting the international slave trade, lapsed in 1808.

92. Although this appears only to be a formal point, since durable shifts in federal authority can occur without constitutional amendments, I would suggest that the formal strongly informs the extra-formal in American politics not only because the United States is a nation bound to a written Constitution, but also because the formal registers the reality that the deepest wells of legitimacy from which political actors must draw in American politics come from the codified principles of our Two Foundings, as I hope the subsequent chapters of this book will demonstrate.

93. Wood, *The Creation of the American Republic*, 562. For Wood, the founding is a bittersweet story of how the Federalists' republican ideology, itself a modification of classical republicanism to remedy its worst evils, was necessarily subverted by the necessity of ratification politics and democratic language.

94. Jackson Turner Main estimated the balance to be 48 percent for the Constitution and 52 percent against; Fink and Riker estimated it at around 50 percent to 46. See Main, *The Anti-Federalists*, 269; William H. Riker and Evelyn Fink, "The Strategy of Ratification," in Bernard Grofman and Donald Wittman (eds.), *The Federalist Papers and the New Institutionalism* (New York: Agathon Press, 1988), 220–255.

95. They are William R. Davie (NC), Oliver Ellsworth (CT), Elbridge Gerry (MA), William C. Houston (NJ), William Houston (GA), John Lansing, Jr. (NY), Alexander Martin (NC), Luther Martin (MD), George Mason (VA), James McClurg (VA), John F. Mercer (MD), William L. Pierce (GA), Edmund J. Randolph (VA), Caleb Strong (MA), George Wythe (VA), and Robert Yates (NY). These were men of considerable reputations too. Among them, for example, was Elbridge Gerry, who was one of only three men who had signed both the Declaration of Independence and the Articles of Confederation (the other two were Robert Morris and Roger Sherman).

96. Ackerman, *We the People: Foundations*, 243, 266.

97. The "paranoid style" of American politics, then, emerges not because, contra Richard Hofstadter, the political Right is always scrambling for a sense of national identity, but because the Anti-Federalist virtue of jealousy has always been a prominent element of the American political mindset. See Richard Hofstadter, *The Paranoid Style in American Politics and Other Essays* (New York: Vintage, 1967), 3–65.

98. Robert V. Remini, *Andrew Jackson and the Course of American Freedom, 1822–1832* (New York: Harper & Row, 1981), 147.

99. Samuel H. Beer, *To Make a Nation: The Rediscovery of American Federalism* (Cambridge, MA: Belknap Press, 1993), 1. For Beer, "the national idea . . . identifies the whole people of the nation as the source of the legitimate powers of any and all governments."

100. James A. Morone, *The Democratic Wish* (New York: Basic Books, 1990).

101. Morone, *The Democratic Wish*, 1.

102. Morone, *The Democratic Wish*, 4.

103. Ronald Reagan, Remarks at the Bicentennial Observance of the Battle of Yorktown in Virginia, 10/19/1981. Available at: http://www.presidency.ucsb.edu/ws/?pid=43151 (accessed 8/27/2011).

104. On the distinction between "political time," which is recurrent, and "secular time," which is conventionally calendric, see Stephen Skowronek, *The Politics Presidents Make: Leadership from John Adams to Bill Clinton* (Cambridge, MA: Belknap Press, 1997), 30.

105. Norman Jacobson, *Pride & Solace* (Berkeley, CA: University of California Press, 1978), 22–23.

Chapter 2

1. Ralph Ketcham, *Presidents Above Party: The First American Presidency, 1789–1829* (Chapel Hill, NC: University of North Carolina Press, 1989).

2. George Washington to Charles Carter, 1/12/1788, in Worthington C. Ford (ed.), *The Writings of George Washington*, 14 vols. (New York: G. P. Putnam's Sons, 1889–1893), 11: 210.

3. George Washington to Charles Carter, 12/14/1787, in Ford (ed.), *The Writings of George Washington*, 11: 210–211.

4. Thomas Jefferson to Mrs. John (Abigail) Adams, 2/22/1787, in Paul L. Ford, *The Works of Thomas Jefferson*, 12 vols. (New York: G. P. Putnam's Sons, 1894), 4: 370.

5. George Washington to James Madison, 5/11/1786, in Jared Sparks (ed.), *The Writings of George Washington* (Boston, MA: Russell, Odiorne, and Metcalf, 1835), 9: 208.

6. George Washington, Farewell Address, 9/19/1796, available online at http://www.presidency.ucsb.edu/ws/index.php?pid=65539 (accessed 6/22/2012).

7. An incumbent president warning against party on the eve of a presidential election where his own Vice President was a candidate, in any case, had to be making a political if not a partisan move. The passages in the address warning of foreign meddling were a reference to France's active intervention in support of Jefferson's candidacy in 1796. See Joseph Charles, *The Origins of the American Party System: Three Essays* (Williamsburg, VA: The Institute of Early American History and Culture, 1956), 48.

8. George Washington, Farewell Address, 9/19/1796.

9. Alexander DeConde, "Washington's Farewell, the French Alliance, and the Election of 1796," *The Mississippi Valley Historical Review* 43 (1957): 641–658.

10. William Giles to Thomas Jefferson, 3/16/1801, in Dice R. Anderson, *William B. Giles: A Study in the Politics of Virginia and the Nation* (Menasha, WI: George Banta Publishing, 1914), 77.

11. For an early account of the different approaches Hamilton and Madison proposed for controlling faction expressed in Federalist 9 and 10, respectively, see John Q. Adams, *An Eulogy on the Life and Character of James Madison* (Boston, MA: John H. Eastburn, 1836), 32.

12. That Washington enjoyed a close relationship with Hamilton is also another inconvenient fact that has been underplayed. Hamilton had served Washington, since 1777, as his aide-de-camp during the Revolutionary War, during which time he quickly earned a place in Washington's trusted inner circle. This relationship persisted when Washington placed him as head of Treasury. According to Martin Van Buren, when Washington was asked to pick between his Secretaries of State and Treasury, "he [Washington] gave the preference to Hamilton, and sustained him in the measures he proposed to carry out the policy he recommended." See Martin Van Buren, *An Inquiry into the Origin and Course of Political Parties in the United States* (New York: Hurd & Houghton, 1867), 73.

13. Stuart Leibiger, *Founding Friendship: George Washington, James Madison, and the Creation of the American Republic* (Charlottesville, VA: University Press of Virginia, 1999), 129.

14. William N. Chambers, *Political Parties in a New Nation: The American Experience, 1776–1809* (New York: Oxford University Press, 1963), 80.

15. George Washington to James McHenry, 9/30/1798, in Ford (ed.), *The Writings of George Washington*, 14: 105.

16. James M. Burns and Susan Dunn, *George Washington* (New York: Times Books, 2004), 68; Jeremy Bailey, *Thomas Jefferson and Executive Power* (New York: Cambridge University Press, 2007), 261; Clement Fatovic, "Constitutionalism and Presidential Prerogative: Jeffersonian and Hamiltonian Perspectives," *American Journal of Political Science* 48 (2004): 429–444.

17. H. W. Brands, *The Money Men* (New York: Atlas Books, 2006), 53; Ron Chernow, *Alexander Hamilton* (New York: Penguin, 2004), 348–352.

18. John Ferling, *The Ascent of George Washington: The Hidden Political Genius of an American Icon* (New York: Bloomsbury, 2009), 298.

19. Burns and Dunn, *George Washington*, 82.

20. Forrest McDonald, *Alexander Hamilton: A Biography* (New York: W.W. Norton & Company, 1979), 110.

21. James Monroe, "Some Observations on the Constitution," 1788, in Herbert J. Storing and Murray Dry (eds.), *The Complete Anti-Federalist*, 7 vols. (Chicago, IL: University of Chicago Press, 1981).

22. James Madison, "The Bank Bill, 2/8/1791," in Gaillard Hunt (ed.), *The Writings of James Madison: 1790–1802*, 9 vols. (New York: G. P. Putnam's Sons, 1900–1910), 6: 41.

23. Antonin Scalia, *A Matter of Interpretation: Federal Courts and the Law* (Princeton, NJ: Princeton University Press, 1998).

24. John C. Hamilton (ed.), *The Works of Alexander Hamilton*, 7 vols. (New York: John F. Trow, 1850), 2: 54.

25. On Madison's loss of faith in the extended republic and his importance in legitimating the Anti-Federalist opposition to Hamilton's policies, see David J. Siemers, *Ratifying the Republic: Anti-Federalists and Federalists in Constitutional Time* (Palo Alto, CA: Stanford University Press, 2002), 77–78.

26. James Madison to George Washington, 4/16/1787, in James Madison, *Letters and Other Writings of James Madison*, 4 vols. (New York: R. Worthington, 1884), 1: 287. It is also in this letter where Madison expresses his strong support of a federal veto, writing, "a negative *in all cases whatsoever* [original emphasis] on the legislative acts of the States, as heretofore exercised by the Kingly prerogative, appears to me to be absolutely necessary." Perhaps Madison was naive going into the Convention, thinking that the federal government would be the impartial umpire adjudicating the "rival and spiteful measures" of states against each other. Nevertheless, even if he came around later, the fact that matters is that Madison was partial going into the Convention and his initially Federalist persuasion was critical to the final equilibrium of the Convention's deliberations. For more on the determined position of the Federalists, including their strategy to force an up-or-down vote on the states without recourse to amendments, see William H. Riker, *The Strategy of Rhetoric: Campaigning for the American Constitution* (New Haven, CT: Yale University Press, 1996). For a different view emphasizing the consistency of Madison's views, see Gary Rosen, *American Compact: James Madison and the Problem of Founding* (Lawrence, KS: University Press of Kansas, 1999).

27. Forrest McDonald, *Novus Ordo Seclorum: The Intellectual Origins of the Constitution* (Lawrence, KS: University Press of Kansas, 1985), 208–209. Indeed, while Madison was the only person who took scrupulous notes of the Convention's proceedings, he was not its most frequent speaker, but the second at 171 speeches, after Gouverneur Morris, who delivered 173. One may hypothesize that Morris has not enjoyed as much attention in our historical accounts because he was, like Hamilton, decidedly of a more Federalist bent than Madison was, and so Madison won the title of fatherhood by virtue of history's median voter ("founder") theory. Having witnessed the horrors of the French Revolution, Morris was an ardent defender of a strong federal government, and as a member of the "Committee of Stile [*sic*] and Arrangement," he played the major role in determining the wording of the Constitution and in particular the united national purpose expressed in its Preamble. On Madison's opponents, see David Brian Robertson, "Madison's Opponents and Constitutional Design," *American Political Science Review* 99 (2005): 225–243.

28. Lynch has argued that the nationalist Madison was the one who had also proposed that state representation in both chambers of Congress would be based on population, which would have guaranteed Virginia's dominance; his views changed after the Great Compromise, which now meant that the small states were disproportionately represented in the Senate. See Joseph M. Lynch, *Negotiating the Constitution: The Earliest Debates over Original Intent* (Ithaca, NY: Cornell University Press, 1999), 2.

29. Richard K. Matthews, *If Men Were Angels: James Madison and the Heartless Empire of Reason* (Lawrence, KS: University Press of Kansas, 1995), 130.

30. James Madison to Thomas Jefferson, 10/17/1788, in James Madison, *Letters and Other Writings of James Madison*, 1: 424.

31. James Madison to George Eve, 1/2/1789, in Gaillard Hunt (ed.), *The Writings of James Madison: 1790–1802*, 9 vols. (G. P. Putnam's Sons, 1900–1910), 5: 320.

32. Charles F. Hobson, "The Negative on State Laws: James Madison, The Constitution, and the Crisis of Republican Government," *William and Mary Quarterly* 36 (1979): 215–223.

33. For an account that potentially reconciles the two Madisons outlined here, see Lance Banning, *The Sacred Fire of Liberty: James Madison & the Founding of the Federal Republic* (Ithaca, NY: Cornell University Press, 1995).

34. James Madison to Thomas Jefferson, 10/24/1787, in Madison, *Letters and Other Writings of James Madison*, 1: 347.

35. William Riker, *Federalism: Origin, Operation, Significance* (Boston, MA: Little, Brown, 1964), 21. The clause said: "*Resolved*, that each branch ought to possess the right of originating acts; that the national legislature ought to be empowered to enjoy the legislative right vested in congress, by the confederation; and moreover to legislate in all cases to which the separate States are incompetent, or in which the harmony of the United States may be interrupted by the exercise of individual legislation; to negative all laws passed by the several States, contravening in the opinion of the national legislature, the articles of union, or any treaty subsisting under the authority of the union; and to call forth the force of the union against any member of the union failing to fulfill its duty under the articles thereof." See Jonathan Elliot (ed.), *The Debates in the Several State Conventions on the Adoption of the Federal Constitution as Recommended by the General Convention at Philadelphia in 1787*, 5 vols. (New York: Burt Franklin, 1888), 5: 190.

36. Jack M. Balkin, *Living Originalism* (Cambridge, MA: Belknap Press, 2011), 3.

37. The future president James Garfield would say, at the end of the Civil War, that the Resolutions "contained the germ of nullification and secession, and we are today reaping the fruits." Cited in Chernow, *Alexander*, 574.

38. James Madison to Thomas Jefferson, 10/24/1787, in Madison, *Letters and Other Writings of James Madison*, 1: 347.

39. James Madison, Report on the Resolutions, 1799–1800, 1/19/1792, in Hunt (ed.), *The Writings of James Madison*, 6: 349.

40. Madison, Report on the Resolutions, 1799–1800, 1/19/1792, in Hunt (ed.), *The Writings of James Madison*, 6: 350.

41. Madison, Report on the Resolutions, 1799–1800, 1/19/1792, in Hunt (ed.), *The Writings of James Madison*, 6: 351.

42. Thomas Jefferson to James Madison, 8/23/1799, Appendix to *Library of Congress Information Bulletin*, August 4–11, 1947.

43. Joseph J. Ellis, *Founding Brothers: The Revolutionary Generation* (New York: Random House, 2000), 200.

44. Ethelbert D. Warfield, *The Kentucky Resolutions of 1798: An Historical Study* (New York: G. P. Putnam's Sons, 1887), 125–126.

45. Thomas Jefferson to Edward Carrington, 5/27/1788, Ford (ed.), *The Writings of Thomas Jefferson*, 5: 20.

46. Thomas Jefferson to Henry Lee, 5/8/1825, in Ford (ed.), *The Writings of Thomas Jefferson*, 10: 342.

47. Wilson Carey McWilliams, *The Idea of Fraternity in America* (Berkeley, CA: University of California Press, 1973), 209.

48. Gordon Wood, "The Political Ideology of the Founders," in Neil L. York (ed.), *Toward a More Perfect Union: Six Essays on the Constitution* (Provo, UT: Brigham Young University Press, 1988), 7–27, 9.

49. Letter to Spencer Roane, 9/6/1819, in Andrew A. Lipscomb (ed.), *Writings of Thomas Jefferson*, 20 vols. (Washington, DC: Thomas Jefferson Memorial Association, 1903–1907), 15: 212.

50. Thomas Jefferson, First Inaugural Address, 3/4/1801, available at http://www.presidency. ucsb.edu/ws/index.php?pid=25803 (accessed 5/25/2012).

51. Charles F. Adams (ed.), *The Works of John Adams, Second President of the United States*, 10 vols. (Boston, MA: Little and Brown, 1851), 4: 194.

52. Stephen Skowronek, *The Politics Presidents Make: Leadership from John Adams to Bill Clinton* (Cambridge, MA: Belknap Press, 1997), 73.

53. Merrill D. Peterson, *Thomas Jefferson and the New Nation* (New York: Oxford University Press, 1970), 687–688; John H. Makin and Norman J. Ornstein, *Debt and Taxes: How America Got into its Budget Mess and What to Do About it* (Washington, DC: American Enterprise Institute, 1994), 65.

54. Thomas Jefferson, Sixth Annual Message, 12/2/1806, available at http://www. presidency.ucsb.edu/ws/index.php?pid=29448 (accessed 5/25/2012).

55. Dumas Malone, *Jefferson and the Rights of Men* (Boston, MA: Little, Brown, 1951), 163–172.

56. Thomas Jefferson to John Adams, 11/13/1787, in Thomas J. Randolph (ed.), *The Writings of Thomas Jefferson: Memoir, Correspondences, and Miscellanies*, 4 vols. (Charlottesville, VA: F. Carr, 1829), 2: 266.

57. Thomas Jefferson to Edward Carrington, 12/21/1787, in Randolph (ed.), *The Writings of Thomas Jefferson*, 2: 278.

58. McWilliams, *The Idea of Fraternity in America*, 210.

59. Norman K. Risjord, *The Old Republicans: Southern Conservatism in the Age of Jefferson* (New York: Columbia University Press, 1965), 1.

60. Thomas Jefferson, Kentucky Resolutions of 1798 and 1799, in Jonathan Elliot (ed.), *The Debates in the Several State Conventions on the Adoption of the Federal Constitution as Recommended by the General Convention at Philadelphia in 1787*, 5 vols. (Philadelphia, PA: J. B. Lippincott, 1881), 4: 543.

61. Thomas Jefferson to Judge Johnson, 6/12/1823, in Ford (ed.), *The Works of Thomas Jefferson*, 12: 254.

62. Thomas Jefferson to M. D. Destutt Tracy, 1/26/1811, in Randolph (ed.), *The Writings of Thomas Jefferson*, 4: 162.

63. Major L. Wilson, "The 'Country' versus the 'Court': A Republican Consensus and Party Debate in the Bank War," *Journal of the Early Republic* 15 (1995): 619–647, 620.

64. Thomas Jefferson to John Jay, 8/23/1785, in Ford (ed.), *The Writings of Thomas Jefferson*, 4: 88.

65. Thomas Jefferson to Brigadier General George Rogers Clark, 12/25/1780, in Ford (ed.), *The Writings of Thomas Jefferson*, 2: 390.

66. Thomas Jefferson to James Madison, 12/20/1787, in Ford (ed.), *The Works of Thomas Jefferson*, 5: 374.

67. John C. Hammond, "'They are Very Much Interested in Obtaining an Unlimited Slavery': Rethinking the Expansion of Slavery in the Louisiana Purchase Territories, 1803-1805," *Journal of the Early Republic* 23 (2003): 353–380.

68. Thomas Jefferson, Second Inaugural Address, 3/4/1805, available at http://www. presidency.ucsb.edu/ws/index.php?pid=25804 (accessed 5/25/2012).

69. Patrick Henry, Virginia Ratifying Convention, 6/4/1788, in Elliot (ed.), *The Debates in the Several State Conventions*, 3: 22.

70. Thomas Jefferson to Samuel Kercheval, 7/12/1816, in Randolph (ed.), *The Writings of Thomas Jefferson*, 4: 287.

71. Kathryn Turner, "Federalist Policy and the Judiciary Act of 1801," *William and Mary Quarterly* 22 (1965): 3–22.

72. William Giles to Thomas Jefferson, 3/16/1801, in Anderson, *William B. Giles*, 77.

73. Samuel Chase, "Charge delivered . . . at a circuit court of the United States," 5/2/1803, in Charles Evans, *Report of the Trial of the Hon. Samuel Chase* (Baltimore, MD: Samuel Butler and Charles Keatinge, 1805), 60, 61.

74. Thomas Jefferson to Henry Lee, 5/8/1825, in Ford (ed.), *The Writings of Thomas Jefferson*, 10: 343.

75. Bruce Ackerman, *The Failure of the Founding Fathers: Jefferson, Marshall, and the Rise of Presidential Democracy* (Cambridge, MA: Belknap Press, 2005), 5. On anti-intellectualism, see Richard Hofstadter, *Anti-intellectualism in American Life* (New York: Alfred Knopf, 1963); Elvin T. Lim, *The Anti-intellectual Presidency: The Decline of Presidential Rhetoric from George Washington to George W. Bush* (New York: Oxford University Press, 2008).

76. The amendment, which directed each Elector to cast separate votes for the President and Vice President, would preempt the possibility of electing a President and Vice President from different parties, as was the case in 1796, and ensure that both officers would always be elected as a ticket.

77. Richard E. Neustadt, *Presidential Power and the Modern Presidents: The Politics of Leadership from Roosevelt to Reagan* (New York: The Free Press, 1990); Arthur M. Schlesinger, Jr., *The Imperial Presidency* (New York: Mariner Books, 2004).

78. The Virginia Plan had provided for legislative election of the executive, which would be limited to one term, while the New Jersey Plan had proposed a plural executive. See Richard J. Ellis (ed.), *Founding the American Presidency* (Lanham, MD: Rowman & Littlefield, 1999), 31–33.

79. A Democratic Federalist, 10/17/1787, in Storing and Dry (eds.), *The Complete Anti-Federalist*, 3: 63 (3.5.13).

80. Letters of Cato IV, 9/1787–1/1788, in Storing and Dry (eds.), *The Complete Anti-Federalist*, 2: 114 (2.6.27).

81. Rawlins Lowndes, 1/16/1788, in Storing and Dry (eds.), *The Complete Anti-Federalist*, 5: 156 (5.12.4).

82. Luther Martin, "The Genuine Information Delivered to the Legislature of the State of Maryland Relative to the Proceedings of the General Convention Lately Held at Philadelphia," 1788, in Storing and Dry (eds.), *The Complete Anti-Federalist*, 2: 65–68 (2.4.80–88).

83. Cornelius, 12/18/1787, in Storing and Dry (eds.), *The Complete Anti-Federalist*, 4: 144 (4.10.12). Indeed, if Hendrickson is correct that distrust of persons outside of each Anti-Federalist's state or region was their modal concern, one may say that this collective fear turned into collective hope for a savior in the White House. See David C. Hendrickson, *Peace Pact: The Lost World of the American Founding* (Lawrence, KS: University Press of Kansas, 2003), 252, 254.

84. R. Gordon Hoxie, "The Presidency in the Constitutional Convention," *Presidential Studies Quarterly* 15 (1985): 25–32, 29–30; Charles C. Thach, *The Creation of the Presidency, 1775–1789* (Baltimore, MD: The Johns Hopkins University Press, 1922), 131–132.

85. A Federal Republican, 10/28/1787, in Storing and Dry (eds.), *The Complete Anti-Federalist*, 3: 83 (3.6.42).

86. John DeWitt III, 10/12/1787, in Storing and Dry (eds.), *The Complete Anti-Federalist*, 4: 26 (4.3.13).

87. George Mason, "Objections to the Constitution of Government formed by the Convention," 1787, in Storing and Dry (eds.), *The Complete Anti-Federalist*, 2: 12 (2.2.6). See also Federal Farmer XII, 1/12/1788, in Storing and Dry (eds.), *The Complete Anti-Federalist*, 2: 306 (2.8.170), who feared that "by giving the senate, directly or indirectly, an undue influence over the representatives, and the improper means of fettering, embarrassing, or controuling [sic] the president or executive, we give the government, in the very out set, a fatal and pernicious tendency to the middle undesirable point—aristocracy."

88. To be sure, this also had something to do with the expectation by almost everyone at the convention, as well as the Anti-Federalists beyond, that George Washington, a man perceived to be in abundant possession of republic virtue, was likely to become the first president.

89. Monroe, "Some Observations on the Constitution," in Storing and Dry (eds.), *The Complete Anti-Federalist*, 5: 296 (5.21.24).

90. Federal Farmer XIV, 1/17/1788, in Storing and Dry (eds.), *The Complete Anti-Federalist*, 2: 314 (2.8.182). Monroe argued similarly, saying, "unless the Executive had a negative on the laws of the legislature, it would soon exist only in name." See Monroe, "Some Observations on the Constitution," in Storing and Dry (eds.), *The Complete Anti-Federalist*, 5: 295 (5.21.22).

91. Brutus XVI, 4/10/1788, in Storing and Dry (eds.), *The Complete Anti-Federalist*, 2: 446 (2.9.198). For similar views against a distinct separation of powers, see Centinel II, 10/1787–4/1788, in Storing and Dry (eds.), *The Complete Anti-Federalist*, 2: 151 (2.7.50); "Observations on the New Constitution and on the Federal and State Conventions by A Columbia Patriot," 1788, in Storing and Dry (eds.), *The Complete Anti-Federalist*, 4: 276 (4.28.4); "A Letter of His Excellency Edmund Randolph, Esquire, on the Federal Constitution," 10/10/1787, in Storing and Dry (eds.), *The Complete Anti-Federalist*, 2: 91–92 (2.5.22); Federal Farmer XIV, 1/17/1788, in Storing and Dry (eds.), *The Complete Anti-Federalist*, 2: 309 (2.8.175). However, "where the members of the government," Federal Farmer also wrote, "are strong and complete, each in itself, the balance is naturally produced, each party may take the powers congenial to it, and we have less need to be anxious about checks, and the subdivision of powers."

92. Stephen Skowronek, *The Politics Presidents Make*, 27.

93. A (Maryland) Farmer I, 2/15/1788, in Storing and Dry (eds.), *The Complete Anti-Federalist*, 5: 21 (5.1.30–31).

94. Federal Farmer XIV, 1/17/1788, in Storing and Dry (eds.), *The Complete Anti-Federalist*, 2: 310 (2.8.178).

95. It has been said that the framers made a mistake in the method of presidential selection, failing to predict the rise of parties, which delivered the debacle of 1796 (when the Democratic-Republican vice-presidential candidate, Jefferson, ended up with more votes than the Federalist candidate) and the near-debacle of 1800 (when Aaron Burr nearly ended up displacing the top of the ticket). And yet, this "mistake" only illuminates the fact that the framers had bigger problems to solve: namely, the battle between the big and the small states for leverage in the Electoral College. The Federalists' scheme, which had failed to designate a separate vote for the presidential and vice-presidential offices, guaranteed that the two conceptions of federalism found expression in Article 2. Electors would be able both to vote for their favorite sons in their respective states, and also to vote for someone of continental reputation, with the expectation that the big states would be more likely to field candidates who would garner a majority vote, while the small states could still win a consolation prize if their candidate managed to obtain a plurality of the votes. The rules of victory codified this by allowing the majority winner to be installed as president and the plurality winner to be installed as vice president. The plan, then, was to present large and small states a fair shot at the office of the *vindex injuriarum* to defend the conception of federalism as they saw fit. This is why even Federal Farmer, after "viewing the principles and checks established in the election of the president" would "confess there appears to be a judicious combination of principles and precautions." On the Federalists' alleged failure, see Ackerman, *The Failure Of The Founding Fathers*; for the quote from Federal Farmer, see Federal Farmer XIV, 1/17/1788, in Storing and Dry (eds.), *The Complete Anti-Federalist*, 2: 310 (2.8.178).

96. Madison comes close to saying this in Federalist 51, where he observes, "A dependence on the people is, no doubt, the primary control on the government; but experience has taught mankind the necessity of auxiliary precautions." See also Ackerman's account of this passage in Bruce Ackerman, *We the People: Foundations* (Cambridge, MA: Belknap Press, 1998), 191.

97. Jeffrey K. Tulis, *The Rhetorical Presidency* (Princeton, NJ: Princeton University Press, 1987).

98. Thomas Jefferson to Doctor Horatio Turpin, 6/10/1807, in Randolph (ed.), *The Writings of Thomas Jefferson*, 4: 79.

99. Samuel Kernell, *Going Public: New Strategies of Presidential Leadership*, 4th Edition (Washington, DC: CQ Press, 2007).

100. Bailey, *Thomas Jefferson and Executive Power*.

101. Adrienne Koch, *Jefferson and Madison: The Great Collaboration* (New York: Oxford University Press, 1976).

102. Matthews, *If Men were Angels*.

103. Jefferson's proposal, which Madison quotes, was "that whenever any two of the three branches of government shall concur in opinion, each by the voices of two thirds of their whole number, that a convention is necessary for altering the constitution, or *correcting breaches of it*, a convention shall be called for the purpose."

104. Thomas Jefferson to William C. Jarvis, 9/28/1820, in Ford (ed.), *The Writings of Thomas Jefferson*, 10: 161.

105. Thomas Jefferson to James Madison, 2/17/1826, in Ford (ed.), *The Writings of Thomas Jefferson*, 10: 376.

106. McWilliams, *The Idea of Fraternity in America*, 222.

107. Thomas Jefferson to John B. Colvin, 9/20/1810, in Ford (ed.), *The Works of Thomas Jefferson*, 11: 146, 148, 149.

108. Thomas Jefferson, First Inaugural Address, 3/4/1801.

109. McWilliams, *The Idea of Fraternity in America*, 219.

110. Thomas Jefferson to John Adams, 28/10/1813, in Lipscombe (ed.), *Writings of Thomas Jefferson*, 13: 396.

111. Darren Staloff, *Hamilton, Adams, Jefferson: The Politics of Enlightenment and the American Founding* (New York: Hill and Wang, 2005), 347.

112. Thomas Jefferson to Mrs. Maria Cosway, 10/12/1786, in Ford (ed.), *The Works of Thomas Jefferson*, 5: 212.

113. Staloff, *Hamilton, Adams, Jefferson*, 300. See also Andrew Burstein, *Sentimental Democracy: The Evolution of America's Romantic Self-Image* (New York: Hill and Wang, 1999), 214.

114. Sheldon Wolin, *The Presence of the Past: Essays on the State and the Constitution* (Baltimore, MD: Johns Hopkins University Press, 1989), 124.

115. Herbert J. Storing, *What the Anti-Federalists Were For: The Political Thought of the Opponents of the Constitution* (Chicago, IL: University of Chicago Press, 1981), 6.

116. Max Lerner, *Thomas Jefferson: America's Philosopher-King* (New Brunswick, NJ: Transaction Publishers, 1997), 125.

Chapter 3

1. Thomas Jefferson to Albert Gallatin, 10/29/1822, in Paul L. Ford, *The Writings of Thomas Jefferson*, 10 vols. (New York: G. P. Putnam's Sons, 1899), 10: 235–236.

2. Robert Yates and John Lansing, 12/21/1787, in Herbert J. Storing and Murray Dry (eds.), *The Complete Anti-Federalist*, 7 vols. (Chicago, IL: University of Chicago Press, 1981), 2: 17 (2.3.8); Centinel V, 11/30/1787, in Storing and Dry (eds.), *The Complete Anti-Federalist*, 2: 167 (2.7.95); Federal Farmer XVII, 1/23/1788, in Storing and Dry (eds.), *The Complete Anti-Federalist*, 2: 331 (2.8.205); Brutus VII, 1/3/1788, in Storing and Dry (eds.), *The Complete Anti-Federalist*, 2: 400 (2.9.84); A (Pennsylvania) Farmer, 4/1788, in Storing and Dry (eds.), *The Complete Anti-Federalist*, 3: 185 (3.14.9); Patrick Henry, 6/5/1788, in Storing and Dry (eds.), *The Complete Anti-Federalist*, 5: 221 (5.16.6); Speech of George Mason in the Virginia State Ratifying Convention, 7/4/1788, in Storing and Dry (eds.), *The Complete Anti-Federalist*, 5: 256 (5.17.1); Melancton Smith, 6/20/1788, in Storing and Dry (eds.), *The Complete Anti-Federalist*, 6: 151 (6.12.15).

3. Norman K. Risjord, *The Old Republicans: Southern Conservatism in the Age of Jefferson* (New York: Columbia University Press, 1965); Jon Meacham, *American Lion: Andrew Jackson in the White House* (New York: Random House, 2009), 48.

4. Almost every Anti-Federalist was also a unionist, it should be said. Federalists and Anti-Federalists were divided only about what *sort* of union was best for the states. As A Plebeian volunteered, "The importance of preserving an union, and of establishing a government equal to the purpose of maintaining that union, is a sentiment deeply impressed on the mind of every citizen of America. It is now no longer doubted, that the confederation, in its present form, is inadequate to that end: Some reform in our government must take place." See A Plebian, Spring 1788, in Storing and Dry (eds.), *The Complete Anti-Federalist*, 6: 134–135 (6.11.12).

5. Stephen Skowronek, *Building a New American State: The Expansion of National Administrative Capacities 1877–1920* (New York: Cambridge University Press, 1982).

6. Cited in Ralph Ketcham, *Presidents Above Party: The First American Presidency, 1789–1829* (Chapel Hill, NC: University of North Carolina Press, 1989), 144–145. As the Democrats added party organization to Jefferson's democratic faith, the Whigs subtracted mercantilism from the commitment to the positive state they shared with the Federalists and National Republicans. See Lee Benson, *The Concept of Jacksonian Democracy* (Princeton, NJ: Princeton University Press, 1961), 86.

7. 17 U.S. 518 (1819), 17 U.S. 122 (1819), 17 U.S. 316 (1819).

8. In the realm of constitutional law, this was affirmed by the landmark case, *Barron v. Baltimore*, 32 U.S. 243 (1833), when a unanimous court, including the nationalist Marshall, would affirm that the Fifth Amendment and the Bill of Rights as a whole applied only to the federal government and not to the states. It has been suggested that the political climate of the January 1833 term had something to do with this decision, as the Court dared not to send down any decision that could encourage the states to join hands in South Carolina's precipitate action. See Daniel W. Howe, *What Hath God Wrought: The Transformation of America, 1815–1848* (New York: Oxford University Press, 2007), 413–414.

9. Senator Daniel Webster (1/20/1830), *Register of Debates in Congress*, 14 vols. (Washington, DC: Gales and Seaton, 1824–1837), 6: 38.

10. Andrew Jackson, Second Inaugural Address, 3/4/1833, available at http://www.presidency.ucsb.edu/ws/?pid=25811 (accessed 10/8/2011).

11. Andrew Jackson, Proclamation, 12/10/1832, available at http://www.presidency.ucsb.edu/ws/?pid=67078 (accessed 9/10/2011).

12. Andrew Jackson to John Sevier, 2/27/1797, in Sam B. Smith and Harriet C. Owsley (eds.), *The Papers of Andrew Jackson*, 6 vols. (Knoxville, TN: University of Tennessee Press, 1980), 1: 126.

13. Andrew Jackson, First Annual Message, 12/8/1829, available at http://www.presidency.ucsb.edu/ws/?pid=29471 (accessed 1/21/2012).

14. Andrew Jackson, Second Annual Message, 12/6/1830, available at http://www.presidency.ucsb.edu/ws/index.php?pid=29472 (accessed 6/30/2012).

15. Andrew Jackson, Veto Message, 7/10/1832, available at http://www.presidency.ucsb.edu/ws/?pid=67043 (accessed 6/6/2012).

16. Alexis de Tocqueville, *Democracy in America*, 2 vols. (New York: Alfred Knopf, [1835–1840] 1945), 1: 169.

17. Henry Clay, "Speech on Internal Improvements," 1/14/1824, in James F. Hopkins (ed.), *The Papers of Henry Clay* (Lexington, KY: University of Kentucky Press, 1963), 3: 587.

18. Andrew Jackson, Second Annual Message, 12/6/1830.

19. Andrew Jackson, First Annual Message, 12/8/1829.

20. Senator Robert Hayne, 1/21/1830, *Register of Debates in Congress*, 6: 34.

21. Andrew Jackson, First Inaugural Address, 3/4/1829, available at http://www.presidency.ucsb.edu/ws/index.php?pid=25810 (accessed 1/21/2012); Andrew Jackson, Second

Annual Message, 12/6/1830. By the end of his second term, his administrations had spent more on internal improvements than previous administrations combined. Nevertheless, the Democratic Party's platform of low tariffs worked in part because of the surplus income the federal government was receiving from land sales. See William Riker, *Federalism: Origin, Operation, Significance* (Boston, MA: Little, Brown, 1964), 54.

22. Andrew Jackson, Sixth Annual Message, 12/1/1834, available at http://www.presidency. ucsb.edu/ws/index.php?pid=29476 (accessed 6/6/2012).

23. Andrew Jackson, Veto Message, 7/10/1832.

24. Richard McCormick, "The Jacksonian Strategy," *Journal of the Early Republic* 10 (1990): 1–17, 4, 12.

25. Consider Calhoun's argument: "There is and always has been in an advanced stage of wealth and civilization, a conflict between labor and capital. The condition of society in the South exempts us from the disorders and dangers resulting from this conflict; and which explains why it is that the political condition of the slaveholding States has been so much more stable and quiet than that of the North." See Senator John C. Calhoun (2/6/1837), *Register of Debates in Congress*, 13: 2187.

26. Andrew Jackson, Veto Message, 7/10/1832.

27. See *Worcester v. Georgia*, 31 U.S. 515 (1832).

28. Horace Greeley, *Hints Towards Reforms* (New York: Fowlers & Wells, 1857), 126.

29. Donald L. Fixico, *Bureau of Indian Affairs* (Santa Barbara, CA: ABC-CLIO, 2012), 170.

30. John Niven, *John C. Calhoun and the Price of Union: A Biography* (Baton Rouge, LA: Louisiana State University Press, 1993), 173.

31. Robert V. Remini, *Henry Clay: Statesmen for the Union* (New York: W. W. Norton, 1991).

32. Charles M. Wiltse, *John C. Calhoun, Nationalist, 1782–1828* (Indianapolis, IN: The Bobbs-Merrill Company, 1944).

33. James A. Hamilton, *Reminiscences: or Men and Events at Home and Abroad* (New York: Charles Scribner, 1869), 62.

34. Charles F. Adams (ed.), *Memoirs of John Quincy Adams*, 12 vols. (New York: J. B. Lippincott, 1874–1878), 5: 361.

35. James L. Hutson, "Virtue Besieged: Virtue, Equality, and the General Welfare in the Tariff Debates of the 1820s," *Journal of the Early Republic* 14 (1994): 523–547.

36. The interesting twist to this story is that Calhoun was publicly for the tariff before he was secretly against it. Together with Martin Van Buren, he had hatched a plan to help Jackson win the presidency by helping to draft a tariff bill that would place especial burden on certain New England imports, and the plan was for Jacksonian allies in the South to vote against it in a bid to win Old Hickory some Northern supporters. The plan, however, backfired because enough New Englanders ignored the bait and voted to support the tariff, at which point Calhoun was forced to pen the Exposition. However, only after he was outmaneuvered by Martin Van Buren to become Jackson's heir apparent did Calhoun break with the president in January 1831, and he publicly identified with the Nullifiers and the Exposition's arguments in July. A year later, he resigned from the Jackson administration in protest to the president's continued support of the tariff. See Frank W. Taussig, *The Tariff History of the United States* (New York: G. P. Putnam's Sons, 1910), 88–89; Forrest McDonald, *States' Rights and the Union: Imperium in Imperio* (Lawrence, KS: University Press of Kansas, 2000), 94–95.

37. David F. Ericson, *The Shaping of American Liberalism: The Debates over Ratification, Nullification, and Slavery* (Chicago, IL: University of Chicago Press, 1993), 73.

38. Richard K. Crallé (ed.), *The Works of John C. Calhoun*, 6 vols. (New York: D. Appleton, 1855), 6: 83.

39. Ericson, *The Shaping of American Liberalism*, 75.

40. It is possibly also why Russell Kirk placed Calhoun on the pantheon of modern conservatism's founding figures. See Russell Kirk, *The Conservative Mind from Burke to Santayana* (Chicago, IL: Henry Regnery, 1953).

41. Crallé (ed.), *The Works of John C. Calhoun*, 6: 107.
42. An Officer of the Late Continental Army, 11/6/1787, in Storing and Dry (eds.), *The Complete Anti-Federalist*, 3: 92 (3.8.3).
43. On "positive good," see Senator John C. Calhoun (2/6/1837), *Register of Debates in Congress*, 13: 2187; William C. Stone, "Confederate States Postal Affairs," *The American Philatelist* 32 (1918): 26–31.
44. Robert V. Remini, *The Legacy of Andrew Jackson: Essays on Democracy, Indian Removal, and Slavery* (Baton Rouge, LA: Louisiana State University Press, 1988), 8.
45. Robert V. Remini, *Andrew Jackson and the Course of American Freedom, 1822–1832* (New York: Harper & Row, 1981), 147.
46. Pauline Maier, *American Scripture: Making the Declaration of Independence* (New York: Vintage, 1998), 212, 197.
47. George S. Camp, *Democracy* (New York: Harper & Brothers, 1841), 9.
48. Jack R. Pole, "Historians and the Problem of Early American Democracy," *American Historical Review* 67 (1962): 626–646.
49. Andrew Jackson, First Annual Message, 12/8/1829.
50. Camp, *Democracy*, 161–162.
51. Ronald Dworkin, "Rights as Trumps," in Jeremy Waldron (ed.), *Theories of Rights* (New York: Oxford University Press, 1984), 153–167; Marc Landy and Sidney M. Milkis, *American Government: Balancing Democracy and Rights*, 2nd Edition (New York: Cambridge University Press, 2008).
52. Gordon S. Wood, *The Creation of the American Republic: 1776–1787* (Chapel Hill, NC: University of North Carolina Press, 1969), 48–70; Akhil R. Amar, *The Bill of Rights: Creation and Reconstruction* (New Haven, CT: Yale University Press, 1998).
53. Richard Hofstadter, *The American Political Tradition and the Men who Made it* (New York: Alfred Knopf, 1948), 90–91.
54. Tocqueville, *Democracy in America*, 1: 254.
55. Storing and Dry (eds.), *The Complete Anti-Federalist*, 1: 19.
56. Madison, in contrast, referred to the Senate as "the great anchor of the government." See James Madison to Thomas Jefferson, 10/24/1787, James Madison, *Letters and Other Writings of James Madison*, 4 vols. (New York: R. Worthington, 1884), 1: 346.
57. Adams had been the former Minister to the Netherlands in the Washington administration, Minister to Prussia in his father's administration, a United States Senator, and the Boylston Professor of Rhetoric at Harvard during Jefferson's presidency, Minister to Russia in the Madison administration, and Secretary of State in the Monroe administration.
58. For a contrary view that party competition was Van Buren's solution to demagoguery, thereby making him "the truer heir to the Founders' intentions," see James W. Ceaser, *Presidential Selection: Theory and Development* (Princeton, NJ: Princeton University Press, 1979), 136.
59. Mark R. Cheathem, *Old Hickory's Nephew: The Political and Private Struggles of Andrew Jackson Donelson* (Baton Rouge, LA: Louisiana State University Press, 2007), 59–60.
60. Speech of Melancton Smith, New York Ratification Convention, 6/21/1788, in Storing and Dry (eds.), *The Complete Anti-Federalist*, 6: 157 (6.12.15).
61. Andrew Jackson, Second Annual Message, 12/6/1830.
62. Andrew Jackson to Andrew Jackson Donelson, 5/12/1835, in Andrew Jackson Donelson Papers, Library of Congress.
63. Andrew Jackson, First Annual Message, 12/8/1829.
64. Martin Van Buren to Andrew Jackson, 17/10/1837, in John S. Bassett (ed.), *Correspondence of Andrew Jackson*, 7 vols. (Washington, DC: Carnegie Institution, 1926–1935), 5: 516.
65. Lawrence F. Kohl, *The Politics of Individualism: Parties and the American Character in the Jacksonian Era* (New York: Oxford University Press, 1989), 178.
66. Quoted in Remini, *Andrew Jackson and the Course of American Freedom*, 157.

67. Library of Congress Rare Book and Special Collections Division, Broadside Collection, portfolio 136, no. 6 c-Rare Bk Coll, Digital ID: cph 3a03214, available at http://hdl.loc. gov/loc.pnp/cph.3a03214 (accessed 2/6/2012).

68. Martin Van Buren, *The Autobiography of Martin Van Buren* (Washington, DC: Government Printing Office, 1920), 125.

69. Richard Henry Lee to Edmund Pendleton, 12/5/1776, in James C. Ballagh (ed.), *The Letters of Richard Henry Lee*, 2 vols. (New York: Macmillan, 1911), 1: 191.

70. Jonathan Elliot (ed.), *The Debates in the Several State Conventions on Adoption of the Federal Constitution*, 5 vols. (Washington, DC: Government Printing Office, 1836), 3: 485.

71. Andrew Jackson, First Annual Message, 12/8/1829.

72. Senator William L. Marcy, 1/25/1832, *Register of Debates in Congress*, 8: 1325.

73. Martin Van Buren, *An Inquiry into the Origin and Course of Political Parties in the United States* (New York: Hurd & Houghton, 1867), 61–62.

74. Richard Hofstadter, *The Idea of a Party System: The Rise of Legitimate Opposition in the United States, 1780–1840* (Berkeley, CA: University of California Press, 1969), 226.

75. Martin Van Buren to Charles Dudley, 1/10/1822, cited in Robert V. Remini, *Martin Van Buren and the Making of the Democratic Party* (New York: Columbia University Press, 1959), 23.

76. Risjord, *The Old Republicans*.

77. Van Buren, *An Inquiry into the Origin and Course of Political Parties in the United States*, 61–62.

78. Van Buren, *An Inquiry into the Origin and Course of Political Parties in the United States*, 59.

79. Van Buren, *An Inquiry into the Origin and Course of Political Parties in the United States*, 61–62.

80. Van Buren, *An Inquiry into the Origin and Course of Political Parties in the United States*, 59.

81. Gunnar Myrdal, *An American Dilemma: The Negro Problem and Modern Democracy* (New York: Harper & Brothers, 1944), 433.

82. Douglas W. Jaenecke, "The Jacksonian Integration of Parties into the Constitutional System," *Political Science Quarterly* 101 (1986): 85–107, 86.

83. James K. Polk, Inaugural Address, 3/4/1835, available at http://www.presidency.ucsb. edu/ws/index.php?pid=25814 (accessed 5/25/2012); Thomas Jefferson, First Inaugural Address, 3/4/1801, available at http://www.presidency.ucsb.edu/ws/index.php?pid=25803 (accessed 5/25/2012).

84. John C. Calhoun to Andrew Jackson, 6/4/1826 in Bassett (ed.), *Correspondence of Andrew Jackson*, 3: 304.

85. Andrew Jackson, Second Inaugural Address.

86. Donald B. Cole, *The Presidency of Andrew Jackson* (Lawrence, KS: University Press of Kansas, 1993), 145–146.

87. Andrew Jackson, Veto Message, 7/10/1832.

88. A (Maryland) Farmer I, 2/15/1788, in Storing and Dry (eds.), *The Complete Anti-Federalist*, 5: 21 (5.1.31).

89. Federal Farmer XIV, 1/17/1788, in Storing and Dry (eds.), *The Complete Anti-Federalist*, 2: 310 (2.8.178).

90. John Whipple, *Substance of a Speech Delivered at the Whig Meeting Held at the Town House, Providence, RI, August 28, 1837* (Providence, RI, 1837), 11.

91. Jackson to Taney, 10/13/1836, in Bassett (ed.), *Correspondence of Andrew Jackson*, 5: 429–430.

92. Cited in Gaillard Hunt, *The Life of James Madison* (New York: Doubleday, 1902), 385.

Chapter 4

1. Harry V. Jaffa, *Crisis of the House Divided: An Interpretation of the Issues of the Lincoln-Douglas Debates* (Chicago, IL: University of Chicago Press, 2009), 14.

2. Alexander H. Stephens, "African Slavery: The Corner-stone of the Southern Confederacy" (3/22/1861), in James W. Loewen and Edward H. Sebesta (eds.), *The Confederate and Neo-Confederate Reader: The "Great Truth" about the "Lost Cause"* (Jackson, MS: University Press of Mississippi, 2010), 188.

3. Robert M. Spector, "Lincoln and Taney: A Study in Constitutional Polarization," *The American Journal of Legal History* 15 (1971): 199–214, 201.

4. Abraham Lincoln, First Inaugural Address, 3/4/1861, available at http://www.presidency.ucsb.edu/ws/index.php?pid=25818 (accessed 9/19/2011).

5. The differences between the Constitution of the United States and the Constitution of the Confederate States are also most stark on the matter of states' rights. First, the Confederate States decided that all appropriation bills must be passed by a supermajority of two thirds of the members in both legislative chambers, and they further insisted that no clause in their constitution "shall ever be construed to delegate the power to Congress to appropriate money for any internal improvement intended to facilitate commerce." Second, as few as just three states would be enough to call for a convention to amend their constitution. Third, the substance of the First and Second Amendments (on speech, religion, and guns), which limit the powers of the federal government and occur in the second half of the U.S. Constitution, were relocated to a dedicated section at the top of the Constitution of the Confederate States, in Article 1, Section 9, while the Ninth and Tenth Amendments were relocated to Article 6, to temper the supremacy clause. Finally, powers not delegated to the central government were now retained by the states "or the people thereof" and not by the "States or the people."

6. Paul D. Escott, *The Confederacy: The Slaveholders' Failed Venture* (Santa Barbara, CA: Praeger, 2010), 8. In 1864, Davis even considered arming the slaves to fight against the North. See Martin Crawford, "Davis and the Confederacy," in Susan-Mary Grant and Brian H. Reid (eds.), *Themes of the American Civil War: The War Between the States* (London: Routledge, 2010), 151–168, 162.

7. E. Merton Coulter, *The Confederate States of America, 1861–1865* (Baton Rouge, LA: Louisiana State University Press, 1950), 401. Historians generally do not have good things to say about Coulter; yet one can be a white supremacist and an authentic follower of the Spirit of '76. Quite a few Anti-Federalists were just that. On Coulter, see Eric Foner, "'The Tocsin of Freedom': The Black Leadership of Radical Reconstruction," in Gabor Borrit and Scott Hancock (eds.), *Slavery, Resistance, Freedom* (New York, University Press, 2007), 118–140, 129.

8. Though rarely used during the war, "War between the States" gained enough currency in the half-century after that the neo-Federalist Franklin Roosevelt would refer, in his own tip of the hat to the principles and *lingua franca* of the First Founding, to the "four-year War between the States" in his annual message to Congress in 1941. See http://www.presidency.ucsb.edu/ws/?pid=16092 (accessed 7/3/2012).

9. Karen Orren and Stephen Skowronek, *The Search for American Political Development* (New York: Cambridge University Press, 2004), 136.

10. Eric Foner, *Reconstruction: America's Unfinished Revolution, 1863–1877* (New York: HarperCollins, 1988), 409.

11. Indeed, McConnell has argued that the period from the end of Reconstruction to the Supreme Court's decision in *Plessy v. Ferguson* was a constitutional moment in its own right. See Michael W. McConnell, "The Forgotten Constitutional Moment," *Constitutional Commentary* 11 (1994): 114–144.

12. William M. Wiecek, *The Lost World of Classical Legal Thought: Law and Ideology in America, 1886–1937* (New York: Oxford University Press, 1998), 84. For the more charitable view that the Republican Party was committed to the civil rights agenda until the ill-fated Lodge (Federal Elections) Bill of 1890–1891, see Pamela Brandwein, *Rethinking the Judicial Settlement of Reconstruction* (New York: Cambridge University Press, 2011). Regardless of timing, the "abandonment" thesis would not need much refurbishment

if one held that the civil rights agenda was never foremost on the Republicans' list of priorities.

13. Akhil R. Amar, *The Bill of Rights: Creation and Reconstruction* (New Haven, CT: Yale University Press, 1998).

14. Orren and Skowronek, *The Search for American Political Development*, 143.

15. 109 U.S. 3 (1993).

16. As I say in Appendix I, the Lovers' Quarrel explains why the United States has always been laggardly, when compared to Europe, with regard to various civil rights issues—it sucks the oxygen out of our other debates, because before Americans can fight for group interests, we must first agree on national identity. And so Tocqueville was right when he said that every political question ends up becoming a legal question in the United States, because the country's highest law is inextricably political.

17. For the view that the war was about Northern capitalism and Southern agrarianism, see Charles A. Beard and Mary R. Beard, *The Rise of American Civilization*, 2 vols. (New York: Macmillan, 1927). For the view that slavery was the leading cause for the war, see James Ford Rhodes, *History of the Civil War, 1861–1865* (New York: Macmillan, 1917), 49; Allan Nevins, *Ordeal of the Union* (New York: Scribners, 1947), *passim*.

18. The text begins, "Articles of Confederation and perpetual Union between the states of New Hampshire, Massachusetts-bay Rhode Island and Providence Plantations, Connecticut, New York, New Jersey, Pennsylvania, Delaware, Maryland, Virginia, North Carolina, South Carolina and Georgia." (See http://avalon.law.yale.edu/18th_century/artconf.asp, accessed 7/3/2012.) The provisional Constitution of the Confederate States drafted after the Montgomery Convention in February 1861 read: "We, the Deputies of the Sovereign and Independent States of South Carolina, Georgia, Florida, Alabama, Mississippi, and Louisiana, invoking the favor of Almighty God." (See http://ia601204.us.archive.org/29/items/provisionalpermaconf/provisionalpermaconf.pdf, accessed 7/2/2012.) This illuminates the significant comma in the "permanent" version, "We, the people of the Confederate States, each State acting in its sovereign and independent character." (See http://www.law.ou.edu/ushistory/csaconstitution/preamble.shtml, accessed 7/2/2012).

19. Jefferson Davis, First Inaugural Address (2/18/1861), in James D. Richardson (ed.), *A Compilation of the Messages and Papers of the Confederacy*, 2 vols. (Nashville, TN: United States Publishing Company, 1906), 1: 33.

20. By another account, Lincoln transforms the Constitution of 1789, committed to freedom and fear, by introducing a "Secret Constitution," committed to security and social justice. Yet this account seems to underestimate the Federalists' strong commitment to a more perfect Union in 1789 that was merely short-circuited by the Anti-Federalists' descendants until the Civil War. See George P. Fletcher, *The Secret Constitution: How Lincoln Redefined American Democracy* (New York: Oxford University Press, 2002).

21. Samuel Johnson, "Taxation no Tyranny," in Samuel Johnson and Arthur Murphy (eds.), *The Works of Samuel Johnson*, 12 vols. (London: Luke Hansard, 1801), 8: 203.

22. These rights supplied what Strauss called the "solid middle ground between antisocial individualism and unnatural universality." See Leo Strauss, *Natural Right and History* (Chicago, IL: University of Chicago Press, 1953), 15.

23. Philadelphiensis I, 11/1787–4/1788, in Herbert J. Storing and Murray Dry (eds.), *The Complete Anti-Federalist*, 7 vols. (Chicago, IL: University of Chicago Press, 1981), 3: 108 (3.9.14).

24. Rawlins Lowndes, 1/16/1788, in Storing and Dry (eds.), *The Complete Anti-Federalist*, 5: 149–150 (5.12.1). There were not many abolitionists on the Federalist side, to be sure; but their moral inconsistency was not as stark as for the Anti-Federalists because the Federalists spoke as much in the language of interests and necessity as in the language of liberty. For an inspiring exception on the Anti-Federalist side, see Republicus, 1/3/1788, in Storing and Dry (eds.), *The Complete Anti-Federalist*, 5: 169–170 (5.13.14).

25. Chilton Williamson, *American Suffrage: From Property to Democracy 1760–1860* (Princeton, NJ: Princeton University Press, 1960).

26. Charles W. Hudson to his mother, 9/14/1861, quoted in James M. McPherson, *What They Fought For, 1861–1865* (Baton Rouge, LA: Louisiana State University Press, 1994), 51.

27. Jonathan Elliot (ed.), *The Debates in the Several State Conventions on the Adoption of the Constitution*, 4 vols. (Philadelphia, PA: J. B. Lippincott, 1876), 3: 137.

28. Elliot (ed.), *The Debates in the Several State Conventions*, 3: 139, 141.

29. Peter S. Onuf, *The Mind of Thomas Jefferson* (Charlottesville, VA: University of Virginia Press, 2007), 10.

30. Daniel J. Boorstin, *The Americans: The National Experience* (New York: Random House, 1988), 400.

31. James Monroe, "Special Message to the House of Representatives Containing the Views of the President of the United States on the Subject of Internal Improvements," 5/4/1822, available at http://www.presidency.ucsb.edu/ws/index.php?pid=66323 (accessed 9/18/2011).

32. William Henry Harrison, Inaugural Address, 3/4/1841, available at http://www.presidency.ucsb.edu/ws/index.php?pid=25813 (accessed 9/18/2011).

33. Zachary Taylor, Special Message, 1/23/1850, available at http://www.presidency.ucsb.edu/ws/index.php?pid=68071 (accessed 9/18/2011).

34. Franklin Pierce, Third Annual Message, 12/31/1855, available at http://www.presidency.ucsb.edu/ws/index.php?pid=29496 (accessed 9/19/2011).

35. Jefferson Davis, Second Inaugural Address, 2/22/1862, in Richardson (ed.), *A Compilation of the Messages and Papers of the Confederacy*, 1: 184.

36. M. E. Bradford, *A Better Guide Than Reason: Federalists and Anti-Federalists* (New Brunswick, NJ: Transaction, [1979] 1994), 157.

37. A Georgian, 11/15/1787, in Storing and Dry (eds.), *The Complete Anti-Federalist*, 5: 135 (5.9.16).

38. Agrippa VIII, 12/25/1787, in Storing and Dry (eds.), *The Complete Anti-Federalist*, 4: 84 (4.6.30).

39. Jefferson Davis, Second Inaugural Address, 2/22/1862, in Richardson (ed.), *A Compilation of the Messages and Papers of the Confederacy*, 1: 188.

40. Jefferson Davis, First Inaugural Address, 2/18/1861, in Richardson (ed.), *A Compilation of the Messages and Papers of the Confederacy*, 1: 33.

41. Susan-Mary Grant, "From Union to Nation? The Civil War and the Development of American Nationalism," in Grant and Reid (eds.), *Themes of the American Civil War*, 295–316, 306.

42. Jefferson Davis, Second Inaugural Address, 2/22/1862, in Richardson (ed.), *A Compilation of the Messages and Papers of the Confederacy*, 1: 185.

43. Brutus XV, 3/20/1788, in Storing and Dry (eds.), *The Complete Anti-Federalist*, 2: 446 (2.9.203).

44. Jefferson Davis, First Inaugural Address, 2/18/1861, in Richardson (ed.), *A Compilation of the Messages and Papers of the Confederacy*, 1: 35.

45. Jefferson Davis, Second Inaugural Address, 2/22/1862, in Richardson (ed.), *A Compilation of the Messages and Papers of the Confederacy*, 1: 185.

46. Brian R. Dirck, *Lincoln and Davis: Imagining America, 1809–1865* (Lawrence, KS: University of Kansas Press, 2001), 87; Thomas Jefferson, First Inaugural Address, 3/4/1801, available at http://www.presidency.ucsb.edu/ws/index.php?pid=25803 (accessed 5/25/2012).

47. Gunnar Myrdal, *An American Dilemma: The Negro Problem and Modern Democracy* (New York: Harper & Brothers, 1944), 49.

48. Karen Orren, *Belated Feudalism: Labor, the Law, and Liberal Development in the United States* (New York: Cambridge University Press, 1991); Louis Hartz, *The Liberal Tradition in America* (New York: Harcourt Brace, 1955), 148.

49. Hartz, *The Liberal Tradition in America*, 151.

50. Hartz, *The Liberal Tradition in America*, 146.

51. Elliot (ed.), *The Debates in the Several State Conventions*, 3: 590.

52. Pierce Butler would declare that "a slave in S. Carola. was as productive & valuable as that of a freeman in Massts." See Max Farrand (ed.), *The Records of the Federal Convention of 1787* (New Haven, CT: Yale University Press, 1911), 581.

53. Thomas Jefferson to the Marquis de La Fayette, 12/26/1820, in Paul L. Ford, *The Works of Thomas Jefferson*, 12 vols. (New York: G. P. Putnam's Sons, 1905), 12: 191.

54. Edmund Burke, *The Works of the Right Hon. Edmund Burke*, 2 vols. (London: Holdsworth and Ball, 1834) 1: 186.

55. Abraham Lincoln and Stephen A. Douglas, *Political Debates between Abraham Lincoln and Stephen A. Douglas* (Cleveland, OH: O. S. Hubbell, 1895), 177.

56. Daniel Boorstin, *The Genius of American Politics* (Chicago, IL: University of Chicago Press, 1953), 84.

57. Myrdal, *An American Dilemma*, li–lii.

58. Sean Wilentz, *The Rise of American Democracy: Jefferson to Lincoln* (New York: W. W. Norton, 2005), 163.

59. Myrdal, *An American Dilemma*, li.

60. Rogers Smith, *Civic Ideals: Conflicting Visions of Citizenship in US History* (New Haven, CT: Yale University Press, 1997), 111. As Smith knows, feminists who have made this same point include Zillah R. Eisenstein, *The Radical Future of Liberal Feminism* (New York: Longman, 1981), 34–49, and Carol Pateman, *The Sexual Contract* (Stanford, CA: Stanford University Press, 1988), 38.

61. Elizabeth Cady Stanton, *A History of Woman Suffrage*, 6 vols. (Rochester, NY: Fowler and Wells, 1889), 1: 70–71; Martin L. King Jr., *I Have a Dream: Writings and Speeches that Changed the World* (New York: HarperCollins, 2011), 101–106.

62. Sonu S. Bedi, *Rejecting Rights* (New York: Cambridge University Press, 2009).

63. Myrdal, *An American Dilemma*.

64. Derrick A. Bell (dissenting), in Jack M. Balkin (ed.), *What Brown v. Board of Education Should Have Said: The Nation's Top Legal Experts Rewrite America's Landmark Civil Rights Decision* (New York: New York University Press, 2001), 185–200; Peggy McIntosh, "White Privilege and Male Privilege," Working Paper 189, Wellesley Center for Research on Women, 1988.

65. Put another way, the statement of the equality of persons as a universal claim must also be a comparative claim for which the question "equal to whom?" must be answered. And to this the Declaration is clear: the standard for comparison is the Englishman or his American cousin. Even today, it is in part because the Declaration asserts that all men are created equal that in order to make good on this promise on those who do not yet enjoy such equality, they must first be marked by the ascriptive categories that were the basis for denying such equality in the first place. (This is, of course, the "color-blind" outcome versus the need to first be "color-conscious" debate surrounding affirmative action.) And so, at every point when the march of democracy extended its welcome to new groups of people, each claim has typically been made in relation to the propertied, Protestant, white males of northern European descent. To move forward has typically required a look backward. No wonder when we say "all-American," our mind wanders against reason and modern practice to the original standard to which Jefferson's words first referred.

66. Myrdal, *An American Dilemma*, 32.

67. Radical abolitionists such as George Mellen and William Goodell were among the first to convert the Declaration into a weapon for their cause, but it took a major statesmen like Lincoln to propagate these arguments before the reinterpretation found traction. On the abolitionists' arguments, see William W. Wiecek, *The Sources of Antislavery Constitutionalism in America, 1760–1848* (Ithaca, NY: Cornell University Press, 1977).

68. Bradford, *A Better Guide Than Reason*, 47.

69. Abraham Lincoln, First Inaugural Address, 3/4/1861.

70. Abraham Lincoln, Address before the Young Men's Lyceum of Springfield, Illinois, 1/27/1837, in John G. Nicolay and John Hay (eds.), *Abraham Lincoln Complete Works*, 2 vols. (New York: The Century Company, 1894), 1: 12.

71. Lincoln, Address before the Young Men's Lyceum of Springfield, Illinois, in Nicolay and Hay (eds.), *Abraham Lincoln Complete Works*, 1: 14.

72. Lincoln, Address before the Young Men's Lyceum of Springfield, Illinois, in Nicolay and Hay (eds.), *Abraham Lincoln Complete Works*, 1: 15.

73. Michael L. Benedict, "The Constitution of the Lincoln Presidency and the Republican Era," in Martin Fausold and Alan Shank (eds.), *The Constitution and the American Presidency* (Albany, NY: State University of New York Press, 1991), 45–63.

74. Glen E. Thurow, *Abraham Lincoln and American Political Religion* (Albany, NY: State University of New York Press, 1976), 34.

75. Lincoln, Lincoln at Peoria, Illinois, 10/16/1854, in Nicolay and Hay (eds.), *Abraham Lincoln Complete Works*, 2: 248.

76. Garry Wills, *Lincoln at Gettysburg: Words that Remade American History* (New York: Touchstone, 1992), 38.

77. Bradford, *A Better Guide Than Reason*, 42.

78. Isaiah Berlin, "Two Concepts of Liberty," in Anthony Quinton (ed.), *Political Philosophy* (New York: Oxford University Press, 1967), 141–152.

79. Jefferson's first draft of the Declaration, which had read "all men are created equal and independent" indicated this understanding of liberty, though his New England colleagues on the drafting committee convinced him to drop the "independent." For a discussion, see Murray N. Rothbard, *Conceived in Liberty* (Auburn, AL: Mises Institute, 2011), 1293.

80. McPherson, *What They Fought For*, 10.

81. David H. Fischer, *Liberty and Freedom* (New York: Oxford University Press, 2005), 5–11. In a different discussion, George Lakoff has argued that conservatives tend to use "liberty" more because it focuses more on individual choices rather than the imposition of that choice on others, while liberals tend not to think that they are at liberty to do anything, but pay more attention to how acts are relational and can limit the freedom of others. See George Lakoff, *Whose Freedom? The Battle over America's Most Important Idea* (New York: Farrar, Straus and Giroux, 2006), 137.

82. Abraham Lincoln, Second Annual Message, 12/1/1862, available at http://www.presidency.ucsb.edu/ws/index.php?pid=29503 (accessed 9/19/2011).

83. Abraham Lincoln, Address at the Dedication of the National Cemetery at Gettysburg, Pennsylvania, 11/19/1863, available at http://www.presidency.ucsb.edu/ws/index.php?pid=73959 (accessed 9/19/2011).

84. Abraham Lincoln, Address at Sanitary Fair in Baltimore, 4/18/1864, in Nicolay and Hay (eds.), *Abraham Lincoln Complete Works*, 2: 513.

85. Michael Kammen has argued that liberty in America has always been explained in relation to some other quality, such as liberty and property in the nineteenth century, and liberty and justice in the twentieth century. See Michael Kammen, *Spheres of Liberty: Changing Perception of Liberty in American Culture* (Ithaca, NY: Cornell University Press, 1986), 5.

86. In similar vein, when King prophesized that freedom shall ring from "the prodigious hilltops of New Hampshire," "the mighty mountains of New York," "the heightening Alleghenies of Pennsylvania," "the snow-capped Rockies of Colorado," "the curvaceous slopes of California," "Stone Mountain of Georgia," "Lookout Mountain of Tennessee," and "from every hill and molehill of Mississippi," he was working with the building blocks of America's First Founding, the "Free and Independent States" of the Union, as the Declaration puts it. See Martin L. King Jr., *I Have a Dream: Writings and Speeches that Changed the World* (New York: HarperCollins, 2011), 101–106.

87. Jonathan O'Neill, *Originalism in American Law and Politics: A Constitutional History* (Baltimore, MD: Johns Hopkins University Press, 2005), 2.

88. Jaffa, *Crisis of the House Divided*, 318.

89. Jaffa, *Crisis of the House Divided*, 324.

90. Jaffa, *Crisis of the House Divided*, 318.

91. Cited in Myrta L. Avary (ed.), *Recollections of Alexander H. Stephens* (New York: Doubleday, 1910), 60; Abraham Lincoln, Fragment on the Constitution and the Union, c.1860, in Roy Basler (ed.), *Abraham Lincoln: His Speeches and Writing* (Cleveland, OH: World Publishing, 1946), 513.

92. Abraham Lincoln, Address at Cooper Institute, New York, 2/27/1860, in Nicolay and Hay (eds.), *Abraham Lincoln Complete Works*, 1: 599.

93. Lincoln, Address at Cooper Institute, New York, 2/27/1860, in Nicolay and Hay (eds.), *Abraham Lincoln Complete Works*, 1: 603.

94. Storing and Dry (eds.), *The Complete Anti-Federalist*, 1: 76.

95. Cecilia Kenyon, "Men of Little Faith: Antifederalists on the Nature of Representative Government," *William and Mary Quarterly* 12 (1955): 3–43.

96. James Smilie, Pennsylvania Ratification Convention, 11/28/1787, available at http://press-pubs.uchicago.edu/founders/documents/v1ch14s28.html (accessed 6/8/2012).

97. John P. Kaminski, "The Constitution Without a Bill of Rights," in Patrick T. Conley and John P. Kaminski (eds.), *The Bill of Rights and the States: The Colonial and Revolutionary Origins of American Liberties* (Madison, WI: Madison House, 1992), 16–45, 19.

98. Elliot (ed.), *The Debates in the Several State Conventions*, 3: 37; 2: 56.

99. Elliot (ed.), *The Debates in the Several State Conventions*, 3: 37, 98.

100. George Washington, Farewell Address, 9/19/1796, available at http://www.presidency.ucsb.edu/ws/index.php?pid=65539 (accessed 10/1/2011).

101. J. David Greenstone, "Political Culture and American Political Development: Liberty, Union, and the Liberal Bipolarity," *Studies in American Political Development* 1 (1986): 1–49, 47.

102. Harry V. Jaffa, *Equality and Liberty* (New York: Oxford University Press, 1965), 15.

103. Like Jaffa, Strauss held back for this reason: "If there is no standard higher than the ideal of our society, we are utterly unable to take a critical distance from that ideal." However, as we know from a well-known passage, Strauss was nevertheless not entirely sure if such a critical standard actually existed. He wrote, "the seriousness of the need of natural right does not prove that the need can be satisfied. A wish is not a fact. Even by proving that a certain view is indispensable for living well, one proves merely that the view in question is a salutary myth: one does not prove it to be true. Utility and truth are two entirely different things." See Strauss, *Natural Right and History*, 3, 6.

104. For a contrary view that posits, as Jaffa does, that the Constitution's purpose was to secure the natural rights affirmed in the Declaration, see Scott Douglas Gerber, *To Secure These Rights: The Declaration of Independence and Constitutional Interpretation* (New York: New York University Press, 1996).

105. This is why some states, such as Rhode Island, had freely and confidently implemented "socialistic and communistic proposals" such as the transfer of property to state governments and the redistribution of property among heads of households every 13 years in 1786. Republicanism and socialism are not so different when the government operating is one created by the people. See Kaminski, "The Constitution Without a Bill of Rights," 21.

106. Daniel Webster, *The Works of Daniel Webster*, 6 vols. (Boston, MA: Little, Brown, 1851), 3: 478.

107. The Federalists have been criticized for having placed the least emphasis on the "of the people" part of the equation, though it is unclear by my account how frontal this criticism was to their republicanism. Perhaps this is what Gordon Wood meant when he argued that Federalists had taken the Whig's democratic theory of politics and turned it into

"an elitist theory of democracy." (See Gordon S. Wood, *The Creation of the American Republic, 1776–1787* [Chapel Hill, NC: University of North Carolina Press, 1969], 517.) It is because the Anti-Federalists were concerned that government worked *for* the people that they called in the help of chartered rights so that a substantive provision could operate alongside a procedural mechanism, and the three branches of government could be guided to seek democratic truth out. But it is precisely in the perceived need for such substantive provisions that a government "by the people" is constrained, so we may now observe how what serves democracy may detract from republicanism. The distinction explains why the Federalists were proudly anti-democratic, and as a result and at the same time, more republican—committed to representative government and institutions—than were the Anti-Federalists.

108. Federal Farmer I, 10/8/1787, in Storing and Dry (eds.), *The Complete Anti-Federalist*, 2: 223 (2.8.1). Gordon Wood, however, has disputed the conventional attribution. See Gordon Wood, "The Authorship of *The Letters from the Federal Farmer*," *William and Mary Quarterly* 31 (1974): 299–308.

109. Among the works that have advanced such arguments are Willmoore Kendall and George W. Carey, *The Basic Symbols of the American Political Tradition* (Baton Rouge, LA: Louisiana State University Press, 1970), 84–95; M. E. Bradford, "The Lincoln Legacy: A Long View," *Modern Age* 24 (1980): 355–363; Michael P. Rogin, "The King's Two Bodies: Abraham Lincoln, Richard Nixon, and Presidential Self-Sacrifice," *Massachusetts Review* 20 (1979): 553–573; Dwight G. Anderson, *Abraham Lincoln: The Quest for Immortality* (New York: Alfred Knopf, 1982); James A. Rawley, "The Nationalism of Abraham Lincoln," *Civil War History* 9 (1963): 283–298.

110. Abraham Lincoln, Fragment of a Speech at a Republican Banquet in Chicago, 12/10/1856, in Nicolay and Hay (eds.), *Abraham Lincoln Complete Works*, 1: 225. On Lincoln's aspirational understanding of the Constitution, see Gary J. Jacobsohn, "Abraham Lincoln 'On This Question of Judicial Authority': The Theory of Constitutional Aspiration," *The Western Political Quarterly* 36 (1983): 52–70; J. David Greenstone, "Political Culture and American Political Development: Liberty, Union, and the Liberal Bipolarity," *Studies in American Political Development* 1 (1986): 1–49, 45.

111. Abraham Lincoln, Second Annual Message, 12/1/1862.

112. Abraham Lincoln, Address at Cooper Institute, New York, 2/27/1860, in Nicolay and Hay (eds.), *Abraham Lincoln Complete Works*, 1: 604.

113. Abraham Lincoln, First Inaugural Address, 3/4/1861.

114. Stephen M. Engel, *American Politicians Confront the Court: Opposition Politics and Changing Responses to Judicial Power* (New York: Cambridge University Press, 2011), 190–192.

115. Abraham Lincoln, Address to the Senate of New Jersey, 2/21/1861, in Nicolay and Hay (eds.), *Abraham Lincoln Complete Works*, 1: 688.

116. Abraham Lincoln, Message to Congress in Special Session, 7/4/1861, in Nicolay and Hay (eds.), *Abraham Lincoln Complete Works*, 2: 64.

117. Jefferson Davis, First Inaugural Address, 2/18/1861, in Richardson (ed.), *A Compilation of the Messages and Papers of the Confederacy*, 1: 33.

118. Alexander H. Stephens, *Recollections of Alexander H. Stephens* (New York: Doubleday, Page, 1910), 169.

119. Drew G. Faust, *The Creation of Southern Nationalism: Ideology and Identity in the Civil War South* (Baton Rouge, LA: Louisiana State University Press, 1988), 84.

120. Abraham Lincoln, First Inaugural Address, 3/4/1861.

121. James M. McPherson, *Lincoln and the Second American Revolution* (New York: Oxford University Press, 1991), 39–40.

122. Hugh Rockoff, "Banking and Finance, 1789–1914," in Stanley L. Engerman and Robert E. Gallman (eds.), *The Cambridge Economic History of the United States: The Long Nineteenth Century* (New York: Cambridge University Press, 2000), 643–684.

123. Daniel J. Elazar, "Civil War and the Preservation of American Federalism," *Publius* 1 (1971): 39–58, 46.

124. Theda Skocpol, "America's First Social Security System: The Expansion of Benefits for Civil War Veterans," *Political Science Quarterly* 108 (1993): 85–116.

125. Although Richard Bensel has argued that "from 1861 to 1877, the American state and the Republican Party were essentially the same thing." See Richard F. Bensel, *Yankee Leviathan: The Origins of Central State Authority in America, 1859–1877* (New York: Cambridge University Press, 1990).

126. Tony A. Freyer, *Forums of Order: The Federal Courts and Business in American History* (Westport, CT: Greenwood, 1979); Justin Crowe, *Building the Judiciary: Law, Courts, and the Politics of Institutional Development* (Princeton, NJ: Princeton University Press, 2012).

127. Clinton L. Rossiter, *Conservatism in America: The Thankless Persuasion* (New York: Vintage), 131.

128. Leonard P. Curry, *Blueprint for Modern America: Nonmilitary Legislation of the First Civil War Congress* (Nashville, TN: Vanderbilt University Press, 1968).

129. Jack Beatty, *Age of Betrayal: The Triumph of Money in America, 1865–1900* (New York: Knopf, 2007); Charles Lane, *The Day Freedom Died: The Colfax Massacre, the Supreme Court, and the Betrayal of Reconstruction* (New York: Henry Holt, 2008).

130. Merle Curti, *Roots of American Loyalty* (New York: Columbia University Press, 1946), 133; James McPherson, *Battle Cry of Freedom* (New York: Oxford University Press, 1988), 859; Wills, *Lincoln at Gettysburg*, 145; Melinda Lawson, *Patriot Fires: Forging a New American Nationalism in the Civil War North* (Lawrence, KS: University Press of Kansas, 2002), 3.

131. McPherson, *Lincoln and the Second American Revolution*.

132. Abraham Lincoln, First Inaugural Address, 3/4/1861.

133. Carl Van Doren, "The Poetical Cult of Lincoln," *The Nation* 106 (1919): 777.

134. Clinton Rossiter, *The American Presidency* (New York: New American Library, 1960), 108.

Chapter 5

1. A version of this chapter appears as "The Anti-Federalist Strand in Progressive Politics," *Political Research Quarterly* 66 (2013): 32–49.

2. George E. Mowry, *Theodore Roosevelt and the Progressive Movement* (Madison, WI: University of Wisconsin Press, 1946), 145. This characterization, of course, came from Roosevelt himself, who in turn had read Herbert Croly. Roosevelt wrote: "Men who understand and practice the deep underlying philosophy of the Lincoln school of American political thought are necessarily Hamiltonian in their belief in a strong and efficient National Government and Jeffersonian in their belief in the people as the ultimate authority, and in the welfare of the people as the end of government." See Theodore Roosevelt, *Theodore Roosevelt: An Autobiography* (New York: Charles Scribner's Sons, [1913] 1920), 423.

3. Edward S. Corwin, "The Passing of Dual Federalism," *Virginia Law Review* 36 (1950): 1–24; Suzanne Mettler, *Dividing Citizens: Gender and Federalism in New Deal Public Policy* (Ithaca, NY: Cornell University Press, 1998).

4. Arthur Mann (ed.), *The Progressive Era: Liberal Renaissance or Liberal Failure* (New York: Holt, Rinehart and Winston, 1963); Otis L. Graham Jr., *An Encore for Reform: The Old Progressives and the New Deal* (New York: Oxford University Press, 1967); E. J. Dionne, *They Only Look Dead: Why Progressives Will Dominate the Next Political Era* (New York: Simon and Schuster, 1996); Martha Derthick and John J. Dinan, "Progressivism and Federalism," in Sidney M. Milkis and Jerome M. Mileur (eds.), *Progressivism and the New Democracy* (Amherst, MA: University of Massachusetts Press, 1999), 81–102; Donald

R. Brand, "Competition and the New Deal Regulatory State," in Sidney M. Milkis and Jerome M. Mileur (eds.), *The New Deal and the Triumph of Liberalism* (Amherst, MA: University of Massachusetts Press, 2002), 166–192; James W. Ceaser, *Nature and History in American Political Development* (Cambridge, MA: Harvard University Press, 2006), 66.

5. For a welcomed dissenting view, see Morton Keller, "The New Deal: A New Look Author," *Polity* 31 (1999): 657–663.

6. Theodore Roosevelt, Speech at Osawatomie, 31/8/1910, in Theodore Roosevelt, *The New Nationalism* (New York: The Outlook Company, 1910), 3: 27–28.

7. William Howard Taft, *Official Report of the Proceedings of the Fifteenth Republican National Convention* (New York: The Tenny Press, 1912), 419.

8. Woodrow Wilson, Speech in Buffalo, NY, 9/2/1912, in Arthur S. Link (ed.), *The Papers of Woodrow Wilson*, 69 vols. (Princeton, NJ: Princeton University Press, 1966–1994), 25: 75.

9. Woodrow Wilson, Speech in Philadelphia, PA, 10/28/1912, in Mario R. Di Nunzio (ed.), *Woodrow Wilson: Essential Writings and Speeches of the Scholar-President* (New York: New York University Press, 2006), 359.

10. Stephen Skowronek, *The Politics Presidents Make: Leadership from John Adams to Bill Clinton* (Cambridge, MA: Belknap Press, 1997), 302; Eldon J. Eisenach, *The Lost Promise of Progressivism* (Lawrence, KS: University Press of Kansas, 1994).

11. Arthur M. Schlesinger, Jr., *The Crisis of the Old Order, 1919–1933* (Boston, MA: Houghton Mifflin, 1957), 81; Harris Gaylord Warren, *Herbert Hoover and the Great Depression* (New York: Oxford University Press, 1959), 24.

12. On Glass and Wilson, see Allan A. Michie and Frank Rhylick, *Dixie Demagogues* (New York: Vanguard Press, 1939), 171; on Bailey, see Elmer L. Puryear, *Democratic Party Dissension in North Carolina, 1928–1936* (Chapel Hill, NC: University of North Carolina Press, 1962); on the American Liberty League see George Wolfskill, *The Revolt of the Conservatives: A History of the American Liberty League, 1934–1940* (New York: Houghton Mifflin, 1962).

13. Martin J. Sklar, "Woodrow Wilson and the Political Economy of Modern United States Liberalism," in Ronald Radosh and Murray N. Rothbard (eds.), *A New History of Leviathan: Essays on the Rise of the American Corporate State* (New York: E. P. Dutton, 1972), 7–65, 10–12.

14. Ellis W. Hawley, "Herbert Hoover, the Commercial Secretariat, and the Vision of an "Associative State, 1921–1928," *Journal of American History* 61 (1974): 116–140.

15. Stephen Skowronek has famously coined the term "the state of courts and parties" to describe the veritable American state of the nineteenth century, rejecting the Tocquevillian and Marxist observations that compared to other industrializing countries of the nineteenth century, America was uniquely stateless. I use the "Party State" here as shorthand. See Stephen Skowronek, *Building a New American State: The Expansion of National Administrative Capacities 1877–1920* (New York: Cambridge University Press, 1982).

16. Vernon L. Parrington, *Main Currents in American Thought: The Colonial Mind, 1620–1800* (New York: Harcourt Brace, 1927).

17. Irving Kristol, "When Virtue Loses All Her Loveliness," in Mark Gerson (ed.), *The Neo-Conservative Reader* (Reading, MA: Addison-Wesley, 1996), 114.

18. Herbert D. Croly, *The Promise of American Life* (Boston, MA: Northeastern University Press, [1909] 1989), 273.

19. Kimberley S. Johnson, *Governing the American State: Congress and the New Federalism, 1877–1929* (Princeton, NJ: Princeton University Press); Martin K. Sklar, *The Corporate Reconstruction of American Capitalism, 1890–1916: The Market, the Law, and Politics* (New York: Cambridge University Press, 1987).

20. Brian Balogh, *A Government Out of Sight: The Mystery of National Authority in Nineteenth-Century America* (New York: Cambridge University Press, 2009), 364.

21. Eisenach, *The Lost Promise of Progressivism*, 18.

22. Martin Shefter, "Parties, Bureaucracy, and Political Change in the United States," in Louis Maisel and Joseph Cooper (eds.), *Political Parties: Development and Decay* (Beverly Hills, CA: Sage, 1978), 211–265.

23. Patrick Henry, 6/5/1788, in Herbert J. Storing and Murray Dry (eds.), *The Complete Anti-Federalist*, 7 vols. (Chicago, IL: University of Chicago Press, 1981), 5: 213 (5.16.2).

24. Croly, *The Promise of American Life*, 274.

25. Michael McGeer, *A Fierce Discontent: The Rise and Fall of the Progressive Movement in America, 1870–1920* (New York: Oxford University Press, 2003), xiii.

26. Carl L. Becker, *The Eve of the Revolution: A Chronicle of the Breach with England* (New Haven, CT: Yale University Press, 1918), 256.

27. Ralph Ketcham (ed.), *The Anti-Federalist Papers and the Constitutional Convention Debates: The Clashes and Compromises that Gave Birth to Our Form of Government* (New York: Penguin Putnam, 1986), 3.

28. Mercy Warren, *History of the Rise, Progress and Termination of the American Revolution* (Boston, MA: Manning and Loring, 1805), in Storing and Dry (eds.), *The Complete Anti-Federalist*, 6: 237 (6.14.148).

29. Robert M. Crunden, *Ministers of Reform: The Progressives' Achievement in American Civilization* (New York: Basic Books, 1982); Eisenach, *The Lost Promise of Progressivism*.

30. Richard Hofstadter, *The Age of Reform: From Bryan to FDR* (New York: Alfred Knopf, [1955] 1959), 152.

31. Gerald Nash, *Creating the West: Historical Interpretations 1890–1990* (Albuquerque, NM: University of New Mexico Press, 1991), 7. The Anti-Federalist and Progressive nostalgia for rural, small-town America, in turn, had roots in one half of the court/country party distinction in Walpolean England espoused by Bolingbroke, Harrington, and others. See James H. Hutson, "Country, Court, and Constitution: Antifederalism and the Historians," *William and Mary Quarterly* 38 (1981): 337–368; Isaac Kramnick, *Bolingbroke and His Circle: The Politics of Nostalgia in the Age of Walpole* (Ithaca, NY: Cornell University Press, 1992); Stanley Elkins and Eric McKitrick, *The Age of Federalism: The Early American Republic, 1788–1800* (New York: Oxford University Press, 1995).

32. George E. Mowry, *The California Progressives* (Berkeley, CA: University of California Press, 1951). More recently, Elizabeth Sanders has highlighted the close relationship between farmers' movements and progressivism in Elizabeth Sanders, *Roots of Reform: Farmers, Workers, and the American State, 1877–1917* (Chicago, IL: University of Chicago Press, 1999).

33. Mowry, *The California Progressives*, 89.

34. Centinel VIII, 12/29/1787, in Storing and Dry (eds.), *The Complete Anti-Federalist*, 2: 178 (2.7.126).

35. The Impartial Examiner I, 3/5/1788, in Storing and Dry (eds.), *The Complete Anti-Federalist*, 5: 187–188 (5.14.15).

36. Cato V, 11/22/1787, in Storing and Dry (eds.), *The Complete Anti-Federalist*, 2: 117 (2.6.34).

37. It is important to note that the Progressives saw political and financial corruption as closely related. As the Progressive economist and social gospelist John R. Commons observed, "The lobby and the machine have grown up together as Siamese Twins. The professional lobbyists are nearly always the managers of the political machine. They carry in their pockets the political fortunes of the legislators. The 'third house' is the legislature." See Malcolm Rutherford and Warren J. Samuels (eds.), *John R. Commons: Selected Essays* (New York: Routledge, 1997), 25.

38. John J. Rumbarger, *Profits, Power and Prohibition: Alcohol Reform and the Industrializing of America, 1800–1930* (Albany, NY: State University of New York Press, 1989), 72. For an account of the moral crusade against alcohol by one of its leading activists, see Henry W. Blair, *The Temperance Movement: or, The Conflict between Man and Alcohol* (Boston, MA: William E. Smythe, 1888).

39. Benjamin Parke De Witt, *The Progressive Movement: A Non-Partisan, Comprehensive Discussion of Current Tendencies in American Politics* (New York: Macmillan, 1915), 4.

40. Woodrow Wilson, *The New Freedom* (New York: Doubleday, Page & Company, 1913), 35.

41. Progressive Party Platform, 11/5/1912, available at http://teachingamericanhistory.org/library/index.asp?document=607 (accessed 7/1/2012).

42. Denatus, 6/11/1788, in Storing and Dry (eds.), *The Complete Anti-Federalist*, 5: 262 (5:18.5).

43. A Columbian Patriot, 1788, in Storing and Dry (eds.), *The Complete Anti-Federalist*, 4: 276 (4.28.4).

44. To be sure, the fact that the Anti-Federalists spilt a good portion of ink on the inadequacy of the checks and balances provided in the proposed Constitution may have been proof that they were for more rather than less checks and balances. But they did so only because they ultimately believed that no checks were ever going to be good enough for a republic as extended as the one the Federalists were proposing. The Anti-Federalists argued that if in a small republic, a vigilant body of citizens would always ensure that no aristocracy would arise, there was no such self-regulating mechanism in a large republic, and some therefore proposed a stronger system of checks and balances than the one the Federalists had proposed. The disagreement between the camps was also intensified by the fact that both sides had different starting assumptions about what needed to be checked and balanced. The Anti-Federalists were, in the main, more concerned with balancing the natural orders of society—in particular the aristocratic and democratic orders—than with balancing the functions and powers of government, as the Federalists were. The Anti-Federalists were more concerned with the tyranny of the natural aristocracy over democracy than with the tyranny of one particular branch over all others (though they recognized that some branches, such as the Senate and the Court, would be more likely to be a captive of aristocratic interests than others). That is why at the center of the Anti-Federalists' criticism of the Constitution was its alleged failure to secure popular responsibility. In their commitment to democratic responsiveness as the ultimate test of a political system, we see the consistency in their call for more checks and balances and a more complex system of government in a large republic on the one hand, and their preferred alternative of a simple government in a small republic on the other.

45. A (Maryland) Farmer II, 2/29/1788, in Storing and Dry (eds.), *The Complete Anti-Federalist*, 5: 23 (5.1.34).

46. Centinel I, 10/5/1787–4/9/1788, in Storing and Dry (eds.), *The Complete Anti-Federalist*, 2: 139 (2.7.9).

47. Woodrow Wilson, *Congressional Government: A Study in American Politics* (Boston, MA: Houghton, Mifflin, [1885] 1901), 284–285.

48. Edward R. Seligman, *The Income Tax: A Study of the History, Theory, and Practice of Income Taxation at Home and Abroad*, 2nd Edition (New York: Macmillan, 1914), 635.

49. Elliot W. Brownlee, *Federal Taxation in America: A Short History*, 2nd Edition (New York: Cambridge University Press, 2004), 55.

50. *The Statutes At Large of the Government of the United States of America from March 15, 1913 to March 15, 1915*, Vol. XXXVIII (Washington, DC: Government Printing Office, 1915), 114. The Act begins with a 51-page schedule of dutiable items, included 21 pages on the administration of the tariffs, and devoted just 16 pages to the income tax. Incidentally, the Progressives shared their objection to tariffs with those who opposed the "tariff of abominations" (1828), who ultimately codified their concerns in Article 1, Section 8 of the Constitution of the Confederate States.

51. Brownlee, *Federal Taxation in America*, 44.

52. In the party period of American politics, which spanned most of the nineteenth century beginning in the Jacksonian era, parties nominated candidates who would promise to allocate economic resources and privileges equally and exactly to all constituents of the

party. Because members of Congress excelled in the distribution of resources, there was an institutional fit between the distributive politics of the nineteenth century and the pork-barreling instinct of Congress. See Richard L. McCormick, *The Party Period and Public Policy: American Politics from the Age of Jackson to the Progressive Era* (New York: Oxford University Press, 1988).

53. In the late 1890s, pensions cost up to 45 percent of federal receipts. See Brownlee, *Federal Taxation in America*, 39. Hence Skocpol has argued, in ways consistent with Skowronek's characterization of the nineteenth-century American state, that the generous federal spending on Civil War pensions belied the conventional view that the early American state was a social policy laggard, but instead was part and parcel of the "precocious" patronage-oriented state of the nineteenth century. See Theda Skocpol, *Protecting Soldiers and Mothers: The Political Origins of Social Policy in the United States* (Cambridge, MA: Harvard University Press, 1992).

54. Seligman, *The Income Tax*, 652.

55. Croly, *The Promise of American Life*, 273–274.

56. *New State Ice Co. v. Liebmann*, 285 U.S. 262, 311 (1932) Brandeis, J. dissenting. On how the Progressives botched their efforts to enhance the administrative capacities of state governments and ended up decentralizing the police power to localities, see Margaret Weir, "States, Race, and the Decline of New Deal Liberalism," *Studies in American Political Development* 19 (2005): 157–172.

57. Roger G. Brooks, "Garcia, the Seventeenth Amendment, and the Role of the Supreme Court in Defending Federalism," *Harvard Journal of Law & Public Policy* 10 (1987): 189–202, 200.

58. Jacob Tanger, "Amending Procedure of Federal Constitution," *American Political Science Review* 10 (1916): 689–699, 697.

59. Henry Jones Ford, *The Rise and Growth of American Politics: A Sketch of Constitutional Development* (New York: Macmillan, 1898), 270.

60. Cited in Laura E. Little, "An Excursion into the Unchartered Waters of the Seventeenth Amendment," *Temple Law Review* 64 (1991): 629–658, 641.

61. Some Progressives even advocated reducing the total number of elected offices so that it would vitiate the need for party competition and elections. See Albert Stickney, *A True Republic* (New York: Harper & Brothers, 1879).

62. William Riker, *Federalism: Origin, Operation, Significance* (Boston, MA: Little, Brown, 1964), 129.

63. The Progressives were open to many other reform ideas, some of which never came to fruition, as long they could deal a blow to the Party State. John R. Commons, for example, believed that upon the adoption of proportional representation of legislative districts, "most important of all, legislative bodies would be transformed from inefficient and corrupt bands of spoilsmen into capable, upright, and representative assemblies of lawmakers." See Rutherford and Samuels (eds.), *John R. Commons*, 28.

64. Even Theodore Roosevelt, champion of "New Nationalism," believed that "the States must be made efficient for the work which concerns only the people of the States; and the nation for that which concerns all the people." See Theodore Roosevelt, *The New Nationalism* (New York: Outlook Publishers, 1910), 27. For a discussion of the states'-rights-oriented, "New Freedom" Progressives and their commitment to communalism, see Derthick and Dinan, "Progressivism and Federalism."

65. Anna L. Harvey, *Votes Without Leverage: Women in American Electoral Politics, 1920–1970* (New York: Cambridge University Press, 1996).

66. Parrington, *Main Currents in American Thought*; J. Allen Smith, *Growth and Decadence of Constitutional Government* (New York: Henry Holt, 1930).

67. Hofstadter, *The Age of Reform*, 214.

68. Wilson Carey McWilliams, "The Anti-Federalists, Representation and Party," *Northwestern Law Review* 85 (1990): 12–38, 22.

69. Theodore Lowi, *The End of Liberalism: The Second Republic of the United States* (New York: W. W. Norton, 1979).

70. Cited in John E. Smith, *John Marshall* (New York: Henry Holt, 1996), 121.

71. Warren, *History of the Rise, Progress and Termination of the American Revolution*, in Storing and Dry (eds.), *The Complete Anti-Federalist*, 6: 240 (6.14.157).

72. Progressives like Louis Brandeis objected to the trusts and favored small business because they believed that the virtues of the petit bourgeois were vital for a democratic polity. See Brand, "Competition and the New Deal Regulatory State," 172.

73. A (Maryland) Farmer, 3/23/1788, in Storing and Dry (eds.), *The Complete Anti-Federalist*, 5: 50 (5.1.82).

74. Storing and Dry (eds.), *The Complete Anti-Federalist*, 1: 21.

75. Federal Farmer XVI, 1/20/1788, in Storing and Dry (eds.), *The Complete Anti-Federalist*, 2: 324 (2.8.196).

76. Federal Farmer XVI, 1/20/1788, in Storing and Dry (eds.), *The Complete Anti-Federalist*, 2: 324–325 (2.8.196).

77. Sheldon Wolin, *The Presence of the Past: Essays on the State and the Constitution* (Baltimore, MD: Johns Hopkins University Press, 1989), 124.

78. Centinel I, 10/5/1787–4/9/1788, in Storing and Dry (eds.), *The Complete Anti-Federalist*, 2: 138 (2.7.8).

79. Hofstadter, *The Age of Reform*, 302; David A. Horowitz, *Beyond Left & Right: Insurgency and the Establishment* (Urbana, IL: University of Illinois Press, 1997).

80. William Howard Taft, "At the Cradle of its Greatness," *American Bar Association Journal* 8 (1922): 333–354, 333.

81. Eileen McDonagh, "The 'Welfare Rights State' and the 'Civil Rights State': Policy Paradox and State Building in the Progressive Era," *Studies in American Political Development* 7 (1993): 225–274.

82. Federal Farmer XII, 1/12/1788, in Storing and Dry (eds.), *The Complete Anti-Federalist*, 2: 298 (2.8.158).

83. Brutus XV, 3/20/1788, in Storing and Dry (eds.), *The Complete Anti-Federalist*, 2: 446 (2.9.203).

84. Brutus I, 10/18/1787, in Storing and Dry (eds.), *The Complete Anti-Federalist*, 2: 370 (2.9.16).

85. Agrippa IX, 12/28/1787, in Storing and Dry (eds.), *The Complete Anti-Federalist*, 4: 86 (4.6.34).

86. Isaac Kramnick and R. Lawrence Moore, *The Godless Constitution: The Case Against Religious Correctness* (New York: W. W. Norton, 1997), 32.

87. Jonathan Elliot (ed.), *The Debates in the Several State Conventions on the Adoption of the Federal Constitution as Recommended by the General Convention at Philadelphia in 1787*, 5 vols. (Philadelphia, PA: J. B. Lippincott, 1891), 4: 199.

88. Edward A. Ross, *The Old World in the New: The Significance of Past and Present Immigration to the American People* (New York: The Century, 1914), 275.

89. Suzanne Marilley, *Woman Suffrage and the Origins of Liberal Feminism in the United States* (Cambridge: Harvard University Press, 1996), 164. A related example would be the Australian secret ballot, which was supported by Progressives to end voter fraud and intimidation but also happened to disenfranchise illiterate voters—many of whom were African American—and newly naturalized voters, who could no longer be accompanied by a literate person to help them identify candidate names on a ballot. See Richard M. Valelly, *The Two Reconstructions: The Struggle for Black Enfranchisement* (Chicago, IL: University of Chicago Press, 2004), 127.

90. David Schmidt, *Citizen Lawmakers: The Ballot Initiative Revolution* (Philadelphia, PA: Temple University Press, 1989); Thomas Goebel, *A Government by the People: Direct Democracy in America, 1890–1940* (Chapel Hill, NC: University of North Carolina Press, 2002); Steven L. Piott, *Giving Voters a Voice: The Origins of the Initiative and Referendum in America* (Columbia, MO: University of Missouri Press, 2003).

91. Gary Gerstle, "Race and Nation in the Thought and Politics of Woodrow Wilson," in John M. Cooper (ed.), *Reconsidering Woodrow Wilson: Progressivism, Internationalism, War, and Peace* (Washington, DC: Woodrow Wilson Center Press, 2008), 93–124, 108–110.

92. Woodrow Wilson, Address at Gettysburg, 7/4/1913, available at http://www.presidency. ucsb.edu/ws/?pid=65370 (accessed 7/1/2012).

93. Edward A Ross, "The Immigrants and Politics: The Political Consequences of Immigration," *The Century* 87 (1914): 392–398, 397.

94. Hans P. Vought, *The Bully Pulpit and the Melting Pot: American Presidents and the Immigrant, 1897–1933* (Macon, GA: Mercer University Press, 2004), 27; United States Immigration Commission (1907–1910), *Brief Statement of the Immigration Commission with conclusions and recommendations and views of the minority*, Vol. 5865 (Washington, DC: Government Printing Office, 1911), 690, also available at http://site.ebrary.com/lib/ stanfordimmigrationdillingham/Doc?id=10006604&ppg=671 (accessed 7/1/2012).

95. Gordon S. Wood, *The Creation of the American Republic, 1776–1787* (Chapel Hill, NC: University of North Carolina Press, 1969), 516.

96. Robert A. Dahl, "Myth of the Presidential Mandate," *Political Science Quarterly* 105 (1990): 355–372, 357.

97. Centinel, in Storing and Dry (eds.), *The Complete Anti-Federalist*, 2: 139.

98. See for example Brutus IV, 11/29/1787, in Storing and Dry (eds.), *The Complete Anti-Federalist*, 2: 382 (2.9.45).

99. Republicus, 3/1/1788, in Storing and Dry (eds.), *The Complete Anti-Federalist*, 5: 168 (5.13.13).

100. Cato IV, 11/8/1787, in Storing and Dry (eds.), *The Complete Anti-Federalist*, 2: 115 (2.6.30).

101. A (Maryland) Farmer IV, 3/21/1788, in Storing and Dry (eds.), *The Complete Anti-Federalist*, 5: 38 (5.1.65).

102. Croly, *The Promise of American Life*, 36.

103. J. Allen Smith, *The Spirit of American Government: A Study of the Constitution: Its Origin, Influence and Relation to Democracy* (New York: Macmillan, 1907), 48.

104. Smith, *The Spirit of American Government*, 57.

105. Croly, *The Promise of American Life*, 41.

106. Herbert D. Croly, *Progressive Democracy* (New York: Macmillan, 1914), 241.

107. Arthur S. Link, *American Epoch: A History of the United States since the 1890s*, 2 vols. (New York: Knopf, [1955] 1967), 2: 115.

108. Progressive Party Platform, 11/5/1912.

109. Robert D. Marcus, *Grand Old Party: Political Structure in the Gilded Age, 1880–1896* (New York: Oxford University Press, 1971); Daniel A. Smith and Dustin Fridkin, "Delegating Direct Democracy: Interparty Legislative Competition and the Adoption of the Initiative in the American States," *American Political Science Review* 102 (2008): 333–350.

110. Eldon J. Eisenach, "Some Second Thoughts on Progressivism and Rights," *Social Philosophy and Policy* 29 (2012): 196–219, 206.

111. Balogh, *A Government Out of Sight*, 364.

112. John Dewey, "The Ethics of Democracy," in Jo Ann Boydston (ed.), *The Early Works of John Dewey* (Carbondale, IL: Southern Illinois University Press, 1969), 227–250, 239.

113. Speech of Melancton Smith, New York Ratification Convention, 6/21/1788, in Storing and Dry (eds.), *The Complete Anti-Federalist*, 6: 157 (6.12.15).

114. James W. Ceaser, *Presidential Selection: Theory and Development* (Princeton, NJ: Princeton University Press, 1979), 190.

115. Jeffrey K. Tulis, *The Rhetorical Presidency* (Princeton, NJ: Princeton University Press, 1987).

116. A Columbia Patriot, 1788, in Storing and Dry (eds.), *The Complete Anti-Federalist*, 4: 284 (4.28.12).

117. A (Maryland) Farmer I, 2/15/1788, in Storing and Dry (eds.), *The Complete Anti-Federalist*, 5: 21 (5.1.31).

118. James Monroe, 1788, in Storing and Dry (eds.), *The Complete Anti-Federalist*, 5: 298 (5.21.27).

119. Roosevelt, *Theodore Roosevelt*, 357.

120. Daniel Carpenter, *The Forging of Bureaucratic Autonomy: Reputations, Networks, and Policy Innovation in Executive Agencies, 1862–1928* (Princeton, NJ: Princeton University Press, 2001). Examples are Sidney M. Milkis, *The President and the Parties: The Transformation of the American Party System since the New Deal* (New York: Oxford University Press, 1993); Peri E. Arnold, "Effecting a Progressive Presidency: Roosevelt, Taft, and the Pursuit of Strategic Resources," *Studies in American Political Development* 17 (2003): 61–81.

121. The parallel to the Confederacy may be illuminating. Like the Anti-Federalists, members of the Confederate States of America were afraid of a powerful consolidated government, yet this fear did *not* lead them to weaken the powers of the Confederate president. Though the president was constitutionally limited to a single six-year term, s/he was given what we would today call a line item veto (Article 7, Section 7, Clause 2) and the explicit power to fire any officer from any department in the executive branch (Article 2, Section 2, Clause 3).

122. See Woodrow Wilson, *Congressional Government: A Study in American Politics* (Boston, MA: Houghton, Mifflin, [1885] 1901) versus Woodrow Wilson, *Constitutional Government in the United States* (New York: Columbia University Press, 1908).

123. Samuel E. Morison, "Faith of a Historian," *American Historical Review* 56 (1951): 261–275, 272.

124. Eisenach, *The Lost Promise of Progressivism*, 6.

125. Henry F. May, *The End of American Innocence: A Study of the First Years of Our Own Time, 1912–1917* (New York: Viking, 1959), 29.

Chapter 6

1. Max M. Edling, *A Revolution in Favor of Government: Origins of the U.S. Constitution and the Making of the American State* (New York: Oxford University Press, 2003).

2. The first session of the 73rd Congress produced a legislative bonanza that has become the lore of modern liberal-statist dreams, including the Emergency Banking Act to address the financial crisis; the Civil Conservation Corps Reforestation Relief Act to create jobs in natural resource conservation; the Agricultural Adjustment Act to bolster farm prices; the Federal Emergency Relief Act, which created the Federal Emergency Relief Administration to provide relief for the needy; the Tennessee Valley Authority to promote economic development in the Valley; the Securities Act, which created the Securities Exchange Commission to monitor the stock market; the Glass-Steagall Act, which created the FDIC to make banking safer; and the National Industrial Recovery Act, which guaranteed the rights of labor and created the Public Works Administration. See E. Pendleton Herring, "First Session of the 73rd Congress," *American Political Science Review* 28 (1934): 65–83; Mario R. DiNunzio, *Franklin D. Roosevelt and the Third American Revolution* (Santa Barbara, CA: Praeger, 2011), 52–58.

3. William E. Leuchtenburg, *The FDR Years* (New York: Columbia University Press, 1995), 279.

4. Lester J. Dickinson, "What's the Matter with Congress?" *American Mercury* 37 (2/1936): 129.

5. Senator Arthur H. Vandenberg, quoted in Arthur M. Schlesinger, Jr., *The Coming of the New Deal* (Boston, MA: Houghton Mifflin, 1959), 3.

6. Franklin D. Roosevelt, Second Inaugural Address, 1/20/1937, available at http://www.presidency.ucsb.edu/ws/index.php?pid=15349 (accessed 11/28/2011).

7. Joseph Alsop and Robert Kintner, "We Shall Make America Over," *Saturday Evening Post*, 11/1938, 19.

8. Suzanne Mettler, "Social Citizens of Separate Sovereignties," in Sidney M. Milkis and Jerome M. Mileur (eds.), *The New Deal and the Triumph of Liberalism* (Amherst, MA: University of Massachusetts Press, 2002), 231–271, 232.

9. Ken I. Kersh, *Constructing Civil Liberties: Discontinuities in the Development of American Constitutional Law* (New York: Cambridge University Press, 2004), 178.

10. Paul T. Homan, "The Pattern of the New Deal," *Political Science Quarterly* 51 (1936): 161–184, 168.

11. Schlesinger, Jr., *The Coming of the New Deal*, 314–315. See also Carl N. Degler, *Out of our Past* (New York: Harper & Row, 1959), 479–416.

12. Franklin D. Roosevelt, Annual Message to Congress, 1/4/1935, available at http://www.presidency.ucsb.edu/ws/index.php?pid=14890 (accessed 11/9/2011).

13. *Helvering v. Davis*, 301 U.S. 619 (1937).

14. For a recent exception to the rule, see Anthony J. Colangelo, "The Foreign Commerce Clause," *Virginia Law Review* 96 (2010): 949–1041. In *Cherokee Nation v. Georgia*, 30 U.S. 1 (1831), the Court limited future debates over the Indian Commerce Clause by denominating the tribes as "domestic dependent nations," thereby subservient to federal authority.

15. 545 U.S. 1 (2005).

16. 295 U.S. 495 (1935).

17. 298 U.S. 238 (1936).

18. 301 U.S. 1 (1937).

19. Bruce Ackerman, *We the People: Foundations* (Cambridge, MA: Belknap Press, 1991), 103.

20. George Thomas, *The Madisonian Constitution* (Baltimore, MD: John Hopkins University Press, 2008), 97.

21. Ronald Rotunda, "The Liberal Label: Roosevelt's Capture of a Symbol," *Public Policy* 17 (1968): 377–408.

22. Franklin D. Roosevelt, First Inaugural Address, 3/4/1933, available at http://www.presidency.ucsb.edu/ws/index.php?pid=14473 (accessed 11/7/2011).

23. Sidney M. Milkis and Jerome M. Mileur, "The New Deal, Then and Now," in Milkis and Mileur (eds.), *The New Deal and the Triumph of Liberalism*, 1–22, 3.

24. Franklin D. Roosevelt, State of the Union Address, 1/3/1937, available at http://www.presidency.ucsb.edu/ws/index.php?pid=15336 (accessed 11/7/2011).

25. James Madison to Thomas Jefferson, 10/24/1787, James Madison, *Letters and Other Writings of James Madison*, 4 vols. (New York: R. Worthington, 1884), 1: 344.

26. Thomas A. Spragens, Jr., *Getting the Left Right: The Transformation, Decline, and Reformation of American Liberalism* (Lawrence, KS: University of Press of Kansas, 2010), 7–8.

27. John Rawls, *A Theory of Justice* (Cambridge, MA: Harvard University Press, 1971), 3.

28. Norman Jacobson, "Political Science and Political Education," *American Political Science Review* 57 (1963): 561–569, 563.

29. John F. Kennedy, Inaugural Address, 1/21/1961, available at http://www.presidency.ucsb.edu/ws/index.php?pid=8032 (accessed 9/12/2011). The distinct understandings of sacrifice between modern conservatives and liberals distinguish two views of the Union that it is either more than or only the sum of its parts that parallel Federalism versus Anti-Federalism. Modern liberals like John Rawls believed in economic redistribution because even in his "original position," individuals were *already* presumed to be part of a community as they set about to decide on the principles of justice that would govern their society. Conservatives and libertarians like Robert Nozick rejected the idea that individuals started off as embedded members of the national community, believing that any talk of redistribution—state-imposed sacrifice on individuals—violates the separateness of persons that Rawls purported to uphold.

30. Abraham Lincoln, Response to a Serenade, 5/9/1864, in John G. Nicolay and John Hay (eds.), *Abraham Lincoln Complete Works*, 2 vols. (New York: The Century Company, 1894), 2: 520.

31. Rexford G. Tugwell and Edward C. Banfield, "Grass Roots Democracy—Myth or Reality?" *Public Administration Review* 10 (1950): 47–55, 54.

32. Frances Perkins, "Basic Idea Behind Social Security Program," *The New York Times*, 11/27/1935, E3.

33. Franklin D. Roosevelt, Fireside Chat, 4/14/1938, available at http://www.presidency. ucsb.edu/ws/index.php?pid=15628 (accessed 11/8/2011).

34. William E. Leuchtenburg, *Franklin D. Roosevelt and the New Deal* (New York: Harper & Row, 1963), 345; Isaac Kramnick and R. Lawrence Moore, *The Godless Constitution: The Case Against Religious Correctness* (New York: W. W. Norton, 1997).

35. Franklin D. Roosevelt, Excerpts from the Press Conference at Warm Springs, GA, 11/28/1934, available at http://www.presidency.ucsb.edu/ws/index.php?pid=14787 (accessed 11/27/2011).

36. Senator Rick Santorum raised a few eyebrows when he made this statement in a forum for Republican presidential candidates in Iowa in late 2011. See Susan Jacoby, "Christian Politicians Exalt Suffering in GOP Campaign," *The Washington Post*, 11/23/2011, available at http://www.washingtonpost.com/blogs/spirited-atheist/post/christian-politicians-exalt-suffering-in-gop-campaign/2011/11/22/gIQAa9HVoN_blog.html (accessed 11/23/2011).

37. Franklin D. Roosevelt, Second Inaugural Address, 1/20/1937.

38. Alan Lawson, *Commonwealth of Hope: The New Deal Response to Crisis* (Baltimore, MD: Johns Hopkins University Press, 2006), 6.

39. David M. Kennedy, *Freedom from Fear: The American People in Depression and War, 1929–1945* (New York: Oxford University Press, 1999), 364.

40. Archibald MacLeish, *A Time to Speak: The Selected Prose of Archibald MacLeish* (Boston, MA: Houghton Mifflin, 1941), 62.

41. Morton Keller, "The New Deal: A New Look," *Polity* 31 (1999): 657–663, 660.

42. Jeffrey Tulis, "The Constitutional Presidency in American Political Development," in Martin Fausold and Alan Shank (eds.), *The Constitution and the American Presidency* (Albany, NY: State University of New York Press, 1991), 133–146, 141.

43. Lawson, *Commonwealth of Hope*.

44. What separates modern, post-New Deal Democrats from Republicans is not an optimism gap in the sense that the former always seem to be griping about the status quo more than the latter, but the tendency of modern Democrats to focus on national problems for which the national government may proactively offer national solutions. Even the "Third Way" Bill Clinton cast his eye to national rather than local problems, even if he punted on whether it was the job of the federal government to address them when he proclaimed, "there is nothing wrong in America that cannot be cured with what is right in America." See William J. Clinton, Inaugural Address, 1/20/1993, available at http://www.presidency.ucsb.edu/ws/index.php?pid=46366#axzz1luqCu9ag (accessed 1/12/2012).

45. Leuchtenburg, *Franklin D. Roosevelt and the New Deal*, 329.

46. Franklin D. Roosevelt, Second Inaugural Address, 1/20/1937.

47. Raymond Moley, *After Seven Years* (New York: Harper & Row, 1939), 184.

48. Rexford G. Tugwell, "The Principles of Planning and the Institution of Laissez-Faire," *American Economic Review* 22 (1932): 75–92, 89.

49. James Madison, *National Gazette*, 3/12/1791, in Gaillard Hunt (ed.), *The Writings of James Madison: 1790–1802*, 9 vols. (New York: G. P. Putnam's Sons, 1900–1910), 6: 69.

50. Richard K. Matthews, *If Men were Angels: James Madison & the Heartless Empire of Reason* (Lawrence, KS: University Press of Kansas, 1995), 8–9.

51. Matthews, *If Men were Angels*, 9.

52. Matthews, *If Men were Angels*, 11.
53. Richard E. Neustadt, *Presidential Power and the Modern Presidents: The Politics of Leadership from Roosevelt to Reagan* (New York: The Free Press, 1990), 29.
54. Franklin D. Roosevelt, Fireside Chat, 3/9/1937, available at http://www.presidency. ucsb.edu/ws/index.php?pid=15381 (accessed 11/9/2011).
55. Franklin D. Roosevelt, Acceptance Speech for the Renomination for the Presidency, 6/27/1936, available at http://www.presidency.ucsb.edu/ws/index.php?pid=15314 (accessed 11/7/2011).
56. Roosevelt, Acceptance Speech for the Renomination for the Presidency, 6/27/1936.
57. Franklin D. Roosevelt, Campaign Address of Progressive Government at the Commonwealth Club in San Francisco, California, 9/23/1932, available at http://www. presidency.ucsb.edu/ws/index.php?pid=88391 (accessed 11/7/2011).
58. Cass Sunstein, *The Second Bill of Rights: FDR's Unfinished Revolution and Why We Need it More than Ever* (New York: Basic Books, 2004), 26.
59. Franklin D. Roosevelt, Campaign Address of Progressive Government at the Commonwealth Club in San Francisco, California, 9/23/1932.
60. Spragens, Jr., *Getting the Left Right*, ix.
61. Tugwell and Banfield, "Grass Roots Democracy," 55.
62. Daniel W. Howe, "The Political Psychology of The Federalist," *William and Mary Quarterly* 44 (1987): 485–509.
63. Tugwell and Banfield, "Grass Roots Democracy," 55.
64. Leuchtenburg, *Franklin D. Roosevelt and the New Deal*, 327.
65. Milkis and Mileur, "The New Deal, Then and Now," 7.
66. Elvin T. Lim, "The Lion and the Lamb: Demythologizing Franklin Roosevelt's Fireside Chats," *Rhetoric & Public Affairs* 6 (2003): 437–464.
67. Wilson Carey McWilliams, *The Idea of Fraternity in America* (Berkeley, CA: University of California Press, 1973), 209.
68. John Kincaid, "From Cooperative to Coercive Federalism," *The Annals of the American Academy of Political and Social Science* 509 (1990): 139–152.
69. Cited in Rexford G. Tugwell, "The Sources of New Deal Reformism," *Ethics* 64 (1954): 249–276, 274–275.
70. Franklin D. Roosevelt, Informal Address at Bowdoin Farm, 8/10/1933, available at http://www.presidency.ucsb.edu/ws/index.php?pid=14499 (accessed 11/12/2011).
71. Franklin D. Roosevelt, Address at the Democratic State Convention, Syracuse, NY, 9/29/1936, available at http://www.presidency.ucsb.edu/ws/index.php?pid=15142 (accessed 11/23/2011).
72. Milkis and Mileur, "The New Deal, Then and Now," 4.
73. Franklin D. Roosevelt, Second Inaugural Address, 1/20/1937.
74. Frances Perkins, *The Roosevelt I Knew* (New York: Viking Press, 1946), 72.
75. H. L. Mencken, *Minority Report: H. L. Mencken's Notebooks* (New York: Alfred Knopf, 1956), 99.
76. Sidney Milkis, *Political Parties and Constitutional Government* (Baltimore, MD: Johns Hopkins University Press, 1998), 84.
77. Leuchtenburg, *Franklin D. Roosevelt and the New Deal*, 331.
78. Theodore Lowi, *The Personal President: Power Invested, Promises Unfulfilled* (Ithaca, NY: Cornell University Press, 1985), 46.
79. Lowi, *The Personal President*, 7.
80. Lowi, *The Personal President*, 20.
81. Clinton Rossiter, *The American Presidency* (New York: Harcourt Brace, 1956), 104.
82. These include the Council of Economic Advisers (1946), the National Security Council (1947), the Office of the U.S. Trade Representative (1963), the Council on Environmental Quality (1970), the Office of Science and Technology Policy (1976), the Office of Administration (1977), the Office of National Drug Control Policy (1989), the Office of

Homeland Security (2001, before it became a cabinet-level Department), and the Office of Faith-based and Community Initiatives (2001). Each succeeding president's trigger-happy proclivity to create new agencies was, as Schlesinger had described of Roosevelt, "a kind of nervous tic," suggesting a relationship between presidential unilateralism and statism that even conservative presidents have failed to resist, as we shall explore in greater detail in Chapter 8. See Schlesinger, Jr., *The Coming of the New Deal*, 535.

83. Herbert Hoover, *American Individualism* (Garden City, NY: Doubleday, Doran, [1922] 1929), 4.

84. For the Whigs' commitment to individualism, see Lawrence F. Kohl, *The Politics of Individualism: Parties and the American Character in the Jacksonian Era* (New York: Oxford University Press, 1989).

85. Herbert Hoover, Statement on Proposed Increases in Federal Expenditures for Employment and Relief, 12/9/1930, available at http://www.presidency.ucsb.edu/ws/index.php?pid=22473 (accessed 11/1/2011).

86. Herbert Hoover, Radio Address on the Drought Relief Campaign of the American National Red Cross, 1/31/1931, available at http://www.presidency.ucsb.edu/ws/index.php?pid=22776 (accessed 11/1/2011).

87. Herbert Hoover, Address at Madison Square Garden in New York City, 10/31/1932, available at http://www.presidency.ucsb.edu http://www.presidency.ucsb.edu/ws/index.php?pid=23317 (accessed 11/7/2011).

88. Rexford G. Tugwell, *The Battle for Democracy* (New York: Columbia University Press, 1935), 319; Edgar Kemler, *Deflation of Ideals: An Ethical Guide for New Dealers* (Seattle, WA: University of Washington Press, 1941), 109–110; Cushing Strout, "The Twentieth-Century Enlightenment," *American Political Science Review* 49 (1955): 321–339.

89. Franklin Roosevelt, Address Accepting the Presidential Nomination at the Democratic National Convention in Chicago, 7/2/1932, available at http://www.presidency.ucsb.edu/ws/index.php?pid=75174 (accessed 11/8/2011).

90. Hoover, *American Individualism*, 23, 22.

91. Hoover, *American Individualism*, 24.

92. Hoover, *American Individualism*, 27.

93. Hoover, *American Individualism*, 40.

94. Hoover, *American Individualism*, 48.

95. Hoover, *American Individualism*, 67.

96. Leuchtenburg, *Franklin D. Roosevelt and the New Deal*, 347.

97. Stephen Skowronek, *Building a New American State: The Expansion of National Administrative Capacities 1877–1920* (New York: Cambridge University Press, 1982).

98. James T. Patterson, *Congressional Conservatism and the New Deal: The Growth of the Conservative Coalition in Congress, 1933–1939* (Lexington, KY: University of Kentucky Press, 1967), 13.

99. Richard Hofstadter, *The Age of Reform* (New York: Knopf, 1955).

100. Patterson, *Congressional Conservatism and the New Deal*, 17.

101. For criticisms of the New Deal, see Howard Zinn, "The Limits of the New Deal," in Howard Zinn, *The Politics of History* (Boston, MA: Beacon Press, 1970), 118–136; Ronald Radosh, "The Myth of the New Deal," in Ronald Radosh and Murray N. Rothbard (eds.), *A New History of Leviathan: Essays on the Rise of the American Corporate State* (New York: E. P. Dutton, 1972), 143–187; Suzanne Mettler, *Dividing Citizens: Gender and Federalism in New Deal Policy* (Ithaca, NY: Cornell University Press, 1998).

102. Charles R. Kesler, "The Public Philosophy of the New Freedom and the New Deal," in Robert Eden (ed.), *The New Deal and its Legacy: Critique and Reappraisal* (Westport, CA: Greenwood Press, 1989), 155–166, 155.

103. James T. Patterson, *The New Deal and the States: Federalism in Transition* (Princeton, NJ: Princeton University Press, 1969); Margaret Weir, "States, Race, and the Decline of New Deal Liberalism," *Studies in American Political Development* 19 (2005): 157–172.

104. Keith D. Revell, "The Road to *Euclid v. Ambler*: City Planning, State-Building, and the Changing Scope of the Police Power," *Studies in American Political Development* 13 (1999): 50–145; Douglas S. Massey and Nancy A. Denton, *American Apartheid: Segregation and the Making of the Underclass* (Cambridge, MA: Harvard University Press, 1993); Nancy Burns, *The Formation of American Local Governments: Private Values in Public Institutions* (New York: Oxford University Press, 1994), 112–116; Thomas J. Sugrue, *The Origins of the Urban Crisis: Race and Inequality in Postwar Detroit* (Princeton, NJ: Princeton University Press, 1996).

105. Alan Dawley, *Struggles for Justice: Social Responsibility and the Liberal State* (Cambridge, MA: Harvard University Press, 1991); Linda Gordon, *Pitied but Not Entitled: Single Mothers and the History of Welfare, 1890–1935* (Cambridge, MA: Harvard University Press, 1994); Alice Kessler-Harris, *In Pursuit of Equity: Women, Men, and the Quest for Economic Citizenship in 20th Century America* (New York: Oxford University Press, 2001).

106. Patterson, *The New Deal and the States*, 3–4; Suzanne Mettler, "Social Citizens of Separate Sovereignties," 243.

107. Tugwell and Banfield, "Grass Roots Democracy," 50.

108. Franklin D. Roosevelt, White House Statement on the National Emergency Council, 12/6/1933, available at http://www.presidency.ucsb.edu/ws/index.php?pid=14571 (accessed 12/1/2011). In 1939, the NEC functions and the State directors were transferred to the Office of Government Reports (OGR) in the Executive Office of the President. For more on the NEC and OGR, see William M. Leiter, "The Presidency and Non-Federal Government: FDR and the Promotion of State Legislative Action," *Presidential Studies Quarterly* 9 (1979): 101–121, 110–111.

109. Ellis W. Hawley, "Herbert Hoover, the Commerce Secretariat, and the Vision of an Associative State, 1921–1928," *Journal of American History* 61 (1974): 116–140; Theda Skocpol and Kenneth Finegold, "State Capacity and Economic Intervention in the Early New Deal," *Political Science Quarterly* 97 (1982): 255–278, 263.

110. 438 U.S. 203 (1987).

111. Frank Freidel, *Franklin D. Roosevelt: A Rendezvous with Destiny* (Boston, MA: Little Brown, 1990), 16–17; Arthur M. Schlesinger, Jr., *The Politics of Upheaval* (Boston, MA: Houghton Mifflin, 1960), 647; Leuchtenburg, *The FDR Years*, 3; Anthony F. Badger, *FDR: The First Hundred Days* (New York: Hill and Wang, 2008), 6.

112. Wallace E. Oates, *Fiscal Federalism* (New York: Harcourt Brace Jovanovitch, 1972); David Brian Robertson, "The Bias of American Federalism: Political Structure and the Development of America's Exceptional Welfare State in the Progressive Era," *Journal of Policy History* 1 (1989): 261–291; Paul E. Peterson, *The Price of Federalism* (Washington, DC: Brookings Institution Press, 1995).

113. See, for example, Lawrence Jacobs and Desmond King (eds.), *The Unsustainable American State* (New York: Oxford University Press, 2009).

Chapter 7

1. Joseph J. Ellis, *First Family: John and Abigail Adams* (New York: Vintage, 2011), 203.

2. Thomas Jefferson, First Inaugural Address, 3/4/1801, available at http://www.presidency.ucsb.edu/ws/?pid=25803 (accessed 6/30/2012).

3. John Higham, *Strangers in the Land: Patterns of American Nativism, 1860–1925* (New Brunswick, NJ: Rutgers University Press, 2002), 9.

4. Louis Hartz, "American Political Thought and the American Revolution," *American Political Science Review* 46 (1952): 321–342, 336.

5. Herbert Hoover, Address at Madison Square Garden in New York City, 10/31/1932, available at http://www.presidency.ucsb.edu/ws/index.php?pid=23317 (accessed 6/30/2012).

6. Herbert Hoover, Radio Address to the Nation From Elko, Nevada, 11/7/1932, available at http://www.presidency.ucsb.edu/ws/?pid=23342 (accessed 6/30/2012).

7. Dwight Eisenhower, Remarks at Luncheon Meeting of the Republican National Committee and the Republican National Finance Committee, 2/17/1955, available at http://www.presidency.ucsb.edu/ws/?pid=10411 (accessed 6/30/2012).

8. Alfred S. Regnery, *Upstream: The Ascendance of American Conservatism* (New York: Simon & Schuster, 2008), xiii–xiv. Many histories of conservatism, like Regnery's, also start in the twentieth century. See, for example, Gregory L. Schneider, *The Conservative Century: From Reaction to Revolution* (Lanham, MD: Rowman & Littlefield, 2009); Stephen Teles, *The Rise of the Conservative Legal Movement* (Princeton, NJ: Princeton University Press, 2008).

9. William Buckley, Jr., "Our Mission Statement," *The National Review*, 11/19/1955, available at http://article.nationalreview.com/?q=NDJhYTJjNWI0MWFiODBhMDc 2MzQwY2JlM2RhZjk5ZjM= (accessed 6/30/2012).

10. Patrick Allitt, *The Conservatives: Ideas and Personalities Throughout American History* (New Haven, CT: Yale University Press, 2009), 3.

11. Seymour M. Lipset, *The First New Nation: The United States in Historical and Comparative Perspective* (New York: W. W. Norton, 1979).

12. Russell Kirk, *The Conservative Mind from Burke to Santayana* (Chicago, IL: Henry Regnery, 1953); Robert Nisbet, *Conservatism: Dream and Reality* (Minneapolis, MN: University of Minnesota Press, 1986).

13. Allitt, *The Conservatives*, 19.

14. Wilson Carey McWilliams, *The Idea of Fraternity in America* (Berkeley, CA: University of California Press, 1973), 203.

15. Bruce Ackerman, *We the People: Transformations* (Cambridge: Belknap Press, 1998), 49–53.

16. Charles R. Kesler and Clinton Rossiter (eds.), *The Federalist Papers* (New York: Penguin Putnam, 2003), xv.

17. Kesler and Rossiter (eds.), *The Federalist Papers*, xx.

18. Kesler and Rossiter (eds.), *The Federalist Papers*, xviii.

19. Whereas Kesler had earlier been at pains to say that Hamilton, Madison, and Jay wrote as one person "to maintain the series' consistent argument and tone," he nevertheless went on to observe, perhaps inconsistently, a "change in tone" between the two volumes. Publius may have been one person, for Kesler, but he nevertheless possessed a split personality. See Kesler and Rossiter (eds.), *The Federalist Papers*, xiii, xix.

20. Kesler and Rossiter (eds.), *The Federalist Papers*, xx.

21. Kesler and Rossiter (eds.), *The Federalist Papers*, xix. This is also how another well-known conservative, Garry Wills, understood *The Federalist Papers*. The fact that the *Federalist* was a partisan tract written to persuade New Yorkers to adopt the proposed constitution is lost in Wills' account: "Publius, as author of the Federalist, comes before us as an impartial judge, without any special role or stake in the transactions at Philadelphia." Wills considered Madison's method of argument as one that "seems to add weights now to one arm of a balance, now to the other, fidgeting it toward perfect equilibrium." See Garry Wills, *Explaining America: The Federalist* (New York: Doubleday, 1981), 22.

22. Consider Lincoln's argument: "The Union is much older than the Constitution. It was formed, in fact, by the Articles of Association in 1774. It was matured and continued by the Declaration of Independence in 1776. It was further matured, and the faith of all the then thirteen States expressly plighted and engaged that it should be perpetual, by the Articles of Confederation in 1778. And finally, in 1787, one of the declared objects for ordaining and establishing the Constitution was 'to form a more perfect Union.'" See Abraham Lincoln, First Inaugural Address, 3/4/1861, available at http://www.presidency.ucsb.edu/ws/?pid=25818 (accessed 9/10/2011).

23. Richard Weaver, "Conservatism and Libertarianism: The Common Ground," in Ted J. Smith III (ed.), *In Defense of Tradition: Collected Shorter Writings of Richard M. Weaver, 1929–1963* (Indianapolis, IN: Liberty Fund, 2000), 479.

24. Kesler and Rossiter (eds.), *The Federalist Papers*, xxix.
25. And thus Brutus was rightly suspicious of (and prescient about) the goal of the "more perfect Union" envisioned in the Preamble of the Constitution, because "it is a union of the people of the United States considered as one body . . . [and] to make a union of this kind perfect, it is necessary to abolish all inferior governments, and to give the general one compleat [*sic*] legislative, executive and judicial powers to every purpose." See Brutus XII, 2/7/1788, in Herbert J. Storing and Murray Dry (eds.), *The Complete Anti-Federalist*, 7 vols. (Chicago, IL: University of Chicago Press, 1981), 2: 425 (2.9.151).
26. Adrienne Koch (ed.), *Notes of the Debates in the Federal Convention of 1787 Reported by James Madison* (New York: W. W. Norton, 1987), 353.
27. Koch (ed.), *Notes of the Debates in the Federal Convention*, 352.
28. Koch (ed.), *Notes of the Debates in the Federal Convention*, 612.
29. Jefferson Davis, First Inaugural Address, 2/18/1861, in James D. Richardson (ed.), *A Compilation of the Messages and Papers of the Confederacy*, 2 vols. (Nashville, TN: United States Publishing Company, 1905), 1: 32.
30. Jefferson Davis, First Inaugural Address, 2/18/1861, in Richardson (ed.), *A Compilation of the Messages and Papers of the Confederacy*, 1: 33.
31. Kesler does not deny that the Constitution is of and by the people, since he argues that "Publius shows us what it means, and what it takes, to live as responsible republicans under a written constitution. This is *The Federalist's* lesson in self government." See Kesler and Rossiter (eds.), *The Federalist Papers*, xxix.
32. Ronald Reagan, Address on Behalf of Senator Goldwater: A Time for Choosing, 10/27/1964, available at http://www.presidency.ucsb.edu/ws/index.php?pid=76121 (accessed 11/9/2011).
33. Jack M. Balkin, *Constitutional Redemption: Political Faith in an Unjust World* (Cambridge, MA: Harvard University Press, 2011), 19.
34. Lee J. Strang, "Originalism, the Declaration of Independence, and the Constitution: A Unique Role in Constitutional Interpretation?" *Penn State Law Review* 111 (2006): 413–479, 438–439.
35. Kesler and Rossiter (eds.), *The Federalist Papers*, xxx.
36. Ronald Reagan, Remarks at the "Prelude to Independence" Celebration in Williamsburg, Virginia, 5/30/1985, available at http://www.presidency.ucsb.edu/ws/?pid=38705 (accessed 6/30/2012).
37. Ronald Reagan, Remarks at the "We the People" Bicentennial Celebration in Philadelphia, Pennsylvania, 9/17/1987, available at http://www.presidency.ucsb.edu/ws/?pid=34801 (accessed 6/30/2012).
38. A (New Hampshire) Farmer, 1/11/1788, in Storing and Dry (eds.), *The Complete Anti-Federalist*, 4: 209 (4.17.9).
39. Ronald Reagan, Remarks at the Annual Meeting of the National Association of Manufacturers, 5/24/1985, available at http://www.presidency.ucsb.edu/ws/?pid=38689 (accessed 6/30/2012).
40. Ronald Reagan, Proclamation 5598–Shays' Rebellion Week and Day, 1987, 1/13/1987, available at http://www.presidency.ucsb.edu/ws/?pid=33942 (accessed 6/30/2012).
41. Patrick Henry, 6/5/1788, in Storing and Dry (eds.), *The Complete Anti-Federalist*, 5: 213 (5.16.2).
42. Candidus, 12/6/1787, in Storing and Dry (eds.), *The Complete Anti-Federalist*, 4: 126 (4.9.5).
43. On the Anti-Federalists' linkage of the Second and Tenth Amendments, see Saul Cornell, *A Well Regulated Militia: The Founding Fathers and the Origin of Gun Control in America* (New York: Oxford University Press, 2008), 73–76.
44. Jonathan Elliot (ed.), *The Debates in the Several State Conventions on the Adoption of the Federal Constitution as Recommended by the General Convention at Philadelphia in 1787*, 5 vols. (Philadelphia, PA: J. B. Lippincott, 1891), 3: 51.

45. Federal Farmer XVIII, 1/25/1788, in Storing and Dry (eds.), *The Complete Anti-Federalist*, 2: 342 (2.8.217).

46. Charles F. Adams (ed.), *The Works of John Adams, Second President of the United States*, 10 vols. (Boston, MA: Little and Brown, 1851), 6: 197.

47. Barry Goldwater, Acceptance Speech, 7/16/1964, available at http://www.washingtonpost.com/wp-srv/politics/daily/may98/goldwaterspeech.htm (accessed 6/30/2012).

48. This quote was taken from Cicero, at the advice of his then speechwriter, the Declarationist and early student of Leo Strauss, Harry Jaffa. See Harry V. Jaffa, "Goldwater's Famous 'Gaffe,'" *National Review* 36 (8/10/1984): 36.

49. See "Essays by None of the Well-Born Conspirators," in Storing and Dry (eds.), *The Complete Anti-Federalist*, 3: 194.

50. Federal Farmer V, 10/13/1787, in Storing and Dry (eds.), *The Complete Anti-Federalist*, 2: 254 (2.8.62).

51. In the third paragraph of Reagan's First Inaugural Address, he would reference "these United States," the first of 29 recorded speeches in which he used the plural demonstrative pronoun in his *Public Papers*, compared to, say, Bill Clinton, who used it in only one. See Ronald Reagan, First Inaugural Address, 1/21/1981, available at http://www.presidency.ucsb.edu/ws/?pid=43130 (accessed 6/25/2012).

52. Ronald Reagan, Remarks at the Bicentennial Observance of the Battle of Yorktown in Virginia, 10/19/1981, available at http://www.presidency.ucsb.edu/ws/?pid=43151 (6/30/2012).

53. Brutus XVI, 4/10/1788, in Storing and Dry (eds.), *The Complete Anti-Federalist*, 2: 444 (2.9.200).

54. Ronald Reagan, Remarks to Participants in the National YMCA Youth Governors' Conference, 6/21/1984, available at http://www.presidency.ucsb.edu/ws/?pid=40081 (accessed 6/30/2012).

55. Ronald Reagan, Address on Behalf of Senator Goldwater: A Time for Choosing, 10/27/1964.

56. Bill O' Reilly and Martin Dugard, *Killing Lincoln: The Shocking Assassination that Changed America Forever* (New York: Henry Holt, 2011), 42. O' Reilly's fundamental misunderstanding of Andrew Johnson's presidency can be seen in his judgment that "Johnson's vengeful policies toward the South were in direct contrast with what Lincoln had hoped for" (285).

57. Brutus IV, 11/29/1787, in Storing and Dry (eds.), *The Complete Anti-Federalist*, 2: 385 (2.9.49).

58. Goldwater, Acceptance Speech, 7/16/1964.

59. Lou Cannon, *President Reagan: The Role of a Lifetime* (New York: PublicAffairs, 2000), 92.

60. Robert D. Meade, *Patrick Henry: Practical Revolutionary* (New York: J. B. Lippincott, 1969), 265.

61. Samuel Kernell, *Going Public: New Strategies of Presidential Leadership* (Washington, DC: CQ Press, 1997); Norman Ornstein and Thomas Mann (eds.), *The Permanent Campaign and Its Future* (Washington, DC: American Enterprise Institute and The Brookings Institution, 2000).

62. Wills, *Explaining America*, 26.

63. Harvey C. Mansfield, Jr., *America's Constitutional Soul* (Baltimore, MD: Johns Hopkins University Press, 1991).

64. Jerry Falwell, *Listen, America!* (New York: Bantam Books, 1981), 1.

65. Federal Farmer XI, 1/10/1788, in Storing and Dry (eds.), *The Complete Anti-Federalist*, 2: 290–291 (2.8.147).

66. Federal Farmer XIV, 1/17/1788, in Storing and Dry (eds.), *The Complete Anti-Federalist*, 2: 313 (2.8.179).

67. George F. Will, *Restoration: Congress, Term Limits, and the Recovery of Deliberative Democracy* (New York: The Free Press, 1992), 141.

68. Federal Farmer XV, 1/18/1788, in Storing and Dry (eds.), *The Complete Anti-Federalist*, 2: 316 (2.8.185).

69. Brutus XII, 2/7/1788, in Storing and Dry (eds.), *The Complete Anti-Federalist*, 2: 422–423 (2.9.145).

70. Federal Farmer XV, 1/18/1788, in Storing and Dry (eds.), *The Complete Anti-Federalist*, 2: 322–323 (2.8.195).

71. 349 U.S. 294 (1955); Gary L. McDowell, "Were the Anti-Federalists Right? Judicial Activism and the Problem of Consolidated Government," *Publius* 12 (1982): 99–108, 105.

72. Federal Farmer XV, 1/18/1788, in Storing and Dry (eds.), *The Complete Anti-Federalist*, 2: 315 (2.8.185).

73. Brutus X, 1/24/1788, in Storing and Dry (eds.), *The Complete Anti-Federalist*, 2: 419 (2.9.137).

74. Brutus XII, 2/7/1788, in Storing and Dry (eds.), *The Complete Anti-Federalist*, 2: 424 (2.9.150).

75. Brutus XI, 1/31/1788, in Storing and Dry (eds.), *The Complete Anti-Federalist*, 2: 421 (2.9.141).

76. Brutus XI, 1/31/1788, in Storing and Dry (eds.), *The Complete Anti-Federalist*, 2: 422 (2.9.144).

77. The quote is from Ackerman, *We the People: Transformations*, 9. For a different account that sees more change in the way politicians have confronted the Court than I do, see Stephen Engel, *American Politicians Confront the Court: Opposition Politics and Changing Responses to Judicial Power* (New York: Cambridge, 2011).

78. Jack M. Balkin and Sanford Levinson, "Understanding The Constitutional Revolution," *Virginia Law Review* 87 (2001): 1045–1109, 1051.

79. Gerald Gunther and Kathleen Sullivan, *Constitutional Law*, 15th Edition (New York: Foundation Press, 2004); Paul Finkelman, "Turning Losers into Winners: What Can We Learn, If Anything, From the Antifederalists?" *Texas Law Review* 79 (2001): 849–894, 878, n169.

80. Robert M. Collins, *Transforming America: Politics and Culture in the Reagan Years* (New York: Columbia University Press, 2007), 76–77.

81. Daniel Patrick Moynihan, *Came the Revolution: Argument in the Reagan Era* (San Diego, CA: Harcourt Brace Jovanovich, 1988), 151.

82. Ronald Reagan, Remarks at the Annual Washington Policy Meeting of the National Association of Manufacturers, 3/18/1982, available at http://www.presidency.ucsb.edu/ws/?pid=42288 (11/24/2013).

83. Ronald Reagan, Remarks at the "Prelude to Independence" Celebration in Williamsburg, Virginia.

84. Ronald Reagan, Remarks at the "Prelude to Independence" Celebration in Williamsburg, Virginia.

85. Manuel Klausner, "Inside Ronald Reagan: A Reason Interview," *Reason*, 7/1975, available at http://reason.com/archives/1975/07/01/inside-ronald-reagan/singlepage (accessed 6/30/2012). Reagan was only nearly right because the federal government has been the constant object of fulmination by Anti-Federalists of every generation. However, whereas libertarians are against all government, the Anti-Federalists were only against the federal government (and rather in favor of state or police powers). Reagan's effort to fuse libertarian thought with modern conservative thought was possible only because the federal government in the second half of the twentieth century had become so powerful, having penetrated the lives of individual citizens, that the old language of states' rights could be combined with a modern language of individual and natural rights against the common enemy of both libertarians and Anti-Federalists. This is also to say that the emergence of libertarianism is evidence that the consolidation that the Anti-Federalists had so feared—that the federal government

would come to have a direct (some say coercive) relationship with the individual—had indeed occurred.

86. Paul Eidelberg, *The Philosophy of the American Constitution* (New York: The Free Press, 1968), 264–271.

87. Elliot (ed.), *The Debates in the Several State Conventions*, 2: 176.

88. Kate Mason Rowland, *The Life of George Mason, 1725–1792* (New York: G. P. Putnam's Sons, 1892), 1: 166.

89. Ronald Reagan, First Inaugural Address, 1/21/1981.

90. Ronald Reagan, Remarks at the Annual Meeting of the National Association of Towns and Townships, 9/12/1983, available at http://www.presidency.ucsb.edu/ws/?pid= 41819 (accessed 9/17/2009).

91. Russell Kirk, *Program for Conservatives* (Chicago, IL: Henry Regnery, 1962), 308.

92. M. E. Bradford, *A Better Guide Than Reason: Federalists and Anti-Federalists* (New Brunswick, NJ: Transaction Publishers, [1979] 1994), 108.

93. Bradford, *A Better Guide Than Reason*, 107.

94. Consider Donald R. Brand, "Competition and the New Deal Regulatory State," in Sidney M. Milkis and Jerome M. Mileur (eds.), *The New Deal and the Triumph of Liberalism* (Amherst, MA: University of Massachusetts Press, 2002), 166–192, 166.

95. Jeffrey M. Jones, "In U.S., Nearly Half Identify as Economically Conservative," 5/25/2012, *Gallup*, available at http://www.gallup.com/poll/154889/nearly-half-identify-economically-conservative.aspx (accessed 6/30/2012).

96. Larry M. Schwab, *The Illusion of A Conservative Reagan Revolution* (New Brunswick, NJ: Transactions Publishers, 1991).

97. Jackson Turner Main, *The Antifederalists: Critics of the Constitution, 1781–1788* (Chapel Hill, NC: University of North Carolina Press, 1951), xl.

Chapter 8

1. John F. Kennedy, "Remarks at Amherst College Upon Receiving an Honorary Degree," 10/26/1963, available at http://www.presidency.ucsb.edu/ws/?pid=9497 (accessed 11/1/2012).

2. The word "federal" (originally spelt "foederal") comes from "foedus," which referred to a treaty between Rome and non-Latin allied states ("foederati"). See Donald W. Baronowski, "Roman Treaties with Communities of Citizens," *The Classical Quarterly* 28 (1988): 172–178.

3. Clinton Rossiter, *Conservatism in America* (New York: Alfred Knopf, 1955), 72.

4. Paul C. Nagel, *One Nation Indivisible: The Union in American Thought* (Westport, CT: Greenwood Press, 1980).

5. "Audio and Transcript: Obama's Victory Speech," 11/7/2012, *NPR*, available at http://www.npr.org/2012/11/06/164540079/transcript-president-obamas-victory-speech (accessed 11/7/12).

6. Richard Weaver, "Conservatism and Libertarianism: The Common Ground," in Ted J. Smith III (ed.), in *Defense of Tradition: Collected Shorter Writings of Richard M. Weaver, 1929–1963* (Indianapolis, IN: Liberty Fund, 2000), 479.

7. Hans Kohn, *American Nationalism: An Interpretive Essay* (New York: Macmillan, 1957).

8. Mark Meckler and Jenny B. Martin, *Tea Party Patriots: The Second American Revolution* (New York: Henry Holt, 2012), 13.

9. Thomas Jefferson to James Monroe, 2/7/1801, in Paul L. Ford, *The Works of Thomas Jefferson*, 12 vols. (New York: G. P. Putnam's Sons, 1905), 9: 203. Among many conservative references to "first principles," perhaps with an unintended pun on the First Founding, see, for example, the Heritage Foundation and the Claremont Institute's websites, at http://www.heritage.org/initiatives/first-principles and http://www.claremont.org/publications/precepts/id.133/precept_detail.asp (accessed 7/2/2012).

The Claremont page explicitly asks and notes, "just what *are* those principles exactly? . . . we believe they are summed up in the Declaration of Independence."

10. Arthur Styron, *The Cast-Iron Man: John C. Calhoun and American Democracy* (New York: Longmans, Green, 1935).

11. Adam Sorensen, "The Top 10 Everything of 2011: 9. Cain Misreads the Constitution," *Time*, 12/17/2011, available at http://www.time.com/time/specials/packages/article/0,28804,2101344_2100826_2100836,00.html #ixzz210btSey7 (accessed 7/2/2012).

12. The two passages exactly quoted in parentheses focus on states' rights ("these United Colonies are, and of Right ought to be Free and Independent States . . . We hold these Truths to be self-evident, that all Men are created equal, that they are endowed by their Creator with certain unalienable Rights, that among these are Life, Liberty, and the Pursuit of Happiness") and the idea of government by consent ("That to secure these Rights, Governments are instituted among Men, deriving their just Powers from the Consent of the Governed"). See http://www.jbs.org/about-jbs/core-principles (accessed 7/2/12).

13. "Mike Huckabee's Remarks at the RNC: 'We Can Do Better' and 'We Will Do Better,'" *FoxNews*, 8/29/2012, available at http://foxnewsinsider.com/2012/08/29/transcript-mike-huckabees-remarks-at-the-rnc/ (accessed 8/29/2012).

14. Gordon S. Wood, *The Creation of the American Republic, 1776–1787* (Chapel Hill, NC: University of North Carolina Press, 1969), 606.

15. Gail Collins, "Parsing Mr. Wilson's Apology," *The New York Times*, 9/11/2009, available at http://www.nytimes.com/2009/09/12/opinion/12collins.html (accessed 7/2/2012); Ann Gerhart, "Joe Wilson's War: A Congressmen Cries 'Lie,'" *The Washington Post*, 9/10/2009, available at http://www.washingtonpost.com/wp-dyn/content/article/2009/09/09/AR2009090903585.html (accessed 7/2/2012).

16. Dan Balz, "Perry warns of Fed treason, challenges Obama," *The Washington Post*, 8/16/2011, available at http://www.washingtonpost.com/politics/perry-warns-of-fed-treason-challenges-obama/2011/08/16/gIQABVScIJ_story.html (accessed 7/1/2012).

17. Mitchell Landsberg, "Gingrich Promises NRA He'll Take the Right to Bear Arms Worldwide," *The Los Angeles Times*, 4/13/2012, available at http://articles.latimes.com/2012/apr/13/news/la-pn-gingrich-promises-nra-hell-take-the-right-to-bear-arms-worldwide-20120413 (accessed 7/2/2012). For a related story on how Sarah Palin turned Paul Revere into a Second Amendment hero who lived before the time when a Bill of Rights was ever contemplated, see Eugene Robinson, "Sarah Palin's Revisionist Ride," *The Washington Post*, 6/6/2011, available at http://www.washingtonpost.com/opinions/sarah-palins-revisionist-ride/2011/06/06/AGVMGbKH_story.html (accessed 7/2/2012).

18. Elizabeth P. Foley, *The Tea Party: Three Principles* (New York: Cambridge University Press, 2012), xi.

19. Rand Paul, *The Tea Party Goes to Washington* (New York: Center Street, 2011), xii–xiii.

20. Jill Lepore, *The Whites of Their Eyes: The Tea Party's Revolution and the Battle over American History* (Princeton, NJ: Princeton University Press, 2010), 9.

21. Lepore, *The Whites of Their Eyes*, 7.

22. The Maine ReFounders have a website at http://themaineteaparty.com/ (accessed 6/30/2012).

23. Jeffrey H. Anderson, "Obama Misquotes Declaration of Independence, Again," *The Weekly Standard*, 10/20/2010, available at http://www.weeklystandard.com/blogs/obama-misquotes-declaration-independence-again_511412.html (accessed 6/30/2012).

24. Samuel Chase, "Charge delivered . . . at a circuit court of the United States," 5/2/1803, *Impeachment of the Hon. Samuel Chase* (Baltimore, MD: Samuel Butler and Charles Keatinge, 1805), 61.

25. Paul, *The Tea Party Goes to Washington*, 62. Similarly, Speaker John Boehner, when asked in a television interview about the House's relentless efforts to repeal President Obama's healthcare law, would say to Bob Schieffer, "We should not be judged by how many new

laws we create . . . We ought to be judged on how many laws we repeal." See http://www.washingtonpost.com/blogs/the-fix/wp/ 2013/07/22/john-boehner-judge-republicans-by-the-laws-they-dont-make/ (accessed 7/22/2013).

26. Paul, *The Tea Party Goes to Washington*, 109.

27. Republican Party Platform of 1964, 7/13/1964, available at http://www.presidency.ucsb.edu/ws/index.php?pid=25840 (accessed 6/30/12).

28. The pledge can be found at http://www.gop.gov/indepth/pledge (accessed 6/30/12).

29. James C. McKinley, Jr., "Texas Governor's Secession Talk Stirs Furor," *The New York Times*, 4/17/2009, available at http://www.nytimes.com/2009/04/18/us/politics/18texas.html (accessed 6/30/12).

30. Robert Marquand, "Is Mitt Romney's Europe-bashing Well Placed?" *The Christian Science Monitor*, 1/11/2012, available at http://www.csmonitor.com/World/Global-News/2012/0111/Is-Mitt-Romney-s-Europe-bashing-well-placed (accessed 6/30/2012).

31. Republican Party Platform of 2012, ii, available at http://www.nytimes.com/interactive/2012/08/28/us/politics/20120812-gop-platform.html?ref=politics (accessed 8/29/2012).

32. Consider Glenn Beck, *Cowards: What Politicians, Radicals, and the Media Refuse to Say* (New York: Threshold Editions, 2012).

33. See, for example, Robin Abcarian, "'Birthers' claim Obama applied to college as a foreigner," *The Los Angeles Times*, 5/30/2012, available at http://articles.latimes.com/2012/may/30/news/la-pn-birthers-claim-obama-applied-to-college-as-a-foreigner-20120529 (accessed 7/3/2012); Frank Newport, "Many Americans Can't Name Obama's Religion," *Gallup*, 6/22/2012, available at http://www.gallup.com/poll/155315/many-americans-cant-name-obamas-religion.aspx (accessed 7/3/2012).

34. James C. McKinley, Jr. and Sam Dillon, "Some Parents Oppose Obama School Speech," *The New York Times*, 9/3/2009, available at http://www.nytimes.com/2009/09/04/us/04school.html (accessed 7/3/2012).

35. Letter, Dwight Eisenhower to Congressman Ralph Gwinn (R-NY), 6/7/1949, in *Public School Assistance Act of 1949*, Hearing before a Special Subcommittee of the Committee on Education and Labor, House of Representatives, 81st Congress, 1st Session (Washington, DC: GPO, 1949), 888.

36. Cited in *Congressional Digest* 25, 2 (2/1946): 49.

37. Republican Party Platform of 2012, ii.

38. Felicia Sonmez, "Santorum: Obama is a `snob' because he wants `everybody in America to go college,'" *The Washington Post*, 2/25/2012, available at http://www.washingtonpost.com/blogs/election-2012/post/santorum-obama-is-a-snob-because-he-wants-everybody-in-america-to-go-to-college/2012/02/25/gIQATJffaR_blog.html (accessed 7/3/2012); Speech of Melancton Smith, New York Ratification Convention, 6/21/1788, in Herbert J. Storing and Murray Dry (eds.), *The Complete Anti-Federalist*, 7 vols. (Chicago, IL: University of Chicago Press, 1981), 6: 157 (6.12.15).

39. Consider Theda Skocpol and Vanessa Williamson, *The Tea Party and the Remaking of Republican Conservatism* (New York: Oxford University Press, 2012), 54–57.

40. For the opposite view, see Anthony DiMaggio, *The Rise of the Tea Party: Political Discontent and Corporate Media in the Age of Obama* (New York: Monthly Review Press, 2011).

41. Skocpol and Williamson, *The Tea Party and the Remaking of Republican Conservatism*, 50.

42. *National Federation of Independent Business v. Sebelius* (2012), available at http://www.supremecourt.gov/opinions/11pdf/11-393c3a2.pdf (accessed 7/3/2012).

43. Barack Obama, *The Audacity of Hope: Thoughts on Reclaiming the American Dream* (New York: Crown Publishers, 2006), 86.

44. Obama, *The Audacity of Hope*, 86–87.

45. On Obama's pragmatism, see James P. Kloppenberg, *Obama: Dreams, Hope, and the American Political Tradition* (Princeton, NJ: Princeton University Press, 2010).

46. Obama, *The Audacity of Hope*, 97.

47. Michael Gerson, "On Sotomayor, Republicans Must Enter Obama's Trap," *The Washington Post*, 5/29/2009, available at http://www.washingtonpost.com/wp-dyn/content/article/2009/05/28/AR2009052803624.html (accessed 7/3/2012).

48. Obama, *The Audacity of Hope*, 90.

49. Obama, *The Audacity of Hope*, 92.

50. Obama, *The Audacity of Hope*, 93.

51. Obama, *The Audacity of Hope*, 362.

52. "Audio and Transcript: Obama's Victory Speech," 11/7/2012.

53. Barack Obama, Second Inaugural Address, 1/21/2013, available at http://www.foxnews.com/politics/2013/01/21/transcript-president-obama-inaugural-address/ (accessed 1/21/2013).

54. "Full Text: President Obama's Speech at MLK Memorial," *The Washington Post*, 10/16/2011, available at http://www.washingtonpost.com/lifestyle/style/full-text-president-obamas-speech-at-mlk-memorial/2011/10/16/gIQAkbl3oL_story.html (accessed 7/3/2012).

55. Barack Obama, First Inaugural Address, 1/20/2009, available at http://www.presidency.ucsb.edu/ws/index.php?pid=44 (accessed 7/2/2012).

56. Bill Clinton's speech to the DNC in 2012 was another more recent example of this, when he said, "We decide to champion the cause for which our founders pledged their lives, their fortunes, their sacred honor—the cause of forming a more perfect union." The pledge he quoted came, of course, from the Declarationists, while the union they turned their pledge toward was of course a creation of the Federalists. See Transcript of Bill Clinton's Speech to the Democratic National Convention, *The New York Times*, 9/5/2012, available at http://www.nytimes.com/2012/09/05/us/politics/transcript-of-bill-clintons-speech-to-the-democratic-national-convention.html?pagewanted=all (accessed 9/5/2012).

57. "Transcript: Robin Roberts ABC Interview with President Obama," *ABC News*, 5/9/2012, available at http://abcnews.go.com/Politics/transcript-robin-roberts-abc-news-interview-president-obama/story?id=16316043#.T_OPBY69w8Y (accessed 7/3/2012).

58. "Transcript: Illinois Senate Candidate Barack Obama," *The Washington Post*, 7/27/2004, available at http://www.washingtonpost.com/wp-dyn/articles/A19751-2004Jul27.html (7/4/2012).

59. "Obama's Healthcare Speech to Congress," *The New York Times*, 9/9/2009, available at http://www.nytimes.com/2009/09/10/us/politics/10obama.text.html?pagewanted=all (accessed 7/3/2012).

60. Jim Geraghty, "Obama: Unemployed Pennsylvanians Cling to Guns, Religion, Anti-Immigrant, Anti-Trade Views," *National Review*, 4/11/2008, available at http://www.nationalreview.com/campaign-spot/9858/obama-unemployed-pennsylvanians-cling-guns-religion-anti-immigrant-anti-trade-vie (accessed 7/3/2012).

61. "Full Text of President Obama's Economic Speech in Kansas," *The Los Angeles Times*, 12/6/2011, available at http://articles.latimes.com/2011/dec/06/news/la-pn-text-obama-speech-kansas-20111206 (accessed 7/3/2012).

62. A case could even be made that we ought not to be celebrating July 4 as *the* national holiday, since we had not yet been *constituted* in 1776. September 17 should figure just as heavily, the day the words that would inaugurate a new order for the ages was finalized at Philadelphia (or March 4, the day government operations began)—though the fact that we do not indicates that if American minds are Federalist, our hearts are still spontaneously Anti-Federalist.

63. Jeff Zeleny, "Thousands Rally in Capital to Protest Big Government," *The New York Times*, 9/12/2009, available at http://www.nytimes.com/2009/09/13/us/politics/13protestweb.html (accessed 6/30/2012).

64. Aaron Wildavsky, "Federalism Means Inequality: Political Geometry, Political Sociology, and Political Culture," in Robert T. Golebiewski and Aaron Wildavsky (eds.), *The Costs of Federalism* (New Brunswick, NJ: Transaction Publishers, 1984), 55–72.

65. Jeffrey Tulis, "The Constitutional Presidency in American Political Development," in Martin Fausold and Alan Shank (eds.), *The Constitution and the American Presidency* (Albany, NY: State University of New York Press, 1991), 133–146, 137. Tulis goes on to argue, correctly, that we need to disentangle the problems of plebiscitary leadership from the development of big government. The first is a Federalist concern, the second an Anti-Federalist one.

66. Lindsey Boerma, "Santorum Calls Romney 'Worst Republican' to Face Obama," *National Journal*, 3/25/2012, available at http://www.nationaljournal.com/2012-presidential-campaign/santorum-calls-romney-worst-republican-to-face-obama-20120325 (accessed 7/3/2012).

67. Paul, *The Tea Party Goes to Washington*, 11.

68. The reason why social conservatives and Tea Partiers can find common ground is that their ideological ancestors were anti-government Anti-Federalists who also believed that the virtue of citizens mattered more than the goodwill of governments. Gun rights, home schooling, and tough state-level immigration laws are all contemporary issues that bear the imprint of Anti-Federalism. Not surprisingly, all of these rights are better understood as majority "privileges," whereas abortion, gay rights, and other rights are derided as "special rights" precisely because the latter are seen as onerous and illegitimate obligations social minorities demand of majorities.

69. *National Federation of Independent Business v. Sebelius* (2012), 5.

70. Russell L. Hanson, "Federal Statebuilding during the New Deal: The Transition from Mothers' Aid to Aid to Dependent Children," in Edward S. Greenberg and Thomas F. Mayer (eds.), *Changes in the State: Causes and Consequences* (Newbury Park, CA: Sage, 1990), 93–113.

71. Frank Newport, "Mississippi Most Conservative State, D.C. Most Liberal," *Gallup*, 2/3/2012, available at http://www.gallup.com/poll/152459/Mississippi-Conservative-State-Liberal.aspx (accessed 6/12/2012).

72. Ronald Reagan, Remarks to Participants in the National YMCA Youth Governors' Conference, 6/21/1984, available at http://www.presidency.ucsb.edu/ws/?pid=40081 (accessed 6/27/2012).

73. Suzanne Mettler, "Social Citizens of Separate Sovereignties," in Sidney M. Milkis and Jerome M. Mileur (eds.), *The New Deal and the Triumph of Liberalism* (Amherst, MA: University of Massachusetts Press, 2002), 231–271, 261.

74. Arthur M. Schlesinger, Jr., "Rating the Presidents: From Washington to Clinton," *Political Science Quarterly* 112 (1997), 179–190; James Lindgren, Steven G. Calabresi, Leonard A. Leo, and C. David Smith, "Rating the Presidents of the United States, 1789–2000: A Survey of Scholars in History, Political Science, and Law," *The Wall Street Journal*, 11/16/2000; CSPAN Historians 2009 Presidential Leadership Survey, available at http://legacy.c-span.org/PresidentialSurvey/Overall-Ranking.aspx (accessed 7/12/2011).

75. John Whipple, *Substance of a Speech Delivered at the Whig Meeting Held at the Town House, Providence, RI, August 28, 1837* (Washington, DC: Library of Congress, 1837).

76. Stephen Skowronek, *The Politics Presidents Make: Leadership from John Adams to Bill Clinton* (Cambridge, MA: Belknap Press, 1997).

77. Herbert Croly, *The Promise of American Life* (Boston, MA: Northeastern University Press, [1909] 1989), 46. For a more expansive reading of Jefferson's actions, see Theodore J. Crackel, "Jefferson, Politics, and the Army: An Examination of the Military Peace Establishment Act of 1802," *Journal of the Early Republic* 2 (1982): 21–38.

78. Bruce Ackerman, *We the People: Transformations* (Cambridge, MA: Belknap Press, 1998), 409.

79. Thomas A. Spragens, Jr., *Getting the Left Right: The Transformation, Decline, and Reformation of American Liberalism* (Lawrence, KS: University Press of Kansas, 2010), xx.

80. For the contrast between the Federalist and Anti-Federalist theories of representation, see Wilson Carey McWilliams, "The Anti-Federalists, Representation and Party," *Northwestern Law Review* 85 (1990): 12–38.

81. Skowronek differentiates between persistent, emergent, and recurrent orders, corresponding to constitutional, secular, and political time. See Skowronek, *The Politics Presidents Make*, 9.

82. Edward S. Corwin, *The President, Office and Powers, 1787–1957: History and Analysis of Practice and Opinion* (New York: New York University Press, 1957); Richard E. Neustadt, *Presidential Power and the Modern Presidents: The Politics of Leadership from Roosevelt to Reagan* (New York: The Free Press, 1990); Skowronek, *The Politics Presidents Make*. The question of legitimacy, in turn, is intimately tied to the ambiguity of the executive power. On this see, Harvey C. Mansfield, Jr., *Taming the Prince: The Ambivalence of the Modern Executive Power* (Baltimore, MD: Johns Hopkins University Press, 1993); Clement Fatovic, "Constitutionalism and Presidential Prerogative: Jeffersonian and Hamiltonian Perspectives," *American Journal of Political Science* 48 (2004): 429–44; J. David Greenstone, *The Lincoln Persuasion: Remaking American Liberalism* (Princeton, NJ: Princeton University Press, 1993); Fred I. Greenstein, *The Hidden-hand Presidency: Eisenhower as Leader* (Baltimore, MD: Johns Hopkins University Press, 1994); Jeffrey K. Tulis, *The Rhetorical Presidency* (Princeton, NJ: Princeton University Press, 1987).

83. James Ceaser, *Presidential Selection: Theory and Development* (Princeton, NJ: Princeton University Press, 1979); Tulis, *The Rhetorical Presidency*.

84. Thomas Jefferson to Colonel Carrington, 5/27/1788, in Adrienne Koch and William Peden (eds.), *The Life and Selected Writings of Thomas Jefferson* (New York: Random House, 1944), 446–447, 447.

85. On the development of democracy and its implication on presidential power, see Stephen Skowronek, "The Conservative Insurgency and Presidential Power: A Developmental Perspective On The Unitary Executive," *Harvard Law Review* 122 (2009): 2070–2103, 2102.

86. Malcolm M. Feeley and Edward Rubin, *Federalism: Political Identity and Tragic Compromise* (Ann Arbor, MI: University of Michigan Press, 2008); William Riker, *Federalism: Origin, Operation, Significance* (Boston, MA: Little, Brown, 1964).

87. Norman Ornstein and Thomas Mann (eds.), *The Permanent Campaign and Its Future* (Washington, DC: American Enterprise Institute and The Brookings Institution, 2000).

88. On the related phenomenon of the "waning of political time," see Skowronek, *The Politics Presidents Make*, Chapter 8.

89. This might, perhaps, be metaphorically represented by the redrawing of the presidential flag and seal by Harry Truman's executive order in 1945, when the eagle's head, which had previously looked to its left, toward a bundle of 13 arrows representing the 13 original states, would henceforth direct its gaze to its right, at the single olive branch. See David McCullough, *Truman* (New York: Simon and Schuster, 1993), 474.

90. Paul West, "In Florida, Paul Ryan warns of Medicare rationing under Obama plan," *The Los Angeles Times*, 8/18/2012, available at http://www.latimes.com/news/politics/la-pn-paul-ryan-in-florida-warns-of-medicare-rationing-20120818,0,6203516.story (accessed 8/18/2012).

91. Aristotle, *Politics*, Book 4, in Benjamin Jowett (trans.), *Aristotle's Politics* (Oxford, UK: Clarendon Press, 1908), 146.

92. Alexis de Tocqueville, *Democracy in America*, 2 vols. (New York: Alfred Knopf, [1835–1840] 1945), 1: 93, 242.

93. Nicolò Machiavelli, *The Prince and the Discourses*, trans. C. Detmold (New York: Random House, 1950), 397.

94. J. G. A. Pocock, *The Machiavellian Moment: Florentine Political Thought and the Atlantic Republican Tradition* (Princeton, NJ: Princeton University Press, 1975), viii.

95. Richard Hofstadter, *The Age of Reform: From Bryan to FDR* (New York: Alfred Knopf, [1955] 1959), 21.

96. Benjamin Franklin, *The Pennsylvania Gazette*, 5/9/1764, in Stephen Hess and Milton Kaplan, *The Ungentlemanly Art: A History of American Political Cartoons* (New York: Macmillan, 1968), 52.

97. Mancur Olson, "Dictatorship, Democracy, and Development," *American Political Science Review* 87 (1993): 567–576.

98. E. E. Schattschneider, *The Semi-Sovereign People: A Realist's View of Democracy in America* (New York: Holt, Rinehart & Winston, 1960), vii.

Appendix 1

1. Karen Orren and Stephen Skowronek, *The Search for American Political Development* (New York: Cambridge University Press, 2004), 123.

2. Orren and Skowronek, *The Search for American Political Development*, 20.

3. Orren and Skowronek, *The Search for American Political Development*, 123.

4. On this point, see John Gerring, "APD from a Methodological Point of View," *Studies in American Political Development* 17 (2003): 82–102, 83–84; Amy Bridges, *A City in the Republic: Antebellum New York and the Origins of Machine Politics* (Ithaca, NY: Cornell University Press, 1984); Karen Orren, *Belated Feudalism: Labor, the Law, and Liberal Development in the United States* (New York: Cambridge University Press, 1991); Louis Hartz, *The Liberal Tradition in America* (New York: Harcourt Brace, 1955); Richard Franklin Bensel, *Yankee Leviathan: The Origins of Central State Authority in America, 1859–1877* (New York: Cambridge University Press, 1990); Stephen Skowronek, *Building a New American State: The Expansion of National Administrative Capacities 1877–1920* (New York: Cambridge University Press, 1982).

5. Samuel P. Huntington, "Political Modernization: America vs. Europe," *World Politics* 18 (1966): 378–414; J. P. Nettl, "The State as a Conceptual Variable," *World Politics* 20 (1968): 559–592; Robert C. Lieberman, "Weak State, Strong Policy: Paradoxes of Race Policy in the United States, Great Britain, and France," *Studies in American Political Development* 16 (2002): 138–161.

6. William J. Novak, "The Myth of the 'Weak' American State," *American Historical Review* 113 (2008): 752–772.

7. Skowronek, *Building a New American State*; Brian Balogh, *A Government Out of Sight: The Mystery of National Authority in Nineteenth-Century America* (New York: Cambridge University Press, 2009).

8. Elisabeth S. Clemens, *The People's Lobby: Organizational Innovation and the Rise of Interest Group Politics in the United States, 1890–1925* (Chicago, IL: University of Chicago Press, 1997); Skowronek, *Building a New American State*; Theda Skocpol, *Protecting Soldiers and Mothers: The Political Origins of Social Policy in the United States* (Cambridge, MA: Harvard University Press, 1992); Daniel Carpenter, *The Forging of Bureaucratic Autonomy: Reputations, Networks, and Policy Innovation in Executive Agencies, 1862–1928* (Princeton, NJ: Princeton University Press, 2001).

9. Peter B. Evans, Dietrich Rueschemeyer, and Theda Skocpol (eds.), *Bringing the State Back In* (New York: Cambridge University Press, 1985).

10. Robert Lieberman, *Shifting the Color Line: Race and the American Welfare State* (Cambridge, MA: Harvard University Press, 1998).

11. Paul Pierson, *Politics in Time: History, Institutions, and Social Analysis* (Princeton, NJ: Princeton University Press, 2004).

12. Pierson, *Politics in Time*, 6.

13. Orren and Skowronek, *The Search for American Political Development*, ix.

14. See also the view espoused in Stephen M. Griffin, "Bringing the State into Constitutional Theory: Public Authority and the Constitution," *Law & Social Inquiry* 16 (1991): 659–710.

15. Orren and Skowronek, *The Search for American Political Development*, 10.

16. Tocqueville may have been drawing out the implications of Madison's caveat when he observed that "the government of the Union depends almost entirely upon legal fictions." See Alexis de Tocqueville, *Democracy in America*, 2 vols. (New York: Alfred Knopf, [1835–1840] 1945), 1: 166. Others who have tried to find a definitive account of what the Federalists were up to may have understated the possibility that despite their efforts, irresolution was a significant outcome in and of itself. For an example of this, consider Vincent Ostrom, "The Meaning of Federalism in 'The Federalist': A Critical Examination of the Diamond Theses," *Publius* 15 (1985): 1–21.

17. Orren and Skowronek, *The Search for American Political Development*, 31.

18. Orren and Skowronek, *The Search for American Political Development*, 33.

19. On institutionalism or the institutional study of politics, see for example, Robert C. Lieberman, "Ideas, Institutions, and Political Order: Explaining Political Change," *American Political Science Review* 96 (2002): 697–712 and Terry M. Moe, "Interests, Institutions, and Positive Theory: The Politics of the NLRB," *Studies in American Political Development* 2 (1987): 236–299. On cultural explanations and a cultural critique, see for example, J. David Greenstone, "Political Culture and American Political Development: Liberty, Union, and the Liberal Bipolarity," *Studies in American Political Development* 1 (1986): 1–49; Rogers M. Smith, "Which Comes First, the Ideas or the Institutions?" in Ian Shapiro, Stephen Skowronek, and Daniel Galvin (eds.), *Rethinking Political Institutions: The Art of the State* (New York: New York University Press, 2006), 91–113; Hartz, *The Liberal Tradition in America*. Indeed, when both approaches are concurrently adopted, such as when scholars think *constitutionally*—both about the formal structures created by the constitution and the legitimating ideas behind them—the synergy has often yielded the finest insights.

20. Greenstone, "Political Culture and Political Development," 2.

21. Max M. Edling, *A Revolution in Favor of Government: Origins of the U.S. Constitution and the Making of the American State* (New York: Oxford University Press, 2003); Richard R. John, *Spreading the News: The American Postal System from Franklin to Morse* (Cambridge, MA: Harvard University Press, 1995); Suzanne Mettler, "Social Citizens of Separate Sovereignties," in Sidney M. Milkis and Jerome M. Mileur (eds.), *The New Deal and the Triumph of Liberalism* (Amherst, MA: University of Massachusetts Press, 2002), 231–271, 244.

22. In America, as the Federalists ensured by their example, political institutionalization has tended to precede social mobilization. See Samuel P. Huntington, *Political Order in Changing Societies* (New Haven, CT: Yale University Press, 1968).

23. Rogers Smith, "Beyond Tocqueville, Myrdal, and Hartz: The Multiple Traditions in America," *American Political Science Review* 87 (1993): 549–566; Skocpol, *Protecting Soldiers and Mothers*; Suzanne Mettler, *Dividing Citizens: Gender and Federalism in New Deal Policy* (Ithaca, NY: Cornell University Press, 1998).

24. Orren and Skowronek, *The Search for American Political Development*, 22.

25. William G. Shade, "'Revolutions Can Go Backwards': The American Civil War and the Problem of Political Development," *Social Science Quarterly* 55 (1974): 753–767.

26. J. David Greenstone, *The Lincoln Persuasion: Remaking American Liberalism* (Princeton, NJ: Princeton University Press, 1993).

27. John R. Commons, *Proportional Representation* (New York: Augustus M. Kelley, [1896] 1967), 359.

28. E. E. Schattschneider, *The Semi-Sovereign People: A Realist's View Of Democracy In America* (New York: Holt, Rinehart & Winston, 1960); Richard L. McCormick, *The Party Period and Public Policy: American Politics from the Age of Jackson to the Progressive*

Era (New York: Oxford University Press, 1986); Douglas W. Jaenecke, "The Jacksonian Integration of Parties into the Constitutional System," *Political Science Quarterly* 101 (1986): 85–107.

29. Elizabeth Sanders, *Roots of Reform: Farmers, Workers, and the American State, 1877–1917* (Chicago, IL: University of Chicago Press, 1999); Eldon J. Eisenach, *The Lost Promise of Progressivism* (Lawrence, KS: University Press of Kansas, 1994); Clemens, *The People's Lobby*; David B. Truman, *The Governmental Process: Political Interests and Public Opinion* (Berkeley, CA: Institute of Governmental Studies, [1951] 1993).

30. Daniel J. Tichenor and Richard A. Harris, "Organized Interests and American Political Development," *Political Science Quarterly* 117 (2003): 587–612.

31. Samuel H. Beer, *To Make a Nation*: The Rediscovery of American Federalism (Cambridge, MA: Belknap Press, 1993), 20. Others, such as Paul Rahe, have even argued that the separation of powers is the "central doctrine" of American constitutionalism. See Paul Rahe, *Republics Ancient and Modern*: Classical Republicanism and the American Revolution (Chapel Hill, NC: University of North Carolina Press, 1992), 604.

32. Richard E. Neustadt, *Presidential Power and the Modern Presidents: The Politics of Leadership from Roosevelt to Reagan* (New York: The Free Press, 1990), 29.

33. Forrest McDonald, *Novus Ordo Seclorum: The Intellectual Origins of the Constitution* (Lawrence, KS: University Press of Kansas, 1985), 240.

34. S. Rufus Davis, *The Federal Principle: A Journey Through Time in Search of a Meaning* (Berkeley, CA: University of California Press, 1977), 77.

35. See, for example, Cynthia L. Gates, "Splitting the Atom of Sovereignty: *Term Limits, Inc.'s* Conflicting Views of Popular Autonomy in a Federal Republic," *Publius* 26 (1996): 127–140.

36. As Chief Justice John Jay wrote in *Chisholm v. Georgia*, 2 U.S. 419 (1793), "Every State Constitution is a compact made by and between the citizens of a State to govern themselves in a certain manner, and the Constitution of the United States is likewise a compact made by the people of the United States to govern themselves as to general objects in a certain manner. By this great compact however, many prerogatives were transferred to the national government, such as those of making war and peace, contracting alliances, coining money, etc. etc." Chief Justice John Marshall would repeat this argument in *McCulloch v. Maryland*, 17 U.S. 316 (1819).

INDEX

Note: The letter 'n' followed by the page numbers refer to notes.